The Medieval Kingdoms of Nubia

The

MEDIEVAL KINGDOMS
OF NUBIA

Pagans, Christians and Muslims along the Middle Nile

DEREK A. WELSBY

THE BRITISH MUSEUM PRESS

First published in 2002 by The British Museum Press
A division of The British Museum Company Ltd
46 Bloomsbury Street, London WC1B 3QQ

A catalogue record for this book is available from the
British Library

ISBN 0 7141 1947 4

Designed and typeset in Centaur by Martin Richards
Printed in Slovenia by Korotan

Acknowledgements

My introduction to the archaeology and history of
Medieval Nubia came as a result of being invited to
participate in a survey of the capital of the kingdom of
Alwa by Mr Charles M. Daniels, then Senior Lecturer
in the Department of Archaeology at the University of
Newcastle upon Tyne. It was the late Sir Laurence P.
Kirwan, at that time President of the British Institute
in Eastern Africa, who was instrumental in setting up
the project and it is a credit to him and the late Mrs
Margaret Shinnie that the work progressed without
hindrance and was continued for many seasons. I am
particularly grateful for all their help and encourage-
ment over the years and it is to be regretted that they
are not still with us to receive these acknowledgements.

I am especially grateful to Drs Julie Anderson and
Bogdan Żurawski who read through a draft of this
book and made many helpful comments on style and
content. Needless to say they are in no way responsible
for any errors in the finished product. Thanks also go
to Isabella Welsby Sjöström and Patricia Usick. A
number of colleagues and institutions have assisted by
allowing their photographs to be reproduced. They are
individually acknowledged in the captions
accompanying the photographs. My Polish colleagues
from the Polish Academy of Sciences have been
particularly helpful over many years and my first-hand
knowledge of Old Dongola in particular is a direct
result of their unstinting hospitality during
innumerable visits to that site. Lastly I would like to
thank my editor Carolyn Jones who saw the typescript
swiftly through to publication.

Frontispiece **Doorway with carved keystone
in the monastery church at el-Ghazali.**

Contents

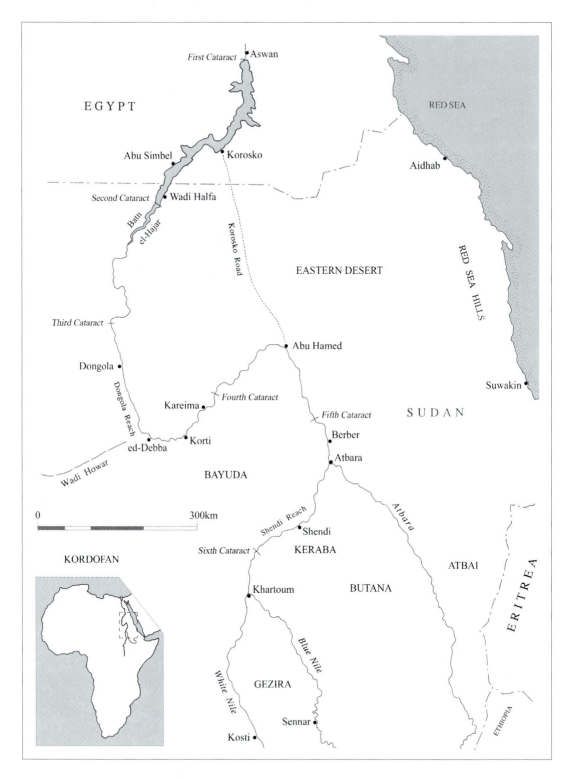

Figure 1 **The Middle Nile.**

CHAPTER 1

Introduction

Nubia and the Nubians

Today the term Nubia has a rather narrow definition and refers to the area occupied by people who speak the modern Nubian language. These people, prior to the construction of the dams at the First Cataract, occupied the Nile Valley between Kubaniya, a little to the north of Aswan, and the region of ed-Debba, and were divided into three groups each with their own dialect, the Kenuzi in the north, the Dongolawi in the south and the Mahasi in between. The northern part of this region, between the First and Second Cataracts, is referred to as Lower Nubia with Upper Nubia lying further to the south, the two separated by the inhospitable Batn el-Hajar (Belly of the Rocks).

The Arab sources in the medieval period generally refer to the people living along the Middle Nile as Nubians. Although in most cases they were referring to the Makurians, with whom virtually all Muslim contacts were confined, it is clear that they considered the people of Alwa also as Nubians. In the early ninth century the geographer el-Khuwarezmi refers both to the Alwa and the Nuba.[1] El-Yaqubi writing in the last quarter of the same century records that the Nuba are divided into two Kingdoms, of Makuria and Alwa.[2] El-Mas'udi in the tenth century describes one branch of the Nuba as having their capital at Dongola and the other branch their capital at Soba[3] while the thirteenth century el-Harrani divides the population of Nubia into two groups, the Nuba and the Alwa.[4] None of the Arab sources refer to the third of the Nubian kingdoms, that of Nobadia, before it became a part of Makuria not later than the early eighth century.

In the modern literature relating to the Nubian kingdoms there is no consistency in the use of the terms Nubia and Nubian. Many writers, simply as a result of the fact that we know so much more about Nobadia and the combined kingdom of Makuria and Nobadia than about the kingdom of Alwa, apply the term only to the kingdoms centred on Old Dongola and Faras and frequently omit reference to Alwa when discussing aspects of Nubia's history and culture. This is clearly inappropriate, from both consideration of the Arab sources and archaeological evidence which indicates that Old Nubian was one of the several languages used throughout the Nile Valley at least from the region of the First Cataract to Soba East on the Blue Nile. By the current definition of the territory of Nubia, and of the ethnicity of the people dwelling within it, Alwa must be integrated into any discussion of Nubia.[5] That it does not take its rightful place in any such discussion is simply a result of the small amount of archaeological work undertaken within its territory.

Figure 2 **The narrow fertile strip along the Nile (view from Jebel Sesi).**

The climate and environment

The medieval kingdoms of Nubia occupied the Nile Valley from the First Cataract at least as far upstream as the Sennar district on the Blue Nile (Fig. 1). Although from the sixth century onwards they were united by a common religion and by the use of common languages there was much diversity, particularly as a result of the very different climatic conditions and environment across this extensive region. In the far north the Nile flows through the eastern edge of the Sahara. This area is characterized by an almost total absence of rainfall and, apart from a thin strip alongside the river (Fig. 2), it is an extremely hostile environment for plants, animals and humans alike. At the latitude of Sennar, on the other hand there is significant seasonal rainfall and extensive vegetation.[6] The opportunities for human activity offered by the increased rainfall are much greater and the river is less significant. Owing to the focus of archaeological activity our knowledge of the Nubian kingdoms decreases dramatically as we move upriver. The Nubian lifestyle known to us is that of the desert regions where it is dominated by the fundamental importance of the Nile. Of the peoples living in the much less hostile regions to the south we know very little.

The behaviour of the Nile and the climatic conditions over time have been far from constant and the dynamic nature of these all-important factors must have adversely, and on occasion advantageously, affected the life of the medieval Nubians. Although we have to study the physical remains left by the Nubians, the world they occupied may have been, at least at some periods, very different from that which we now observe. Periods of high

Niles, caused by variations in the amount of rain falling in the headwaters of the Blue Nile, its tributaries and the Atbara in particular, which will have affected flood levels, were of fundamental importance to the agriculturists along the river banks. A superabundance of water was certainly not a blessing: the disastrous consequences of this were illustrated by the very high Nile flood in 1988 and the extensive damage it caused throughout the Middle Nile valley. Fluctuations in the often meagre rainfall may also have been disastrous in the short term in some of the more marginal areas. Humans have also had a profound effect on the flora and fauna. All the big game has now disappeared from Nubia, apart from isolated areas where crocodiles still survive, while overutilization of timber resources for building materials and fuel has adversely effected certain areas and speeded up the desertification of the north.

Sources for the Nubian Kingdoms

A wide range of written sources is available from which to reconstruct the history of the Nubian Kingdoms and the lifestyles of their populations. Of the indigenous sources the most common are graffiti, scratched in particular onto pottery and the walls of buildings. Inscriptions, especially funerary *stelae*, are common, but inscriptions with a historical content are few and far between. Some of the most useful material, discovered mainly at Qasr Ibrim, consists of legal texts, documents and correspondence. The potential of this material to elucidate many facets of Nubian life and commercial and political dealings, particularly with their Muslim neighbours, is immense but unfortunately much of it remains to be published.

For the early period of medieval Nubian history Roman and Byzantine writers provide details of contacts with the north of Nubia in the political and diplomatic spheres, and about the introduction of Christianity to the three kingdoms. The Nubian kingdoms co-existed with the Muslim world for several centuries and many Muslim writers, a number of whom actually travelled in Nubia, have left not only often detailed accounts of Muslim/Nubian relations but also topographic information, details of political organization, of the economy and of local customs. Among the Arab writers who concerned themselves with Nubia Ibn Selim el-Aswani is by far the most useful although his account has only come down to us in part as it is extensively quoted by the fifteenth century historian el-Maqrizi. The earliest translation into a European language was made by the great Swiss traveller Burckhardt who describes Ibn Selim's account as 'more detailed, more accurate, and more satisfactory with regard to Nubia than that of any other Arabian geographer or historian'.[7]

What we totally lack are any Nubian accounts of Nubia. No history written by a Nubian has been found, nor do we have any indication that such works were ever produced. The literary texts that we do have are all religious in content. However, the Nubians certainly maintained archives although, apart from at Qasr Ibrim, little of this material survives. The Ibrim archives have yielded detailed records that are invaluable for writing history when taken in combination with other types of evidence. For the latest history of the Kingdom of Alwa we are forced to turn to the Funj Chronicle, an originally oral history only committed to paper in the later nineteenth century. For the modern scholar access to the literary material dealing with Nubia is not always easy. Individual site reports include sections on the epigraphic material of all types from those sites and there are several volumes publishing a portion of the material from Qasr Ibrim. A corpus of inscriptions from Nubia as a whole is not available. However, the epigraphic and literary material relating to the earliest Nubian period has now been collected together and published with detailed commentaries in *Fontes Historiae Nubiorum* which is invaluable. All the other literary sources relating to Nubia have been translated by G. Vantini and are published in his *Oriental Sources Concerning Nubia*.

The fastest growing body of evidence comes from, and will continue to come from, archaeology. Not only do archaeologists uncover epigraphic material, but their investigations of Nubian settlements, cemeteries and fortresses, with the abundant artefacts to be found on many of these sites, promise to vastly increase our data-base. Most of the archaeological work, however, has been focused in the north of Nubia in response to the dams constructed and reconstructed at the First Cataract. Further south the archaeological activity has been patchy and within the Kingdom of Alwa there has been very little indeed. This necessarily contributes to the northern bias already found in the written sources. The Romans, Byzantines and Arabs were much more interested in the regions close to the southern frontiers of Egypt than they were in the situation in Central Sudan. In 1928 Griffith wrote, 'Of the southern kingdom, which received Christianity in 580, almost nothing is known except that it was more barbarous than that of Dongola ...'[8] We now know a little more but his comments remain, apart from his suggestion of the greater barbarity of Alwa, as true today as they were seventy years ago.

There has been considerable interest in medieval Nubia since the reopening of Sudan to the outside world following the Anglo-Egyptian conquest of the country between 1896 and 1898. Along with reports on excavations a number of archaeologists sought to synthesize the available date. The earliest general works focused on the upstanding monuments. Mileham's *Churches in Lower Nubia* appeared in 1910 to be followed in 1912 by Somers Clarke's *Christian Antiquities in the Nile Valley* which included sites as far upstream as Soba East. In the 1930s the Italian Ugo Monneret de Villard wrote what is the standard work on the archaeological remains known at his time in four volumes, *La Nubia Medieovale*, volume I appearing in 1935, volume IV some twenty-two years later. He also produced a general synthesis of medieval Nubian history entitled *Storia della Nubia Cristiana* in 1938. Both these works remain essential starting points for any study of the subject. Thereafter, although medieval Nubia is discussed in general works on the Middle Nile, often in some detail – Adams devotes 113 pages to the period in his magisterial history of the region, *Nubia: Corridor to Africa* – monographs dealing with the whole period of the Nubian kingdoms are extremely rare.

There is still much data from excavations, some completed over a quarter of a century ago, yet to be published in detail. Several excavations on medieval sites are currently in progress and the information recovered, although alluded to in preliminary reports, is not yet fully available. In the light of this any attempt to write about the medieval Kingdoms of Nubia is bound to be inadequate and will certainly be out of date even before the last words are typed, let alone by the time it is published. However, this is a situation which pertains in archaeology as in many other fields of research the world over and should not dissuade us from attempting to synthesize the vast amount of data currently available. This book is a humble attempt to do just that. It is certainly not the last word on this fascinating period which embraces the transition from pagan 'Pharaonic' culture to Islam through one of the highest points of Nubian civilization, that of the Christians on the Middle Nile.

Chronology

In the literary and epigraphic sources several different dating systems were used, most of which can be converted with some precision to years AD which will be used throughout this book. The Arab sources used dates relating to the time subsequent to the Hegira, the flight of the prophet Mohammed from Mecca, that is beginning in AD 622 according to the Christian calendar, abbreviated to AH. Coptic and Nubian writers most frequently use the Era of Diocletian, the number of years after the accession of the Roman emperor Diocletian during whose reign there were great persecutions of the Christians in the Roman Empire. This began on 29 August 284. From the mid ninth century onwards this term began to be replaced by the Era of the Martyrs, which gradually superseded the earlier term.[9] Other eras are also referred to. A graffito in the temple/church at Wadi es-Sebua is dated by reference to the Era of the Martyrs, i.e. AD 795 and is also equated with 91 of another era, beginning in 704 – a local era the significance of which is uncertain.[10] Other eras include the Ethiopian era which began in AD 7/8, the Protobyzantine era (the Chronicon Paschale era) which is 16 years different, and the date after the creation of the world, i.e. after 5493/2 BC.[11] The indiction system and years after the birth of Christ also appear. On funerary *stelae* the date of death is sometimes given by several different systems. For example, the presbyter Thomas died at Old Dongola '(in the) 7th indiction, (in the year) 6290 from the creation of the world, (in the year) from Christ's stay (on earth) 890, (in the year) from Diocletian 515'.[12] Increasingly, as the influence of the Muslims grew, Hegira dates were used even on Christian tombstones, the earliest example found together with a date after Diocletian is of 906-7. Another of the same year is dated solely by the Hegira system.[13]

Dating is also frequently given by reference to the particular years of a particular ruler which may or may not allow us to precisely pinpoint the date in years AD. Nubian letters were often dated by the reign of the king and by a list of the officials then holding office, e.g. '[In] the reign of our god-loving king Cyricus; when the illustrious (?) lord Zacharias was *domesticos*; when the most God-beloved Cyri-Nosk (?) was bishop; when Paulos-Kolla the priest (?) was *eparch* of the land (?) of Nobadia; when the God-fearing Petrus was *domesticos*'.[14] To contemporaries such a dating method must have caused no problems, but to us it is far from ideal.

Archaeological data also is not precisely datable in most cases. Apart from association with events directly dated by inscriptions or by the literary sources, the greatest precision comes from dendrochronology followed by a number of other scientific techniques, the most common of which is radiocarbon dating. Dendrochronology has not yet been used in the archaeology of the Middle Nile and the necessary comparative data is not available. Also much of the timber utilized in that area is palm, which owing to its fibrous structure, without annual growth rings, cannot be used for dendrochronology. Radiocarbon dating is widely used and archaeomagnetic dating has also been utilized. The dates provided by these techniques have a range of probability which varies from one sample to another.

Hence dates may be given such as 1270±70 BP where BP stands for 'before the present', that is before 1950. Such a date can then be calibrated. With the example here, a charcoal sample from within Church A at Soba East, a calibration which gives a 68% probability for the date of the death of the timber, i.e. when the tree was first cut down or when the particular timber was removed from the tree, lay between 665 and 810 or 840 to 850. At a higher probability of 95% the date range expands, in this case giving the dates 640-895 or 925-930.[15] With a radiocarbon date taken from part of a human or animal the date centres on the time of death. However it must be borne in mind that with a single date there is a significant possibility that the date one is seeking may lie beyond the date range quoted, hence the need for multiple dates from closely associated material, if possible, to reduce the probability of this occurring.

Much archaeological data cannot be directly related to calendar years and a date range has to be given. This is especially the case with pottery where material of a particular shape, style of decoration, method of manufacture etc. may be dated to a cultural phase such as Early Christian, itself imprecisely dated to 650-850. The imprecise nature of archaeological dating makes it extremely difficult to integrate fully 'historical' data on the one hand and archaeological data on the other. Hence history tends to concentrate on fixed events, and the narrative jumps from one to another, while archaeology provides information on gradual changes over long periods of time.

A wide range of cultural/chronological terms will be found throughout the following pages and reflect the lack of consensus among scholars studying the period. The Kushite period is divided between an earlier phase known as Napatan and a later phase known as Meroitic with the divide placed in the fourth century BC. In northern Nubia the Meroitic period is followed by the X-Group, a term first coined by Reisner in 1907. It is contemporary with the post-Meroitic further to the south.[16] Both of these terms have been superseded to some extent in the more recent literature. The Ballana Culture has been used instead of the X-Group, which itself embraced both the early Nubian and the Blemmyan cultures in the Nile Valley of Lower Nubia. The suitability of the term post-Meroitic has been called into question in the light of the clear continuities from the earlier Meroitic period, and the term post-pyramidal Meroitic has been invented to cover what was the earlier part of the post-Meroitic. The next major division was occasioned by the arrival of Christianity which certainly did bring in its train considerable cultural changes. However, 'medieval' is generally preferred here to stress the continuity between the pagan phases of the Nubian kingdoms and their Christian phases. In a purely chronological context Meroitic, X-Group, post-Meroitic and Christian, divided into Transitional, Early, Classic, Late and Terminal are well understood and cannot be avoided. The table below gives a rough indication of the chronological span encompassed by these terms. The chronological phases for the Christian Period were first proposed by Adams in his 'Seven Ages of Christian Nubia'[17] although these were subsequently modified.[18] All the dates are approximate.

Table 1. The chronology of the cultures on the Middle Nile, ninth century BC to sixteenth century AD.

Culture	Phases	Date	Extent
Kushite	Napatan	ninth – fourth century BC	
	Meroitic	fourth century BC – fourth century AD	
post-Meroitic	post-pyramidal Meroitic	fourth – sixth century AD	upstream of the third cataract
X-Group	Ballana culture	fourth – sixth century AD	first – third cataract
Christian	Transitional	AD 550-600	
	Early I	AD 600-750	
	Early II	AD 750-850	
	Classic I	AD 850-1000	
	Classic II	AD 1000-1100	
	Late I	AD 1100-1300	
	Late II	AD 1300-1400	
	Terminal	AD 1400-1500	

What is clear from a study of the remains of the era immediately after the collapse of the Kushite Empire is that we are not entering a barbarous dark age during which the Kushite civilization disintegrated in the face of the onslaught of uncultured barbarians. Although the Kushite state religious institutions seems to have survived only in a very much reduced form, and the Kushite written and (presumably) spoken language disappears, a consideration of settlement patterns, architecture and artefacts of the post-Kushite period tends rather to demonstrate that it was a rich, cultured society. There appears to have been a population explosion at least in Lower Nubia, while large architectural projects, such as the massive fortifications constructed in the heartlands of the Kushite state and in Lower Nubia, indicate the ability of the local rulers to marshal considerable resources and have access to architects and builders as skilled as their Kushite predecessors. The vast numbers of artefacts recovered from X-Group settlements indicates that pottery vessels in particular were so abundant and affordable that large numbers were discarded while still in perfect condition. Even the most 'barbarous' of their practices, the slaughter or sacrifice of humans and animals on the occasion of the funerals of their rulers and elite, is a continuation of the practices of the 'civilized' Kushites. This is, therefore, not an account of collapse and degeneration but of a renaissance in the fortunes of the Middle Nile dwellers which was only to crumble in the face of protracted conflict with their Muslim neighbours.

CHAPTER 2

The emergence of the Nubian kingdoms

The origins of the Nubians

Kushite inscriptions name a large number of enemies of the state, among them the tribes living in the deserts to the east and west of the Nile Valley with whom the Kushites interacted and occasionally fought. Most of these inscriptions date to the earlier Kushite period and there is no mention among them of any group which may be identified as the ancestors of the Nubians. However, there are representations in Kushite art of individuals of high rank depicted with a single upright feather headdress. In a New Kingdom context such iconography was used to denote one of Egypt's enemies living on the Middle Nile. A few figures of bound captives, represented with the feather, bear inscriptions identifying them as Nubians.[1] A people known as Nubai are first mentioned during the third century BC by the Hellenistic geographer Eratosthenes. Strabo, deriving his information from Eratosthenes' lost work, describes the situation thus, 'The parts on the left side of the course of the Nile are inhabited by Nubae, a large tribe, who, beginning at Meroe, extend as far as the bends of the river, and are not subject to the Aethiopians [Kushites] but are divided into separate kingdoms.'[2] The Nubae are described by Strabo as nomads and brigands. Pliny, writing in the latter half of the first century AD records that the Nubian Aethiopians inhabited a town on the Nile called Tenupsis but the whereabouts of this is uncertain.[3] It has been suggested that some Nubian speakers had already settled in the Nile Valley by the New Kingdom, in the latter half of the second millennium BC.[4]

The Noba are mentioned on the victory inscription erected by the Aksumite king Aezanes in the mid fourth century AD which has been interpreted as recording an account of his invasion of the Nile Valley and of his activities in the Island of Meroe, the area bounded in part by the lower Blue Nile, the Lower Atbara and the main Nile. The geographical location of the campaign, and of the tribes and peoples recorded as affected by it, depends on modern identifications of the toponyms contained within the text and there is no certainty that these have been correctly identified. One radical interpretation even argues that the campaign was confined to the Ethiopian highlands where, the supporters of that interpretation argue, many of the toponyms and tribal names can be identified from other sources.[5] However, if one follows the generally accepted interpretation the inscription provides evidence for the Noba living in the Gezira, the triangle of land between the White and Blue Niles. They dwelt in masonry towns including two captured from the Kasu. They owned temples and images, included gold and silver vessels among their possessions, and practised agriculture. To the north lived the Kasu, usually identified with the Kushites, the rump of the once great Empire. Further to the north again lived the

'Red Noba'.[6] The Byzantine historian Procopius, writing in the sixth century AD, notes that before the Noba entered the Nile Valley in Lower Nubia, an event which he dates to the late third century AD, they were living in the oases to the west of the Nile.[7]

In the sources we have a plethora of names which may refer to a single people, among them Nubae, Nobades, Nobates, Annoubades, Noba, Nouba and Red Noba. The significance of these names is unclear, they may be different names used loosely by our sources, Greek, Roman, Aksumite, Byzantine and Arab, for the same people, refer to sub-groups, or refer to different peoples altogether. Certainly archaeologically we cannot recognise different cultural assemblages to match each name, but we do not have a single culture covering the whole of the area occupied by these peoples. It is these people or peoples who coalesced into the three Nubian kingdoms first attested in the sixth century.

It is assumed that the Nubians gradually infiltrated the Kushite state, with or without the acquiescence of the Kushite rulers, and that, with the weakening of Kushite central authority, they were able to take over the reins of power and eclipse the Kushite ruling class. Another manifestation of this rise to prominence is the sudden appearance on the one hand of their traditional hand-made ceramics in the southern part of the middle Nile Valley, and the demise of the finer Kushite pottery as well as the apparent demise of the Kushite state and religious institutions, Kushite art, architecture, and literacy in the Meroitic language.

A graffito in Greek, carved on the wall of the former Temple of Isis at Philae some time after 537, reads 'I, Theodosios, a Nubian' (Nouba) and provides evidence for the name used by the Nubians to describe their ethnicity.[8]

The end of the Kushite state

According to Procopius it was Diocletian who ordered the withdrawal of Roman forces from the *Dodekaschoinos* (the region of the Nile Valley between Maharaqa and Philae), back to the First Cataract in the late third century, at which point the frontier remained until the end of Romano/Byzantine control of Egypt. Procopius also recorded that Diocletian invited a people from the Great or Kharqa Oasis, the Nobatai, to occupy the vacated territory as *foederati*, that is, a group tied by treaty obligations to Rome on the understanding that it would maintain the peace immediately beyond the Roman frontier.[9] Such an approach to frontier defence was typical of the late Roman period. However, Procopius was writing over two centuries after the events he describes, and it has been suggested that his description is rather anachronistic. There is some evidence to argue that it was in fact the Kushites who stepped into the vacuum left by the withdrawing Roman garrisons, if such a vacuum ever existed. By the third century the Kushite state was entering its terminal phase, but it was still the major power on the Middle Nile and was strong enough to reassert its control over an area where it may well have been in *de facto* if not *de jure* control for much of the third century.[10] Diocletian's withdrawal of the frontier may simply have been a formal recognition, couched in the appropriate terms necessary to avoid any adverse propaganda, of a pre-existing situation.

The exact date of the collapse of the Kushite state is impossible to fix and it is highly unlikely that any single catastrophic event brought about a rapid destruction of the political structure. It is more plausible to consider that the state split into a number of its constituent parts: such a fate must always have been inherent in the geography of the state, which was, over large areas, confined to a narrow strip along the banks of the Nile for well over 1000 km of its course. A study of the latest royal graves at Meroe in the Northern royal cemetery, of the latest rich Kushite burials in the western cemetery, and of the very rich burials of the earliest Nubian rulers, suggests that the political hegemony of the Kushite ruling elite at Meroe no longer held sway over the northern part of the Kingdom by the later fourth century.[11]

Both the Romans and the Kushites had long experienced trouble from the people occupying the eastern desert, the Blemmyes. Literary and epigraphic evidence relating to the late fourth and fifth centuries makes it clear that Kushite control of Lower Nubia had lapsed, and two groups, the Nobadae and the Blemmyes, were locked in a bitter struggle for supremacy in the region.

The problems posed by the sources

For Lower (northern) Nubia, in the period between the late fourth century and the later sixth century we have an embarrassing richness of sources, literary, epigraphic, textual and archaeological. However, this superabundance of source material poses its own special problems. Almost none of the events recorded by the written sources can be precisely dated and, given the dramatically fluid situation that seems to have been characteristic of Lower Nubia and the Egyptian borderlands at this time, it is extremely difficult to write a coherent and consistent narrative of events. This is exacerbated by the loose nature of the tribal confederacies among the Blemmyes in particular. It is perfectly possible for one section of the Blemmyes to have been bound by treaty obligations to the Romans while other elements of the same people continued to wage war against them. The relationship of the main barbarian protagonists is equally confusing. There is abundant evidence for warfare between the Blemmyes and the Nobades in the Nile Valley, yet also evidence for both groups acting either in concert or separately against the Romans in the region of Aswan. The purely archaeological evidence for royal burials with their abundant fine Roman artefacts cannot be synchronized with the historical data except in the most general terms. For the south, apart from the inscriptions of Aezanes, and a few fragments of other Aksumite inscriptions from Meroe, we have to rely on archaeology alone.

The Blemmyes and the Nobadae

The Blemmyes had for centuries controlled the eastern deserts and from their desert fastness had harassed both Roman Egypt and Kushite Lower Nubia. In the later fourth century, however, a section of the Blemmyes was able to take over part of the Nile Valley. Epiphanius, a monk from Palestine, incidentally records that the Blemmyes had, apparently very recently, occupied the emerald mines in the Eastern Desert near Kalabsha, and internal evidence suggests that this event happened close to 392-394.[12] According to Olympiodorus, who visited Blemmyan Lower Nubia around 423, they occupied five towns, Phoinikon (el-Laqeita in the Eastern Desert), Khiris which has not been identified, Thapis (Taifa), Talmis (Kalabsha) and Prima, which has been identified as Qirta.[13] Kalabsha, with its temple dedicated to the god Mandulis, appears to have been the major religious centre in the region to the south of Philae and was probably the capital of the

Blemmyan Nile state. The names of four Blemmyan kings, Tamal, Isemne, Degou and Phonen (recorded as Phonoin when he was *phylarch*) appear on the walls of the temple. The inscription of Phonoin indicates the continuance of the Romanized cult life in at least one urban centre in the *Dodekaschoinos*[14] and the presence of cult societies of the type known from Roman Egypt.[15] Below the king were the *phylarchs*, the chiefs of the separate tribes who made up the Blemmyan state,[16] among whom was the heir to the throne, and there were also lower status officials, the *hypotyrannoi*, who were tribal dignitaries.[17]

The inscriptions carved on the walls of the Temple of Mandulis furnish us with considerable information on the history of this region in the fifth century. One of the most intriguing, carved on the facade of the hypostyle hall, is that of Kharamadoye which is the latest known inscription written in cursive Meroitic script.[18] As Meroitic is a language little understood, what it says is obscure, but some details can be made out. It was inscribed on the orders of Kharamadoye who is described as *'qore'* ruler. Kharamadoye, who invokes the Kushite state god Amun in his inscription, clearly considered himself an independent ruler and this has led to the suggestion that he is likely to be one of the kings buried at Ballana between *c.* 410-420 rather than one of the incumbents of the earlier burials at Qustul where, on the evidence of the funerary regalia, the individuals do not appear to have claimed royal status.[19] The use of the Kushite imperial language, Meroitic, however, stresses his links with the old regime. The inscription appears to commemorate his presumably successful campaign against a king Yismeniye who may be the Blemmyan king Isemne noted above. If this is correct it indicates that the Nobadae, who were presumably the subjects of Kharamadoye, took Kalabsha from the Blemmyes, although subsequent events make it clear that the Blemmyes regained control of the region later.

The latest important inscription in the Temple of Mandulis is that of Silko. This inscription, which is in Greek, has been dated to the sixth century on the mistaken interpretation of the reference to God, which has been thought to indicate that Silko was a Christian and, hence, that it must post-date the conversion of the Nobadian king in the mid sixth century. The 'God' referred to may be Mandulis, upon the walls of whose temple the inscription was carved, or perhaps the scribe was a Christian.[20] The inscription is now usually dated much earlier, perhaps to the earlier fifth century, after that of Kharamadoye, but before *c.* 450. Silko describes himself as 'King of the Noubades and all the Aithiopians' and recounts the conduct of three campaigns against the Blemmyes. I 'came to Talmis (Kalabsha) and Taphis (Taifa). On two occasions I fought with the Blemmyes; and God gave me the victory. On the third occasion I was again victorious and took control of their cities.' He goes on to state that he fought with the Blemmyes from Primis (Qasr Ibrim) to Telelis, which may be Shellal at the First Cataract. This campaign appears to mark the end of Blemmyan control of the Nile Valley in Lower Nubia.

Further evidence is shed on this campaign by a letter found during excavations in 1976 by the Egypt Exploration Society at Qasr Ibrim. This letter, written on papyrus, was one of several discovered in a storeroom in House X-19 and presumably came from a royal archive. It is written by the Blemmyan king Phonen and his son, the *phylarch* Breytek, to Aburni, king of the Nobades and to his sons Nakase and Mouses, in reply to a letter from the Nobadian king. Phonen is probably to be identified with the *phylarch* Phonoin whose inscription at Kalabsha has already been referred to. The letter makes it clear that Phonen was the enemy of Silko: he presents a summary of his conflicts with Silko and with his successor, his correspondent Aburni. In the letter Phonen recounts how he had opened negotiations with Silko to recover the lost Blemmyan territory and that a treaty had been agreed whereby sheep, cattle and camels would be exchanged for the land. Silko reneged on the deal after receiving the animals, killed the Blemmyan *phylarch* Yeny, and imprisoned a number of Blemmyan prophets. It is not clear whether Phonen was able to recover the lost territory but, if so, he certainly lost it to Aburni at some later date, and the survival of the victory inscription of Silko rather suggests that the Blemmyes never again occupied Kalabsha.[21]

War and peace with Rome

With the demise of the Kushites the Romans were left to contend with the aggressive activities of the Blemmyes supplemented by the Nobades. In time-honoured Roman fashion attempts were made to secure peace through a combination of the carrot and the stick, by offering subsidies for a guarantee of peace, backed up by the ultimate sanction of military force if this failed. In the words of John of Ephesus, subsidies were paid to the Nobadae 'who are not only not subject to the authority of the Roman Empire, but even receive a subsidy on condition that they do not enter nor pillage Egypt'.[22] Increasingly during the later Roman Empire the system came unstuck because the threat of military force was not always a credible deterrent. Procopius succinctly describes another aspect of standard Roman frontier policy, the neutralization of one hostile neighbour by the formation of a buffer zone occupied by another hostile neighbour, in the hope that one former enemy would, after being accepted into land previously controlled by Rome, equate their well-being with that of the Romans and incidentally assist in protecting the Empire's frontier from the other hostile group. He recounts that 'the Nobatai ... were forever ravaging and plundering all the places there. ... Diocletian persuaded those barbarians to migrate ... and to settle on either side of the Nile, promising to present them with great cities and with a large territory. ... So they took possession of both the Roman cities and all the country on both sides of the river beyond the city of Elephantine.' The rationale behind this was that 'he [Diocletian] supposed that they would stop harassing the territories ... and also, taking possession of the land which was given to them probably drive off the Blemmyes and the other barbarians, since the land was now their own.'[23] Our sources give us a very detailed picture of the workings, apparently with limited success, of this system of frontier policy on Egypt's southern border and its eastern flanks.

In around 423, the Roman diplomat and historian Olympiodorus, according to his own reports was invited, while in the Thebaid, to visit the Blemmyan territory along the Nile. However, it seems not unlikely that he was in actual fact sent by the Roman government on a diplomatic mission which may have resulted in the Blemmyes accepting federate status.[24] Further evidence to support this comes from Phonoin's inscription on the walls of the Mandulis temple at Kalabsha where there is recorded the receipt of a letter at Kalabsha from the *comes*, who was presumably the commander of the Roman frontier forces, highlighting the close relations between the Blemmyes and the Romans.[25]

The Nobadae were also *foederati* and the abundant fine objects of Roman manufacture in the tombs at Qustul and Ballana may, in part at least, be derived from the exchange of gifts between the Romans and their allies. In the tombs at Ballana are examples of folding chairs, a symbol of royal authority also seen in the graves of Rome's allies along the northern and western borders of the Empire. The federate status may be indicated in the inscription of Silko at Kalabsha, where he is styled *basiliskos*, perhaps denoting his lower status relative to the Roman emperor, while in the context of his relations with the subsidiary rulers under his control he is referred to as king (*basileus*).[26] A letter in Coptic on papyrus, found at Qasr Ibrim, also suggests that negotiations between the Romans and the *phylarch* Tantani were in the context of a federate relationship, with references to peace, friendship and the exchanging of oaths.

Although both the Blemmyes and Nobadae were tied to Rome by treaty obligations, and received annual subsidies,[27] they continued to harass Egypt. Among the sources for information on these attacks is the so-called Leiden papyrus, a petition from Appion, bishop of the region of Syene (Aswan) and Contra Syene, to the Roman emperors Theodosius II and Valentinian III, dating to the period *c.* 425-450. Appion bemoans the fact that 'since I find myself with my churches in the midst of these merciless barbarians, between Blemmyes and the Anoubades, we suffer many attacks from them, coming upon us as if from nowhere, with no soldiers to protect our places.'[28] This was the worse case scenario for the Romans: the uniting of their two enemies in either concerted or alternating attacks. Some at least of the Roman objects found in the royal tombs of the Nobades dating to this period may represent loot from these attacks into Egypt.[29] As a last resort the Romans were forced to retaliate in strength and in 452 ' – through Florus, the procurator of the city of Alexandria, he checked the Nubians and Blemmyes who fell in from Aithiopia and expelled them from the territory of the Romans'.[30] In the account of Priscus it is Maximinus who is approached by the barbarians to conclude a peace treaty to be binding for the duration of his term of office. By the terms of the peace treaty, ratified in the temple at Philae, they agreed to return the prisoners and livestock they had captured in Egypt, to pay war damages, and to surrender as hostages the children of their elite families. On the Romans' part they allowed their erstwhile enemies to cross the frontier as pilgrims to the Temple of Isis at Philae and agreed that the cult statue of the goddess could resume its annual voyage by barque to Lower Nubia, a tradition dating back many centuries. However, on the death of Maximinus, shortly afterwards, the Nobades and Blemmyes no longer felt bound by the treaty and they overran the country and released the hostages.[31]

That the federate status was reinstated, despite the apparent recalcitrance of the Nobades and Blemmyes, is illustrated by the offer of the Emperor Justin of Nubian troops from the Nile Valley and of Beja nomads[32] to assist the Aksumite king, Kaleb, in his campaign in Southern Arabia in 523-5.[33]

As noted, according to Procopius, it was in the reign of Diocletian that the Nobades were invited to occupy Lower Nubia upstream of Elephantine. That this actually took place in the late third century goes against the considerable body of contemporary evidence. Such an agreement between Rome and the Nobades is more likely to date to the mid fifth century and may reflect the Roman propaganda machine making the best out of the final victory of the Nobades under Silko over the Blemmyes, an event probably totally beyond the control of Rome in any event. However, the Romans may have had good reason to feel pleased with this development as the Nobadian state may well have been a more coherent political entity than the looser tribal groupings of the Blemmyes, and hence easier to deal with.

Although we cannot be in any doubt of Blemmyan political control of parts of Lower Nubia for perhaps half a century, archaeologically they are virtually invisible. At Qasr Ibrim, for example, which they are known to have controlled, and where there has been a considerable amount of excavation within the levels which span the whole of the X-Group period, the presence of these different groups cannot be distinguished in the cultural assemblage.[34] The entry of the relatively artefact-impoverished nomadic Blemmyes into the extremely artefact-rich Nile Valley may have had no influence on the everyday lives of the more abundant Romano-Nubian, Kushite and Nubian inhabitants and evidence for their presence may, therefore, be missing. This suggests that the X-Group cultural assemblage was a development of that of the later Kushite period and as such was produced and used by the indigenous inhabitants who presumably remained in the region throughout the period of political upheaval. The impact of the Blemmyes on the culture of Lower Nubia must have been minimal, with them assimilating the culture of those they controlled rather than directly influencing the physical manifestations of that culture. However, in the realms of funerary culture we would expect to be able to recognize them and this may be possible in some cases. In the X-Group cemetery at Sayala there is a very high rate of trauma among the adult population, rising to 45%, most thought to be of battle origin. It is suggested that these people are Blemmyes.[35]

Nobadia

Kharamadoye's inscription implies that during his reign, after his successful campaign against the Blemmyes, he controlled the Nile Valley from Philae as far upstream as Soleb, between the Dal and Third Cataracts. The northern part of this region, however, was regained by the Blemmyes only to be finally lost by them in the mid fifth century, after which date the Nobadae were in firm control of the whole of Lower Nubia.

Although the late fourth and early fifth century Nobadian overlords of Lower Nubia were presumably buried at Qustul, the identification of individual burials is uncertain. None of the burials at that site appear to be of individuals who considered themselves independent rulers.[36] It has been suggested that they considered themselves vassals of the Kushite royal house, with whom they were perhaps connected by intermarriage. Török has used a number of characteristics of the burials here (and at Ballana) in an attempt to identify the number of royal generations present.[37] He considers that there are five royal generations buried at Qustul which was in use for approximately fifty years from c. 370 until 410-20. The funerary rituals and the grave goods show that there was a marked change with the move of burials across the river to Ballana in the early fifth century where they are buried as kings wearing royal crowns.[38] Silko uses Greek as the language for his victory inscription at Kalabsha, the official language of Roman Egypt within which for over two centuries Kalabsha lay. Adjacent to the inscription are two images, both of which probably depict Silko portrayed in Roman military garb but with a number of traditional Pharaonic elements, an amalgam of imported and local, but not distinctly Kushite, motifs. In one representation he is shown on horseback spearing an enemy, imagery known throughout the Roman Empire from tombstones of cavalry troopers as early as the first century (Fig. 3).

Figure 3 **Representation of the Nobadian king Silko(?) on the wall of the Temple of Mandulis at Kalabsha.**

At Ballana the burials of seven generations of rulers have been identified up to *c.* 490-500,[39] one of which is presumably that of Silko.[40] At the time of the excavation of most of the tumuli at Qustul and Ballana by Emery and Kirwan from 1931 to 1934 a number of signs of continuity with Kushite royal burial practices was noted. The crowns, the most distinctive of the royal furnishings, have attracted much attention (Fig. 4). Although they are clearly heavily influenced by Kushite (and Pharaonic) artistic and iconographic tradition, Török has drawn attention to the fact that they are more closely related to the crowns worn by royal princes than to those of Kushite rulers, a crown type perhaps also used by Kushite viceroys in Lower Nubia. He further suggests that it was these viceregal crowns that were being copied, and that it was the power of these viceroys that the Ballana kings aspired to, rather than to be successors to the Kushite king.[41]

A penetrating new analysis of the evidence by Patrice Lenoble[42] has shown a much greater degree of continuity and, concomitantly, a much greater understanding of Kushite royal iconography, religion and funerary ritual by the Nobadian elite than has hitherto been appreciated. This strengthens the view that the Nobadian rulers considered themselves the heirs of the Kushite state.

The terminal date suggested for the burial of rulers at Ballana brings us close to the

Figure 4 **A crown from Tomb B.80 at Ballana (courtesy of the SARS Kirwan Archive).**

date of the official conversion of the Nobadian kings to Christianity. Where later kings were buried is unknown, but it is clear that the tradition of providing elaborate tomb monuments, built to mark the place of burial of rulers, ended with the arrival of Christianity. We may probably seek later royal burials in one of the ecclesiastical centres of the Kingdom, of which Faras, the capital of the state, is the most likely.

Broadly contemporary with the Qustul and Ballana cemeteries were similar high status burials, in Lower Nubia at Gemai, Firka, Kosha and Wawa,[43] the graves of regional elites, perhaps of *phylarchs* or of kinglets under the control of the Kings of Ballana. One such official exercising local control was Tantani, who is described on a letter in Coptic from the Roman Viventius, perhaps commander of the frontier troops, as '*phylarch* of the people of the Anouba'. He was of sufficient status to conclude an international treaty.[44]

Makuria and Alwa

In contrast with the wealth of information available for events in Lower Nubia, we have virtually no information on the early development of the regions further to the south, and hence no way of explaining the changes within the fledgling states of Makuria and Alwa.

As in Nobadia the presence of high status burials at a number of sites suggests that there were regional centres dominated by an elite class. There is assumed to be a direct correlation between the size of tumuli and the political status and wealth of those buried

Figure 5 **Tumuli at ez-Zuma.**

beneath them. If this is valid then the massive tumuli noted within what came to be the territory of Makuria at ez-Zuma (Fig. 5) and Tanqasi near Jebel Barkal and at Khizeinah and Hajar el-Beida must be significant, as is the absence of comparable tumuli on this scale near Old Dongola. Within the later Kingdom of Alwa massive tumuli are found at el-Hobagi and Jebel Qisi (Sururab) near the Sixth Cataract, with possibly another one at Meroe.[45] In the case of Alwa are we justified in seeing continuity from the el-Hobagi burials to those individuals who held sway from Soba East, or was the move from the el-Hobagi region to the Blue Nile the result of a rival power base being established which eclipsed that in the Shendi reach?

The Nubian hegemony

The Kushite state had been in existence for well over 1000 years and, as with those invaders who swept into the western provinces of the Roman Empire at exactly this period, the new rulers will have sought legitimacy by associating themselves with much of the paraphernalia of the old regime. Although at first sight the cultural break between the Kushite period and that of its successors appears overwhelming, detailed studies show that there was a marked degree of continuity. This apparent contradiction is clearly visible at Ballana where the rulers are buried under tumuli rather than pyramids, yet with crowns showing clear Kushite iconography, and many details of their funerary rituals can be closely paralleled with Kushite practice, as pointed out by Lenoble. An exactly similar situation is seen at el-Hobagi where certain aspects of Kushite funerary beliefs were actively practised, the significance of which was presumably understood by those in charge of the funerary ceremonies. Continuity in funerary ritual demands some religious, as well as the implicit ideological, continuity. What was thought to be one of the distinguishing features between the Kushite and post-Meroitic periods was the apparent abandonment of an organized state religion based on the temple. However, recent archaeological discoveries have provided evidence for the continued construction and use of temples into the post-Meroitic period. Temple 1 at Qasr Ibrim is built over a grave pit containing pottery of the mid fourth century[46] and another temple at Jebel Adda was claimed by its excavator as the latest temple in Nubia.[47] At Soba East a structure which closely parallels in form a Kushite temple was not built until the sixth century at the earliest.[48] At Qasr Ibrim votive offerings of Roman coins dating from the early second to the early fifth century have been found in Temple 4, providing a *terminus post quem* for the continuance of pagan ritual at that temple.[49] Temple 6, possibly constructed during the XXVth Dynasty, remained in use as a place of pagan worship into the sixth or early seventh century at which time it appears to have been violently destroyed, perhaps by zealous early Christian converts.[50] The continued veneration of Isis of Philae is well documented and this was maintained into the sixth century. The late Roman historian Priscus recorded that, by the terms of the treaty between the Romans and the Blemmyes and Nobades in 452-3, 'in accordance with the ancient law, their crossing to the temple of Isis be unhindered, Egyptians having control of the river boat in which the statue of the goddess is placed and ferried across the river. For at a stated time the barbarians bring the wooden statue to their own country and, after having consulted it, return it safely to the island.'[51]

The temple evidence is one of a number of different indicators suggesting considerable cultural continuity from the late Kushite into the X-Group period. At a small number of urban sites there is cultural and political continuity, largely maintained by the priesthood of some temples in Lower Nubia, which continued to flourish into the fifth century.[52]

In the settlement at Arminna West the excavators found deposits containing both Meroitic and Ballana styles of pottery which they considered to belong to a single contemporary culture, either to be considered as the end of the Meroitic tradition or the beginning of the Ballana tradition: there was no clear break between the two.[53] Trigger considered 'that the transition between the Meroitic and Ballana cultures took place gradually and that Meroitic elements either evolved into Ballana ones or were replaced by traits of Egyptian origin. Several stages can be defined in this process, but since the process was a continuous one all of them are necessarily somewhat arbitrary.'[54] Evidence for continuity between the two cultures had been noted long ago by Junker who wrote:

> There is no striking difference between the X-Group and Meroitic cultures. The grave forms
> are almost the same in both, the differences being mainly in the preference for individual
> types. Numerous pottery types were found in both as well as iron spears, arrowheads and
> tools. Thus both represent in Nubia a single culture which either directly or indirectly
> developed into that of the Christian period.[55]

The Nubian kingdoms in the early sixth century

By the mid sixth century literary sources indicate that there were three Nubian kingdoms, Nobadia in the north, Alodia/Alwa in the south, and Makuria in between. Archaeologically, however, only two cultural assemblages can be identified. In the north we have a highly distinctive material culture first described by George Reisner and called by him the X-Group. The pottery is particularly characteristic with red ware goblets decorated with blobs of paint (Fig. 6), typical artefacts found in large numbers on habitation sites but particularly in burials. South of the Third Cataract, however, the assemblages are very different. This culture has been called the post-Meroitic culture and the distinctive

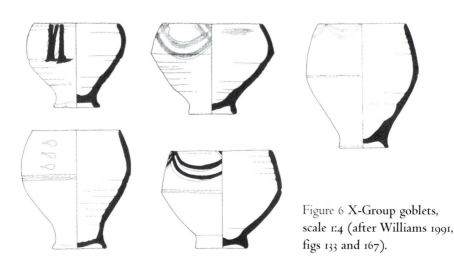

Figure 6 **X-Group goblets, scale 1:4 (after Williams 1991, figs 133 and 167).**

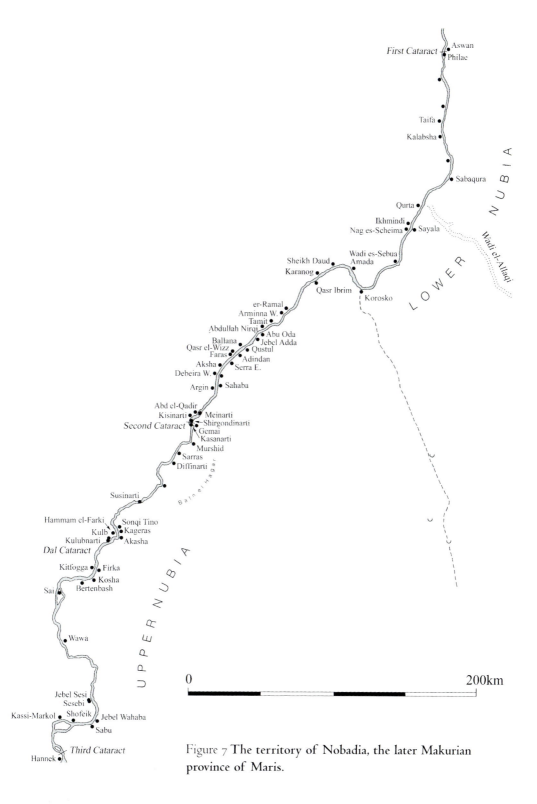

First Cataract
Aswan
Philae

Taifa
Kalabsha

Sabaqura

LOWER NUBIA

Qurta
Ikhmindi
Nag es-Scheima ● Sayala

Wadi el-Allaqi

Wadi es-Sebua
Sheikh Daud ● Amada
Karanog

Qasr Ibrim
Korosko

er-Ramal
Arminna W.
Tamit
Abdullah Nirqi ● Abu Oda
Ballana ● Jebel Adda
Qasr el-Wizz ● Qustul
Faras ● Adindan
Aksha ● Serra E.
Debeira W.
Argin ● Sahaba

Abd el-Qadir
Kisinarti ● Meinarti
Second Cataract Shirgondinarti
Gemai
Kasanarti
Murshid
Sarras
Diffinarti

Susinarti

Bain el hagar

Hammam el-Farki
Kulb ● Sonqi Tino ● Kageras
Kulubnarti ● Akasha
Dal Cataract

Kitfogga ● Firka
● Kosha
Sai ● Bertenbash

● Wawa

UPPER NUBIA

Jebel Sesi
Sesebi
Kassi-Markol ● Shofeik ● Jebel Wahaba
● Sabu

Third Cataract
Hannek ●

0   200km

Figure 7 The territory of Nobadia, the later Makurian
province of Maris.

where the northern border of Alwan territory was, nor how far it was from there to the capital.[58]

The literary sources concerning the conversion of the region to Christianity, to be recounted in the next chapter, incidentally throw light on the relationship between the three kingdoms. It appears that the Kings of Alwa and Nobadia enjoyed cordial relations, while Nobadia and Makuria were not on the best of terms. In the Silko inscription at Kalabsha the Nobadian king recounts how he fought against the Blemmyes and 'on one occasion I ravaged the country of the others too, above the Noubades because they contended with me'. This may be a reference to an attack on Makuria, although it may refer to regions elsewhere where 'above' would mean 'away from the river'.[59] Ibn Selim records that in pre-Christian times the two states were often at war. One can assume that the friendship of the northern and southern states posed a serious threat to Makuria, although whether Makuria was actively hostile to Alwa is unknown.

By the mid sixth century the metropoli of the three kingdoms lay at Faras, Old Dongola, and Soba East.[60] Apart from Faras, which is a short distance upstream of Ballana and Qustul, the other sites are far from the large tumuli cemeteries of the earlier post-Meroitic/X-Group periods, and their choice as capitals may date to a later phase in the reorganization of political control in the region. This suggests that the Nubian Kingdoms of the sixth century were rather different from the fledgling states of the late fourth and fifth centuries known from funerary evidence. The material culture of Nobadia shows a degree of continuity through this period, in spite of the clear literary evidence for both the Blemmyes and the Nobadians in the region. However, differences have been noted between the ceramics of the early and late Ballana phases with the Nubian potters diverging from the Egyptian prototypes of many of the pottery types which had been faithfully adhered to in the earlier X-Group.[61] It has been noted that the late Ballana material appears to be more common in the southern part of Nobadia than in the areas closer to the Egyptian frontier.[62]

Further to the south there is a common ceramic tradition throughout the region from the upper Blue Nile to the Northern Dongola Reach (Fig. 10) at a time when a number of regional power bases are known, at Old Dongola, el-Hobagi and Soba East. El-Hobagi clearly dates to the Kushite to post-Meroitic transition whereas at Soba East occupation began in the later post-Meroitic. In the mid fourth century the centre of power presumably still lay at Meroe. By the end of the century high status burials are no longer found at Meroe, but their presence at el-Hobagi suggests that the power base had shifted upstream to that region, while by the sixth century the very considerable size of the settlement at Soba East, over 150 km further upstream implies that it had shifted yet further south. The status of the old capital at Meroe remains uncertain. Excavations by Garstang before the First World War found extensive cemeteries of the 'post-Meroitic' period but there is very little evidence for occupation within the Kushite town at that time.[63] However the latest structures and occupation deposits may have been either totally lost or heavily denuded. The large amounts of red-brick fragments on the surface of the occupation mounds, where almost all the underlying structures where excavated were of mud bricks, offers support to this observation. According to Bradley, post-Meroitic pottery is present on the surface and is associated with numerous indications of squatter occupation within the temples excavated to the east of the Temple of Amun.[64]

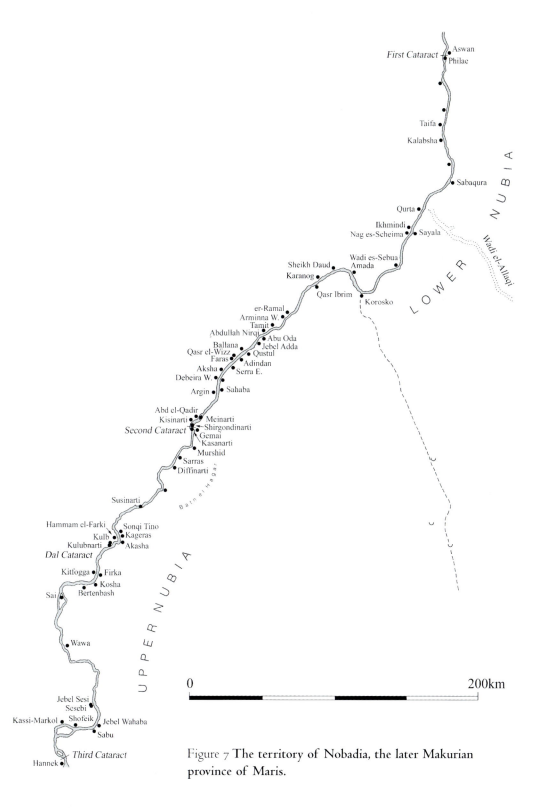

Figure 7 **The territory of Nobadia, the later Makurian province of Maris.**

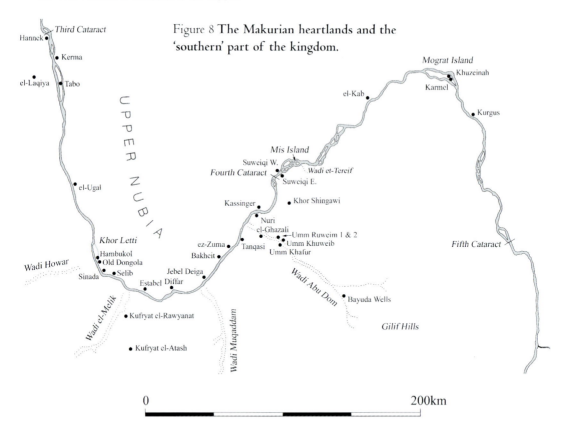

Figure 8 **The Makurian heartlands and the 'southern' part of the kingdom.**

pottery has been called Alwa Ware although this is a rather confusing term as the pottery is certainly not confined to the area which may have been under the control of the kings of Alwa, but is found also throughout the Kingdom of Makuria. The political boundary between Nobadia and Makuria presumably lay around the Third Cataract in the same area as the cultural boundary.[56] The northern limit of Nobadia will have lain at the First Cataract, the border of late Roman, Byzantine, Persian and Muslim Egypt (Fig. 7).

Owing to the homogeneity at this time of the material culture of the Kingdoms of Makuria and Alwa, and to the lack of archaeological work in the border region between the two states, the limits of their respective control is uncertain. It is likely that it lay somewhere between the Fourth and Fifth Cataracts (Figs 8 and 9) although a number of scholars maintain that the actual border lay in the region of Atbara. While this seems inherently unlikely, there is virtually no evidence which can be used to refute such a claim. A single sherd of the highly distinctive Soba Ware, the pottery par excellence of the metropolis of the Kingdom of Alwa, has been found at Jebel Nakharu[57] but cannot be used to argue for political hegemony of that area immediately upstream of the Fifth Cataract. The presence of the chain of fortresses stretching from Jebel Umm Marrihi in the Khartoum Reach as far downstream as Jebel Nakharu, if not as far as Kurgus, may, however, suggest that these reaches of the river were at that time under the same political control. A number of the arguments have hinged on the accounts of Longinus' journey to Alwa in around 580, yet there is nothing in that account that can be used to ascertain

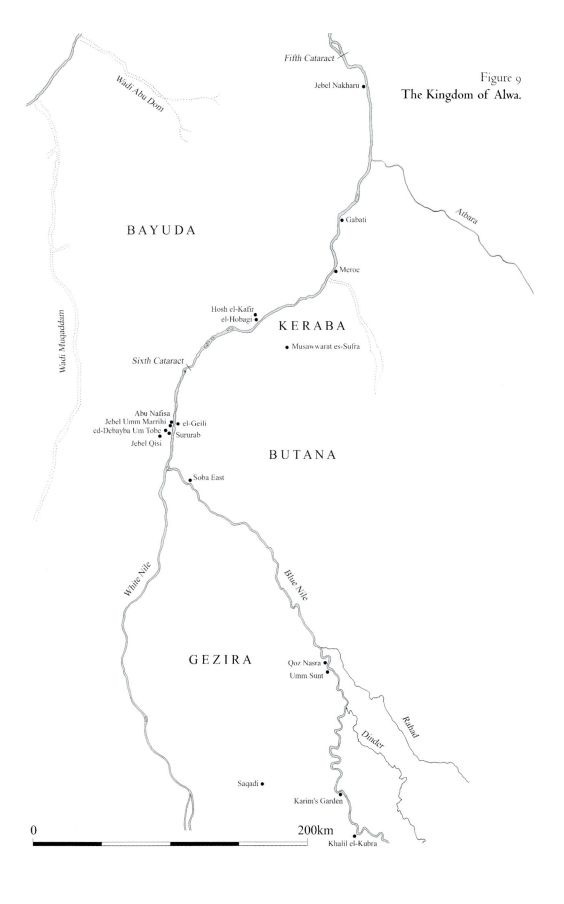

Figure 9
The Kingdom of Alwa.

where the northern border of Alwan territory was, nor how far it was from there to the capital.[58]

The literary sources concerning the conversion of the region to Christianity, to be recounted in the next chapter, incidentally throw light on the relationship between the three kingdoms. It appears that the Kings of Alwa and Nobadia enjoyed cordial relations, while Nobadia and Makuria were not on the best of terms. In the Silko inscription at Kalabsha the Nobadian king recounts how he fought against the Blemmyes and 'on one occasion I ravaged the country of the others too, above the Noubades because they contended with me'. This may be a reference to an attack on Makuria, although it may refer to regions elsewhere where 'above' would mean 'away from the river'.[59] Ibn Selim records that in pre-Christian times the two states were often at war. One can assume that the friendship of the northern and southern states posed a serious threat to Makuria, although whether Makuria was actively hostile to Alwa is unknown.

By the mid sixth century the metropoli of the three kingdoms lay at Faras, Old Dongola, and Soba East.[60] Apart from Faras, which is a short distance upstream of Ballana and Qustul, the other sites are far from the large tumuli cemeteries of the earlier post-Meroitic/X-Group periods, and their choice as capitals may date to a later phase in the reorganization of political control in the region. This suggests that the Nubian Kingdoms of the sixth century were rather different from the fledgling states of the late fourth and fifth centuries known from funerary evidence. The material culture of Nobadia shows a degree of continuity through this period, in spite of the clear literary evidence for both the Blemmyes and the Nobadians in the region. However, differences have been noted between the ceramics of the early and late Ballana phases with the Nubian potters diverging from the Egyptian prototypes of many of the pottery types which had been faithfully adhered to in the earlier X-Group.[61] It has been noted that the late Ballana material appears to be more common in the southern part of Nobadia than in the areas closer to the Egyptian frontier.[62]

Further to the south there is a common ceramic tradition throughout the region from the upper Blue Nile to the Northern Dongola Reach (Fig. 10) at a time when a number of regional power bases are known, at Old Dongola, el-Hobagi and Soba East. El-Hobagi clearly dates to the Kushite to post-Meroitic transition whereas at Soba East occupation began in the later post-Meroitic. In the mid fourth century the centre of power presumably still lay at Meroe. By the end of the century high status burials are no longer found at Meroe, but their presence at el-Hobagi suggests that the power base had shifted upstream to that region, while by the sixth century the very considerable size of the settlement at Soba East, over 150 km further upstream implies that it had shifted yet further south. The status of the old capital at Meroe remains uncertain. Excavations by Garstang before the First World War found extensive cemeteries of the 'post-Meroitic' period but there is very little evidence for occupation within the Kushite town at that time.[63] However the latest structures and occupation deposits may have been either totally lost or heavily denuded. The large amounts of red-brick fragments on the surface of the occupation mounds, where almost all the underlying structures where excavated were of mud bricks, offers support to this observation. According to Bradley, post-Meroitic pottery is present on the surface and is associated with numerous indications of squatter occupation within the temples excavated to the east of the Temple of Amun.[64]

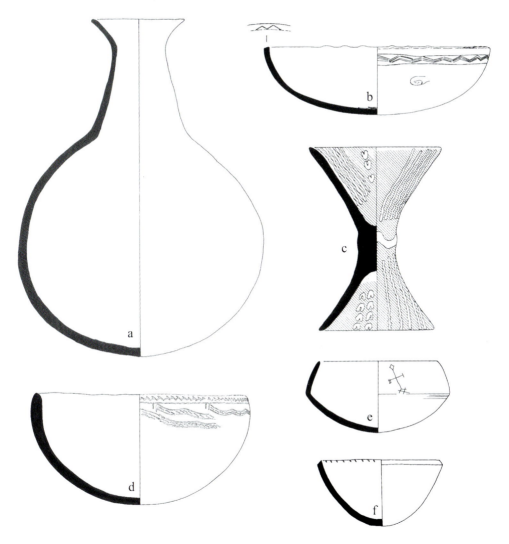

Figure 10 **Pottery of the post-Meroitic period from Karim's Garden (a and f), Gabati (c) and Soba East (b, d and e), scale 1:4 (after Edwards 1991, pls II and IV; Smith 1998, fig. 6.28; Welsby and Daniels 1991, fig. 111; Welsby 1998, figs 46 and 48).**

The political landscape of Nubia thus appears, within the space of two hundred years and perhaps much less, to have undergone two major upheavals. In many ways the changes from the Late Kushite period through into the early post-Meroitic period are more understandable. The loss of political power of the ruling elite at Meroe and its usurpation by those individuals buried at Ballana and Qustul in the north, at el-Hobagi in the south, and perhaps to a lesser extent by those individuals buried at the other centres known from their large burial mounds, brought a number of new localities to the fore. The incomparable richness of the Ballana rulers, where their status is unambiguously stated by the presence of their crowns, indicates their local pre-eminence. How far their writ extended cannot be precisely ascertained although it is very clear that the limits of the culture within which they operated extended to the Third Cataract and the distinctly different material culture immediately beyond does point to the border having lain in that area. The exact status of the el-Hobagi people is a matter of some debate. Although their excavator, Patrice Lenoble, has convincingly argued that they were holders of *imperium*, it cannot be certain whether this was *imperium* delegated from some higher status individuals, i.e., a king, or whether they exercised it in their own right.

The burials at el-Hobagi have perhaps assumed a rather greater importance than is justified in the historiography of the Middle Nile, as they are the only graves marked by massive tumuli to have been extensively excavated in the region south of the Third Cataract. Small-scale excavations were conducted by Shinnie at Tanqasi near Jebel Barkal but the poor nature of the burials uncovered does not seem to be commensurate with the large tumuli which covered them. The tumuli at ez-Zuma have not been investigated. If they are of this date, a likely but at present unproved hypothesis, they must have some relationship with the Tanqasi burials which lie a little over 10 km away across the Nile. The subsequent rise of the Kingdom of Makuria in the Dongola Reach does suggest the possibility that there was an early post-Meroitic power base in that area with burials comparable with those at el-Hobagi if not with those at Ballana.

CHAPTER 3

The arrival and impact of Christianity

One of the first inhabitants of the Middle Nile region to have embraced Christianity was a man described as 'a eunuch and an officer at the court of the Kandake, or queen of Ethiopia', in around 37, recorded in the *Acts of the Apostles*. However, there is no archaeological evidence for the presence of Christianity in the Kingdom of Kush. Although Christianity was adopted as the official religion of the Roman Empire in 312 by the emperor Constantine, a process culminating in the Edict of Theodosius, promulgated in 390, which ordered the closure of all pagan temples, we have little evidence for Christianity in the Nile Valley south of Aswan until the sixth century. In fact, so important were the old pagan cults that the Temple of Isis was uniquely exempt from the terms of Theodosius' edict and continued to function as a major cult centre for the peoples living beyond the Roman frontier. This special treatment of the Isis temple highlights the importance of the relations between Rome and the peoples of Lower Nubia. It would appear that every effort was made to accommodate these peoples in an attempt to maintain stability on the frontier and to protect against incursions into the Roman province of Egypt. As we have seen this policy was only partially successful. Large numbers of Roman artefacts produced in a Christian milieu are found in the graves of the early Nubian elites, but there is no reason to think that these had any religious significance to the individuals who chose to have these high status and valuable objects buried with them in typical pagan fashion. However, one Nobadian prince in the mid fifth century was called Mouses, a popular name in Christian Egypt at that time and one held by several bishops perhaps (but by no means certainly), indicating that he was a Christian.[1] The *phylarch* of the Nobades, Tantani, also appears to have been a Christian by this date.[2]

Political considerations

The sources concerning the introduction of Christianity to Nubia are remarkably full through the good fortune of the survival of a number of accounts written by near contemporary church historians. In the Roman world religion had always been highly political and the late Roman and Byzantine periods saw no change in this. It was clearly felt to be advantageous to bring the peoples beyond the Empire into the Roman state religion, establishing bonds of similar beliefs and also, perhaps, implying at least a spiritual conquest where physical conquest was no longer a practical option. From the Nubian perspective there may well also have been real benefits in a closer association with the Roman rulers. Much reduced territorially during the fifth century with the loss of most of the western provinces of the Empire, the Eastern Roman Empire with its capital at

Constantinople, mounted a vigorous expansionist policy under the emperor Justinian in the 530s which brought about the reconquest of much of North Africa and Italy. It is precisely at this time that we find the first moves being made by the Nubians to adopt the new religion. The official nature of this conversion is borne out by the sources, which clearly state that the impetus for the changeover to Christianity came, in the case of Nobadia, as a direct imperial initiative, in the case of Alwa from the Alwan royal family. Procopius, in the *History of the Wars* states that in 531 Justinian 'got the idea of making the Aithiopians and Homeritae his allies with a view to damage the Persians'.[3] The conversion of the Nubians to Christianity was a part of this process.

The conversion of Nubia: the literary evidence

At the time of Nubia's conversion there were two major denominations within the Byzantine Empire, the Melkites and the Monophysites. The Melkites adhered to the dogma of the separate human and divine natures of Christ but united into One Person, and it was this interpretation which was accepted at the Council of Chalcedon in 451 as the correct doctrine, while the Monophysites, heretics after 451, believed in the single nature of Christ, partly divine, partly human. The supporters of the dual nature of Christ were known as Dyophysites or Chalcedonians and, as they were supported by the emperor, were also called *basilikoi*, the Arabic version of which, *maliki*, has given us the term Melkite. The Monophysites were also known as Jacobites after Jacob Baradai who organized them in Egypt, where most of them resided, around 530.[4]

According to the sources there were three stages in the conversion of Nubia. The northern Kingdom of Nobadia with its close geographical proximity to Roman Egypt was, not surprisingly, the first target of missionary activities. John of Ephesus, a native of Amida, modern Diyabikir in eastern Turkey, is the main source for these events, but his account must be understood in the context of his profession of Monophysite beliefs and is hence inevitably biased. He resided in Constantinople where he held a number of important offices at Court and enjoyed the friendship of Justinian, despite being a Monophysite. He was thus well placed to receive information about contemporary affairs. He had also worked as a missionary in Anatolia and would have been well informed on the difficulties of such activities.[5] According to him there was intense rivalry at the imperial court between the Monophysite Empress Theodora and the Melkite Emperor Justinian and they sent rival missions to Nobadia. The Empress, by intimidating the Byzantine officials in Southern Egypt, was able to ensure that it was her Monophysite mission that reached Nobadia first, around 543, and was able to influence the Nobadian king so that he politely refused the advances of the subsequent Melkite missionaries.[6] The Monophysite mission was led by Julian, an Egyptian monk, 'an old man of great worth … who conceived an earnest spiritual desire to christianize the wandering people who dwell on the eastern borders of the Thebais beyond Egypt'.[7] Although this does not seem a good geographical description of the location of Nobadia it is clear that Nobadia was the subject of Julian's fervour.

Julian and his fellow ambassadors were apparently received with joy; an army was sent to meet them and they were shown into the presence of the Nobadian king who received them gladly. The ambassadorial nature of the missionaries' visit is underlined by the letters they bore from the Empress and also by the great gifts they presented to the Nobadian ruler. They also brought numerous baptismal garments to expedite the task of enrolling the Nubians into the Christian faith. The Melkite missionaries on their arrival were faced with a *fait accompli* and, although the gifts they brought from Justinian were accepted, and letters and gifts were exchanged, the Melkite faith was not accepted. Julian remained in Nobadia for two years, suffering greatly from the rigours of the climate. 'He used to sit from the whole of the third to the tenth hour in caves full of water with the whole people of the region, naked or, better, wearing only a cloth, while he could perspire only with the help of water.'[8] During his stay he baptized the king and his nobles and many other people and entrusted them to Theodore, Bishop of Philae[9] before he returned to Constantinople. After Theodore returned to Philae around 551 it was several years before Longinus, who was detained for three years in Constantinople as a result of Melkite opposition, arrived in Nobadia where he continued the work of the earlier missionaries, Julian having died in the meantime. During his six-year sojourn he instructed all the people in the Christian religion, built what was presumably the first church in Nubia, established the clergy and organized the liturgy, and set up all the church institutions.

John of Ephesus is totally silent about the conversion of Makuria and this, it has been generally accepted, underlines his partisan stance on religious matters. The conversion of Makuria is recorded by John of Biclar who, while in Constantinople in 568, notes that 'about this time, the people of the Maccurritae received the faith of Christ'. In 573 a delegation arrived in the capital from Makuria bearing gifts for the emperor Justin 'of elephant tusks and a giraffe, and stated their friendship with the Romans'.[10] No further details are known but it is assumed that Makuria was converted to Melkite Christianity (as the silence of John of Ephesus would suggest) although nowhere is this explicitly stated. This has led some scholars to doubt that Makuria was Melkite at this time.[11] The enmity between Makuria and Nobadia is confirmed by the accounts of the conversion of Alwa. The adoption of the differing Christian dogmas, and presumably the concomitant alliance with different factions at the Byzantine court may be a manifestation of these poor relations. It can have been of no comfort to the Makurian king to have both his northern and southern neighbours on friendly terms, as they evidently had been for some time,[12] and also for both those states to have close relations with the Byzantine court. The close relations between Makuria and Byzantium are highlighted by the early ecclesiastical architecture at Old Dongola which is in marked contrast to the early churches so far known from Nobadia.[13]

According to John of Ephesus, 'when the people of Alodia knew that the Nobades had been converted, their king sent a letter to the king of the Nobades, asking to send him (the bishop) who had taught and baptized the Nobades, that he might instruct and baptize also the Alodaei.'[14] John of Ephesus has much to say about intrigues against Longinus by certain clerics in Alexandria and of an attempt by those individuals to send a rival mission to Alwa (Alodia) which, however, was rejected by the Alwan king being enjoined to 'depart, therefore, from our land, that you die not miserably'.[15] No details are given as to how these missionaries travelled to and from Alwa. Longinus's journey to Alwa was fraught with difficulties. He left Nobadia in the company 'of some people who know the desert' and under the protection of the King of the Blemmyes, and took one of the cross-desert routes which apparently avoided Makuria. Although John of Ephesus records that the Makuritae sought to impede Longinus's journey 'moved by satanic envy' the choice of a cross-desert route would have been the obvious one for anyone travelling from Nobadia to Alwa. The most suitable route may have been the Korosko Road which left the Nile at Korosko and headed directly across the desert, rejoining the Nile in the region of Abu Hamed, a journey of approximately eight days by camel in the nineteenth century.[16] All does not appear to have gone well on Longinus' journey; he and many other of his companions became ill and seventeen camels died because of the heat.

When Longinus arrived at the borders of Alwa, the Alwan king sent one of his noblest men, Itiqya who received him with great attention and introduced him into the country with great honours. He then proceeded to the capital by ship, and was there met by the king. The name of the Alwan capital is nowhere mentioned but there is no good reason to doubt that it was already at Soba East. Within a few days Longinus had baptized the king, all his nobles and the greater part of the population, or by the king's own admission in a letter of thanks to the King of the Nobades, himself, his nobles and all of his family. The Nobadian king is called Orfiulo or Awarfiulai and is perhaps to be identified with Eirpanome who was on the throne in 559. In his letter to the King of the Nobades the Alwan ruler requests that church furniture be readied for dispatch to him.

Longinus and his followers were not the only Christians in the Alwan capital in 580. They met there 'certain Aksumites who had fallen into the malady of the fancy of Halicarnassus'. It is often assumed that these were a rival mission but this is not supported by Longinus' account as published by John of Ephesus. The ease with which these individuals were won over to the 'true' faith does suggest that they were not missionaries.[17] We have no other evidence to suggest what relations there may have been at that time between the Aksumite state, converted to Christianity in the mid fourth century AD, and the fledgling Nubian state of Alwa.

Nubian Christianity

In Byzantine Egypt the rival Christian doctrines of the Monophysites and Melkites had come to symbolize two groups with different political ideologies. The Monophysites were Egyptian 'nationalists' and Monophysitism was professed as a mark of opposition to Byzantine rule. The Melkites, on the other hand, were imperialists closely tied to the Byzantine state. Whether these political nuances were understood by the Nubians is unclear, and it would perhaps have been surprising if the Nobadian and Alwan rulers sought to associate themselves with the anti-imperial *fellaheen* of Egypt rather that with the imperial administration.

Archaeologically the two doctrines are difficult to distinguish. We might expect differences in the internal arrangements in churches but the early churches in Nobadia and Makuria do not exhibit any features which can be confidently associated with one or other of the two beliefs. Some have suggested that the prayer for the dead to be found on funerary *stelae* is indicative of the Christian doctrine adhered to. In early Christian Makuria the commonly used prayer, written in Greek, might have Melkite associations. However, with the union of the two kingdoms the same prayer is also to be found in the north in both a Greek and a Coptic version. It became accepted throughout the united kingdoms and was then used in a Monophysite context. It then certainly, and perhaps also earlier, had no doctrinal connotations.[18] Other traits held to indicate one or other doctrine have been advanced at Faras. Among them are the liturgical vestments worn by clerics depicted in the paintings on the walls of the cathedral which were thought to provide evidence for a change from Monophysite to Melkite practice in the late tenth to early eleventh century.[19]

Although politically Makuria came to dominate Nobadia Monophysitism appears to have become the dominant creed. This was presumably the result of the Nubian church being cut off from Constantinople with the arrival of the Arabs in Egypt in the seventh century and, thereafter, the closest religious ties remained with the Monophysite patriarch and church at Alexandria.

THE ARCHAEOLOGICAL EVIDENCE FOR CHRISTIANITY IN NUBIA

The arrival of Christianity brought about profound changes in Nubia. Nubia had a rich pagan heritage which, for many millennia in the north of Nubia, and at least from the early Kushite period in the south, had been exposed to Egyptian theology which was modified and assimilated with the local cults to form a highly complex syncretic religion. The state religions of the Kingdoms of Kush, based firstly on Kerma and latterly on Napata and Meroe, exhibit many Pharaonic aspects. Whereas the ancient religion of the Egyptian pharaohs was displaced by Christianity in the first few centuries AD in Egypt the Middle Nile remained a bastion of the old religion which continued to be practised until the sixth century. As noted above political considerations may have been more important than religious fervour in the early stages of the introduction of Christianity which then had a trickle-down effect eventually being professed by most, if not all, of the native population of medieval Nubia. However, it has been suggested that Christianity may have made inroads into Nubia well before the date of the conversion of the rulers, spread as a result of 'wandering monks' and perhaps also by Christian merchants[20] although this is difficult, if not impossible, to document on the ground. There is certainly continuance of pagan practices and pre-Christian culture after that date making it extremely difficult to be certain whether the latest pagan and the earliest Christian graves in particular pre- or post-date the arrival of the official missionaries.

The impact of Christianity in the archaeological record is most obvious in the architectural field with the construction of churches, in the advent of Christian motifs in art, and in funerary culture. Although objects bearing Christian-inspired decoration are common in early tombs they cannot by themselves be used as evidence for the introduction of Christianity.

Churches

It is the construction of churches and the changes in burial customs which are the clearest indicators of the arrival of Christianity. Church construction may be more a reflection of official sanction of the new religion, while funerary practices are a more sensitive indicator of the beliefs of the individual. According to John of Ephesus, Longinus built a church in Nobadia at some date between 569 and 575 and, in the context of the conversion of the Nubian states, it can be assumed that this was the first church in the region to have been constructed. Until the early sixth century the Temple of Isis had remained in use for

Figure 11 **The church inserted within the temple built by the Kushite king Taharqo (690-664 BC) at Qasr Ibrim.**

pagan worship. It was the first of many Nubian temples to be converted to church use, by *c.* 535-7.[21] The dedicatory inscription reads:

'This place became, in the na[me of the holy a]nd consubstanti[al Trinity, the ho]use of [St Stephen u]nder [o]ur [most God-loving father], B[ishop Apa Theodoros. May God] pre[serve him for a very lo]ng ti[me].'[22]

The Temple of Taharqo at Qasr Ibrim was converted into a church (Fig. 11) and it has been claimed that this event took place well before the historically attested date of 543 for the introduction of Christianity to the area. The claim is based on the date of the ceramics in the fill at the back of the curved wall of the apse inserted into the temple's sanctuary chamber, part of the modifications associated with its conversion to Christian use. All this material is dateable to the late X-Group period suggesting a date for this fill in the very early sixth century.[23] However the relevance of this ceramic material to the date of the construction of the apse wall is far from certain. The filling material was presumably quarried from elsewhere on the site and the incorporation of the latest material in this dump need not have immediately pre-dated its re-deposition in the temple/church.

The date of the conversion of temples into churches may have varied widely from one site to another and we cannot assume that they all necessarily date to the immediate aftermath of the first arrival of Christianity. The temple at Taifa was not used for Christian worship until the eighth century while the church at Tabo was built on the site of the XXVth dynasty temple, which continued in use into the later Kushite period, only after over 1 m of earth had formed over the denuded ruins.[24]

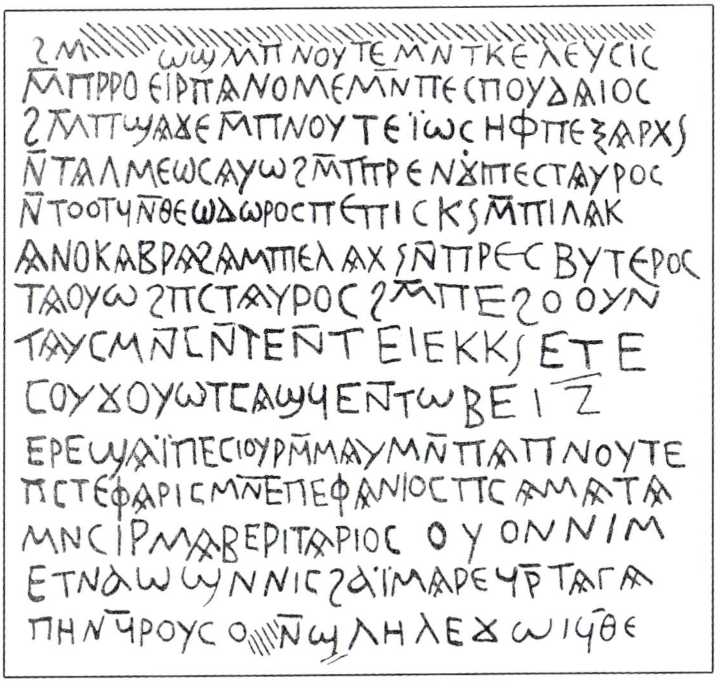

Figure 12 **The foundation inscription set up by Eirpanome in the church at Dendur (after Monneret de Villard 1935, fig. 34).**

The earliest epigraphic evidence we have for the construction of a church is an inscription (Fig. 12) dated to the reign of the Nobadian king Eirpanome.[25] It records that,

> By [the w]ill of god and the decree
> of King Eirpanome and the [man] zealous
> in the word of god, Joseph, the *exarch* of
> Talmis, and by our receiving the cross
> from Theodore, the bish[op] of Philae,
> I, Abraham, the most hum[ble] priest,
> [it is] who set up the cross on the day
> they founded this church, ... [26]

This inscription in Coptic commemorating the conversion of the Temple at Dendur into a church probably dates either to 559 or 574.[27] The dating of many of the other temple conversions cannot be precisely fixed. As noted above, the temple built by Taharqo at Qasr Ibrim in the seventh century BC may possibly have been used for Christian worship much earlier. Not all temples were converted, although this may have been influenced by practical considerations rather than a lingering sense of pagan sanctity as has been suggested to explain the lack of use of the temples built by Ramesses II at Abu Simbel.[28]

At Faras, the Nobadian capital, we might expect to find evidence for the earliest church, perhaps that built by Longinus. However, this site had a long history of settlement during the medieval period, little of which could be investigated before the site disappeared beneath the waters of Lake Nubia. Limited excavations under the floors of the later cathedral revealed a mud-brick church which has been dated to around the time of the official conversion of Nobadia in the mid sixth century.[29]

Within the fortress of Ikhmindi one of the two churches was founded by the king or kinglet Tokiltoeton and was completed by 577 by the same Joseph who is recorded at Dendur.[30] This is the earliest closely-dated purpose-built church in Nubia. Excavations are continuing at Old Dongola, the Makurian capital. To date a large number of churches have been located of which the earliest has been dated to mid sixth century.[31]

Few churches are known in the Kingdom of Alwa. At Soba East the earliest of the churches excavated at the western end of mound B does not predate the mid seventh century[32] although the church on mound C, with its stone columns, may well be earlier. However, the developments in ecclesiastical architecture as documented by excavations at Old Dongola must make one wary of assuming that columnar supports are necessarily earlier than brick piers. Earlier churches may lie buried elsewhere on the site. The vitality of early Christianity in the town must be considered in the light of the large structure, apparently a temple, which is not earlier than the sixth century,[33] and can hardly have been built on the outskirts of this major urban centre without official sanction.

Archaeological evidence to suggest a gradual infiltration of Christianity into Nobadia, perhaps before the official conversion of the kingdom, comes from Christian symbols carved on pottery, after firing, presumably by the owners. This is common in Lower Nubia, and quite frequent at Ballana.[34] What are thought to be locally-made leather quivers from Jebel Adda, with the cross as a decorative motif, were found in what may be fifth-century graves.[35] The carving of a cross motif on the wall of a rock-cut tomb at Qasr Ibrim, which contained pottery of the late fourth or fifth centuries, above the head of the deceased,[36] is further proof of the gradual infiltration of Christianity, something that was inevitable in areas close to the Egyptian border where there must have been considerable contact between the local inhabitants and traders from Christian Egypt. A shift from pagan to Christian funerary beliefs at Sesebi has been dated on ceramic evidence to the late fifth to early sixth century[37] but attempts to closely date the pottery of this period must be treated with caution.

At Soba East at least one early Christian scratched a cross on two pottery vessels of typical pre-Christian type.[38] The evidence provided by the fine painted ceramics from Soba, which have been named Soba Ware, is indicative of the co-existence of Christian and pagan culture. The motifs in general and in detail seem firmly tied to styles of decoration employed on Christian wall paintings. However, Soba Ware is found closely associated with typical later post-Meroitic ceramics, and its presence at Soba pre-dates the construction of what was probably a temple on the outskirts of the town.[39]

It has been suggested that a major factor in the conversion of Nubia to Christianity may have been the activities of monks, rather than the activities of the official missionaries recorded in the ancient sources.[40] However, there is no literary evidence to support this suggestion, nor can any definite monastic community be dated earlier than the dates recorded for the official missions. This must remain a hypothesis which may be given greater credence by further archaeological work. The duration of the conversion phase may have spanned some considerable time. The Makurian king Mercurios, reigning around 700, was named the 'New Constantine' in *The Annals of the Coptic Patriarchs*. It has been suggested that this may well have been as a result of his zeal in stamping out paganism.[41]

Funerary culture

One of the greatest changes was connected with funerary culture. From the earliest burials known archaeologically in the Middle Nile, that is from the Khartoum Mesolithic (*c.* 8000–5000 BC), grave goods had been included with the deceased[42] implying some concept of an afterlife and the need of worldly provisions, either to be used in that after-life, or to assist in the passage to the afterlife. In Egypt the survival of the physical body became a prerequisite for life beyond death. Although mummification did not dominate the funerary scene on the Middle Nile, the provision of grave goods is manifest at many levels of society. The plundering of most of the richest tombs allows us only to glimpse the range and value of the objects provided for the afterlife and those associated with the rituals at the graveside. Some of the best preserved burials to have survived come, as we have seen, from the early phases of the Nubian Kingdoms, from Ballana and Qustul, from Firka and Gemai, and from el-Hobagi. The arrival of Christianity brought an immediate stop to these practices at least in the graves of those professing the new faith. Also, whereas the burial of a high status individual demanded an impressive tomb monument in the pagan milieu, the ideology of the Christians on the Middle Nile eschewed such symbols. It is a startling fact that although we know the tombs of the latest rulers at Kerma, of almost all the rulers of the Kushite state, and of many of the earliest Nubian kings, after the arrival of Christianity in the sixth century we do not have even one tomb which can be identified with certainty as that of any subsequent monarch, and only a handful of royal tombstones have been recovered. This may partly be the result of the difficulties of recognizing such individuals, particularly if the royal regalia was not buried with them.

Żurawski, considering the burials of the eighteen high-ranking ecclesiastics in the three tombs in the north-western part of the Monastery of the Holy Trinity at Old Dongola, noted that all but one were wrapped in coarse shrouds and tightly tied. By contrast, the individual placed in the northern tomb beneath the templon arch was clad in an extremely elaborate garb consisting of costly textiles of various fabrics and including gold thread. These garments have nothing in common with the modest burials of ecclesiastics known from several sites in Makuria, among them those of archbishops at Faras, men who occupied the very upper echelons in the church hierarchy. The imported textiles, which do not resemble the liturgical vestments depicted on the bishops' portraits, may be on the body of a layman, and Żurawski is of the opinion that the only layman who would be buried in such a holy area would be a king of Makuria, who was perhaps also the founder of the Monastery and of the adjacent *xenon*.[43] If this burial is that of a Makurian king it raises the possibility that those individuals buried in fine clothing, including items with gold thread, at Soba East may have held similar rank.[44]

As one might expect, where there is continuity of settlement, there is frequently continuity in cemetery use from the pagan into the Christian phases and evidence for respect by the later Christian population for their pagan ancestors. This has been demonstrated at a number of sites among them Sesebi. Tumulus 201 a little to the north of the Pharaonic town has many features in common with pagan X-Group burials further to the north. The nearby tumulus 101 seems to be of very similar date but appears to be ideologically transitional. The body is buried without grave goods, is aligned east-west with the head to the west, but is placed on a bed. Immediately to the west of the tumulus is a tight cluster

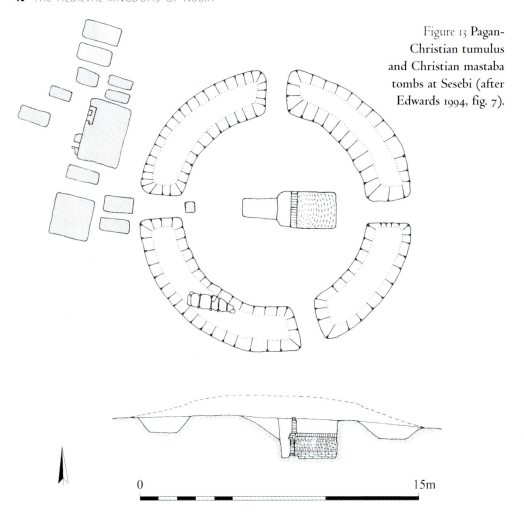

Figure 13 **Pagan-Christian tumulus and Christian mastaba tombs at Sesebi (after Edwards 1994, fig. 7).**

0   15m

of 12 mud-brick mastabas (Fig. 13), marking the positions of typical Christian graves, suggesting the possibility of some familial relationship between the individuals whose final resting places were marked by the traditional, and by the new, tomb monument types.[45] A very similar situation was noted in the cemetery at Jebel Ghaddar North where Christian burials cluster around a post-Meroitic tumulus.[46] The earliest Christian mastaba burials were placed in close proximity to the latest tumulus dating to the seventh century, the burial beneath which is devoid of grave goods although it was in other ways typical of post-Meroitic burials in the cemetery.[47] Close physical proximity between X-Group north-south burials and Christian east-west burials have also been noted in other cemeteries.

FUNERARY RITUAL

There is a considerable degree of continuity in the funerary ritual of the late Kushite and the earliest phases of the Nubian kingdoms and the significance of this has been the focus of considerable debate since the excavation of the X-Group tombs at Ballana and Qustul between 1931 and 1934. More recent work, at el-Hobagi in particular, to the south west

of Meroe, has led to a reassessment of just what was changing at the time of the undoubted political collapse of the Kushite state in the fourth century. As we have seen, one of the most dramatic differences between the burials of Christians and those of the earlier pagan inhabitants along the Middle Nile was the absence of grave goods. The burials at el-Hobagi, Qustul, Ballana and elsewhere contain abundant grave goods as did the late Kushite elite burials. Many of these grave goods not only bear similarities in style to Kushite material, but the types suggest that there was a continuity of ritual and an appreciation of the significance of the objects buried. Patrice Lenoble has made a very detailed and penetrating analysis of the material from el-Hobagi and has recognized the survival of libating and censing rituals, clearly indicating an understanding of Kushite funerary ritual by the people who buried their dead there. In the graves are bottles and cups associated with this Isiac ritual.[48] He has further established the high political status of the individuals by drawing attention to their similar perception of the symbols of power, though expressed in a different way to that of their predecessors, the Kushite kings. They were buried with a vast array of weaponry including lances, swords and archery equipment (fig. 14) with over 306 arrowheads recovered from grave HBG VI/1 and over 425 from HBG III/1, which can be compared to the importance of archery in Kushite royal iconography where bows and arrows are depicted in reliefs and are also found in royal tombs.[49]

One of the hallmarks of burials of this period is the presence of human and animal sacrifices. It is the presence of the human sacrifices in particular, first uncovered in large numbers during the excavations at Qustul and Ballana, which was held to underscore the barbaric nature of the X-Group culture. The excavators described the scene in emotive terms: 'The silver trappings glinting in the Nubian sun, the horses stumbling on the uneven surface of the ramp, then the axe blows, the slumping animals, the anguished stifled cries of the slaves, drowned by the warling and chanting of mourners and the rhythmic beat of the drums.'[50] 'Cleaning those charnel houses with their mixture of human

Figure 14 **Weaponry in Tomb HBG III/1 at el-Hobagi (after Lenoble 1997, fig. 2).**

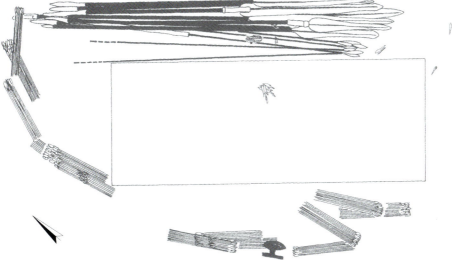

0   5m

Figure 15 **Tomb Q.3 at Qustul**
(after Emery and Kirwan
1938, fig. 8).

pomp and human suffering, it was not difficult to visualize that scene of horror as the body of the king was laid on the bed in his tomb, followed by the terror-stricken men and women, dragged down in the darkness by their slayers.'[51] However, this was not a re-emergence of the practice of human and animal sacrifice after a long period of abeyance but a continuation of a tradition found in the later Kushite period. From generation 46-7 onwards (first century BC) in Kushite elite and royal burials in the North and West cemeteries at Meroe, up to seven additional burials have been noted. In some of the royal X-Group burials the numbers are higher, a maximum of nineteen at Qustul, nine at Ballana and four in one of the elite burials at Firka.[52] Lenoble, referring to the human victims, suggests that, rather than this being the sacrifice of the deceased's retainers, it actually represented a continuation of the practice of ritual slaughter of enemies on the occasion of the funeral, and is another 'symbol of power' surviving from the Kushite period. The sacrifice of animals also displays continuity from the Kushite period and has a similar meaning.[53]

At Qustul the greatest number of sacrificed animals was in Tomb Q.3 (Fig. 15), and consisted of the following:

Species	Total no.	No.	Location
dogs	45	1	lowest level of the tumulus above the filled ramp
		1	head of the ramp
		2	forecourt
		1	ramp
		40	Room 1
donkeys	2	1	ramp
		1	forecourt
camels	4	4	ramp
horses	17	4	ramp
		5	forecourt
		2	Room 1
		6	Room 2
sheep	2	2	forecourt
cow	1	1	plundered area
bull	1	1	plundered area

As well as animals sacrificed in the installations under the tumuli, there were also others buried in one to three pits between 20 and 45 m away to the west. These contained the remains of horses, donkeys and camels, either intact, decapitated, dismembered or partly burnt. Of the three pits associated with Tomb Q.3 two each contained two layers of animal bones, the remains of several camels, donkeys and many horses, or at least bits of them, with an insufficient number of hooves to go around, separated by a layer of clean sand. All the eight to ten horses in each pit were headless and the heads were not included in the pit. Some remains of saddles and other fittings were present. The third pit, really a double pit, had one part totally empty, the other with four complete horses.[54] In the elite cemetery at Firka camels were sacrificed on the stairways leading to Tombs A.11 and A.12, there was a horse towards the bottom of the stairway in Tomb A.11, a donkey at the bottom of the stairway and another in one of the two chambers in Tomb A.14, and a cow between rooms I and II in A.11.[55] At Gemai were camels and horses.[56]

No human sacrificial victims have been found at el-Hobagi in contrast to Qustul and Ballana, and only one sacrificed animal, a horse, was found in Tumulus HBG III/1.[57] No sacrifices were found in the albeit limited excavations of the large tumuli at Tanqasi.

Away from the high status cemeteries sacrificial victims are rare. Dogs were sacrificed at a number of sites, for example at the bottom of the ramp leading to the grave under tumulus 201 at Sesebi.[58] Lenoble's study of these animal sacrifices has linked them to Kushite ritual, where the dog in particular has an important role in royal iconography, and he suggests that in the post-Meroitic period they retained this role in a royal and elite context.[59] Their significance in the tombs of lower status individuals is more difficult to access. Do they still imply some official rank or do they have an entirely different meaning? To the list of species sacrificed may be added two cats at Tabo.[60]

Some elements of funerary ritual at the interface between pagan and Christian funerary culture may be visible at tumulus 101 at Sesebi.[61] The deceased is buried without grave goods, and is aligned in the Christian manner. To the west of the grave, immediately within the ditch at a point where a pathway leads across it, was a small mud-brick platform reminiscent of the offering table stands within the Kushite cemetery at Karanog.[62] The small group of ceramics close by, later sealed by the tumulus, and the ceramics in the adjacent stretch of ditch, suggest that there was a funerary feast of some sort. The three lamps sealed under the tumulus, however, can be compared with the common practice of associating lamps with Christian burials.

Burials on beds are a post-Meroitic feature which can also be observed, albeit rarely, in the very earliest Christian period, perhaps in burial B6 at Firka, an extended inhumation of a female of about thirty years placed in a mud-brick vaulted chamber.[63] At Kulubnarti a vaulted tomb within the Christian cemetery contains a bed burial, the individual covered with a brightly coloured blanket and with a *qulla* (water jar), probably with a lamp resting on top of it, by the head. It dates to the Classic or Late Christian periods.[64]

Although, with the establishment of Christianity, grave goods were not usually included with Christian burials, this is not invariably the case and items of clothing, footwear and personal jewellery in particular were sometimes left on the body. There are also a number of graves, particularly at Faras and Old Dongola, where grave goods are an important feature. In the vicinity of the Faras cathedral all the tombs of the earlier bishops are devoid of grave goods. However, starting with the burial of Ioannes in 1005, grave furnishings are provided. In his tomb, which also contained the burials of four of his successors, each body was accompanied by a consistent array of goods. By the head was placed a water jar and a small lamp of the 'saucer' type. Two of the jars were undecorated, but the other three were painted with wavy-line motifs, fish and dots.[65] Near the head and feet of the latest occupant were two large jars. In one of the crypts in the Monastery of the Holy Trinity[66] at Old Dongola were three *qullas* and three lamps at the western end close to the heads of the deceased, while two *qulla* stood in the western corners. There were also baskets and abundant textiles. Another *qulla* stood upright in the access shaft.[67]

Żurawski has suggested that the placing of a *qulla* close to the mouth, to provide for the refreshment of the deceased, is a tradition seen much earlier in Graeco-Roman Egypt, and that the appearance of this custom in the later phases of Nubian Christianity is to be connected with a weakening of the Christian doctrines and the 'nationalization' of the Nubian Church.[68] However, these vessels may have had a liturgical and protective function and contained holy water.[69] Żurawski draws attention to another survival of a pre-Christian tradition, the symbolic protection of the head using upright bricks and stones seen throughout Nubia (see p. 66). Grave goods consisting of a lamp with a segmental dish over it and another carinated dish were found among the disturbed burials dumped into the crypt of Church A at Soba East.[70]

Grave goods in more humble burials are extremely rare. One grave within the disused church on the North Kom at Hambukol contained a leather cup and a ceramic bowl placed by the head of the deceased.[71] At nearby Old Dongola grave goods in similar graves are confined 'to some bricks, huge mud stopper and some jar sealings of smaller size piled above the head of the deceased'.[72] In northern Nubia many early Christian graves contained date stones. They may represent a survival of pre-Christian offerings of food for the dead, and such deposits have also been found in the Old Dongola area in post-Meroitic graves.[73] At Kulubnarti ten out of the twelve burials accompanied by personal jewellery were of juveniles and this is a feature noted at other Christian cemeteries.[74]

Grave types

KUSHITE GRAVES

During the Kushite period a range of grave types had been in vogue. Among the more humble members of society side- and end-niche graves, approached down a sloping ramp, were common, as also were simple elongated pit graves. Higher status burials were placed within rock-cut chambers sometimes with one or more antechambers, as in the royal burials at Meroe, or were within barrel-vaulted tombs, again usually with descendaries. Although in the earlier Kushite period crouched inhumations were ubiquitous many later burials contained individuals laid in an extended position, most frequently on their back. There was variation in the orientation with the graves usually aligned east-west but with little preference being displayed in the placement of the head, whether to the east or west.

PAGAN NUBIAN GRAVES

In the pagan phase of the Nubian kingdoms crouched inhumations are once again common. In what had been the heartlands of the Kushite state the early Nubian graves were very similar to many of those which had preceded them. At Meroe in the northern necropolis, thought to date from the first century BC into the second century AD, the graves had small chambers entered down a narrow flight of steps. One body was slightly flexed, laid on its left side, head to the east.[75] The late Kushite through to post-Meroitic graves in the middle and southern necropolises, on the other hand, had tombs with double descendaries giving access to a single oval tomb chamber set transversely to the descendaries, and similar tombs but with a single descendary and two chambers.[76] The position of the bodies was uncertain although the excavator, John Garstang, considered that in the middle necropolis the bodies had been placed on beds with the head to the south, while in the southern necropolis they were generally contracted.[77] A major feature of interest is the reuse of offering tables and pyramid finials in the walls built to block the entrances to the burial chambers, indicating that some of the practices of the earlier funerary cults were no longer observed, or at least that earlier Kushite burials were no longer respected although too much significance should perhaps not be attached to it. During the Kushite period a number of earlier tomb monuments in the North and West cemeteries at Meroe, among other sites, were demolished and the stonework reused, though we do not know the circumstances surrounding the destruction of the earlier monuments. A similar lack of respect can also be documented within Christian cemeteries of the medieval period but the implication of this behaviour is uncertain. The reuse of material derived from earlier Kushite funerary monuments may be partly opportunistic, and need not imply the arrival of a new group with scant regard for the earlier inhabitants of the area. Pragmatic considerations may have been more important; the reuse of a collapsed monument or the demolition of one inconveniently placed, although the lack of provision of offering tables, in particular at Meroe, and of ba-statues and *stelae* in northern Nubia for the new burials, does indicate a change in attitude towards some of the physical manifestations of the funerary practices of the earlier inhabitants.

At Arminna West during the X-Group most people continued to be buried in reused late Kushite graves beneath mastaba and pyramids.[78] This may simply have been the continuation of earlier practice where tombs were frequently reused, in some cases clearly for the burials of descendants or relations of the individual for whom the grave and its monument were originally erected. Elsewhere there is considerable variation. In the Kalabsha region the typical X-Group tomb monument was the stone cairn[79] and these have also been noted at Arminna West. Similar monuments are widespread in Nubia but when not excavated their dates remain open to question. Also in the Kalabsha region are well-built cylindrical cairns which have the burial chamber contained within the superstructure in contrast to what is found at most other periods of Nubian history.[80]

In Lower Nubia many poor individuals were buried with the minimum of effort in so-called 'crevice burials'. In some of the examples at Arminna West the natural crevices were enlarged to accept the body and then covered by piles of stones to form the tumuli.[81]

Figure 16 **Post-Meroitic burial in tomb T.83 at Gabati (photo D. N. Edwards; courtesy of the SARS Gabati Archive).**

The elite and royal burials at Qustul and Ballana were placed within elaborate tombs. Although they all differ in detail they can be divided into a number of general types.[82] The earliest, at Qustul, is very similar to late Kushite tombs with a lateral chamber opening off a pit which was subsequently closed by a mud-brick wall. Subsequent types have multi-roomed chambers, the earliest being Q.3 which uniquely is constructed of red brick on a socle of roughly cut stone. Entry is via a sloping ramp. The tomb was a rectangular structure, 9.75 x 7 m in size, with six vaulted rooms (Fig. 15).[83] The next type has a linear arrangement of rooms and exhibits a wide range of variability. It is found at Qustul and also at Ballana. With the move of the burials to Ballana we see the re-

Figure 17 **The burial shaft under Tumulus VI at el-Hobagi (photo P. Lenoble).**

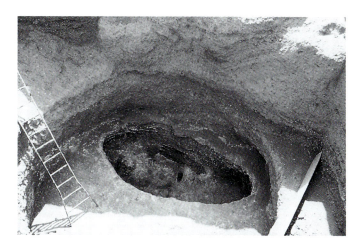

emergence of the tradition of bed burials, the deceased placed on an *angareeb* as in the Kerma period, together with the burial of a 'retainer queen'. The tradition of bed burials is not widespread at this period but has been noted in cemeteries as far upstream as Gabati (Fig. 16) and Meroe.[84] A distinctive feature of the next phase was that the main burial is placed within a pit dug into the floor of the burial chamber. Orientation of the bodies varied considerably over time.

Other elite burials of this period, all under large tumuli, have been excavated at Gemai, Firka, and Kosha. A number of the tombs at Gemai are similar to the earliest examples at Qustul with a shaft and side niche. Others are provided with a ramp or stairway, as in mound E, the largest of the tumuli, leading to a hollowed-out chamber roughly 8 x 9 m in size, the western part divided by a narrow wall into two chambers.[85] The larger tombs at Firka and Kosha were entered down a sloping stairway or ramp giving access to the two or three chambers hollowed out in the alluvium. Typologically they can be related to the tombs at Qustul and to those of the earlier phases at Ballana.[86] What may have been a particularly rich tomb at Wawa made extensive use of red brick in its construction.[87]

The elite burial under Tumulus VI at el-Hobagi was placed within a niche opening off an oval pit 3.5 x 1.5 m in size, accessed via a vertical cylindrical shaft 4 m in diameter and 2 m deep (Fig. 17).[88] The only other elite burials of this period excavated to the south of the Third Cataract are at Tanqasi. Although the tumuli are of considerable size the graves that were excavated were notable for their poor nature. Mound I was chosen for excavation on account of its large size, it was 16 m in diameter and 8 m high. It covered a rectangular pit at the bottom of which were three graves, consisting of shafts filled with mud bricks, opening off each of which was a side-niche grave.[89] The graves had been robbed, but their small size suggests that they did not contain large quantities of grave goods. The other tumulus excavated, mound II, covered a side-niche grave containing the body of a woman laid on her left side, head to the south east, and accompanied by a small number of pots and personal jewellery.[90]

CHRISTIAN NUBIAN GRAVES

With the introduction of Christianity there was a greater degree of homogeneity.[91] Graves were invariably orientated east-west, although within this there is a range of variability even in the same cemetery. At Kulubnarti the actual orientation lay between 220° and 290°, at Soba East it fell into the range 248° to 275.5°.[92] In many areas the alignment was determined by river north rather than by cardinal north. The most common grave type was a long, often extremely narrow, pit with rounded ends, sometimes over 1.5 m in depth. Individuals were placed directly on the earth at the bottom of the grave, with the body almost invariably extended usually, though by no means always, on the back with the head to the west. The arms lie alongside the torso with the hands by the hips, together on the pelvis, or with the arms crossed on the chest. The legs are either placed side by side, or are crossed at the ankle. This grave type is the norm, but there is a wide range of variation. Many individuals, for example, are placed in east-west graves with the head to the east. Although this has led one recent commentator to urge caution in the identification of these graves as those of Christians,[93] the intimate association of east-west and west-east orientated burials suggests that both conformed to a recognised Christian practice in at least certain areas of Nubia. At Soba East for example, one child in the cemetery to the east of Building G was buried with the head to the east, but in all other respects the burial can be compared directly with the west-east burials which surround it.[94] The close proximity of the

Figure 18 **Christian grave (B2)250 at Soba East. The body is placed face down and bricks placed on the neck and across the thighs.**

two types makes it difficult to accept that the east-west individual was not of the same religious persuasion. Burials with the head to the east have been noted at a number of sites in what can be assumed to have been territory under the control of the kings of Alwa, or of their immediate predecessors, as for example at el-Hobagi, Jebel Makbor, Gabati and el-Geili.[95] Where there is dating evidence available these burials fall firmly within the medieval period and, at el-Geili, a number were provided with small pendants in the form of crosses.[96]

A further range of variation was observed at Soba East where, in a number of child burials to the east of mound (UA3)1, the body was placed in a crouched position or, more rarely, sitting up with the back resting against the end of the grave.[97] In the cemetery to the east of the northern church on mound B a number of adult burials had been placed face down (Fig. 18). Some of these had had a red brick placed on the body as though to hold it down and, in grave (Z3)163, a stone had been placed on the abdomen of a child. Two individuals were found at Kulubnarti buried in a ventral position, one at Meinarti and a few others in Lower Nubian cemeteries. The significance of the dorsal or ventral positions is not clear and does not seem to be related to the sex of the individual nor, apparently, to their social status, as bodies in different positions are found in adjacent graves. Adams suggests that ventral burials represent some form of execration,[98] although if this was so one might expect that such burials would not have been placed within a Christian cemetery, and at Soba East in very close proximity to a major church. Among the other burials at Kulubnarti a significant proportion were placed on their left sides (34%) and some on their right sides (4%). Where the bodies were in the dorsal position (the other 61%) the largest numbers had the head turned to face left, facing upwards was the next most common position, others faced to the right. Adams noted that these arrangements are rather different than those observed in Lower Nubian cemeteries where there is a marked preference among the non-dorsal burials for the bodies to be on their right sides and for the heads of the dorsal burials, which usually face upwards, but are otherwise turned to the right rather than to the left.[99]

An arrangement of three bricks set on edge around the skull, to symbolically protect it, is a common feature of the Soba East graves.[100] Bricks or stones placed in this way are also common elsewhere in Nubia, as is the presence of one to each side with a third laid across them to cover the face.[101] However, north of the Second Cataract this has only been recorded at one site, el-Kubanieh in the extreme north of Nubia downstream of the First Cataract.[102] At a number of sites bodies have been found wrapped in textile from head to toe and often tightly bound with cords or tapes.[103] This was probably a very widespread practice although, in many cases, due to post-depositional factors, no trace of the textile survives. At Kulubnarti textiles were very well preserved. In the two cemeteries excavated there, a total of 241 graves, only 36 contained professionally made shrouds; textiles made exclusively to wrap the dead. Most individuals were wrapped in whatever was available, light blankets, mantles and other items of untailored clothing. Some individuals, mostly children, were buried in fragments of garments or pieces of cloth roughly tacked together. A sixteen-year-old woman wore a very finely made cotton tunic. Several bodies were also wrapped in sheepskin or leather. Three graves contained mats made from human hair, the use of which is, at the time of writing, unique in Nubia.[104] From several graves at Soba

East leather sandals and shoes survived and one individual was buried with a particularly fine pair of sandals (Fig. 83).[105] It seems very unlikely that an individual would be buried wearing footwear and nothing else, but no trace of a shroud or clothing remained. A range of fine textiles, including some with interwoven gold thread, must have been placed in graves to the east of Church A at Soba. When these graves were robbed the bodies, along with their decayed finery, were dumped into the church's crypt.[106] Among the best preserved clothing is that found in the burial of Bishop Timotheos at Qasr Ibrim (Figs. 84 and 85). Timotheos was laid to rest in his normal garb under a linen shroud and he wore a fine iron benedictional cross at his breast.[107]

Figure 19 **Red-brick vaulted grave at Soba East. The deceased was placed in a coffin made from acacia, Ziziphus spina-christi and Ficus sp.**

In many interments the body, after being placed in the grave, was covered with earth. However, greater elaboration was common. Wooden coffins, made from acacia, fig, Christ's thorn, *Cassia* and tamarisk are a feature of some of the graves at Soba East (Fig. 19).[108] The body of a child was placed in a wooden chest which had the corners strengthened with iron angle-brackets and was closed by an elaborate lock. The chest had been wrapped in textile before being placed in the grave.[109] Elsewhere, to protect the body, slabs of stone or very large bricks,[110] and probably in some cases horizontal timbers,[111] were supported on two ledges cut into the side of the grave a little above the body. Graves of this type, which have been called 'bottom-niche' graves are thought to be of Early Christian date and are especially common in Lower Nubia between Taifa and Arminna.[112] A rather symbolic protection of the body is seen in some graves at Old Dongola where a layer of mud bricks are placed part way up in the filling of the shaft.[113] Some of the early graves at Old Dongola, which are cut down into the bedrock, have an anthropoid-shaped slot in the bottom.[114] Many burials in northern Nubia have a narrow lateral niche, at the same level as the base of the shaft, into which only one side of the body would fit. The body is then protected by bricks or stone slabs laid at an angle against the side of the grave.[115] End-niche graves are a survival from the earlier pagan tradition and were not used for long into the Christian period.[116]

Within the simple grave pits single burials were the norm although there are some instances where two individuals were buried together, perhaps an opportunistic practice when two people happened to die within a very short period of each other. Double burials of this type are often of a mother and child, sometimes probably the result of death during childbirth.[117] An unusual grave at Old Dongola was of the simple pit type but contained three successive burials, one above another, the earliest of a woman aged between nineteen and twenty-eight years, the next of a woman of over fifty years, the uppermost of a child.[118]

Many grave pits were rather larger and contained a barrel-vaulted chamber of mud or red brick. Such grave sub-structures have a long history in Nubia and are known from the C-Group, as in the cemetery at Aniba,[119] and in the Kushite period, for example at Sedeinga, where, however, the chamber was entered down a sloping ramp. No such ramp was provided in the medieval Christian graves except in some very early burials,[120] and there was frequently very little room between the end of the vault and the end of the grave pit. Inserting the body must on occasion have been a rather tortuous process. In some graves it is clear that the interment may have been placed in the tomb before the vault was built. The wooden coffins at Soba East must have been inserted at a very early stage in the construction of the vault. The vaults are of typical Nubian type, and would be constructed without any form of centring, hence their construction after the body was placed in the grave would not have posed any insurmountable difficulties. The ends of the vaults were roughly sealed before the grave pit was filled with earth.[121]

It was in the more monumental vaulted chamber tombs that multiple burials were common. At Faras from the early tenth century onwards provision was made for later burials within the tombs of bishops.[122] At Soba East a red-brick barrel-vaulted tomb, 2.5-2.55 m x 1.5-1.54 m internally, one of a pair located immediately to the east of mound (UA3)1, contained the bodies of sixteen adults and one foetus (Fig. 20). There were five males, seven probable males, two females and two probable females. Five of the skeletons showed evidence for weathering suggesting that they were not interred in this tomb immediately after their death. The archaeological evidence indicated that all the skeletons had been placed in the tomb at the same time.[123] Żurawski has drawn attention to the necessity in the extremely hot climate for burial very soon after death, usually a matter of a few hours. Where a new but sumptuous tomb was to be provided the deceased must have been interred elsewhere for a time before being transferred to the final resting place. The speed of the initial burial will not have allowed for the extended ceremonies prescribed by the *Euchologium*, but the elaborate commemoration and post-burial practices will have made up for this.[124] Reuse of pre-existing tombs will have had, in this context, very definite advantages.

Rock-cut tombs of this period are rare. Two fine examples were however, found at Old Dongola. Tomb 1 has a stepped *dromos* leading to a single chamber into the floor of which

Figure 20 **Red-brick vaulted tomb at Soba East containing the bodies of sixteen adults and one foetus.**

was an anthropoid-shaped 'sarcophagus' to take an extended inhumation laid with the head to the west. The entrance to the chamber had a carefully carved portal with a large Greek cross in a roundel carved in the centre of the 'lintel' and there was a similar cross carved in a niche at the eastern end of the chamber. Tomb 2 was of similar type but at the bottom of the *dromos* with its rock-cut steps were two parallel chambers each with a single 'sarcophagus' as in Tomb 1. Unfortunately both tombs had been thoroughly cleared and no indication remained as to who was buried within them. They are thought to date to the sixth century and were presumably the graves of nobility, or even of Makurian kings.[125] Tombs with *dromoi* are known within the settlement at Qasr Ibrim dating to the tenth to eleventh centuries, consisting of a chamber on average 3.5 m long by 2 m wide with narrower doorways at the west end which could be closed by stone slabs. The *dromoi* are dug through the earth fill up against the rock face into which the tombs were excavated, and are, therefore, lined with masonry. *Stelae* associated with them indicated that they were tombs of bishops of Ibrim and Qirta.[126] Other rock-cut tombs were entered down a vertical shaft. That immediately to the north of Church R-44 at Debeira West had a shaft 2 m deep, off the bottom of which opened a rectangular chamber containing the bodies of four adults.[127]

Falling into a special category of tombs were the subterranean crypts which have been found in a small number of Nubian churches. What may have been the earliest were in Building X at Old Dongola constructed in the mid sixth century. The two parallel chambers were entered via a flight of steps from the eastern passage behind the apse, and lay directly beneath the sanctuary. Each contained a single inhumation within the plastered and whitewashed chambers.[128] Building X was presumably a great memorial church constructed in honour of the men buried beneath it. These tombs, which were respected through the various rebuildings on this site, were venerated until the end of the medieval period. They must have been of the very greatest importance to the people of Old Dongola and may even have been the apostles of the kingdom or perhaps the apostle and a king of Makuria.[129] No evidence was found to establish the actual identities of the individuals. A study of their remains indicated that both were males probably of local origin, and were between thirty-five to forty and sixty to sixty-five when they died.[130]

At Soba East the crypt in the northern church on mound B was of rather different form being entered down a flight of steps from outside the building to the east. At the foot of the steps, to each side, were the vaulted burial chambers dug a further 400 mm into the ground. The vaults, with spans of 1.8 and 1.88 m, were constructed of red brick with the use of timber centring. In one of the chambers, which remained open to the central area, was a single inhumation which, although not robbed, had the lower arm bones of the left arm placed by the right arm. The chamber appeared to have been rendered with a mud plaster but there was no trace of whitewash.[131] This crypt was under a room immediately to the east of the apse of the church. A similar arrangement seen in the early Byzantine churches of Hagia Ioannes and Hagia Polyeuktos in Constantinople, it has been suggested, was to allow access to the crypts by the laity without them having to pass through the *bema* and this may be the explanation for the arrangement at Soba East.[132] No crypt was found in the cathedral at Faras but they were a feature of the cathedral at Qasr Ibrim. The two crypts flanking the sanctuary chamber were entered through stone arched doorways at the foot of stone stairways from the aisles to the west and each consisted of whitewashed brick vaulted chambers 3 m in height. The crypt's floors were formed by the bedrock and there were four rock-cut tombs dug into the floor of the southern crypt and two in the northern crypts. No grave goods were found with the three intact burials. It was on the stairway leading to the north crypt, after it had filled with debris, that Bishop Timotheos was buried.[133]

Crypts are not confined to the largest Nubian churches. The monastic church at Qasr el-Wizz had two crypts hewn into the bedrock entered via a vertical shaft from the central of a range of three rooms immediately to the east of the sanctuary chamber, an identical location to that observed at Soba East.[134] There are also a few smaller churches which have burials occupying a similar position to the crypts noted above. In Church R-2 at Debeira West a rock-cut grave was found on the north side of the sanctuary chamber sealed by the tribune. It was presumably the grave of the deacon Peter whose gravestone, recording his death in 1029, was found close by.[135] The northern church at Faras has a shaft immediately to the east of the church close to its main axis which extends 1.7 m beneath the apse and contained the remains of five or six individuals.[136]

As well as individuals buried in crypts a number of churches contained other burials within them, some being simple graves but others being much more elaborate chambered tombs. At Sahaba a vertical shaft in the centre of the nave gave access to four chambers arranged towards the cardinal points.[137] Another four-chambered tomb entered via a vertical shaft was located in the north aisle of the southern church at Faras. Here two parallel chambers opened off each of the long sides of the rectangular shaft.[138] In the Church of the Granite Columns at Old Dongola were nine tombs and the same number were found in the nearby Cruciform Church. These contained not only men but also women and children.[139] How they came to qualify for burial in such hallowed surroundings is unknown. In the south-eastern room of the Church of the Granite Columns, which contained the baptismal font, was found a *stela* set into the floor of the *Eparch* of Gaderon, Yoannes. Less than 1 m from the *stela* was a grave which may well be that of the *eparch*.[140] The late Church Four at Jebel Adda was constructed atop an earlier house, the small narrow rooms of which were cleared out providing crypts under much of the building which were used for the burials of the 'town notables'.[141]

Crypt tombs have also been discovered recently in the Monastery of Holy Trinity at Old Dongola. Three have been found so far, one of which can be associated with a tombstone recording the death of archbishop Giorgios which was set into the wall of a small chapel through the floor of which the crypt was entered. The single vaulted chamber contained the remains not only of the bishop but of four other individuals.[142] The standard of preservation was so high that the archaeologists who made the discovery were loath to disturb the burials, hence they remain intact but unstudied. The whole of the chamber was rendered, white-washed and then covered in texts written in black (colour plate I). The other two crypts lie adjacent to each other a little to the north. All three are within one wing of the massive monastic complex which seems to have consisted of a series of commemorative chapels.

Tomb monuments
It is likely that many medieval graves had some sort of superstructure marking their position on the surface although this was certainly not invariably the case. Many of the X-

Group graves at Jebel Adda do not appear to have ever been marked by a monument.[143] At Arminna and Meinarti large numbers of graves lacked any sort of grave monument, and Adams suggests that at the latter site this may have been in part a response to overcrowding in the cemetery.[144] Some individuals continued to be buried under the traditional Middle Nile grave monument, the tumulus, which is known from all periods from the A-Group onwards and this monument type probably continued in use throughout the medieval period. A wide range of tumuli types is used during the medieval period, from very small piles of earth, the surplus fill derived from the excavation of the grave pit, to substantial monuments, sometimes with a kerb of larger stones and covered in quartzite pebbles or stone fragments as at earlier periods. Some graves were marked by cairns, piles of stones, which, although they tend to be of small size, are of considerable height relative to the area they cover and form prominent monuments. Few of these have been excavated and their ascription to the medieval Christian period is in most cases uncertain.[145] Some of the largest tumuli in the Middle Nile Valley date to the period from the fourth to the sixth century at a time when the fashion for pyramids waned.

At el-Hobagi the elite burials were marked by large tumuli still surviving to a height of 3.75 m. The largest, Tumulus VI, was constructed of a mound made from the white sediments excavated from the burial pit over which was heaped red sediments quarried from the surrounding area and bounded by a rough wall approximately 500 mm high enclosing an area 30 m in diameter with an entrance through it from the east. After over 1,500 years of erosion the mound has slumped and attains a diameter of 40 m. The tumulus lay within an elliptical enclosure *c.* 70 x 55 m in size, defined by a stone wall constructed of large stones, some up to 1.5 m in length. It was originally 2-2.5 m thick, built without foundations, and perhaps stood to a height of 1 m.[146] Other tumuli within enclosures of this type have been noted at Jebel Qisi a little to the south and perhaps also at Meroe.[147] At Qustul and Ballana the tumuli were much bigger, the largest, at Ballana B3 was 77 m in

Figure 21 **Tumulus B.3 at Ballana (courtesy of the SARS Kirwan Archive).**

diameter and 11.92 m high (Fig. 21), B10 although a little smaller at 74 m in diameter was 13 m high.[148]

The tumuli at Sesebi were surrounded by a ditch (Fig. 13), from which some of the spoil to build the mound presumably came, and there were also traces of a ditch around tumulus A.11 at Firka and tumulus K.I at Kosha.[149] The Jebel Adda tumuli were constructed from earth scraped up from the surrounding area although a shallow trench was dug to mark the proposed limits of the mound prior to its construction.[150] Many tumuli had pebbles placed on their surface, which may in some cases have been an attempt to enhance the feature but was also a necessary precaution against aeolian erosion.

Among the more unusual tumuli types is a group from Tabo where, before the excavation of the burial chamber, a slightly dished circular or oval area 10 to 15 m in diameter was paved with mud brick and earth. The burial shaft was then cut through this 'saucer' and the burial placed in the chamber and the shaft refilled. In some cases offerings were placed on the surface of the 'saucer', such as a camel, cats, a small bowl and a dom nut, before the whole feature was covered by a mound of stones and sand.[151] Another group of tumuli which are certainly broadly if not directly contemporary at the same site were simple mounds lacking the mud-brick 'foundation'.

A little upstream of the Fourth Cataract is a distinctive type of tumulus. These tumuli are markedly egg-shaped, are revetted in stone, the revetment often being very carefully laid to form a smooth, angled slope, and the pointed end of the mound attains a considerably greater elevation (Fig. 22).[152] They are found in cemeteries associated with the more common tumuli types.

Figure 22 **'Egg'-shaped tumulus at site N-45-F/3-O-I near the Fourth Cataract.**

Continuity of religious practices manifest in the continuing use of, as well as the construction of, new temples in the X-Group period has been observed at a number of sites. There is also a very limited amount of evidence to suggest that the archetypal, though by no means universally used, Kushite grave monument, the pyramid, may have continued into the period where the X-Group cultural assemblage takes over from that of the late Kushite period. At Jebel Adda X-Group burials were placed under pyramids (although the excavator suggested that this was a reuse of an earlier grave for the local elite). In some cases to have effected such a reuse would have involved partial dismantlement, the pyramid then evidently being reinstated to its original condition.[153] Elsewhere however, the excavator suggested that the pyramid and chapel were actually constructed during X-Group times but in the Meroitic tradition.[154]

Fuller suggests that the Kushite tomb monuments at Arminna West and elsewhere recalled symbolically the royal pyramids far to the south, and that with the loss of the political influence of the Kushite state, this symbolic association with the centre of power

Figure 23 Area QE in the
Qustul cemetery with tumuli
and chapels (after Williams
1991, pl. 8).

0   100m

would have ceased to have any relevance. Rid of the traditional funerary monuments, local innovation came to the fore; at Arminna West there appeared a new type of monument, an oval mound framed and perhaps completely paved with mud-bricks.[155] The substructure of the grave and the placement of the body, however, retained Kushite practices.

The continuing need for a funerary chapel is highlighted by the construction of these at a number of sites associated with tumuli, although the physical relationship of the chapel to the tomb monument is not always as direct as in C-Group and early Kushite tumuli or as in the case of the pyramid and funerary chapel. At Qustul very large numbers of chapels appear to be associated with individual tumuli, 51 by Qu.31, 54 to the north of Qu.48 and 14 by Qu.36 arranged in east-west rows (relative to river north) extending a symmetrical distance to each side of the tumuli and facing south (Fig. 23). Variation among the orientation of the chapels within each row suggests that they were not all built at the same time. Some showed evidence of having been rebuilt. Each chapel was a simple rectangular room with walls of mud brick, the doorways had wooden thresholds and pivot stones and there were remains of a number of wooden doors. Stone jambs and lintels and sandstone plaques bearing painted decoration suggest that the chapels may have been rather elaborate. Some had the side walls extending a little in front of the entrance, forming a small porch which was paved with mud. In front of a number of chapel doors were small brick *podia* on at least two of which were libation tables. Why such a large number of chapels was associated with a single royal burial is unknown and contrasts markedly with the situation among the royal tumuli at Kerma and those observed in a Kushite context. Williams' suggestion that the chapels were erected by members of the Court to worship the dead king but also to serve as cult places for the sacrificed persons in the tumulus is perhaps unlikely.[156] No similar chapels are known at Ballana but a roughly kidney-shaped enclosure delimited by a wall of *jalous* or of mud brick was presumably a ritual structure, perhaps with a similar function, and was associated with tumulus Ba.80.[157] At Tabo rectangular mud-brick chapels may actually have been attached to the tumuli[158] but the poor preservation of these features makes certainty impossible.

The typically medieval Christian funerary monument is the box grave where a basically rectangular structure with almost vertical sides covers the site of the grave pit. These are usually of small size approximating to the size of the grave itself. The types of mastaba varied both geographically and over time, and even within the same cemetery variation can be considerable as illustrated at Meinarti where the excavator recognized eight major types, a total of twenty-five sub-types.[159] Between Aswan and Faras the most common type, at least in the earlier medieval period, was of similar form, built from stone or mud brick but capped by a semi-circular 'vault' running along the long axis a little narrower than the monument on which it rests. Mastaba of the same type but with a flat top are found at Sakinya and between Faras and the Second Cataract. As with the 'vaulted' type the earlier examples tend to be of stone; both stone and mud-brick mastaba were often whitewashed. In Upper Nubia, both along the Nile Valley and in the Bayuda and Butana/Keraba similar types abound. Rarely are they well enough preserved to indicate whether the top was flat or of some other form. In these areas away from the main urban centres they are almost invariably made from rough pieces of stone forming the faces and filled either with stones of a similar size or with earth and small stones (Fig. 24). There is rarely any evidence to

Figure 24 **Box graves in the upper Wadi Abu Dom in the Bayuda.**

indicate that they were rendered in any way. A variation on the type is the square mastaba.[160] The use of mud and red brick is common at Old Dongola and has been noted elsewhere. On Mis Island a little upstream from the Fourth Cataract, for example, there are six cemeteries with a minimum of about 850 graves marked by stone mastaba, while close to the church are approximately thirty graves with red-brick, lime-mortar rendered mastaba.[161] At Soba East the mastaba are rectangular, range in size between 3.8 x 2.4 m and 1.33 x 0.82 m, and are constructed of a wall of mud brick one course thick within which earth was deposited to form the platform. One of these had a small post-hole in each corner which may have supported vertical poles and similar 'flag' poles are a feature of Christian graves in Egypt, as at Arsinoë and Aswan.[162]

Less common are mastaba with a cross in relief on the top (Fig. 25).[163] The whole is often rendered in a mud mortar or lime plaster and whitewashed although a number of early mastaba at Old Dongola, for example, do not appear to have been rendered.[164] Fine examples at Meinarti have the cruciform top but also a slightly raised pylon at the west end.[165] A variation on the type is seen in the cemetery at Abdullah Nirqi where one monument is square, another oval; both are covered in mud, have sides sloping at about 45° and the cross in low relief.[166] The cruciform-topped mastaba in some cases are tall monuments with the cross formed by two intersecting 'barrel-vaults' sometimes with a cupola at the intersection and crowned on occasion by a terracotta cross. The resemblance to church architecture is striking and is also seen in another mastaba type with a central 'vault' flanked by lower 'naves'.[167] By the Church of the Granite Columns the earlier monuments were cruciform-shaped;[168] it is the later variety which has the cruciform shape set on a rectangular mastaba. The latest form in this cemetery is termed a 'chest mastaba' and has no cruciform embellishment.[169] In Lower Nubia the cruciform mastaba has a restricted location mainly between Qasr Ibrim and Tamit but others have been noted at Faras, Argin and Meinarti.[170]

An unusual form of the mastaba-type tomb is to be found at Sonqi Tino where it is crowned by a small onion-dome.[171] In the vicinity of Old Dongola it has been noted that the early mastaba are rather elongated (e.g., 2.9 x 0.8 m) those of the Classic Christian period much less so.[172] The provision of a lamp box usually consisting of a small rectangular chamber projecting from the mastaba and open to the west, is a not uncommon feature (Fig. 26). Other forms include a sealed chamber containing the pot and occasionally a freestanding 'lamp house' set a little apart from the grave monument.[173] The Terminal Christian mastaba at Old Dongola are again of elongated form but lack the lamp box and have no western platform.[174]

Another 'superstructure' type is constructed from a single layer of stones or bricks forming a pavement on the surface above the grave. At Kulubnarti a range of types have been found. Those utilizing stone slabs are irregular in shape as are the stones from which they are made. This monument type is common in the Second Cataract and Batn el-Hajar region and has not been recorded to the north of Debeira. It appears to be largely confined to the Early Christian period although a few may have been constructed in Classic Christian times.[175] Brick pavements are quadrangular, those made from bricks laid flat having the bricks laid in a combination of 'headers' and 'stretchers' forming a pattern. Others were made from bricks set on edge (rollag) with one or two rows of 'stretchers' down the centre and 'headers' to either side. The most elaborate monument has four rows of 'stretchers' each flanked by a row of 'headers' and with a row of 'stretchers' along each end.[176] Many graves at Soba East also had rectangular pavement monuments constructed of fragmentary red bricks.[177] Other simple monuments include a line of stones and a row of stones marking the outline of the grave sometimes with the interior filled with earth and small stone fragments, a type of feature also seen in post-medieval graves.[178]

The most elaborate monuments were reserved for the tombs of bishops and several very well-preserved examples were excavated at Faras. The graves of the earlier bishops in the eighth and ninth centuries, were marked by mastaba, initially flat topped and later with the front raised a little above the level of the rest of the mastaba top. From the eleventh to the thirteenth century they were much more elaborate.[179] The Tomb of Ioannes, set on the main axis of the cathedral and 1.9 m beyond its east wall, had a cuboid superstructure constructed of fired brick 2.7 x 2 m in size by 1.5 m high capped by a dome 1.2 m in diameter and 1.4 m high. The vaulted burial chamber built of mud brick, 2 m long by 1.2 m wide and 1.2 m high, lay immediately below the monument and was entered down a flight of two steps giving onto a vertical shaft at the bottom of which was a low doorway. The five occupants of the tomb were identified by their *stelae* set into the inner face of the wall of the tomb.[180] In the bishop's graves at Faras lamp boxes were not provided but a lamp was placed within the tomb, invariably to the right of the skull.

Prior to the construction of the Aswan High Dam many well-preserved monuments remained in the cemetery at Jebel Adda (Fig. 100). These were cuboid, with an arched opening in each face surmounted by a dome. Although these are usually considered to be of post-medieval (Islamic) date[181] the lower parts of what were probably very similar monuments have been noted in a medieval context at Debeira West, Arminna West and Old Dongola to name but a few.[182] The excavator noted that all the graves under these tomb monuments at Jebel Adda had been reopened after the original burial and that there was no way to determine which if any of the bodies belonged to the original burials.[183] At Faras a tomb of this type, of the bishop Petros, stood immediately to the north-east of the Church on the South Slope of the Kom (colour plate II) and a well preserved example survived at Abdullah Nirqi.[184] Another, extant, monument at Qasr Ibrim surmounts an earlier mastaba of medieval date although it is suggested that the arched and domed monument is Islamic, but was constructed during the Christian period.[185] Similar *qubba*, but with small arched windows in the centre of each face, were considered to be Christian in the cemetery at Meinarti.[186]

Found mainly, but not exclusively, in the most northerly part of Lower Nubia were rectangular barrel-vaulted structures, 'vaulted *qubbas*' some of which contained burials while others were occupied only by votive lamps, the burials being in a vault beneath.[187]

A unique tomb monument existed at Soba East immediately to the east of the central church on mound B (colour plate X).[188] Unfortunately it had been totally robbed out, only 12 bricks remaining *in situ*. In form it was a circular monument 4 m in diameter constructed of specially shaped trapezoidal red bricks.[189] Some pieces of red brick found in the robber fill, were covered in lime mortar render on three faces indicating that there were rectilinear elements higher on the superstructure. The burial pit lay under the monument and had contained a barrel-vaulted chamber. The position of this tomb, immediately to the east of the sanctuary of a church suggests that the individual to whom it belonged had a similar status to the individuals buried in the crypts of the other churches noted above. It is tempting to suggest that, with the presence of the tombstone of King David at Soba 40 m to the south east of the circular tomb, it may have been a royal tomb, but the evidence is not sufficient to indicate that this was actually the case.

Cemeteries are very frequently found closely associated with churches with burials particularly located to the east of these buildings. However at Old Dongola on Kom H graves with fine quality grave monuments (Figs 25 and 26) appear to be clustered around the area containing the memorial chapels and crypt graves of ecclesiastical dignitaries,

Figure 25 **A mastaba overbuilt by the south wall of room 21 of the Monastery of the Holy Trinity at Old Dongola.**

Figure 26 **A mastaba by the Monastery of the Holy Trinity at Old Dongola.**

presumably to associate them with the sanctity of the area.[190] It has been noted at Old Dongola that whereas the grave monuments are uniform their layout within the cemeteries is haphazard.[191] This is what one might expect given the often considerable period of use of many cemeteries.

In a number of cemeteries the arrangement of the tomb monuments, or certain features of the grave goods in the graves, suggest that there was some association between the deceased. It has been noted that Christian graves are placed in close association with post-Meroitic tumuli at Sesebi. In what is almost certainly a post-Meroitic cemetery in Wadi et-Tereif near the Fourth Cataract (Site 3-O-1) there were several instances where individual tumuli were linked by stone walls, up to a maximum of four tumuli being linked in this way. A single instance of the same phenomenon was noted in another cemetery (3-N-302), undoubtedly of Christians, where two box graves were linked by what appears to be a contemporary wall.[192]

At Wadi Qitna, in the cemetery dating from the late Kushite into the X-Group period, familial relationships are indicated by tumuli clusters in some cases with more than one adult female appearing to be related to an adult male suggesting the possibility of polygamy, or of the male having had two successive wives. There are many burials where more than one individual has been interred in the same grave but at a different time. There are also what may be family graves which contain more than one individual. These may be one of the following combinations, parents and children, brothers and sisters, or husbands and wives. Frequently graves designed to take a small infant later have a much larger body of a juvenile or adult stuffed into them. Only single male and female adults were placed in the same grave.[193] Within the cemeteries at Kulubnarti three groups of contiguous graves can be associated on account of the textile found within them and these may also represent family plots.[194]

Tombstones

Tombstones are not uncommon but were presumably restricted to a relatively small section of society. Christian tombstones usually bear a formulaic text and several distinct types are known.[195] Those bearing a prayer of the *Euchologion Mega* type are the most characteristic of funerary inscription in Greek.[196] The general formula is for the epitaph to begin with an invocation followed by a request for the soul of the deceased to rest in peace and summary information on the dead person, their name, sometimes with the name of the father and, more rarely, details of the titles and functions of the individual. There is then another sequence of the prayer and more details on the deceased with age and date of death.[197] An example of this type at Soba East (Fig. 97), which is also the only royal tombstone found in Nubia, reads:

> O God of the spirits and all flesh, Thou who hast rendered death ineffectual and has trodden down Hades, and hast given life to the world, rest the soul of (Thy) servant David, the King, in the bosom of Abraham and Isaac and Jacob, in a place of light, in a place of verdure, in a place of refreshment, whence pain and grief and mourning hath fled. Pardon [every sin committed] by him in word or deed [or thought; remit and annul,] because [there is no man who will live] and will not sin. For [Thou only, O God, art without] sin, and Thy justice [is justice for]ever.
>
> O Lord, Thy word [is truth,] for Thou art the rest and resurrection of Thy servant and to Thee we sing the glory of the Father and the Son and the Holy Ghost, now and always and forever. Amen.
>
> The years from his birth when he was not a king (were) [..] whereas he was king 16 years 3 months. After the Martyrs 732 he completed (his life) in the month of Hathor the 2nd; Thursday.[198]

Another from Arminna West reads:

> According to the statement which the creator spoke, 'Adam thou art dust and unto dust thou shalt again return,' such was the way in which the blessed Maria went to rest, who was the daughter of Ptoou and the daughter of Miriam in the month of Hathor in the year (of the martyrs) 637. Her years were 39. The good god will give her rest in the bosom of Abraham, Isaac, and Jacob beneath the tree of life which is in the paradise of joy with all his saints, who cried out, 'Amen, so be it, Amen'.[199]

A very rare example with the opening formulae stating that the deceased met his death as a result of divine intervention comes from Old Dongola. Dating from 798 the tombstone of the *eparch* of Nobadia, Petros reads:

> By the inclination and command of God who created all things, the blessed Petros, *eparch* of the land of Nobadians fell asleep, the 12th (day) of the month Tybi, 6th indiction, year after Diocletian 514. God of spirits and all flesh, rest his soul in the bosom of Abraham and Isaac and Jacob, (in the place) where all your saints ... take their rest.[200]

Infant burials

One category of burials is set apart from all those discussed above. The burials of newly-born and very young individuals were treated rather differently. Many may have received no burial at all, if the exposure of newly-born infants was practised in Nubia as it certainly was in many other areas of the world over a very long period.[201] However, it was also the custom to bury very young children within the confines of, or immediately outside of, the house. At Debeira West they were placed in ordinary cooking pots;[202] at Arminna West a foetus of about seven month was buried in a *qadus*.[203] Early this century the Copts still practised this tradition and according to Blackman 'Among the Copts, if a child dies before it is baptised it is placed naked in a *kadus* [*qadus*]. This jar is then buried under the floor of one of the rooms of the house, it does not matter which, and is covered again with mud of which the floors are usually made in the houses of the Fellahin. This is believed to ensure that mother of having another child.'[204] A very young individual who, from the evidence of the deformed skull, probably died or was fatally injured during childbirth was buried in a small elongated pit within an X-Group house at Qasr Ibrim and a sandal was placed upside down over it. The body had been wrapped in a cotton cloth stitched up to form a boat-shaped bag closed by a patch made of the same material sewn across the opening.[205] Elsewhere very young babies or foetuses were buried in cemeteries along with the rest of the population. At Kulubnarti infants were buried within jars in graves of the same types as those occupied by older individuals. The vessels used were Egyptian amphorae, a locally-made copy of a vessel of this type, and handmade pots.[206]

Respect for the Dead
At Gabati the Kushite tombs were robbed systematically in the later Kushite period, it was the work of fellow pagans. By contrast the post-Meroitic graves with their grave goods remained intact.[207] Clearly their Christian descendants did not wreak a similar fate on the post-Meroitic graves. This, however, is by no means invariably the case. At many other cemeteries it appears to have been during the medieval period that the X-Group graves were systematically robbed.[208]

The medieval Nubians seem to have had a very pragmatic view of the need to preserve grave monuments. Burial under a substantial grave monument in no way guaranteed that one's final resting place would be marked and respected forever. At Old Dongola when monuments began to disappear under the wind-blown sand they were frequently demolished and their building materials reused. No attempt was made to restore decayed monuments, they were also demolished. The amount of reused material in the grave monuments of Old Dongola is enormous. Żurawski has estimated that grave monuments may have had an average life of as little as fifty years and that they lost their sacral importance with the ending of the commemorative cycle.[209] On the extension of the Monastery of the Holy Trinity mastabas that got in the way of the new building works were sometimes bodily incorporated into the new walls, where they extended beyond the building line they were ruthlessly chopped through. At Meinarti the cemetery grew vertically, new graves being dug on the site of earlier graves then covered in sand. No compunction was shown by the grave diggers who were perfectly happy to cut through earlier grave monuments while digging later graves.[210] What is, however, noteworthy about Nubian Christian graves is that the dead were left in peace. The absence of grave goods made the disturbance of the burial unproductive and it may have been this practical consideration rather than a greater respect for their ancestors which ensured the survival of the bodies in marked contrast to those of many earlier periods.

In the Church of the Granite Columns (Church of the Brick Pillars) at Old Dongola there are a number of *stelae* set into the floor of the nave which do not appear to be associated with burials within the building. It has been suggested that where tomb monuments of ecclesiastical dignitaries were demolished the *stelae* were recovered and set in the church floor. A similar situation has been noted at Hammam el-Farki, in the church on the north kom at Hambukol and perhaps at Soba East, where the tombstone of King David was worn as though it had been used as a floor slab.[211]

POPULAR RELIGION, PAGAN TRADITIONS AND MAGIC

Lamp boxes are a common feature of medieval Christian graves and are associated with funerary ritual. In the early Christian cemetery at Jebel Ghaddar North the lamp boxes are closed on all sides although they may have been open above, whereas in the Classic Christian period at Old Dongola one side of the lamp box was always open (Fig. 26).[212] Petrie drew attention to the modern Egyptian practice of placing a lamp upon the grave in a shelter and also to Jewish practice where a light is provided for some weeks after the burial.[213] The substitution in some 'lamp boxes' of a bowl, plate, goblet or cup may be connected with their use as water containers 'poured *pietatis et commemorationis causa* on the third, seventh, ninth (etc.) day after death as in modern Muslim practice' although there is no direct evidence for this usage.[214] At Faras Griffith thought that the cups had been used as censers although the presence of burnt material within them was only recorded in a few instances.[215] At Old Dongola charred twigs and berries are frequently found within the lamp boxes.[216] Lamps found within sealed lamp boxes suggest that they were only placed there at the end of the commemorative cycle.[217]

One of the most important apotropaic devices used by the Nubian Christians was the symbol of the cross and the branding of a cross on the forehead is recorded as part of the

Figure 27 **Inscribed stone cross from the northern cemetery at Tamit (after Monneret de Villard 1935, 149).**

baptismal ceremony.[218] The cross was important in funerary practices and when scratched or painted on the walls of the burial chamber could be efficacious in keeping away the forces of evil which might appear from four directions, a response to what must have been a widely held belief that demonic forces had to be thwarted from taking possession of everything that was not 'impregnated with *sacrum*'.[219] The cross was also used to form the superstructure of many Nubian mastaba tombs while stone, terracotta and probably wooden crosses (Fig. 27), some of the ceramic examples inscribed before firing, were used as *stelae* at Tamit and Old Dongola,[220] and have also been noted in the Wadi Abu Dom at el-Ghazali and Umm Ruweim, at Wadi el-Kab west of Dongola and from Site 3-J-18 on Mis Island near the Fourth Cataract.[221] They were probably set into the top of mastabas

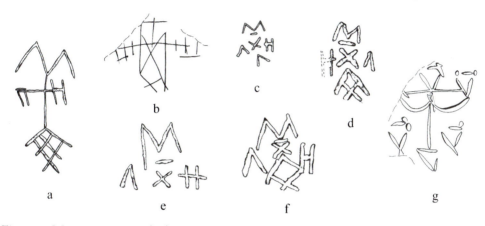

Figure 28 **Monograms scratched on pottery at Soba East; a-f monograms of** MIXAHA, **g alpha - omega monogram with additional alphas (after Jakobielski 1991; Anderson 1998).**

and the stump of what may have been a cross of this type was found in situ at el-Ghazali.[222] Additional protection was often provided by carving a cross or a Solomon's Seal above the entrance to the burial chamber.[223] Crosses were also frequently carved as graffiti on buildings and on ceramics.[224]

Equally common were invocations to the archangel Michael who appears to have been extremely popular throughout Nubia. His name is found carved on walls and on pottery, either written out in full, as a monogram based on the form of the cross (Fig. 28), or as a cryptogram. A Coptic text from Upper Egypt describes the rationale behind the use of the name of Michael

Because the name of Michael will be for them a strong armour. If a man writes these glorious letters upon the (?wall) of his house that is nothing of the enemy will come upon the house nor will the device of wicked men have power over it. But let everyone who shall write it for himself as an amulet take care concerning the compact lest he place it in a place where there is defilement, because great is the power of these marvellous names.

Timothy, Archbishop of Alexandria[225]

Cryptograms are based on the fact that many letters in Greek have a numerical equivalent: those forming the name Michael add up to 689 which is then written again in letters, hence $MIXAE\Lambda = 40$ (M) + 10 (I) + 600 (X) + 1 (A) + 8 (E) + 30 (Λ) = 689 = X$\Pi\Theta$.[226] The monks in the Monastery of the Holy Trinity at Old Dongola decorated their personal eating vessels with both a cross and many cryptograms of Michael, presumably an attempt to protect their pottery, their food and themselves from evil powers (Fig. 96).[227]

The protection of the head and face of the deceased is another manifestation of the importance of superstition and magic to Nubian Christians. The face protection may have been to guard against the evil spirits flying in the air entering the body through the orifices of the face.[228] At a number of the bishop's tombs at Faras the mastaba is pierced by a hole directly above the head of the interment, presumably connected with the pouring of libations to the dead, linking the funerary beliefs of the Nubian Christians with their predecessors and with much later African practice.[229] In the so-called Nubian Queen's grave near the eastern room in the Cruciform Church at Old Dongola there is evidence to suggest artificial mummification and the Egyptian custom of tying the limbs together.[230] The custom of inscribing texts on the shrouds and bandages of the deceased as at Jebel Adda,[231] may also have a more magical than religious significance and can be compared to similar practices in Ethiopia.[232] In a number of tombs the walls are inscribed with magico-religious texts, the most impressive of which is the crypt probably belonging to the archbishop Giorgios, who died in 1113, recently discovered in the Monastery of the Holy Trinity in Old Dongola where all the walls are covered in texts (colour plate I).[233]

From Late Christian contexts at Qasr Ibrim come magical texts in Old Nubian and in Arabic. The Old Nubian texts, like the earlier Greek magical texts, have strings of certain letters particularly vowels, repeated without any obvious meaning; some of the letters have circles appended to them. One of these has been translated as 'A man of bad birth ...' followed by strings of the letters 'O', 'A' and 'E'.[234] A white painted inscription in Coptic on an unusual pottery vessel of rectangular shape from Aksha was designed to provide divine protection for the contents.[235] It calls for divine damnation – and promises blindness to anyone who dared to touch the contents of the vat, without however, specifying what they were.

A widespread practice, particularly during the Pharaonic and Kushite periods in Nubia, was the burying of foundation deposits which it was hoped would magically protect and maintain the building with which they were associated for eternity. The discovery of foundation deposits in the medieval period is infrequent, perhaps because they have rarely been looked for. At Hambukol 'magic bowls' were placed as foundation deposits beneath three of the four corners of the original building known as Building One. The shallow bowls are decorated in the interior with a list of names of the seventy-two disciples of Christ and the twelve apostles as related in the Book of Luke, in Greek and applied in ink.[236] Another foundation deposit might have been buried at the intersection of the main axes of the building where a robber pit had subsequently been dug, but this is by no means certain.[237] An uninscribed bowl was found buried under the mud threshold in the nearby House C-One.[238]

Not dissimilar discoveries have been made at Serra East where ten deposits have been recorded. One building of modest plan had an upturned footed bowl under three of its corners. Each of these covered an *ostracon* bearing the names written in Greek of Abba Klous Theodoros Leontios Panigiros Phēmamon followed by a number of symbols which are known from Coptic magical texts. Among the other foundation deposits at the site was an inverted bowl but with no *ostracon* underneath, while different types of bowls under two corners of a building again were without *ostraca* but in the sand within one were organic remains, and in the others were the remains of a small fish.[239] Under the four corners of another building were deposits of small unfired jars and cups.[240] Large numbers of 'cheap' cups and saucers of Egyptian manufacture were similarly buried beneath the floors and foundations of the houses at Meinarti, often in groups of twos and threes, in the period between 1000 and 1150.[241] The practice of making foundation deposits continued up to the end of Nubian Christianity if the evidence from Jebel Adda is representative. When the late church, Church Seven, was occupied by a Christian family as a dwelling inscribed sherds were placed under the two new door sills they laid.[242]

Within House PCH.1 at Old Dongola were a number of deposits of pottery which defy attempts to suggest a rational explanation for them, nor were there any features in common between them. Among the pots are two filled with sand and pottery sherds, the mouth of one sealed with mud and both placed upside-down then sealed within a mastaba.[243]

Foundation deposits are also known in a religious context at Old Dongola. In Church ED a globular jar containing earth and 100 beads was found together with a lump of iron beneath the flooring. In the North-West Church a number of deposits were located although not all the likely positions were investigated. Those recovered were found in prominent locations from a structural point of view: in the apse of the sanctuary chamber, under the western and southern apses, and at the intersection of the two main axes of the building. They consisted respectively of a water jar (*qulla*), two red bricks, a pot containing *jir* and a pot containing clean gravel. Also in the nave was found a large lump of mud set in clean sand.[244] Other deposits have also been noted from the Cruciform Church and the Church of the Granite Columns although, as much of the structure of these buildings survives, not all locations could be examined in detail.[245] It would seem, therefore, that they were a common if not an ubiquitous feature of churches in the city.

No foundation deposits were found in the churches at the western end of mound B at Soba East. Within the north aisle in Church E, however, was a pit filled exclusively with pebbles and water-worn pottery which can have had no structural function and is presumably to be associated with the types of deposits noted above.[246]

The presence of foundation deposits indicates that the Christian Nubians performed foundation ceremonies which lie more in the realms of magic than in the mainstream of Christian religious practices. Like their pagan forefathers they presumably sought to placate the spirits of the locality of the building to be constructed and to secure the protection of the structure against demons, concepts in no way confined to the Middle and Lower Nile Valleys.[247]

CHAPTER 4

The Nubians and their neighbours, seventh to early thirteenth centuries

By the beginning of the seventh century relations between the Nubian kings and the Late Roman (Byzantine) Empire appear to have been amicable. The international situation was dramatically changed in 619 when the Persians under King Chosroes swept into Egypt and remained in control until ousted by the Byzantines nine years later. Very little is known about relations between Egypt's new pagan rulers and the Nubians although one later Arab source records that the Nubians sent a gift of a giraffe to the kings of the Persians.[1]

In the midst of renewed struggles between two of the superpowers of the ancient world, the Byzantine and the Persian empires, there emerged a new contender, the Arabs. Mohammed began a *jihad*, a holy war to proselytize the new religion of Islam, which stimulated the meteoric rise of the Arabs as a military force second to none. Within five years of Mohammed's death in 632 the Arab tribesmen, fanning out from what is now western Saudi Arabia, defeated the Field Army of the Byzantines at the second battle of Yarmuk on 20 August 636 while another Arab force dealt an equally mortal blow to the Persians at the battle of Qadasiya probably in February of the following year.[2] The Arab forces, fresh from their victories over the Byzantines in Jordan, swept into Egypt in December 639 ending in 2 years over 600 years of Roman rule, and rapidly marched beyond Egypt's frontiers to the west and south intent on further conquests. To the west they overran the Byzantine possessions in Libya, Tunisia and Algeria, moved through northern Morocco and on into Spain and France only being halted at the battle of Tours by the armies of Charles Martel in October 732. Alone of all the enemies who stood against the all-conquering Muslim armies in the early phases of their expansion, the Nubians survived the onslaught.

The first Arab invasions of Nubia and the Baqt

The Byzantine governor of Egypt, Aristulis, sought the aid of the Beja and the Nubians against the Arab invaders but an outbreak of hostilities between these two allies led to no help being sent[3] and sealed the fate of the Byzantine garrison who withdrew from Egypt under the terms of a treaty engineered by the Patriarch Cyrus, leaving Alexandria on 12 September 642. In 641 or 642 the emir Amru b. El-As dispatched Abdallah b. Sa'id Abi Sarh with an army of 20,000 men into Nubia. Few details of the campaign are known, although Ahmad el-Kufi records that the Muslim soldiers scattered in all directions killing and plundering. The Nubian response was to amass a large army, 100,000 men according to el-Kufi, which attacked the Muslims so bravely that 'the Muslims had never suffered a loss like the one they had in Nubia'.[4] Hostilities were brought to a close without significant

Muslim gains. According to el-Maqrizi and Qalqashandi a peace treaty was signed, a *baqt*,[5] although other writers do not record such an agreement at the conclusion of this campaign.

An episode recorded in a number of Arab sources which refer to Zacharias, son of Barky, may be relevant to Arab/Nubian relations at this time. Zacharias is described as a king by some of the sources but his exact status is impossible to determine. Munro-Hay suggests that he may have been King of Nobadia. In the context of the hostilities between the Nubians and the Arabs at this time, the story of his presentation of a carved minbar, one of a number of 'legends' connected with this minbar, to the mosque at Fustat during the governorship of Abdallah b. Saad (645-55) is noteworthy.[6]

El-Maqrizi relates that the Nubians subsequently broke the *Baqt* and raided Upper Egypt causing damage and devastation, Aswan and Philae remaining in their hands in 652.[7] This led to a second campaign against them in 652, again led by Abdallah b. Sa'id Abi Sarh. The Muslims advanced on the Makurian capital at Dongola, today known as Old Dongola, with an army of 5,000 horsemen according to some sources. They laid siege to the town which was defended by stout walls (Fig. 29), attacking with their catapults and destroying the roof of one of the city's churches.[8] However, not every-thing appears to have gone in favour of the Muslims. A sheikh from the tribe of the Himyar who participated in both of these campaigns reported:

Figure 29 **The formidable defences of Old Dongola. Several metres of sand still obscure the lower parts of the walls and towers.**

> I never saw a people who were sharper in war than they [the Nubians]. I heard one
> of them say to the Muslims: 'Where do you want me to hit you with my arrows?'
> and in case the Muslim would disdainfully say: 'In such a spot', the Nubian would
> never miss it. They were fond of fighting with arrows; but their arrows would
> scarcely ever hit on the ground. One day, they arrayed themselves against us and we
> were desirous to carry the conflict with the sword; but they were too quick for us
> and shot their arrows, putting out our eyes.[9]

The prowess of the Nubians as archers made a profound impact on the attackers and they nicknamed the Nubians, 'pupil smiters' and 'archers of the eyes'. Presumably it was in the aftermath of the attack that the defences of Old Dongola were extended a short distance along the bluff overlooking the river bank to enclose a triangular terrace immediately beyond the north-west tower. The foundations of one of the towers on this new section of curtain is constructed of *spolia*, many damaged fragments of granite columns and capitals (Fig. 30) which, it has been plausibly suggested, came from the Church of the Stone

Figure 30 **Tower constructed on a foundation of reused column shafts and capitals at Old Dongola** (photo W. Godlewski).

Pavement, built in the early seventh century in the plain to the north. This church was presumably destroyed during the second Muslim invasion.[10]

In the light of the determined resistance of the Makurians, the Muslims, on being approached by the Makurian king, Qalidurut who, entering the enemies' camp sued for peace, readily granted his request and another *Baqt* was drawn up. This *Baqt* is mentioned, often in considerable detail, by most of the Arab authors who wrote on Muslim/Makurian relations and they are broadly in agreement as to its terms. It is described as a gift exchange, an exchange of goods of equal value,[11] rather than as tribute and its terms did not imply that Makuria was anything but an independent sovereign state.[12] It was a bilateral agreement of non-aggression and non-intervention rather than a formal treaty, a *sulh*, which at this period in the rise of Islam would have implied that the Makurians were in a markedly subservient position.[13] It was to be of fundamental importance in the relations between the two states for many centuries. The annual exchange of the *Baqt* took place at el-Qasr a few kilometres south of Philae on the border between Makuria and Egypt.

According to the tenth-century writer el-Mas'udi the *Baqt* stipulated that the Makurians supplied annually

365 slaves (other sources record the number as 360), to the treasury of the Muslims
40 slaves to the emir of Egypt
20 slaves to his delegate who resides in Aswan who is in charge of overseeing the *Baqt*
5 slaves to the judge of Aswan, who together with the emir of Aswan presides over the delivery of the *Baqt*
1 slave to each of the 12 court witnesses chosen from among the people of Aswan to supervise the delivery of the *Baqt* [14]

In the most detailed list of provisions of the *Baqt* it is recorded that in return the Muslims undertook to provide the Makurians with the following

1000 *ardeb* of wheat
300 *ardeb* of wheat to the delegates of the Makurian king
1000 *ardeb* of barley
1000 jugs for the king
300 jugs for the king's delegates
2 horses of the breed used by the emir
4 pieces of *qabati* cloth for the king
3 pieces of *qabati* cloth for his delegates
8 pieces of *buqturiyyah* cloth
5 pieces of *mu'lama* cloth
a mantle of *mukhmala* silk (velvet or wool)
10 pieces of *Abu Buqtor* cloth
10 pieces of *Ahasi* cloth

Other sources mention lentils, olive oil, and 'food and drink', carpets and perhaps wine and vinegar, although the latter may be a misreading for horses.[15] The occasional (or annual) gift of a giraffe to the caliph is also mentioned by several sources.[16] The *Baqt* also stipulated that there be freedom of travel for Nubians in the country of the Muslims and vice versa, but that settlement was forbidden. Additionally any slaves who sought refuge in Nubia were to be handed back. The eleventh-century writer Ibn Hazm records that on the conclusion of peace with the Makurians Abdallah b. Saad 'built a mosque at the gate of the capital of their kingdom and made it a condition that they should look after it always'.[17] El-Maqrizi also refers to the same mosque constructed 'in the enclosure of your town' and that Muslims must be allowed free access to it to pray and to stay in its vicinity.[18] It has been suggested that the reference to a mosque in 652 is in error and that such a mosque must date to a much later period.[19] No archaeological remains of a mosque of this date have been found at Old Dongola although it should be noted that the town covers a vast area, little of which has so far been excavated.

The *Baqt* of 652 marked an acceptance by the Muslims of the independence of Makuria. In the centuries thereafter much of the friction between the two states was ostensibly about infringements of the terms of the *Baqt* by one side or the other, usually by the Makurians. Muslim complaints about non-payment of the *Baqt* are recorded on several occasions up until the twelfth century. One of the most interesting of these, because its veracity cannot be in doubt, is a letter in Arabic found at Qasr Ibrim registering a complaint by the Governor of Egypt to the King of Makuria, presumably Cyriacus, and dated November 758. According to the governor, although the Muslims had complied with the terms of the *Baqt*, the Makurians had not. They had hindered Muslim messengers and robbed and ill-treated Muslim merchants. They had granted refuge to runaway slaves and they had failed to supply the stipulated number of slaves or had sent 'the one-eyed, the lame, weak old men or young boys'. Reprisals were promised if the terms were not complied with.[20] As late as 1292 we find the Nubian king regaling the Egyptian Sultan with excuses as to why the *Baqt* had not been paid.[21] The provision of slaves seems to have placed a heavy burden on the Makurians. The main source of the slaves stipulated in the *Baqt* was war prisoners furnished by the raids conducted by the Makurian king on other parts of the country of the Nuba.[22] However, on occasion the Makurians had to resort to selling their own women and children into slavery to comply with its terms.[23]

Table 2 The states in Nubia and the rulers of Egypt from the fourth to the sixteenth centuries.

Data (century)	NUBIA	EGYPT
4th	KUSH	
5th	BLEMMYES	Romans
6th		Byzantines
7th	NOBADIA	Persians / Byzantines / Rashidun
8th		Ummayads
9th	MAKURIA	Abbasids
10th		Tulunids / Abbasids / Ikhshidids
11th		Fatimids
12th		
13th		Ayyubids
14th		Mamelukes
15th	DOTAWO / ALWA	
16th	FUNJI	Ottomans

In the reign of King Zacharias I the *Baqt* had fallen fourteen years into arrears and its non-payment was seen by the Muslims as a *casus belli*. Faced with the demand for what must have totalled over 5,000 slaves, in 835 the king dispatched his son Giorgios to Egypt and on to the court of the caliph at Baghdad to seek a remittance of the agreed terms. Giorgios was received with honour by the caliph, el-Mutasim and was presumably successful in his mission. He is described as a clever young man of about twenty years of age, well-mannered, educated and handsome, worthy of the royal rank on account of his manners.[24]

One excuse the Makurians used during the Abbasid rule in Egypt was that the *Baqt* was only payable once every three years.[25] Ibn Selim notes that el-Mutasim decreed, following Giorgios' visit to Baghdad, that the *Baqt* should only be paid every three years and confirmed this in a document which remained in the hands of the Makurians.[26]

Military conflicts in the eighth to twelfth centuries

Although the *Baqt* regulated Makurian/Muslim relations it did not guarantee peace. During the eighth to twelfth centuries there were several raids, both sides being the aggressors on occasion. In the period 723-742 Nubia was raided although no permanent conquests were made. One 'battle of pillage' was fought and a number of captives were taken.[27] By the middle of the century the balance of power had swung dramatically towards the Makurians. Around 748 their king Cyriacus was able to intervene directly in Egyptian affairs. Abba Michael, patriarch of Alexandria, had been imprisoned by the Egyptian emir Abd el-Malik, on account of his communicating with the Makurian king by letter and in order to extort money from him. Cyriacus demanded the patriarch's release. When the emir did not comply Cyriacus invaded Egypt 'with a great army, including a hundred thousand horsemen, with a hundred thousand horses and a hundred thousand camels', pillaging and killing the Muslim inhabitants as he advanced on Cairo where he encamped outside the city. During his advance he had sent his *eparch* as an envoy to demand the release of the patriarch but he had been seized and imprisoned. On the arrival of Cyriacus' army at Cairo Abd el-Malik, with no means to resist him, released his prisoners and the Makurians withdrew within their own borders.[28] It has been suggested that the weakness of the Muslims at this time may have been partly the result of internal troubles in Egypt, caused by the high taxes imposed on the Copts.[29] Renewed Muslim aggression followed with raids under Abd al A'la b. Hamid between 762-70.

EL-OMARI

The episode of Mohammed Abdallah el-Omari, of which two very different accounts survive, stands out from the 'official' hostilities between the Tulunids and the Makurians. The story told by the tenth-century writer el-Balawi[30] is that during a Beja raid into Upper Egypt in 854-5 el-Omari, 'full of zeal for God and for the Muslims', laid ambush for and killed the Beja leader and his companions. He followed up this success by advancing into Beja territory and killing a great number of people. 'He became for them like a bone planted in their ribs' and to finally rid themselves of him the Beja agreed to pay the *jizya*, the Muslim tax imposed on infidels. According to et-Taghribirdi,[31] el-Omari was fighting a motley force of the Sudan under the command of the king Ali Baba. It is unclear whether the Makurians were directly involved at this stage. El-Omari, initially at peace with Makuria, was provoked into reprisals when attacked, probably by the *eparch* from Maris, and drove him out of his country and burnt his towns, capturing so many prisoners that his 'men could buy goods from a green-grocer and pay him with a Nubian slave'. Ibn Hawqal mentions that el-Omari demanded the submission of the Makurian king Giorgios who was then dispatched along with the Beja king Ali Baba to Baghdad. [32] Whether this account is mistaken, confusing the visit by the then crown-prince Giorgios twenty years earlier, or is a separate incident is unclear. [33] If it is correct it directly conflicts with the very detailed account of el-Omari's activities as recounted by el-Maqrizi.

According to el-Maqrizi, drawing his information from *The Great Chronicle of Egypt*, el-Omari moved into the eastern Desert beyond Aswan with a group of slaves to work a gold mine but, owing to hostile action from the Rabi Arabs, withdrew to another mining area further away. From there some of his men, entering the Nile Valley in search of water, were arrested by the Nubians and subsequently murdered. Then el-Omari, equipping his men with weapons forged from the mining tools they had available, marched on the Nubians somewhere in the region of Abu Hamed and defeated them, the remnants of the Nubian army crossing to the west bank. El-Omari's men, under cover of darkness, crossed the river, routed the Nubians and stole their boats which were then used to raid the islands in the area. The Makurian king Giorgios appointed his nephew Nyuti to lead an elite force against el-Omari. After a number of skirmishes a treaty was agreed between the two sides whereby el-Omari would settle with his men in a designated area of the country. However, on Nyuti turning against Giorgios, the king sent his eldest son to continue the fight but he was several times defeated and finally fled to Alwa where the king of that country offered him sanctuary.

Giorgios then appointed another of his sons, Zacharias as commander of the army. Zacharias succeeded in persuading el-Omari to remain neutral in the Makurian civil war, while he concentrated his forces against Nyuti. In several engagements Zacharias was worsted and was forced to place himself at the mercy of el-Omari. He won el-Omari's support in the fight against Nyuti by lavish gifts of money, by the promise of the hand of Nyuti's soon to be widowed wife (who was the sister of Zacharias), if all went according to plan, and by confirming el-Omari in control of all the land he at present occupied. Zacharias through treachery succeeded in capturing and murdering Nyuti and was then able to win over Nyuti's army to his cause, planning to turn against el-Omari. By subterfuge Zacharias succeeded in bringing his army into the Muslims' camp where it fell upon its unsuspecting allies causing considerable devastation. El-Omari, who still remained at liberty, was forced, after dissensions within his remaining troops fuelled by the intrigue of Zacharias, to abandon his position and move away from the Nile. He continued to raid Makuria and reappeared in the Nile Valley, in Maris, but was forced to retreat northwards to Aswan by the arrival of Zacharias at the head of a numerous army and finally passed out of Nubian history. It is recorded that he had occupied a part of Makuria for seven years. [34]

This account provides our first evidence for the tendency of Makuria to degenerate into a state of civil war and for one of the parties involved to seek the assistance of the Muslims. The degree of duplicity that Zacharias is credited with appears in accounts of similar events over the next several centuries. Whether the Makurians were as unprincipled

as the Muslim writers would have us believe, or whether this is the bias of our sources, is unclear but the Arab writers do not attempt to take the moral high ground so perhaps their accounts of Makurian politics come close to the mark. Zacharias' duplicity seems to have achieved for him the desired result, but for many of his successors the involvement of Muslims in Makuria's dynastic squabbles was to prove disastrous in the long term.

Around 910-15 Abu Mansur Makin raided both Nubia and Barqa in Libya in the same year[35] but no further details are known.

In the mid tenth century the Makurians again went on the offensive. A raid against the Oases was followed in April/May 956 by a devastating attack on Aswan, the Muslim frontier town where a garrison of the regular army was stationed as a bulwark against the Makurians.[36] Why the Makurians launched these attacks is unknown, although it has been suggested that it was a response to the economic hardship caused by high Nile floods at that time destroying the agricultural infrastructure.[37] This campaign, however, ended disastrously. A Muslim army, advancing both by land and on the river, counter-attacked, entered Nubia and defeated the Makurian king in battle, killing and taking many prisoners. The Muslims then went on to capture the citadel of Ibrim located 233 km upstream from Aswan. The discovery in 1969 of a number of manuscript fragments by the steps leading up to the west facade of the cathedral at Ibrim, ecclesiastical works in Coptic mainly written on papyrus and probably all pre-dating the tenth century, found lying under a layer containing signs of burning, has been associated with the destruction of the settlement and the ransacking of the cathedral library at this time.[38] No attempt was made to occupy the newly conquered territory and the Muslims returned to Egypt by late August with 150 prisoners and a great number of heads! [39]

In 1066 Nasir ed-Dawla raided Nubia 'but the Sudan crushed him, plundered his army and took all his equipment'.[40]

THE CAMPAIGN OF SHAMS ED-DAWLA TURANSHAH IN 1172-73

The first contacts between Makuria and the new Ayyubid dynasty in Egypt was a Makurian attack in 1172 towards Aswan, as far north as the country of Sa'id, possibly in support of the Fatimids. However, the attack was not pressed home and the reinforcements sent to Aswan by Salah ed-Din found that the enemy had already withdrawn. Salah ed-Din then ordered his brother Shams ed-Dawla Turanshah to march against Nubia. The rationale behind this campaign, according to el-Athir, was that Salah ed-Din and his brother were expecting Nureddin, King of Mosul, to invade Egypt and they were looking for a safe haven either in Nubia or in Yemen if they were unable to stand against him.[41] Shams ed-Dawla, conveyed by boat some at least of his troops and stores collected above the First Cataract. He captured Qasr Ibrim in 1173, which contained many provisions including, apparently, 700 pigs, cotton, arms and ammunition, and took booty and prisoners, whom he incarcerated in the fortress, before returning to Aswan.

While at Ibrim Shams ed-Dawla ordered that the cross on the dome of the church should be burnt and that the muezzin call the faithful to prayer from its summit indicating that the church was converted into a mosque. As well as killing the pigs he tortured a bishop who was found in the city, presumably to ascertain the location of the ecclesiastical treasure but without result. Two other sources provide us with contemporary evidence for these events. On a graffito written in Coptic within one of the rock-cut tombs at Aswan an unknown informant records,

> On this day, the 22nd of Tobe, the first day of the moon, the year of the Martyrs 889 [1173] it happened that the rule of the Turkos over all the land of Egypt, while Amba Markos was the Archbishop of Alexandria, and in the days of Theodorus, the Bishop of Aswan. The Turkos came south. They went to Ibrim and captured it on the seventh day of Tobe ... [42]

In Ibrim itself the director of the excavations conducted in the 1960s found, in the rock-cut tombs to the south of the cathedral, a deposit of written material including religious texts on parchment in Greek and Coptic. There were also non-literary texts in Old Nubian and Arabic written on paper, none of which dated to later then the twelfth century. He considered that the religious works probably came from the Cathedral library, the paper documents from an archive, perhaps belonging to the *eparch*. This deposit was sealed by five funerary *stelae* inscribed in Greek, most of them of bishops, dating to the period 1037-1132. It is possible that the destruction of the Library and archive, and the vandalism of the bishop's tombs, may have been by the troops of the Ayyubids. [43]

Shams ed-Dawla gave Ibrim in fief to Ibrahim el-Kurdi who occupied the fortress with a company of Kurdish horsemen and used it as a base to raid into Makurian territory. Enemy activity at this time has been tentatively linked with the partial destruction of the Faras cathedral. [44] The last bishop noted on the Bishop's List in the cathedral is one Iesu who died at some time between 1170 and 1175. Iesu was buried in a tomb which ultimately contained five individuals, but only four skulls were found on its excavation, which has led to the suggestion that it is perhaps Iesu's head that is missing and that he was killed by the troops of el-Kurdi. [45]

The Makurian king sent an ambassador bearing a letter requesting a peace treaty and a present of a male and female slave to Shams ed-Dawla who was at Qoz. The ambassador was received with honour but Shams ed-Dawla's reply to the king was to hand to the ambassador two pairs of arrows saying 'Tell the king:- I have no reply for him other than this.' The ambassador was then dispatched back to Old Dongola together with a Muslim, Mas'ud from Aleppo, who was to act as a spy reporting on the state of Makuria. The hapless Mas'ud was branded by the king with a cross and given a present of fifty pounds of flour before being sent on his way. The poor resources of the country and the hard life led by the Nubians persuaded Shams ed-Dawla to abandon any attempts at further conquest.

Ibrim was abandoned by the Muslims after two years, following the drowning of Ibrahim and a number of his companions while swimming across to the Island of Adindan. Thereupon the Makurians reoccupied the fortress. [46]

Within a few years of these events Salah ed-Din was locked in a fierce struggle with the western troops of the Fourth Crusade. There is very little evidence for any contact between, or even direct knowledge of, the Crusaders by the Christian Nubians. However, in 1203 or 1204 a Nubian ruler on pilgrimage to Jerusalem went on to Constantinople which was then under the control of the Crusaders. [47] Any cooperation between the

Crusaders and the Nubians is inherently unlikely. The Crusaders were just as hostile to other non-Catholic branches of the Church as they were to the Muslims; their treatment of the Copts amply bears this out. However, other Nubian pilgrims to Jerusalem are mentioned by Burchard of Mount Sion in 1280 and it may have been in that century that the Nubians obtained possession of Adam's Chapel in the Church of the Holy Sepulchre. This had passed out of their hands by the later fifteenth century but there were apparently at that time still Nubian pilgrims in the city.[48]

Alwa

All the events noted above affected Makuria and its northern province of Maris, the one time independent state of Nobadia. The terms of the *Baqt* specifically excluded the territory of the Alwans. At this period we know virtually nothing of military matters relating to the Alwan kingdom.

Nubia as a refuge

Salah ed-Din and Shams ed-Dawla were not the first inhabitants of Egypt who sought to use Nubia as a refuge from their enemies. In the mid eighth century Abdallah b. Marwan, the last Umayyad caliph, and his followers fled from Damascus into Nubia, but on meeting with the Makurian king his request for residence was denied and he was given three days to vacate the kingdom, which he did.[49] Abu Rakwa, who was a member of the Spanish Umayyad family, came to North Africa in 1003 and raised an army made up of Berbers and Arabs with which he proceeded to defeat the troops of the caliph el-Hakim in several battles. His power was broken when he was defeated by the caliph's forces in 1006, at Fayyum, whereupon he fled to the 'Lord of Nubia' or, according to another source, to the envoy of the king in 'the Fortress of the Mountain of the Nuba'. However, after repeated requests for his extradition by el-Hakim, Abu Rakwa was handed back to his countrymen by the Makurian king who sent one of the princes bringing presents to the Egyptian caliph.[50]

Kanz ed-Dawla, the leader of the powerful tribe of the Beni Kanz who effectively controlled the Aswan region, at some time between 1046 and 1077 sought to avoid retribution for his misdeeds by fleeing to Nubia, but he, like Abu Rakwa was handed over to the Egyptian authorities and was subsequently crucified in Cairo.[51] The last refugee to flee to medieval Nubia was Janim el-Ajrud el-Ainani, the Kashif of Manfalut, in 1486.[52] There is no mention of any contact with a Nubian king and by this time much of Nubia had probably slipped from the control of the Nubian kings of Dotawo, el-Abwab and Alwa.

Relations with the peoples to the east and west of the Nile

In June 950 the Makurian king plundered a number of oases in the territory of Egypt and caused great damage. According to Ibn Hawqal, writing in the tenth century a peace treaty was signed between the Nubians and the ruler of the Oases after a time of continued warfare and raids.[53] This may be related to the Nubian activities of 950 although the events recounted by Ibn Hawqal are not dated by him. At other times the Makurians and Beja raided each other although until the tenth century Makuria was reckoned to be the more powerful of the two states. According to el-Mas'udi the balance of power shifted with the reinforcement of the Beja by the infiltration of Muslims into their lands. These Muslims intermarried with Beja women and posed an increasing threat to the Makurians.[54]

Other enemies of the Nubians recorded in the Arab sources are the Damadim, whose whereabouts are uncertain,[55] and the Monophysite Christian Balliyin situated between the Beja and the Nubians of whom it was said 'all their neighbours fear them and make alliance treaties with them'.[56]

Of the raids made by the Makurian king to furnish slaves for the *Baqt* little is known. The Nubians, mounted on camels, raided the trade and pilgrimage route through the lands of the Beja from Qoz on the Nile along the Wadi el-Allaqi to Aidhab on the Red Sea,[57] but any captives from such activities, being largely Muslim, could not have been supplied to Egypt as slaves. More fruitful may have been raids to the south-west of Makuria into the Bayuda and northern Kordofan.

Whether there were offensive actions between Alwa and Makuria is not recorded although in the late thirteenth century there were attacks by Adur, king of the independent state of el-Abwab which lay between the two, on Makuria.[58] Alwa and Makuria on occasion were ruled by the same dynasty (see p. 89).

The Christian kingdoms of Alwa and of Ethiopia, both under the authority of the Patriarch in Alexandria, were close neighbours although separated by the steep western and north-western edge of the Ethiopian plateau, making communication difficult. There were Aksumites at the Alwan capital in 580 and we might expect there to have been close relations between the two states, but evidence for this is lacking, as it is for earlier contacts between the Kushites and the Aksumites, except perhaps in the mid fourth century AD. Direct contact between the King of Ethiopia and the King of the Nubians, which would usually be the designation of the Makurian rather than the Alwan ruler, is recorded during the life of the Patriarch Philotheus (980-1003).[59] Nubian objects in an Ethiopian context and vice versa are extremely rare.[60] Although Nubia and Ethiopia were geographically close the international outlook of the two areas was very different. The dwellers along the Nile looked principally north and south along the valley itself while the Ethiopians had strong contacts with the Red Sea littoral. Their spheres of interest were, therefore, largely mutually exclusive.

The army of the Nubians

We have little detailed information on the armies fielded by the Nubians. The reference to the effectiveness of the Makurian archers during the earliest Muslim invasions in the mid seventh century has already been mentioned. Although we have no relevant archaeological evidence from this period the importance of archery is well documented in graves pre-dating the conversion of Nubia to Christianity. That this evidence is no longer available after the sixth century presumably reflects changing funerary customs rather than changes in the weaponry used. Finds of archery equipment include remains of bows, arrows (Fig. 31), archer's looses, quivers (Fig. 32) and wrist guards are extremely common. At Qustul and Ballana bows have been found, both wooden self bows and the more powerful but complex compound bows with a wooden core covered with coarse textile, wrapped with leather and with a bone element bound against the belly of the bow.[61] Vegetable fibre bow strings have been recovered from Jebel Adda.[62] From the graves at

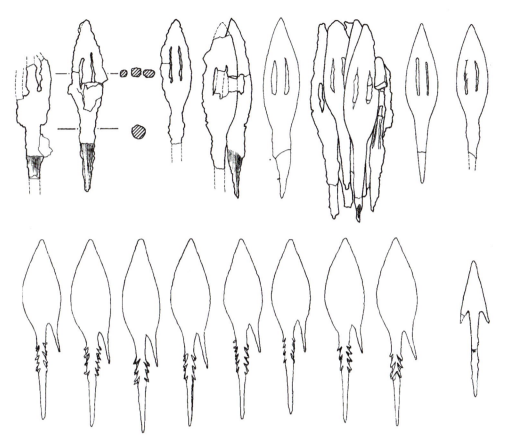

Figure 31 **Arrowheads from tombs HBG III/1 and HBG VI/1 at el-Hobagi (after Lenoble 1997, figs 3 and 4).**

el-Hobagi vast numbers of arrowheads were recovered; over 425 from HBG III/1 of which 388 were of iron and 37 of copper-alloy.[63] These were found in bundles and had presumably been buried in quivers which have not survived (Fig. 14). Elaborate leather quivers are found in some numbers in the contemporary graves, at Qustul, Ballana and Jebel Adda in particular, in Lower Nubia.[64] Archer's looses are a common find and leather wrist-protectors are also recovered. Arrowheads, which have a much higher rate of survival than archery equipment made from organic materials, are found on settlement sites throughout the medieval period although it is usually impossible to say whether they were associated with the military or were used for hunting. They could, of course, be used for either as the occasion demanded.[65] Most of the archer's looses are of the ceremonial type and testify to the status of archery rather than to its ubiquity. There is no mention of archery as a major arm of Nubian armies after 652. That archery remained important, however, is suggested by the use of the bow as a symbol of power: a number of wall paintings of the *eparch* resident in the north of Maris show him holding a bow.[66]

Other weaponry includes halberds and lances although these are probably ceremonial rather than for use in battle. They have been found in the elite burials at Qustul, Ballana,

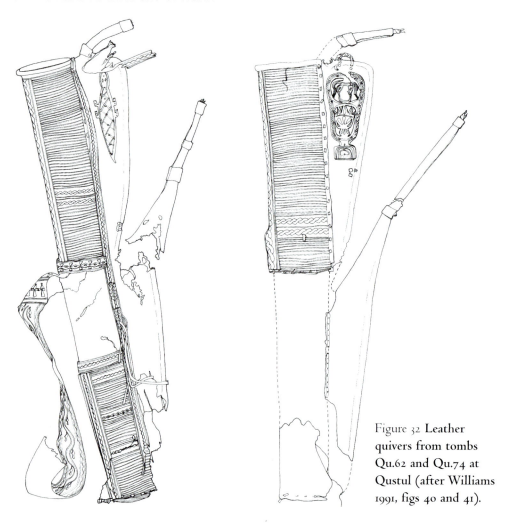

Figure 32 **Leather quivers from tombs Qu.62 and Qu.74 at Qustul (after Williams 1991, figs 40 and 41).**

Firka and el-Hobagi.[67] There was also a range of smaller spear-heads which may have been used for fighting or hunting, including a barbed type. One of these, from Qustul, is inscribed in Meroitic characters on one side and has two incised lions on the other.[68] Short swords are known from some graves including examples from Qustul, Ballana and Qasr Ibrim. Those at Qustul and Ballana are all very similar weapons with a straight hollow-ground blade, a tang which fitted into the wooden hilt covered with sheet silver and with five grooves to aid grip. In place of a pommel was a precious stone set in silver. The swords were only sharpened along one side of the blade and were clearly designed for hacking rather than thrusting (if they were anything other than ceremonial). They were contained in a wooden scabbard strengthened with embossed silver sheet.[69]

Finds of body armour are rare, perhaps because most of it was made from perishable leather as were shields. A fine, complete, breastplate made of thick oxhide, moulded and decorated into a complex pattern of raised bosses and ribbed surfaces, was recovered from near the main gate at Qasr Ibrim.[70] Pieces of what may have been leather body armour were also found in tomb Q.3 at Qustul and small fragments of thick leather from other tombs suggests that the principal interment was usually buried in armour.[71] Another piece from Qustul was made of several layers of hide decorated with rosettes, perhaps of lead.[72] Two shields were found at Qustul. The better preserved was of leather decorated with embossed spiral designs and was 700 mm in diameter. A simple wooden grip was threaded through slits cut in the shield either side of the conical central boss. The other had suffered some damage in use. It had been partly split, presumably by a sword cut, and repaired with iron staples.[73] Another shield of strange shape comes from Jebel Adda.[74] Fragments of iron chain mail from Soba East were found in the palatial building, Building D,[75] whether of Nubian manufacture or an 'exotic' imported item is unknown.

Cavalry appears to have been important and was a major component of Cyriacus' army along with troops mounted on camels, and camel troops are mentioned by the thirteenth-century writer el-Andalusi.[76] The Makurian cavalry was said to be mounted on small horses the size of asses.[77] There is mention of the presence of armoured cavalry, the horses with breastplates, at the battle before Old Dongola in 652, although it is unclear whether this is a reference to the Muslim or Makurian forces.[78] The chamfron discovered at Soba East was presumably for ceremonial use rather than being effective horse armour.[79]

Although we have no representations of cavalry from this period a number of wall paintings depict horses as mounts for the Three Kings in nativity scenes and for saints. Details of their harnesses can be seen and compared with the archaeological evidence. The most extensive finds of horse harnesses come from Qustul where a number of fully equipped horses were sacrificed at the grave. Two types of bridle were found. One type is well known from the wall paintings, with a headband, headpiece, cheek straps, noseband, jaw strap and an additional strap running down between the horse's eyes from headband to noseband. The other type is very different and dispenses with the noseband but has straps running down from the headband, crossing between the eyes and running down to the bit.[80] Also found in many graves was an unusual type of kerb bit parallels for which in Luristan in Central Asia, were noted by the excavators.[81] Two horses from Qustul each had a saddle with leather girth straps,[82] breeching and breast strap, but there was no provision for stirrups. However, on later wall paintings dating from the eleventh century onwards, for example that of the Three Kings on the Nativity scene in the Faras Cathedral, stirrups are seen. They had presumably been introduced into Nubia from Egypt. On later wall paintings stirrups are no longer depicted, leading to the suggestion that when relations with Egypt worsened an embargo on the supply of harnesses with stirrups was imposed. This, however, presupposes that, once acquainted with the idea of the stirrup, the Nubians were unable to manufacture their own, which seems rather implausible.[83] Horse harnesses were frequently adorned with rows of small bells which may have had as much a military as a decorative function. In a battle between the Muslims and the Beja in the ninth century the Muslim commander el-Omari ordered that bells be tied to the necks of his horses. During the battle with the Beja, who were mounted on camels, the sound of the bells, contributing to the cacophony of sound, led to the camels of the enemy turning back in utter confusion and panic.[84] The straps from around the horse's neck at Qustul were hung with small round bells and shells threaded onto leather thongs provided additional decoration.

One camel sacrificed and buried in the approach to Tomb A.11 at Firka had a saddle of leather stuffed with straw with no trace of a wooden frame. It was covered in a linen cloth over which was another linen saddle cloth with a coloured tapestry border of a continuous scroll of vine leaves and tendrils.[85]

The saddles from Qustul and Ballana, whether associated with camels or horses, were all of similar type with wooden pommel and cantle to which the wooden seat and skirt rods were lashed with strips of hide. Leather girth straps terminating in a copper-alloy or leather ring secured the saddle. The leather skirt cushion was stuffed with 'tibn' and the leather seat cushion had loops at both ends to pass over the pommel and cantle. Associated with many saddles were saddle cloths and sheepskins dyed blue.[86]

All we know of the Alwan army, from the written sources, is that, in the later tenth century, according to Ibn Selim, the Alwan king had a larger army with more horses than the Makurian king.[87]

Of the organization of the Nubian army we know nothing. Presumably there was a permanent component comprising both a royal guard and frontier garrisons forming a counterpart to the Muslim garrison at Aswan. The only garrison mentioned in the sources was stationed at Upper Maqs (Akasha) at the head of the Batn el-Hajar where it controlled movement from the north of Maris into the central part of the Kingdom.[88] A chain of fortified sites is known along the Nile over a distance of 250 km between Faras and Kalabsha although in the sources the only Makurian citadels recorded are at Qasr Ibrim and Jebel Adda. These, and other fortified sites, are discussed in detail in Chapter 6.

Dating from the eleventh and fourteenth centuries are two *nauarchoi* indicating that a navy was in existence at that time.[89] Water transport was certainly used by the Muslims during some of their invasions of Nubia and a Makurian navy would have been essential to combat this threat. Of naval actions, other naval personnel and of the ships themselves we know nothing.

An interesting find from Qasr Ibrim, from a deposit perhaps to be associated with the capture of the fortress by Shams ed-Dawla, was the remains of a flag bearing a painted device and the Greek word λεων, lion, perhaps the remains of a battle ensign.[90]

It was the military prowess of the Makurian army, perhaps aided in no small measure by the poor impression that the country made on the Muslim invaders, that ensured the survival of the independent Nubian kingdoms for many centuries. Throughout much of its history Makuria was able to field forces of sufficient numbers and calibre to defeat the unwary Muslims. However, in the later medieval period, apart from the impressive offensive mounted by David, the Makurians were on the defensive, and the severe damage wrought by the movement of Muslim armies through the length of the kingdom must have done much to sap its strength and bring about the demise of its army as an organized fighting force.

CHAPTER 5

The heyday of the Nubian kingdoms

The *Baqt* of 652 established peaceful relations with the Muslims in Egypt which were maintained, almost unbroken, until the rise of the Ayyubids in the later twelfth century brought about renewed aggression against Nubia. During the four centuries of peace, Nubia attained a considerable degree of prosperity, and developed a rich Christian culture from the First Cataract at least as far south as Soba East. Although it is the northern kingdom of Makuria which is best known to us through the Arab sources and through archaeology, it is noteworthy that Alwa may have been the more important. Ibn Selim, who travelled from Egypt along the Nile to Old Dongola and on to Soba East in the tenth century, and who appears to have been a reliable observer of all he saw, wrote, 'The king of Alwa is more powerful than the king of Maqurra, has a larger army and more horses than the Maqurran: his country is more fertile and larger…'[1] Another eyewitness Ibn Hawqal writing in the same century, considered Alwa the most prosperous part of the whole of Nubia.[2]

Frontiers

Several Arab writers provide information on the topography of the Nubian kingdoms and from this it is possible, with a considerable degree of confidence, to define the boundaries of each state, at least in the Nile Valley. The picture presented below appears static, but it must be borne in mind that over the 1000-year history of these kingdoms there may well have been changes in the areas controlled by each state.

Ibn Selim is one of our best sources. He records that the northernmost town in Nubia is the village of el-Qasr, 8 km from Aswan.[3] Philae is described as the last fortress of the Muslims, lying one mile from the village of el-Qasr.[4] Ibn Hawqal, who visited Nubia around 955, notes that on the east bank of the Nile, across from Philae, stand a mosque and a fortress and below the mosque a church, property of the Nuba, which marks the frontier between the two nations.[5]

Descriptions of the Muslim campaigns into Nubia in the mid seventh century make no mention of Nobadia. Clearly their goal was Old Dongola, the capital of Makuria. In the terms of the *Baqt* of 652 there is no reference to a sovereign state of Nobadia, implying that it had ceased to exist by that date. The *Baqt* 'applied to the land of Nubia as far as the frontier of Alwa'.[6] Although Nobadia may have been subsumed into the Makurian state, we have no details as to how this came about. It may have been a direct response to the Muslim threat from the north, although the interval between the first arrival of the Muslims in Egypt in 639 and their first invasion of Nubia in 641 or 642, during which there is no mention of Nobadia, leaves little time for such a unification to have taken place. The last mention of Nobadia as an independent state dates to 580, and the unification of Nobadia and Makuria may have taken place between that date and 652 if not 641-2.[7]

Notwithstanding the evidence of the sources referring to the terms of the *Baqt* many scholars have argued for a much later date for the unification of the two states. The silence of the Arab sources regarding Nobadia, although compelling, must be treated with some caution. It is salutary to note that the Kingdom of Dotawo, which is mentioned frequently in documents from Qasr Ibrim in the late medieval period, is also never mentioned in the literary sources. Epigraphic evidence proves that by 707 Nobadia and Makuria were certainly united as in that year, Mercurios, who was King of Makuria, is mentioned on the inscription perhaps recording the construction of the cathedral at Faras, and is again mentioned on the foundation stone of a church at Taifa in 710. In *The Life of the Patriarch Isaac* (690-93) written by Bishop Mena, a contemporary of these events, it is recorded that the king of Makuria was unable to get bishops for his country on account of the enmity of the king of Mauritania who was an ally of the Saracens, themselves enemies of the Makurian king. It has been suggested that for Mauritania we should read Nobadia, and that this literary evidence and the epigraphic evidence just noted provides the chronological parameters within which the unification of the two kingdoms lie.[8] Monneret de Villard suggested that the inscription in the temple-church at Wadi es-Sebua, which is dated by a new era beginning in 704, may be connected with this unification.[9] King Mercurios, according to John the Deacon, was held in high regard and was called the New Constantine; 'on account of his beautiful conduct he became like one of the disciples'.[10] Was this on account of his unification of the Churches of Makuria and Nobadia?

The Arab sources which describe the terms of the *Baqt* all date to well after the date of the unification of Nobadia and Makuria. They may be referring to the situation in their own day rather than to that of the mid seventh century. The absence of any mention of conflicts between the Muslim invaders and the kingdom of Nobadia may be the result, as the author of *The Life of the Patriarch Isaac* records, of those two states being already allies. The possibility of enmity between Nobadia and Makuria at this time is entirely plausible in the light of the situation known to have existed not too much earlier, during the later sixth century.

Archaeological evidence from the cemetery at Ballana suggests that the latest royal burial of a Nobadian king dates to around 480-90, with one tomb of a queen perhaps a decade later.[11] This however need have no relevance for the dating of the unification of Nobadia and Makuria, but may be a reflection of the conversion of the royal house to Christianity and the changes in burial practices which this brought about. The last royal burial at Ballana may be that of the last pagan ruler of Nobadia.

Although Nobadia had long ceased to exist as an independent political unit by the time the earliest Arab writers reported on the situation in Nubia, the territory of Nobadia appears to have been retained as a distinct territorial unit within the Makurian state with the name of Maris. As late as 1186 the term Nobadia is still used.[12] Ibn Hawqal says that Maris is the area between the frontier of Aswan and the frontier of Makuria.[13] Ibn Selim, describing his journey upstream through Nubia, entered the Third Cataract region and the details of his journey at this point can be directly equated with the topography visible on

Figure 33 **The Kajbar rapids from Jebel Wahaba.**

the ground today. After describing the beginning of the cataract where there is a fortress which he calls Astanum by which the water gushes through with a terrible roar, clearly Jebel Wahaba and the Kajbar rapids (Fig. 33), [14] there are rocks lying in the bed of the Nile for a distance of three day's journey, until one reaches the village of Bastu, 'the last village of the Maris and the beginning of the country of the Muqurra'.[15] The exact location of Bastu is not known, but it must have stood at the head of the Third Cataract in the region of Tumbus and Hannek. The status of this region as a frontier was perpetuated into the post-medieval period. The Ottoman Turks invading from the north and the Funj expanding from the south fought a decisive battle at Hannek, and after the battle the frontier between the two states was fixed eight miles south of Hannek.[16]

In the account of the Muslim invasion of Makuria in 1289-90 it is recorded that the king fled from Old Dongola, a distance of fifteen day's journey to a large island three day's journey in length. That the boats of the Muslims were unable to follow 'because of the many rocks cropping up from the river bed'[17] indicates that the large island was beyond the Fourth Cataract and the most suitable candidate for it is Mograt, the largest island in the Nile. From there the king withdrew upstream for three day's journey which took him to el-Abwab which lay beyond the bounds of his kingdom.[18] The journey from Mograt would take him towards the Fifth Cataract which is 138 km along the river or 123 km as the crow flies. The border between Makuria and el-Abwab thus lay in this region.[19] A king named Johannes, who is not precisely dated but is assumed to have reigned around 850, ruled 'all the Ethiopians ... from Tilimauara until the fortress of Peilak (Philae).[20] The location of Tilimauara is unknown.

According to Ibn Selim the northern frontier of Alwa is marked by some villages on the east bank of the river called el-Abwab.[21] The southern border lay in the land of the Tubli (Tubula) 'This is the extreme limit of Alwa on the Nile.'[22] Where these peoples lived is unknown. On the White Nile the swamps of the Sudd lay beyond Nubian control.[23] Large areas of the Gezira, which was 'inhabited by Nuba, Kursa and other people about which it is impossible to know [more] because they are inaccessible', were under Alwan control.[24] Pottery of types familiar from Soba East has been found at a number of cemeteries along the Blue Nile, at Qoz Nasra, Umm Sunt and Karim's Garden,[25] and a pottery vessel, of a type almost certainly made at Soba, has been recovered from Khalil el-Kubra 40 km upstream of Sennar.[26] Mounds covered in red brick, traditionally assumed to cover the remains of churches, have been noted on many sites upstream of Soba although none have been tested by excavation.[27] The most southerly church known, which presumably was within the kingdom of Alwa, lay at Saqadi 50 km to the west of Sennar.[28]

The limit of control of the Nubian kingdoms to the east and west of the Nile, to the east of the Blue Nile, and to the west of the White Nile, is difficult to determine. Like the states in Lower Nubia before them, the writ of the kings of Nobadia probably extended only a little to the east and west of the Nile, although presumably some attempt was made to coexist peacefully with the desert dwellers who had long been troublesome to the sedentary riverine population. Further to the south the potential for settlement well away from the river will have made control of those areas both more desirable and important for the security of the riverine states.[29]

To date virtually no sites of this period are known outside of the Nile Valley, notwith-standing the claims of Arkell for a medieval Nubian presence in Darfur. A Christian monastic community may have been living at Selima Oasis, 90 km to the west of the Nile Valley from Sakiat el-'Abd. Krump, who passed through Selima in 1700, recorded the presence there of an ancient monastery with strong stone walls within which eight cells were visible; the site was in ruins.[30] Reference to two monasteries, perhaps in this region,[31] described as 'in the desert between the Nuba and the Sudan' are to be found in the tenth century Persian geographical work, *Hudud el-Alam*.[32] Medieval occupation is attested at the oasis of el-Laqiya about 24 km to the west of the Northern Dongola Reach of the Nile, and 16 km south of el-Laqiya, there are number of structures of stone and earth and a cemetery surrounded by a circular enclosure wall.[33] Immediately to the east of el-Laqiya itself are extensive remains of a settlement with two prominent mud-brick buildings surviving.[34]

A fortress over 100 km up the Wadi Howar from Old Dongola appears to be Kushite rather than of medieval date.[35] Nuwabiya, said by a twelfth-century writer to have been one of the famous Nubian towns, lay four days journey from the Nile.[36] It presumably lay to the west of the Nile but its whereabouts is unknown. At the time of Zacharias the Makurian king bemoans the fact that a barbarian group was in rebellion against him, presumably a people living outside of the Nile Valley though exactly where is unknown. The king was fearful that they might be in a position to take Old Dongola if he were to leave the capital.[37]

Medieval graves, often the typical tumuli and box graves associated with medieval ceramics, are common in the Bayuda, a region where control may have been essential to safeguard the cross-desert trade from Soba East to Old Dongola and beyond.[38] Possibly connected with these cross-desert routes are a number of fortified sites in the lower Wadi

Abu Dom which may be of post-Meroitic date. The juxtaposition of these, however, all four within as many kilometres of each other, and the absence of similar enclosures further along the route, calls this explanation of their function into question.[39] Another stone-walled enclosure with at least one red-brick building within it, at Kufryat el-Atash 41 km to the south of ed-Debba, is of uncertain date although a few sherds identified as of Christian date were noted there. It stands close to a number of wells which it was presumably placed to control. Other wells along the same route, at Kufriyat el-Rawyanat 19 km south of ed-Debba, do not have any structure associated with them.[40]

Ibn Hawqal in the tenth century records that to the west of the White Nile is a race known as the Highlanders, who are subjects of the Lord of Dongola.[41] He goes on to state that between the Highlanders and the kingdom of Alwa is a sandy desert, but with innumerable villages and various people speaking a range of languages. These people are Christians and are under the control of the Alwan king. If Ibn Hawqal is to be believed, one could suggest that the most likely locality to be occupied by the Highlanders would be the Gilif Hills in the centre of the Bayuda. It is perhaps also in the Bayuda, or in northern Kordofan, that the Zanj lived. They are described as being to the south and west of Dongola and as being subjects of the Nubians.[42] A graffito in Old Nubian at Awadun close to the Wadi el-Melik,[43] 200 km upstream from its confluence with the Nile at ed-Debba, indicates that at least one speaker of this Nile Valley language, closely associated with the medieval kingdoms, may have used this route on his way to places further west and south-west where Abu Sufyan and Zankor lie. Red-brick structures, which are traditionally dated to the medieval period along the Nile Valley, occur at Abu Sufyan, over 400 km to the south west of ed-Debba. These are circular and the largest is 150 x 130 ft (46 x 40 m) at the base, 70 x 55 ft (21 x 17 m) at the flat top and stands 15-20 ft (4.6-6.1 m) above the plain. The sides are revetted in red brick (300 x 170 x 80 mm in size) while the top is of mud brick. No dating material has been recovered from the site.[44] Two hundred kilometres to the south are red-brick mounds at Zankor in the Kaja Serug hills. The pottery from this site has been dated to the seventh century.[45] It does not, however, appear to be closely related to Nubian pottery types current in the Nile Valley during the medieval period. In Darfur there are other red-brick structures, some of which have been claimed as of medieval date. Although there is little evidence for this attribution, or at least for the implied contact with medieval Nubia,[46] two undoubtedly Nubian sherds of pottery have been found at Ain Farah, but these do not, along with the structural evidence, support the claim that there was a church and monastery on the site.[47] Some contact has been suggested between Nubia and Chad, via the Zaghawa tribe, leading to the transmission of a number of 'Nubian' features, among them one element of royal regalia, the purse.[48]

The builders of the church, and the occupants of the post-Meroitic and Christian graves, at the old Kushite royal and religious centre of Musawwarat es-Sufra 28 km to the south-east of the Nile in the Keraba,[49] were presumably subjects of Alwa. Along the Atbara were the Dihiyyun, said to be the offspring of intermarriages between Alwans and Beja.[50] How far up the Atbara direct Alwan control extended is uncertain. Numerous 'Christian' sites have been claimed along that river, at one of these, Goz Regeb, there was a settlement and two cemeteries. In the latter were some fired bricks bearing incised stars, crosses, fish(?) and part of the name Petros in Greek.[51] In a region known as Dujn is Taflin, a fertile area to which nomads bring their flocks during the rainy season. Ibn Hawqal states that their king is a Muslim but is a vassal of the King of Alwa.[52] It has been suggested that Dujn may be in the southern Atbai to the east of the river Atbara. Pottery, thought to be related to medieval Nile Valley wares, along with fired bricks decorated with crosses, fish and bearing Greek letters, has been found in this area in the Gash Delta and there was possibly also Christian occupation at Khatmiya near Kassala.[53] Further south the banks of the tributaries of the Blue Nile were inhabited and cultivated[54] by people who may also have been Alwan subjects. Leo Africanus, writing a short time after the final extinction of the Nubian kingdoms, records that the peoples living between the Nile and the Red Sea with whom the king of Nubia was often at war, were paid a subsidy sometime from the Lord of Suwakin and sometimes from Dongola.[55] The veracity of this statement, and the period to which it refers, cannot be ascertained, but the payment of subsidies as a means of maintaining peace between a sedentary state and a nomadic enemy finds numerous parallels. Leo Africanus could, however, be referring to money exacted from caravans by the Beja who sat athwart the trade route, which seems to have shifted south from the Nile-Aidhab route to another from Old Dongola to Suwakin during the fourteenth century.[56]

Royalty

On the takeover of Nobadia by Makuria we have no information on the fate of the Nobadian royal family. Makurian royalty appear frequently in the Arab sources. It is very clear that the succession passed through the matrilineal line, as it had in Nobadia in the later sixth century. It was the son of the sister of the reigning monarch who was heir to the throne, and the same principle also applied in Alwa, at least in the mid tenth century.[57] In Makuria many of the nephews of the reigning king appear to have been rather impatient to ascend the throne, and the crown prince usurping his uncle's throne is a common theme in Makurian history. According to Abu Salih if there was no nephew to whom the throne could pass the king's son was next in line.[58] On other occasions, presumably when there was no eligible candidate, other members of the royal family, or even people from outside it, were acceptable.

Two episodes illustrate the complexity of the succession. Zacharias, the son of King Mercurios, was crown prince in the eighth century, but he chose not to become king, instead devoting his life to God, and chose in his stead one of his kinsmen, Simon. On the death of Simon, Zacharias once again assumed the role of kingmaker and adopted one Ibrahim, who was attached to the palace staff. However, Ibrahim proved to be unsuitable and following a serious clash with the bishop of Dongola he was deposed by Zacharias, who appointed Mark in his place. To consolidate his power Mark sought to kill Ibrahim but was himself assassinated, while he was praying in a church before the sanctuary, after a rule of only six months. A man called Cyriacus was then placed on the throne, bringing to an end this particularly unsuccessful episode of royal succession.[59] In the mid ninth century royal power was exercised by a prince called Zacharias, who we are told was not of royal descent, without which it was unlawful to become king. Zacharias assumed the position of regent for his son Giorgios, whose mother was of royal descent and was hence eligible to ascend the throne.[60] During the 1000 years of Makurian history we are not dealing with a single royal family. Usurpers are recorded who, when successful, set up their own dynasties.

Of the fate which generally lay in wait for the king's son on the succession of his cousin we have no information. However, according to Severus, who specifically states the principles of matrilineal succession, the Makurian king Basil sent his son to the Patriarch in order that he might be made a bishop. The Church certainly appears to have had a strong attraction for the Makurian royal house. In the eleventh century the Makurian king Solomon abdicated to lead a life of worship and handed over the kingdom to his nephew Giorgios. He retired to a wadi known as Saint Onuphrius, worshiping there in a church dedicated to his name, ten days journey from Aswan, from whence he was abducted by the *wali* and sent to Cairo where he died a year later.[61]

The Makurian kings bore an hereditary title, Kasil, Kamil or Kabil.[62] On a *stela* from Old Dongola is an individual called Zacharios Augustus, presumably King Zacharias of Makuria although the use of the title is not known from elsewhere.[63]

THE ALWAN AND MAKURIAN ROYAL FAMILIES

The written sources demonstrate the very close relations at certain periods between the royal families of Makuria and Alwa. In December 943 we are told by el-Mas'udi that Kubra Ibn Surur,[64] King of Dongola, ruled over Alwa,[65] while Ibn Hawqal, writing at about the same time, records that the king of el-Maqurra, who is also the king of Dongola, was under the king of Alwa.[66] At the time of Ibn Hawqal's visit to Nubia the sister of the Alwan king was married to Yurki and the son of that union, Stephanos, succeeded to the throne. The suggestion that Yurki was Giorgios II, king of Makuria cannot be proven although chronologically it is a possibility.[67] If there was intermarriage between the two royal houses the principle of matrilineal succession may frequently have caused the throne to pass to a king whose father was of the royal family of the other state. As so few Alwan kings are known it is difficult to suggest when the two kingdoms may have been united. It is only in the period *c.* 1000 to 1006 that we know the names of the contemporary Makurian and Alwan kings, Raphael and David.

An inscription found at Soba East of 'Giorgi, Christ-loving king' with its unusual form of the king's name also seen on inscriptions of King Giorgios I of Makuria, suggests the possibility that the same ruler may be referred to.[68] If this were the case the implications of an inscription bearing the name of a Makurian king in the capital of Alwa is uncertain. Griffith suggested that the Giorgios mentioned on a marble *stela* from Soba in Berlin, may have been a king.[69] Dating from the late twelfth century is an inscription identifying the accompanying painting in the cathedral at Faras as King Moses Giorgios. He is described as 'King of (the) Nobadians and Alwa and Makuria'.[70] Moses Giorgios may also have been the king of that name who was ruler of the kingdom of Dotawo.

Among the kings known to us is Giorgios who is recorded on a large circular dish or tray of marble found in the Monastery of the Syrians in the Wadi en-Natrun in northern Egypt which is inscribed in Greek around the rim and has a twenty-four line inscription in Old Nubian within (Fig. 34). It records that he was born in 1106, came to the throne in 1130 and died in 1158.[71] Although the kingdom he ruled is not stated the language of the inscription indicates that it was Makuria, Alwa or perhaps the Kingdom of Dotawo,

Figure 34 **The inscription of a Nubian king Giorgios from the Monastery of the Syrians in the Wadi en-Natrun in northern Egypt inscribed in Greek and Old Nubian (after Griffith 1928, 124).**

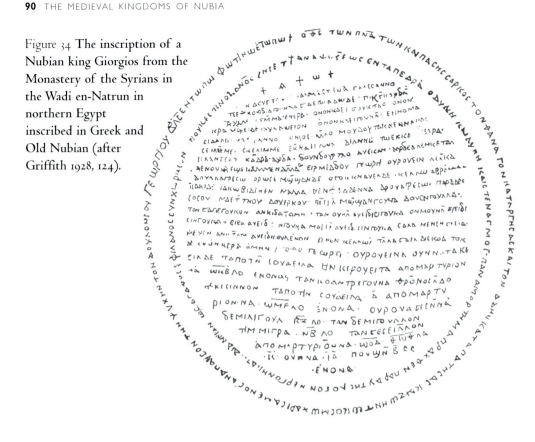

although there is the possibility that he may have been one of the other kinglets in Nubia. Why his funerary inscription should have been found in the Wadi en-Natrun, over 900 km from the Nubian border, is something of a mystery.

El-Mas'udi records that the Nubian kings claimed Himyarite descent[72] but there is no further evidence to shed light on this.

REGALIA

We have very disparate evidence for the regalia of the Nubian kings. The earliest Nubian kings were pagans and adhered to the age-old practice of burial with elaborate funerary rituals, many of the artefacts associated with these being buried in the tomb, along with abundant grave goods. With the arrival of Christianity all our evidence for regalia is iconographic, from the wall paintings in churches and monasteries. We have no artefacts which can be directly associated with any Nubian Christian ruler.

The only crowns to have been discovered are those of the pagan Nobadian rulers buried at Ballana. Five crown types were found, two clearly derived from Kushite crowns. All are formed of a simple band of two sheets of silver over a plaster core with one or a combination of decorative embellishments, embossed decoration, inset stones (beryl, carnelian, garnet) or glass, and/or with the circlet surmounted by ram's heads, *uraei* and plumed crests. According to Török, four crowns belonging to kings, six to queens and three to princes were discovered.[73] The quality of the crowns is poor and Török suggests that they may have been made specifically for funerary use. Their Kushite royal predecessors had crowns of gold, but it is impossible to say whether similar crowns were used by the early Nubian kings. The iconography displayed on some of the crowns suggests that there was an understanding by the Nobadian rulers, or by the craftsmen who fashioned the crowns, of their significance in a Kushite context.[74] Two reliefs, probably of Silko on the Temple of Mandulis at Kalabsha, show the king wearing a Egyptian double crown with Kushite accoutrements, and a skullcap-diadem with *hmhm* superstructure and streamers (Fig. 3), again underlining the continuing appreciation of the symbolism inherent in these crown types.[75]

A number of representations of Christian Makurian kings are preserved on wall paintings and we have several eyewitness accounts of Makurian kings from Muslim travellers. According to Michael the Syrian during the crown-prince Giorgios' visit to Egypt, on his way to Baghdad, he wore a crown composed of a tiara with a cross on top of it,[76] elsewhere it is noted that the king wore a crown of gold.[77] On the wall paintings in the Faras cathedral crowns are worn by both heavenly and earthly individuals and the form of the crowns is not, in many cases, exclusive to one group or the other. King Giorgios II wears a tiara which is surmounted by a six-pointed star on top of which is a cross of gold. The whole tiara is highly decorated with coloured stones and pearls.[78] Queen Martha wears a crown of unusual form, a diadem surmounted at each side by elements perhaps representing plumes, again richly decorated with stones and pearls, while the Virgin in the same scene wears a crown of Byzantine type, the *kamelaukion*.[79] A Nubian princess wears a diadem surmounted by four low 'dome'-shaped projections.

Among the objects buried in the royal tombs of the Nobadian ruling elite at Ballana, and in the high status (royal?) tombs at el-Hobagi, archery equipment forms a significant proportion (see p. 80). Within many of these elite burials were other weapons, lances with long leaf-shaped blades, swords and axes. The discovery of archery equipment in a funerary context can be documented from the Kerma period when bows and arrows were buried in graves which were probably not of members of the highest echelons of society.[80] In the Kushite period archery equipment — bows, arrows, quivers and archer's looses — is commonly associated on reliefs with the ruler[81] and with the gods, particularly the war god Apedemak. Finds of archery equipment have been made in Kushite royal and elite burials in the north and west cemeteries at Meroe. In the post-Meroitic period relief decoration of tombs is unknown, but the absence of representations of archery equipment and other weaponry is made up for by the provision of the actual objects. Lenoble considers that the importance of the archery equipment and lances in particular, in the burials at el-Hobagi, demonstrates the continuity of the symbols of *imperium* from the Kushite period.[82] Although the importance of archery as a weapon of war continued at least into the mid seventh century, and was used to great effect against the earliest Arab invaders, there is no evidence that in the Christian milieu military prowess was celebrated as a royal accomplishment, and representations of Christian Nubian rulers do not feature weaponry and triumph over worldly foes.

Most of the symbols associated with the Christian Makurian kings, as depicted on wall paintings, are derived from Byzantine imperial iconography, although there are a few which link the Makurian royal iconography with the local African traditions. The king is frequently shown wearing a purse or a water skin. The former object is used in other

African kingdoms to symbolize the control of the ruler over his subjects. Żurawski suggests that the depictions of the king handling this levy purse during the accession ceremonies may symbolize his power over the petty rulers within his kingdom. If the object is a water skin it can be compared with that carried by a number of Kushite gods, and another continuation of Kushite iconography is the wearing of the thumb ring. The headcloth is also alien to Byzantine tradition, but appears to be, in Nubian art, an attribute both of heavenly and earthly royalty.[83]

In 1172 a messenger from Shams ed-Dawla reported that the Makurian king rode out to him almost naked and completely hairless, wrapped only in a silk robe and mounted on an unsaddled horse.[84] On wall paintings, however, rulers wear elaborate, highly decorated, clothing. Giorgios II, both on his painting in the cathedral at Faras and on another in one of the churches at Sonqi Tino, wears a cloak in the form of a *paludamentum* beneath which is a *dalmatica* and tunic, Queen Martha has a cloak of *paenula* type and a tunic covered with very rich ornamentation.[85]

Administration and officials

THE KING

The king was the undisputed head of state holding absolute authority over all his subjects. Ibn Selim states that the Makurian king has the power to reduce any of his subjects to slavery, whether that individual is guilty of any wrongdoing or not, and that his rule is unopposed.[86] It is possible that the subjects of the king of Makuria were legally regarded as his slaves and, therefore, that they had no right of land ownership, being technically, as slaves of the king, his tenants. However, in the early ninth century this status was successfully challenged in the Egyptian courts by a number of Muslim residents of Aswan who had bought land in northern Makuria from citizens of that country. The Makurian king claimed that this land had been sold illegally and that it really belonged to him.[87] As a result of this ruling the status of Maris was different thereafter than that of the rest of Makuria. In Maris estates could be passed on by inheritance while elsewhere the inhabitants remained technically the slaves of the king.[88]

KINGLETS

John the Deacon and Abu Salih refer, in the mid eighth century, to the Makurian king Cyriacus as king of the Nubians, under whom were thirteen kings ruling the kingdom and country; Cyriacus was the 'Great King'.[89] These kinglets were all priests, but if they killed someone they were no longer allowed to celebrate the liturgy. Throughout the history of Makuria there are no references to these kinglets in the Arab sources. Whereas the *eparch* features prominently in the historical sources the absence of the kinglets suggests that they exercised no important administrative role at an international level and did not, independently, control military forces with whom the Muslims may have come into conflict. A graffito from Jebel Adda, written by an individual called Grailekor, the town-mayor or castellan of Akirimip, records 'Ameud's son Taanengo the king …'.[90] This king is not otherwise recorded and may be a kinglet rather than a Makurian Great King. As discussed further in Chapter 10, the King of Dotawo, known mainly from inscriptions and texts found at Qasr Ibrim and Jebel Adda, was presumably also one of these kinglets. In the fifteenth century, after the demise of the kingdom of Makuria, the Dotawan kings seem to have taken the position of the Great King and adopted the same administrative arrangements. Joel is described as King of Kings of Dotawo and one of the kinglets was King Tienossi of Ilenat.[91]

THE EPARCH

The authority of the Makurian king was delegated to a number of officials, chief among whom was the *eparch*, a title which, as the Greek equivalent of the Latin *praefectus*, was widely used in the Roman and Byzantine Empires.[92] The prominence of the *eparch* based in the north of the kingdom is in part presumably due to his function and the locality where he held office. He is referred to in the Arab sources as the 'Lord of the Mountain' or the 'Lord of the Horses'; texts in Old Nubian indicate that he held both titles as well as 'Lord of the King's Horses' and many others.[93] This *eparch* was resident in the north of Makuria and appears to have been charged with relations between Makuria and the Muslims. Ibn Selim describes the Lord of the Mountain as dealing with anyone who entered the land of the Nuba from the land of the Muslims.[94] Under Cyriacus in the eighth century he is referred to as 'one of the great men of the kingdom';[95] Ibn Selim describes him as among the highest ranking governors in the kingdom[96] while under king David he is described as having 'power over one half of the Nubian territory'.[97] The court of the *eparch* was modelled on that of the monarch and used the same court titles, derived in both cases from the imperial court at Byzantium.[98]

The earliest reference to an *eparch* is during the reign of Mercurios. Whether that *eparch*, Markos, was the first person to hold that office, a particularly attractive suggestion if one accepts that Nobadia and Makuria were united during Mercurios' reign, is unknown.[99] The tombstone of the *eparch* Petros (died 798) has been found at Old Dongola. On it he is described as 'eparch of the land of Nobadia' or 'eparch of the land of the Nobadians'. Similar phraseology is to be found on an inscription of the *eparch* Paulos-Kolla dated to around 750 and one of Johannes who died in 883. The latter was 'eparch of Gaderon' and, as he was the king's son, it has been suggested that he was the chief administrator of the southern part of the kingdom, the counterpart of the *eparch* of Nobadia. The *eparch palatium* may have been a separate office, [100] perhaps the chief administrator of the whole realm.[101]

A tombstone, found within the Church of the Granite Columns at Old Dongola and dated to 883, of Johannes, son of Zacharias (presumably the king of that name, and hence brother of Giorgios I), describes him as *Eparch* of Gaderon. The meaning of Gaderon is uncertain, it has been suggested that it may mean 'the Countries' (from the Greek *gadera*, country) hence implying control over large territories, or that it refers to the village of el-Ghaddar near Old Dongola.[102] Among the documents relating to the Kingdom of Dotawo there is evidence for two eparchal offices, one, the *eparch* of Nobadia, the other the *eparch* of a place called $\tau^\pi\varepsilon\rho$ the location of which is unknown,[103] while the *eparch* of Palagi is also mentioned. A Greek *stela* from Meinarti, dated 1161, commemorated Goassi, *Eparch* of Nobadia and Choiakeikšil.[104] The latter is probably not an eparchal office; Papasa who died in 1181 is described as a priest and Choiakeikšil.

Of the eparchal offices known the bulk of the evidence relates to the northern eparchate. The relationship of this office to the royal family and administration of the Kingdom of Nobadia is unclear. Originally the *eparch* may have resided at Faras, probably the old Nobadian capital, and Abu Salih records that that was the capital of Maris and contained the dwelling place of Jawsar 'who wore turban and two horns and the gold bracelets'.[105] The *eparch* was certainly resident for centuries at Qasr Ibrim, confirmed by a number of Arab sources and also by the discovery of a large amount of correspondence on the site. During the events of 1275/6 and 1287 he occupied Jebel Adda[106] and also Meinarti,[107] although at least some of the eparchal correspondence and the archaeological evidence from houses considered to be the dwellings of *eparchs* at Qasr Ibrim indicate that it continued to be his headquarters long afterwards.[108]

In the cathedral and Rivergate Church at Faras, and in the churches at Abd el-Qadir and the Church of the Angels at Tamit, there are wall paintings most frequently showing the *eparch* under the protection of Christ, the Virgin or Angels. The *eparchs* wear a distinctly Nubian style of costume, with a wide skirt, a caftan, veil and voluminous white robe beneath. They also wear a distinctive crown consisting of a skullcap or helmet sometimes with one or two horns to either side and with a central projection topped by a crescent (Fig. 52).[109] Another variant has the cap and horns with a circular feature between. Yet a third incorporates a bucranium with two pairs of horns.[110] A sack hangs from their right shoulder and they frequently hold a bow in their right hand.[111] The origin of the *eparch*'s crown is uncertain and is not closely paralleled by either the crown types well known from Pharaonic Egypt and the Kushite Empire, or those found in the graves of the early Nobadian rulers at Ballana. A very similar crown type was worn by the Sassanian Persians who came in direct contact with Nobadia in the earlier part of the seventh century.[112]

According to Ibn Selim the *eparch* received all visitors entering the kingdom for the purposes of trade or to bring gifts to him or to the king and that the *eparch* allowed no one to travel upstream to visit the king.[113] The limit of free access into Makuria seems to have lain at Upper Maqs, probably to be equated with the modern settlement at Akasha at the downstream end of the Dal Cataract. There the garrison was charged to refuse access upriver to anyone except with the permission of the king (presumably through his delegated official the *eparch*). Whoever transgressed this law was to be put to death, no matter who they were.[114] Ibn Selim explains this law as guaranteeing secrecy about what was happening within the kingdom, allowing the Makurians to invade a neighbouring country or move into the deserts without warning.

The correspondence of the *eparch* from Qasr Ibrim furnishes a wealth of detail regarding his activities and responsibilities. Many of the letters refer to disbursement of grain either from the public stores or from the *eparch*'s personal store. Some of these were directly authorized by the *eparch* himself, others signed on his behalf by a vice-*eparch*. The recipients in many cases are individuals and the amounts are small. Some of the correspondence appears to be of so trivial a nature as to make the direct involvement of the *eparch*, one of the most important officials of Makuria, rather surprising unless some of this correspondence is of a more personal nature, recording the *eparch*'s interaction with his extended family and friends.[115] Among these is a letter from *eparch* Adam to a man described as an *architriclinus* which concerns one bale of hay which a third party gave to the *eparch*'s mother, another bale of hay belonging to the *architriclinus*' mother and an admission by the *eparch* that he had 'gulped down' some dates.[116] Other letters of the late medieval period, found among the *eparch*'s archive, concern matters relating to Muslim inhabitants of Maris, the confirmation of land title and a problem relating to land rentals. Another, probably from a member of the Beni Kanz, requests the return of two slaves according to the terms of existing agreements, presumably the *Baqt*.[117]

The *eparch* also played a prominent role in international trade between the Nubian kingdoms and the Islamic world and these matters are discussed in Chapter 8.

A number of *eparchs* held other offices concurrently. The title Governor of Ibrim causes little surprise. The Late Christian *eparch* Adam describes himself as *eparch* of Nobadia and *domesticos* of Pachoras, as was the *eparch* Darme.[118] Adam also held the office of *Migin sonoj* for nearly forty years, although it has been suggested that this is simply the Old Nubian term for *eparch*.[119] In 1155, Moses Giorgios, King of Dotawo, was also *Eparch* of Palagi.[120] Among the extensive eparchal correspondence from Qasr Ibrim there is no hint that the eparchal office was hereditary. One document does recorded the establishment of one Gabrielinkouda as *Eparch* of Nobadia 'holding all authority over Nobadia, Adama the *Eparch* establishing him in the Church of the Holy Trinity in the Town of Ibrim'. However as Adama continues to be attested as *eparch* Bill Adams suggests that Gabrielinkouda was only a temporary replacement and that this need not indicate that the *eparch* nominated his successor.[121]

The loyalty of the *eparch* was not always to be counted upon. In the time of Giorgios, son of Zacharias Israel the king had cause to put out the eyes of the Lord of the Mountain but no further details are given.[122] The *Eparch* Jorays in the late thirteenth century, after first supporting the Makurian king defected to the Muslims only to be finally captured and executed by the Nubian king Semamun.

OTHER STATE OFFICIALS

During the period of Blemmyan control the chiefs of the separate tribes were termed *phylarchs*,[123] while *hypotyrannoi* were tribal dignitaries.[124] Only one *exarch* is known in Nobadia before its loss of independence, Joseph, who is referred to on royal building inscriptions at Ikhmindi and Dendur. He was *exarch* of Talmis, presumably a high official of the town, but his exact function is unclear.[125]

Among the officials of Makuria recorded in the sources are the *primicerius*, the *promeizon* and the *protodomesticos* of the palace and the *protomeizoteros*.[126] The *eparch* of Gaderon noted above was also *protomeizoteros*. Staurophorus was *nauarchos* of Nobadia and the Seven Lands[127] and Iesonsinkouda was *domesticos* of Faras and *nauarches* of the Nobadae.[128] A recent discovery is a round marble plaque dating to the late ninth century, set into the floor of the church on the North Kom at Hambukol, bearing the name of Mariankouda, who was *tetrarchos*. No details of his office are known.[129] A letter from the kinglet, Moses Giorgios, King of Dotawo, dated to 1155 records the following list of state officials without elaborating their functions:

> *Tricliniaris* of the *Domesticos*
> *Tricliniaris* of No
> *Domesticos* of Pachoras
> *Potentiary* (?) of Nan-Nokko

> *Meizoteros* (?) of Adauou
> *Silentiary* (?) of Nobatia
> *Ness* of Nobatia
> *Ness* of the *Domesticos*
> *Tot* of Michaêlko(l) and (?) *Motiko(l)* of Ibrim.[130]

Very many more officials are recorded on contemporary documents found at Qasr Ibrim among which are several mentions of 'shoemaker', which appears from the context of its use to be some sort of title.[131] The *tot* is the most commonly found of these officials and is always associated with a locality, of which a total of fifteen are recorded. Adams suggests that the *tot* may have been a wealthy local worthy deputed by the state to oversee a community[132] although the presence of *tot* at settlements of very differing status may suggest that the situation was rather more complicated. Another official mentioned on documents is the *nonnen*.[133] One holder of this post, Mari was in office from 1155 until just before 1199. He was succeeded in that year by Iesusikol.[134]

Many of these titles are familiar from the Byzantine Court but we cannot assume that they necessarily had a similar function in Makuria. The *domesticos* was a deputy and we find *domesticoi* of the king and of the *eparch*. However in some cases the *domesticos* must have had an independent role, as some holders of that position were also *eparchs*. *Nauarchos* is the early Byzantine title of an admiral, an inscription dating to 1322 can be reasonably securely translated as 'the admiral supreme on the water'. On the Debeira inscription, dated 1069, the title may be *meizonauarchos* 'admiral supreme'. By the time these terms are attested in Nubia they had been obsolete in the Byzantine navy since at least the ninth century.[135]

At a local level the architecture of dwellings might be expected to give a hint of the presence of minor officials within a community. However, the lack of large-scale excavations severely hampers the use of this type of evidence. In the early medieval period several substantial dwellings are known, among them two at Faras and two at Debeira West (see p. 161). In the later medieval period a number of settlements contain castle houses but the presence of several in some settlements suggests that they were occupied by people of a particular financial status rather than being the dwellings/refuges of a class of officials. There appears to be no provision of protection for the surrounding peoples who lived in undefended houses although the castle houses could have been used as temporary refuges for the owner's extended family. This is good evidence for an absence of feudalization at this time.[136] It may be contrasted with the situation further upstream where the presence of heavily fortified enclosures indicates the ability of the state or the local official/ruler to mobilize or coerce significant numbers of people to construct and to defend them in times of danger. The corollary to this is that the maintenance of the peasant population was essential to the well-being of the person responsible for these structures. The exact nature of these relationships, however, eludes us.

Of the administration and officials of Alwa we have virtually no information. The only official referred to by the Muslim sources is the *wali* of el-Abwab who is described by Ibn Selim as subject to the Lord of Alwa.[137] In the Kingdom of Dotawo, the latest of the Nubian Christian kingdoms, there is little differentiation between civil and religious officials, prompting the suggestion that the church and state were largely combined.[138]

The Church

After the monarchy the Church was the next most important state institution. The high status of the Church is apparent from the direct participation of the monarchy in its activities. The Makurian king and the kinglets under his control were also priests who celebrated the liturgy, at least while they remained untainted by having taken human life.[139] The desire of members of the royal family to choose a life in the Church rather than to take, or continue to hold, supreme power again indicates the high status of the Church and the piety of the Makurian ruling class. However, at least one episode makes it clear that it was the king who was the undisputed head of state and that he was able to dictate his will to the Church. In the eighth century, during a dispute between King Ibrahim and the Bishop of Dongola, Cyriacus, the King threatened that, if the Patriarch did not excommunicate his Bishop, 'I will make all my country worship idols', and was able to intimidate the Patriarch in Alexandria into removing Cyriacus and appointing his nominee in his place.[140] However, this incident demonstrates, and many other sources indicate, that the Nubian Church, as the Ethiopian Church, came firmly under the control of the patriarch of Alexandria whose appointee was charged with ordaining the other bishops and priests in the land. It was he alone who had the authority to appoint the metropolitan and this authority was never usurped by the Nubian kings. A remarkable find made at Qasr Ibrim in 1964 proves the continuing pre-eminent position of the Alexandrian patriarch over the Nubian Church. One of the latest holders of an episcopacy, Timotheos, died at Qasr Ibrim and was buried in the stairway leading to the north crypt of the cathedral in 1371-2. Buried with him were two copies of his letter testimonial confirming his appointment by the Patriarch as Bishop of Pachoras and signed by a number of witnesses in the Hanging Church of St Mary in Old Cairo, one in Coptic with a Greek postscript, and the other in Arabic. In the former he is described as bishop of 'Apachoras [Faras] which is in the country of Nubia', Ibrim has however, been later inserted in the latter. Timotheos died before taking up office.[141] He was by no means the only Bishop of Pachoras to have died away from his episcopal seat. Among the others were Bishop Marianos of Pachoras, buried at Ibrim in 1036,[142] and Bishop Martyroforos, the son of Goassi, the son of Marian(?)a, dated to 1158-9, who was presumably bishop of Faras. His tombstone was found at Debeira East.[143]

It would appear that there were regular contacts between the patriarch and the Nubian Church. Severus, in *The Life of Cyril* (1077-93), describes the many messages passing back and forth between Alexandria and Nubia (and Ethiopia).[144] However, according to Abu Salih writing in the twelfth century, el-Hakim forbade the practice of the fathers and patriarch writing letters twice a year to the kings of Ethiopia and Nubia and this prohibition remained in force down to his own time.[145]

In the first few years after the introduction of Christianity into Nobadia the fledgling church was under the control of the Bishop of Philae. During the 550s Longinus was appointed the first Bishop of Nubia. The earliest bishop attested on the Faras episcopal list is thought to date to the second or third decade of the seventh century.[146] However, it was only in the ninth century that Faras became a metropolitan see, the first holder of the office being Abba Kyros (866-902). Prior to that the metropolitan see of Nubia was based

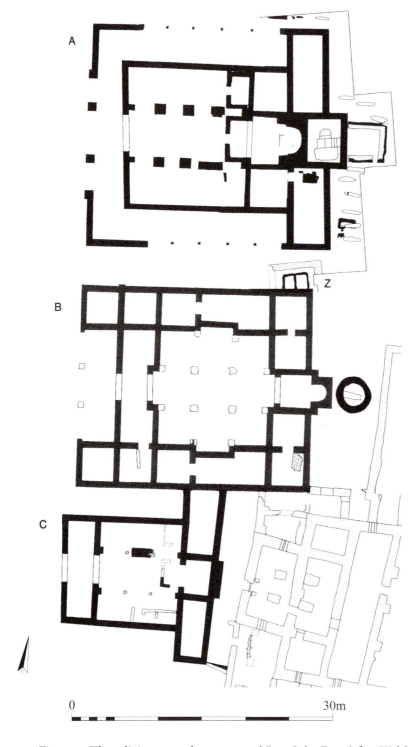

A

Z

B

C

0   30m

Figure 35 The religious complex on mound B at Soba East (after Welsby and Daniels 1991, fig. 2).

at Old Dongola.[147] Whether it held authority over Alwa is unknown. According to Abu Salih the metropolitan of Dongola had the authority to consecrate the bishops and priests in Nubia (Makuria).

Among the bishoprics known in Nubia are those at Taifa (replaced by Talmis after 710),[148] Qurta, Qasr Ibrim, Faras, Sai, Old Dongola, Shanqir, Kallama and Merka, the latter three of which are not located although it has been suggested that Shanqir may have been near present day Abu Hamed and the other two are somewhere in Makuria.[149] In Vansleb's *Histoire de l'église d'Alexandrie* ..., published in 1677, are recorded six bishopics in the Kingdom of Alwa, at Borra, Gagara, Martin, Arodias, Banazi and Menkesa. Monneret de Villard suggested that Arodias be equated with Alodia and there certainly must have been a bishopric located at the capital of the kingdom, Soba East. The location of the other places is unknown.[150] At Ibrim, Faras, Old Dongola and Soba East, churches are known which on account of their size, considerably larger than churches known elsewhere, may have been the cathedrals of those bishoprics. At Sai, which is recorded in one source as Tripolis Sai,[151] the location of a church is known and four of its granite columns still stand but in the absence of excavation attempts to reconstruct its plan, such as that published by Gartkiewicz,[152] are premature. At Old Dongola and Soba East there is more than one church of this size. Building X at Old Dongola and the subsequent buildings on its site all appear to be memorial churches,[153] and the seat of the bishop presumably lay in the adjacent Old Church a little over 20 m to the north where there was again a succession of buildings: the original church, the Church of the Granite Columns and the later modification of it, the Church of the Brick Pillars.[154] At Soba East three large churches have been found but that on mound C, although partly investigated by Somers Clarke in 1910 and by Shinnie in 1951-2, is very poorly known.[155] The other two churches of this size, standing close to the centre of the site lie parallel to each other and only 4 m apart (Fig. 35). Their close juxtaposition suggest that they may be considered as two elements of a double cathedral of a type seen throughout the Late Roman Empire.

We have most information about the bishopric of Pachoras at Faras. Within the cathedral painted on the wall of the south-eastern room was a list of the twenty-eight bishops who held office between the early seventh century and the late twelfth century. Marianos is missing but a gap has been left for his name. His funerary *stela* has been found at Qasr Ibrim and is dated to 1037. Iesu, the last bishop on the list, was not the last incumbent of the office as bishops of Pachoras are known as late as Timotheos. Many of these bishops are depicted on the walls of the Faras cathedral and also at other churches within the diocese, which was bounded to the north by that of Qasr Ibrim and to the south by that at Sai.[156] On the wall paintings they are shown richly attired in vestments which differ in detail from those of the Coptic Church and which contain a number of elements of monastic origin.[157]

As was the tradition in the Coptic Church bishops seem to have been recruited largely from among the monastic orders, and a number of those depicted on the Faras wall paintings wear elements of monastic vestments.[158] In keeping with their monastic origins the bishops were celibate in contrast to the lesser clergy who were not sworn to celibacy.[159]

Among the late Christian documents from Qasr Ibrim are mentioned the following church officials: bishops (*papas*) of Ibrim, Kourte, Sai and Ori, great priests (*sorto daoul*), priests (*sorto*), archimandrites, archdeacons, deacons, liturgists (*jalligatt*), *chartelarius*, elders (*gort*) and a fire-sacrificer? (*eigla mosil*). Most are named as witnesses to or writers of documents and there is no further information on what their functions may have been.[160] In the monastery on Kom H at Old Dongola are references to *archiepiscopos* and *archpresbyter*.

A number of inscriptions from Lower Nubia and one from Old Dongola indicate that, in the Byzantine tradition, private persons could be the legal owners of ecclesiastical buildings, both churches and monasteries. They might be the founders of the establishments they owned although ownership could be legally transferred. Among the owners attested are a number of women and Abba Marianos, 'orthodox bishop of Faras and *archimandrite* of Pouko and envoy to Babylon [Old Cairo] having (the Church of) the Four Living Creatures (on) the Island (of) Teme'. An inscription in the cathedral at Faras appears to record the ownership by a king of the Church of the Virgin Mary, a name well attested for the cathedral itself.[161]

The gradual reduction in the size of churches and the exclusion of the laity from them entirely in the Late Medieval period has been thought to indicate the increasingly esoteric nature of Nubian Christianity which sowed the seeds for its demise in the fifteenth century. This was a general trend in medieval Christianity but in Nubia it happened against the background of a weakening of the state, a disastrous combination.[162] Another factor, however, is the increasing importance of Islam and the material benefits which accrued from converting to that faith.

MELKITE AND MONOPHYSITE CHRISTIANITY

In the accounts of the conversion of Nubia to Christianity it is clearly stated that Nobadia and Alwa became Monophysite and Makuria, Melkite. If one accepts this as a true record of the state of affairs, what was the result of the unification of Nobadia and Makuria during the seventh century? As noted above many sources of later date indicate that the whole of Nubia was under the jurisdiction of the Monophysite patriarch of Alexandria. El-Makin, writing in the thirteenth century, but quoting an early eighth century source, notes that from the caliphate of Umar ibn el-Khattab (634-44) there was no Melkite patriarch at Alexandria for 97 years and that it was during this period that the Jacobites occupied the whole of Egypt and appointed Jacobite bishops in all the sees including Nubia and that it was from that time that Nubia turned Monophysite.[163] Munro-Hay suggests that the conversion of Melkite Makuria to Monophysitism took place under Mercurios' predecessor.[164]

If Makuria had been Melkite up to that time this is not clear from the archaeological record. The use of the *Euchologion Mega* formula on funerary *stelae* was thought to be indicative of an adherence to the Melkite doctrine as were a number of the scenes depicted on wall paintings in Nubian churches, but this is no longer considered to be the case.[165] However there are some indications that Melkite doctrines were not entirely banished from Nubia by the eighth century. The twelfth-century writer Michael the Syrian records that the Melkite patriarchs and bishops troubled and misled Syria, Palestine and Egypt 'and even when they had the opportunity, the Nubians and the Abyssinians'.[166] Large numbers of wall paintings depict ecclesiastical officials with full details of their attire. It can be seen that on these there is a mixture of elements derived both from the Coptic (Monophysite) and the Byzantine (Melkite) churches. According to Innemée one should not assume that the wearing of these reflects a sympathy with either belief.[167] The wall paintings do not allow us to ascertain whether the individual professed the Monophysite or Melkite doctrine.

The sources tell us little of the liturgy of the Nubian Church. Certainly in the earliest period it presumably closely followed the liturgy of its parent churches, both Melkite and Monophysite.[168] It was celebrated in Greek although evidence from Qasr Ibrim indicates that at least parts of the liturgy, especially lessons from the New Testament, were read in Old Nubian, the language of the people.[169] Among the inscriptions in a chapel in the Monastery of the Holy Trinity at Old Dongola was Psalm 97, each verse written both in Greek and in Old Nubian. The chapel also contained a fragmentary inscription of an *inter-cessio* in Greek, a prayer for the liturgy of the Holy Mass.[170] Elsewhere in this complex have been found two inscriptions of the *oratio oblationis* in Greek, a text which can only be used when Holy Communion is given on a day other than Sunday, the usual practice in the Nubian Church.[171] The celebration of the Eucharist in a monastic chapel rather than in church requires some explanation. Łajtar has suggested that this may have been done on account of monks who were otherwise unable to attend the Sunday mass. Other evidence suggests that the Eucharist may have been celebrated at an altar associated with each of the crypts in this part of the monastery.[172] The large number of Coptic documents at Ibrim, particularly from the eighth and ninth centuries may relate to Ibrim being a refuge for Copts fleeing persecution in Egypt in the aftermath of the revolts against their Muslim overlords in 725, 739 and 750.[173] In the time of Giorgios it was the practice to strike a wooden gong on the roof of the church at the time of the liturgy.[174]

The wall paintings at Faras, along with graffiti, indicate that the cult of the Christ, the Virgin, archangel Michael and the martyrs, especially the military martyrs Mercurios and

Figure 36 **Crosses of shell (a and d), of copper alloy (b and c) and of iron (e) from Soba East (after Allason-Jones 1991, figs 59, 62, 70; 1998, fig. 28).**

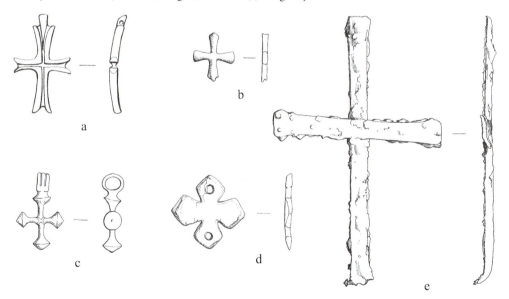

barrel-vaulted crypts including that of the Giorgios who was archbishop of Old Dongola for fifty years and died in 1113. He may well have been the man responsible for the construction of this part of the building which was decorated not earlier than the mid eleventh century.[195] Among the rooms in this complex was a chapel (Room 29) decorated with a wall painting of Christ as well as inscriptions in Greek and Old Nubian.[196] It has been suggested that the North-Western annex may have been, from the twelfth century, a *xenon*, an institution of Byzantine origin which was a combination of a hospice and a hospital where the efficacy of the treatment was assisted by its proximity to the burials of Holy Men.[197] The patients had access to small rooms for meditation, could receive Holy Communion in Rooms 7 and 27 on weekdays, and could participate in the liturgical services held in the numerous chapels (Rooms 3, 5, 29 and possibly 13).[198] Probably associated with this new function are two unique wall paintings, one depicting the saints Cosmas and Damianus receiving bags with medicants from an angel, the other showing Christ healing a blind man at the Pool of Siloam (colour plate III).[199]

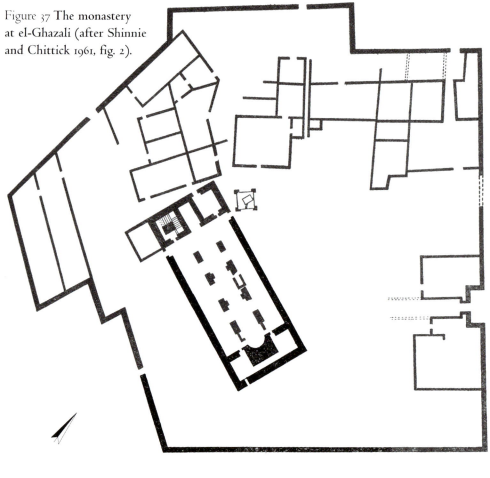

Figure 37 **The monastery at el-Ghazali** (after Shinnie and Chittick 1961, fig. 2).

0   50m

and the Byzantine (Melkite) churches. According to Innemée one should not assume that the wearing of these reflects a sympathy with either belief.[167] The wall paintings do not allow us to ascertain whether the individual professed the Monophysite or Melkite doctrine.

The sources tell us little of the liturgy of the Nubian Church. Certainly in the earliest period it presumably closely followed the liturgy of its parent churches, both Melkite and Monophysite.[168] It was celebrated in Greek although evidence from Qasr Ibrim indicates that at least parts of the liturgy, especially lessons from the New Testament, were read in Old Nubian, the language of the people.[169] Among the inscriptions in a chapel in the Monastery of the Holy Trinity at Old Dongola was Psalm 97, each verse written both in Greek and in Old Nubian. The chapel also contained a fragmentary inscription of an *intercessio* in Greek, a prayer for the liturgy of the Holy Mass.[170] Elsewhere in this complex have been found two inscriptions of the *oratio oblationis* in Greek, a text which can only be used when Holy Communion is given on a day other than Sunday, the usual practice in the Nubian Church.[171] The celebration of the Eucharist in a monastic chapel rather than in church requires some explanation. Łajtar has suggested that this may have been done on account of monks who were otherwise unable to attend the Sunday mass. Other evidence suggests that the Eucharist may have been celebrated at an altar associated with each of the crypts in this part of the monastery.[172] The large number of Coptic documents at Ibrim, particularly from the eighth and ninth centuries may relate to Ibrim being a refuge for Copts fleeing persecution in Egypt in the aftermath of the revolts against their Muslim overlords in 725, 739 and 750.[173] In the time of Giorgios it was the practice to strike a wooden gong on the roof of the church at the time of the liturgy.[174]

The wall paintings at Faras, along with graffiti, indicate that the cult of the Christ, the Virgin, archangel Michael and the martyrs, especially the military martyrs Mercurios and

Figure 36 **Crosses of shell (a and d), of copper alloy (b and c) and of iron (e) from Soba East (after Allason-Jones 1991, figs 59, 62, 70; 1998, fig. 28).**

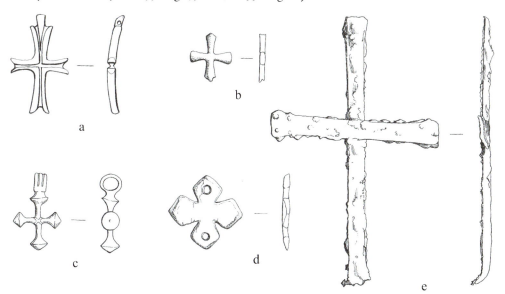

Demetrius were particularly important. The liturgy appears to have been based on that of St Mark but in an abbreviated and simpler form, perhaps reflecting an adherence to older liturgical forms rather than those which developed elsewhere. The internal evidence suggests that the liturgy was Monophysite at all periods.[175] The cross was an important element and it was Christ who was always the one shown fighting sin and death. The symbol of the cross represented this victory and as such it held a special role in the life of Nubian Christians, 'a cult object representing power as opposed to temporal life, hope of the redemption of all Christians believing in the cross, instruction for the future and the right basis for the present.'[176] This great interest in the cross is manifest in the numerous representations of it on wall paintings, on painted pottery and as graffiti, and crosses made from a wide variety of materials which are found throughout Nubia (Fig. 36).[177] A wide range of cross types is known and they vary greatly in size and function. Very small crosses with suspension loops were presumably worn round the neck. Other, larger examples were also worn around the neck, carried in the hand or were provided with a wooden haft. A fine pectoral cross of bronze, with splayed arms terminating in a roundel, with a roundel occupying the centre of the cross, each occupied by a silver ball, and with smaller roundels at the exterior angles of the arms, was found at Faras within the grave of the bishop Ioannes. This *crux gemmata* may have been of Egyptian or Byzantine manufacture.[178] An arm from an equally fine cross of not dissimilar form was found at Soba East. This came from a gilded cross with oval copper-alloy mounts at each outer corner surrounded by a silver collar in which were set blue glass inserts.[179] A number of the crosses on the Faras wall paintings are painted yellow presumably to indicate that they were gold or gilded. Pectoral crosses may have been worn as a symbol of faith, but also as a talisman, as was the practice in the Coptic Church until the recent past.[180] One of the functions of the Cruciform Church at Old Dongola may have been for the veneration of the Holy Cross.[181]

Finds of crosses made from palm leaves and of palm-leaf amulets and wreaths may be associated with Palm Sunday and Easter Sunday processions. They have been found in churches at Qasr Ibrim but also in private houses. Some of the wreaths were buried as a cache beneath the floor of a Late Christian building identified as a storehouse.[182]

In early Nubian churches the percentage of the building reserved for the clergy was small implying that a large congregation was to be expected. By the end of Nubian Christianity the whole of the church may have been usurped by the clergy, either a reflection of the increasingly esoteric nature of the Church and of the isolation of the clergy from the populace, or of a change in practice with the congregation remaining outside the building.

THE ROLE OF THE CHURCH IN THE ADMINISTRATION

The large numbers of churches known and the large numbers of monasteries referred to in the sources testify to the wealth of the Nubian Church. This is illustrated by the account of the destruction of a church at Sus in the later thirteenth century when the Muslims carried off golden crosses and other objects of gold, the whole of which was valued at 4,640½ dinars, the silver vases also taken were valued at 8,660 dinars.[183] The Church was clearly a major force in the State, but how it was maintained and what secular role it played in the administration is unclear. The Church certainly owned land, as is

indicated by an Old Nubian document from Qasr Ibrim where the land holdings (*saqia*) of the Jesus Church at Touggili are enumerated and the boundaries to each property given. Many of the adjacent landowners are also churches, the Raphael Church of Kopagi, the Michael and Gabriel Churches of Ibrim, the Andrew Church of Touggili, the George Church of Ibrim West and the Kollouthos Church.[184] Fragments of Coptic texts from Kulb appear to be concerned with a land donation or land lease in which a monastery is involved.[185] There is a suggestion that monastic institutions were directly involved in manufacturing, especially of pottery but also possibly of other goods, and, along with members of the clergy, in the provision of services, legal, medical and secretarial.[186] The monks and clerics were presumably among the best educated and literate members of Nubian society and hence would have been an invaluable resource for the administration of the State, although their abilities alone do not constitute proof that they were so employed. There was clearly also a civil administration with its own scribes, separate from the Church.[187]

MONASTICISM

Ibn Selim during his visit to Alwa in the tenth century notes that at the capital, Soba, there were large monasteries.[188] Although none of these have been discovered there is considerable evidence from elsewhere in Nubia for monastic establishments. Abu Salih describes a finely built monastery at Taifa called the Monastery of Ansūn,[189] and records several others in the region of the Second Cataract and a large monastery near the Fourth Cataract 'upon a high mountain which overlooks the blessed Nile'.[190] Several of these have been extensively excavated. The monastery at Qasr el-Wizz was founded some time between 850 and 950 and may have been the successor to that at Faras, which was at about that time utilized for pottery production.[191] At Old Dongola two monasteries are known. The earlier was on Kom D close to the river and 1.5 km to the north of the early fortified centre. The site is badly preserved having suffered extensively from flood damage and it may have been this problem which caused the monastery to be abandoned and replaced by the monastery currently under excavation on Kom H, although there are indications that this was already established by the seventh century in an area where there is an extensive cemetery of the Early and Classic Christian periods.[192] Qasr el-Wizz appears to have been abandoned after the Classic Christian period and el-Ghazali, which lies 16 km from the Nile in the Wadi Abu Dom, ceased to be occupied some time after the eleventh century, the church thereafter being used for domestic activities which were associated with pottery of medieval type.[193] The monastery on Kom H at Old Dongola may have remained in use as late as the fifteenth century, close to the date of the final demise of Christianity in the area.

Although little of the Monastery of the Holy Trinity on Kom H at Old Dongola has yet been excavated it is clear that it is rather more complex than the other monasteries so far known in Nubia. On the west side of the monastery a number of additional buildings dating from the tenth century abut the outside of the enclosure wall; these were extensively modified and extended over the next few centuries (Fig. 66). There were originally two buildings of uncertain function with a passageway between them. One, with later modifications and additions, was used as a commemorative complex, the other was possibly of a residential character.[194] The former complex included a number of burials in barrel-vaulted crypts including that of the Giorgios who was archbishop of Old Dongola for fifty years and died in 1113. He may well have been the man responsible for the construction of this part of the building which was decorated not earlier than the mid eleventh century.[195] Among the rooms in this complex was a chapel (Room 29) decorated with a wall painting of Christ as well as inscriptions in Greek and Old Nubian.[196] It has been suggested that the North-Western annex may have been, from the twelfth century, a *xenon*, an institution of Byzantine origin which was a combination of a hospice and a hospital where the efficacy of the treatment was assisted by its proximity to the burials of Holy Men.[197] The patients had access to small rooms for meditation, could receive Holy Communion in Rooms 7 and 27 on weekdays, and could participate in the liturgical services held in the numerous chapels (Rooms 3, 5, 29 and possibly 13).[198] Probably associated with this new function are two unique wall paintings, one depicting the saints Cosmas and Damianus receiving bags with medicants from an angel, the other showing Christ healing a blind man at the Pool of Siloam (colour plate III).[199]

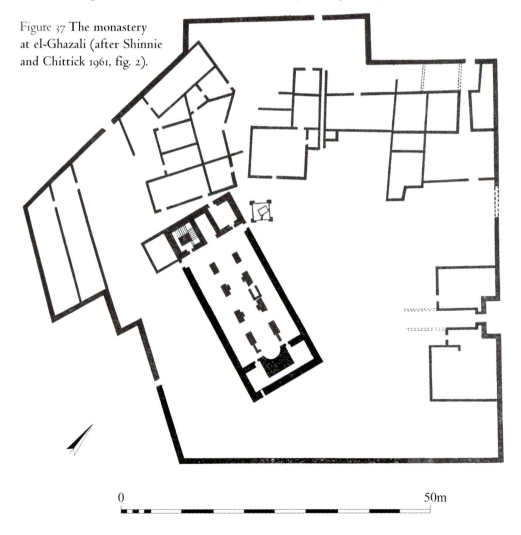

Figure 37 **The monastery at el-Ghazali (after Shinnie and Chittick 1961, fig. 2).**

0   50m

In Egypt, Syria and Palestine, monasteries of the Byzantine period are of two types, the *coenobium* and the *laura*. All of the Nubian monasteries which have been either certainly or probably identified are of coenobic type.[200] In a coenobic monastery all the monks live a communal life with a daily routine of communal prayer, work and meals.[201] They are compact installations contained within an enclosure wall comprising a church, refectory, work and service areas and accommodation, the monk's cells (Fig. 37, colour plate XII). The other type of monastery, the *laura*, is much more dispersed with monks living in separate cells and spending most of their time in solitude only assembling at the weekend for communal prayer and to receive their weekly provisions. Typically the two core buildings of these complexes are a church and a bakery.[202] *Laura*s are more difficult to identify archaeologically but they are to be expected in Nubia and they may have accounted for some of the abundant monastic communities recorded in the literary sources. There are a number of walled sites in the Batn el-Hajar, dating to the Classic Christian period, which might be *laura*s although some of these sites do not appear to have had a church. If they were not monastic it is difficult to suggest what other function they may have served.[203] At present, although Nubian *laura*s are likely none have been securely identified.[204]

Attempts to assess the size of Nubian monastic communities have been based on the eating and sleeping accommodation available but assume that space was available for all members of the community to eat and sleep at the same time, while the possibility of upper floors providing additional accommodation adds a complicating factor. The figures arrived at for Qasr el-Wizz, twenty to twenty-four,[205] should be taken as a minimum as should those calculated using similar criteria elsewhere, thirty-six to forty-eight at el-Ghazali and eighteen at Old Dongola DM.[206]

ANCHORITES

Hermits were a feature of Nubian Christianity and a number of much earlier rock-cut tombs and caves were used as cells (Fig. 38). Evidence for this comes from the scatters of medieval pottery sherds within a number of tombs, and crosses carved within them, as well as modifications such as the addition of ledges cut in the rock.[207] A little to the west of Faras in the hillside on the edge of the desert the largest of the group of four New

Figure 38 **The anchorite cell at ez-Zuma.**

Kingdom tombs was used by monks and several inscriptions on the walls have been studied by Griffith among others.[208] These include the name of Paulos, one of the most famous of the Faras bishops. One occupant wrote on 4 December 738 'I, Theophilos, this least of monks, am he who hath written these writings on my dwelling place.'[209] The latest dated evidence for the use of this tomb is from 933.[210]

The population of Nubia

On the collapse of the Kushite state we have no direct evidence for the fate of the Kushite population along the Middle Nile. In Lower Nubia, where it has been suggested that only the upper echelons of society were actually Kushites[211] it is possible that they were withdrawn or moved back towards the heartlands of the Empire before its collapse. However, the archaeological evidence suggests, on the one hand with the traces of remaining Kushite culture and on the other with the appearance everywhere of traits associated with the Nubians, that there were no dramatic population movements on the collapse of centralized Kushite authority. We need not envisage a massive influx of invaders within a short period of time as occurred into the western provinces of the Roman Empire at this period. By the later sixth century, with the arrival of Christianity throughout Nubia, the culture was relatively homogenous.

Over the next several hundred years the racial and cultural composition of Nubia was gradually modified by the arrival of Muslims from the north and east and by the conversion of certain sectors of the Christian population to Islam. Muslims certainly had access to Makuria and Alwa as traders and diplomats and although the *Baqt* specifically excluded the possibilities of settlement of Muslims within Makuria, this prohibition was not maintained. As early as the tenth century Muslims owned land south of the Aswan frontier.[212] When Ibn Selim travelled through Nubia in 985 he mentions Muslim Nubians between the First and Second Cataract and he found a large Muslim community resident in the capital of Alwa.[213] He also saw a Beja group, known as az-Zanafil, who lived on the Nile in the region of Berber. They had apparently moved into Nubia long before his time, retained their pastoral lifestyle and language and kept separate from the Nubians. They were governed by a *wali* who was appointed by the Nubian (Alwan) king.[214] In *The Life of the Patriarch Christodoulus* is recounted a story in which the Metropolitan Victor is accused, falsely as it turned out, of destroying a mosque in the lands of Nubia.[215] That the story was treated at first as credible suggest that there may well have been a mosque in Nubia in the third quarter of the eleventh century. Archaeological evidence for the presence of a mosque may have been recovered from Jebel Adda. This consisted of tiny fragments of painted plaster bearing Kufic inscriptions in a deposit predating the Late Christian rebuilding of the town in the thirteenth century.[216] As a result of the treaty enacted in 1276 the northern part of Maris came under the direct control of the Sultan and an influx of Muslims might be expected thereafter.

The discovery of a number of Muslim tombstones in Nubia provides further evidence for the presence, and presumably in most cases for the permanent residence, of Muslims within Makuria. At Meinarti tombstones inscribed in Arabic, of two women who were apparently sisters, have been found dated to 1061 and 1063 associated with archaeological levels firmly within the Christian occupation of the site and suggest that Muslims were resident on the island or in its immediate vicinity at that time. Within one of the houses dating to the period 1100-50 was a bilingual inscription scored into the wet plaster, in Old Nubian and Arabic.[217] From the region of Debeira a little downstream are two Islamic *stelae*, of Mahmuda Bint Muhamad Ibn Yusuf who died on a Saturday, Safar 1 in 913 and of Ishaq Ibn Ahmed dated to 978. The date of the Arabic *ostraca* found close by is not recorded.[218] A tombstone from Taifa dates to 832, others from Kalabsha and Qertassi date to the first half of the tenth century and four from Jebel Adda are of the early eleventh century.[219] At el-Geili Christians and Muslims were being buried in the same cemetery during the twelfth century and this continued for a considerable period. One of the latest Christian graves, within which was a cross made from two strips of camel hide placed above the head at the east end, was radiocarbon dated to the early sixteenth century, but in some other respects is directly comparable to contemporary Muslim graves in the cemetery. [220]

At Debeira West, where occupation is thought to have ceased in the twelfth century, *ostraca* bearing Arabic texts are found in some of the buildings as are graffiti inscribed on the walls; one bears a painting which appears to be a Muslim depiction of Noah's Ark, the names Adam and Eve are written in Arabic close by and appear to be contemporary with the painting.[221] At Arminna West an Arabic graffito was scratched onto the plaster within the side chapel in the church prior to the application of the whitewash.[222] Ibn Selim mentions converts to Islam among the local population in Lower Nubia; 'there is also a number of Muslim inhabitants but none of them speak Arabic'.[223] He further records an attempt made to convert the Makurian king Giorgios to Islam and recounts the discourse between the envoy Jawhar and the king. While Ibn Selim was at Old Dongola it was the time of the *Iid el-Adha* which the king allowed him and his entourage to celebrate outside the city against the opposition of some of his advisors.[224]

In the late medieval period letters written in Arabic by Muslim inhabitants residing in Maris to the *eparch* at Ibrim indicate that they regarded the *eparch* as their suzerain.[225] At this time some Egyptians, or Muslims from elsewhere, resided in Qasr Ibrim.[226] Another letter to the *eparch*, written at the end of the thirteenth or beginning of the fourteenth century, is from a Muslim who is sending two of his sons to the King of Dongola and is hoping eventually to join them. He requests the *eparch* to ask the king for permission for him to build houses at a number of places in Makuria.[227]

The earliest Arab settlers in Sudan may have entered the region directly from Arabia across the Red Sea. Tombstones from Khor Nubt near Sinkat, several of them of women, date to the period 861-3 to 941.[228] It was the subsequent immigration of Muslims into the regions to the east of the Nile Valley from Egypt and via the Red Sea which led to the gradual conversion of the tribes in that area, among them the Blemmyes/Beja, to Islam. Their incursions into the Nile Valley at a later date will have been instrumental in the penetration of Islam into the Nubian kingdoms.

The regions to the south of Egypt acted as a refuge for dissident factions. Eminent political refugees are noted elsewhere (p. 77). Under the Mamelukes in particular harsh treatment of their nomadic Arab subjects provided an impetus for migration into the Eastern Desert and many ultimately found their way into the Nile Valley and central and western Sudan.[229] Nubia will have also acted as a refuge to Copts fleeing persecution by their Muslim overlords in Egypt, and they may have had a significant presence at Qasr

Ibrim and elsewhere.[230] In the Persian geography, *Hudud el-Alam*, written in the tenth century, it is stated that there was a constant flow of Egyptian monks from Upper Egypt to the monasteries of Sudan.[231]

Among the bishops of Faras depicted on the wall paintings are a number who are clearly of African, i.e. local origin, among them Kyros (+ 902) and Petros (+ 999). Marianos who died in 1037, on the other hand, bears definite Egyptian characteristics.[232]

Nubians in Egypt

There were also Nubians living in Egypt, who by treaty were still obliged to pay taxes to the Makurian king. In 835-6 there is reference to a Nubian who was in charge of collecting dues from the Nubian subjects in the country of the Tayâyê (Egypt), who rebelled and became a Muslim but was captured by the King, Giorgios.[233] Nubians formed a major component of the army in Egypt, being recruited along with troops from among the Turks and the Rum (Byzantines) in preference to fellow Arabs who were deemed untrustworthy. In the time of Ibn Tulun (860-881) there were 24,000 Turks and 40,000 blacks in the army, although how many of the latter were Nubians, or were the slaves furnished to Egypt in compliance with the *Baqt*, is unknown. They were said to come from a region south of Nubia where there were large pastures and strong people.[234] Although Salah ed-Din disbanded these Sudanese troops in the later twelfth century they are again in evidence under the Mamelukes who came to power in Egypt in 1260. Nubians also enjoyed positions of great power within the Egyptian government. In the mid tenth century the Nubian Kafur, who was captured in Nubia in his youth, was vizier to Abu Bakr Tughj el-Ikhshid, and between 960 and 966 actually came to rule Egypt.[235] In the twelfth century the Nubian el-Mutamen was a confidential adviser of the last Fatimid Caliph el-Adid and was executed by Salah ed-Din.[236]

Contacts between the Nubians and the Muslims go back to the very earliest period of Islam. Mohammed himself held the Nubians in high regard and is quoted as saying 'If anyone has no brother, let him take one from among the Nuba,' and again, 'the best slave for you is the Nuba'.[237] Nubian women were held in equally high esteem. Ibn Butlan considered that they were of all the Sudanese 'the most agreeable, tender and polite and that their bodies are slim with a smooth skin, steady and well-proportioned.' He also considered them ideal as nurses.[238] They were recognized as very distinct from the peoples of central Africa, and are described as having thin lips, small mouths, white teeth and hair which is short and not curly. As a result of this high regard they were much sought after as slaves in Egypt.[239]

LONGEVITY AND DISEASE

The medieval Nubians appear to have enjoyed reasonable health and exhibit the typical survival pattern of a pre-modern developed society with a high mortality rate among infants levelling off slightly among young adults and increasing sharply among older adults. Mortality was higher for females during the childbearing years up until around or shortly after thirty at which time there is a relative increase in male mortality rates.[240] Among the most common health problems, at least of those which have left a record on the skeletal material, are the onset of arthritis and osteophytosis which can be directly correlated with longevity.[241] These two ailments are common to most societies the world over and to most periods. Osteoporosis was also observed affecting older females. Many of the bishops buried at Faras enjoyed a long life. Bishop Petros died at the age of ninety-three and Ignatios at seventy-eight. Although their social position may have served to protect them from many of the hardships of life they still suffered from bone deformation and degeneration causing, in some cases, severe loss of mobility and pain.[242] There does appear, according to one study conducted on Lower Nubian populations, to have been increased longevity in the medieval period when compared to Mesolithic, Late Kushite and X-Group populations and this is reflected in the increased percentage of traumatic lesions on that population, some due in part to intentional injuries. There was no evidence for a decline in health and life expectancy in the aftermath of the collapse of the Kushite Empire.[243] However, a recently published study on two closely-related communities at Kulubnarti showed a marked difference in survival and biological wellbeing.[244] The reasons for this are unclear but it highlights the dangers of extrapolating from our limited data and the pitfalls of making generalizations about health and longevity.

In the second half of the sixth century and after 1348 plague appears to have wiped out vast numbers of the population of Egypt and Nubia may well have been affected by these catastrophes.[245] However, such rapidly fatal diseases leave little trace in the archaeological record and their impact can only be assumed rather than proved. In Lower Nubia a study of an X-Group population where tissue and hair had survived showed that 40% of the sample was infested with head lice (*Pediculus humanus capitis*) which are known to be a vector for disease. Both external and internal parasites were probably common although a study of material recovered from the pelvic area of burials at Soba East failed to locate any evidence for the latter.[246]

Like the Ancient Egyptians before them and their contemporaries, the Muslims, the Nubians practised circumcision, both of males and females.[247] Female circumcision in particular will have held many attendant risks of infection and may well have been a significant cause of premature death among young women.

COIFFURE

It is only very rarely that bodies are well enough preserved so that the coiffure can be studied directly. One of the best examples is the hair of a young female buried at Sai. It is arranged in a double range of small plaits brought towards the back. The first, with 29 tresses 150 mm in length started at the front of the head. The second, of 36 tresses between 120 and 160 mm in length, began at the sides of the head and extend to the nape of the neck.[248] Another female adult of post-Meroitic date at Gabati has an elaborate plaited hairdo (Fig. 39).[249] Finds of long-tined combs of ivory, bone and wood have been made on a number of sites. Some of those from Qasr Ibrim have very elaborate handles and it is suggested that they were designed principally as hair ornaments for men. Hair pins of wood, ivory or bone and copper-alloy have also been found at Ibrim.[250] Few details of coiffure can be gleaned from wall paintings. Many of the individuals portrayed are religious figures who are frequently veiled or wear some other head adornment masking their hairstyle and in any event these may be stereotypical representations not necessarily bearing any relation to current Nubian hairstyles. Many of the portraits of Nubians, be

Figure 39 **An adult female with plaited hair, buried at Gabati (photo D. N. Edwards; courtesy of the SARS Gabati Archive).**

they members of the royal family or of the ecclesiastical elite, also have much of their hair hidden under crowns, helmets or headcloths of various sorts. However, occasionally details of the coiffure are visible which probably represent contemporary styles, among them what appears to be a top knot.[251]

PASTIMES

Among the most common evidence for games are counters, usually made from a pottery sherd the finest examples of which are made from the central stamped roundels found on some Nubian fine ware bowls. Some from House PCH.1 at Old Dongola seem to have been especially made and are decorated with engraved dots. In the same house were small pottery balls with varying numbers of dots marked on particular 'sides'.[252] It is not clear what games these were used for. In Tomb Q.3 at Qustul a wooden gaming board, fifteen ivory and the same number of ebony gaming pieces contained in a leather bag, five ivory dice and a wood and silver dice box were found. The basic design of the board is very similar to that used for 'Egyptian draughts' but how exactly this game was played is unclear. Dice are found on many sites made from a variety of materials. An elongated dice known as a *talus*, a type used in a number of Greek and Roman games, was found in Late Christian levels at Qasr Ibrim.[253] A pair of knuckle bones were recovered from the Ballana Tomb B.50 and balls made from rags sewn or tied together have been found at Qasr Ibrim.[254]

From a number of sites of X-Group date in Nubia and also from contemporary Egypt are pottery figurines of ladies and of horses. The female figurines all wear a tiara-like headdress or coiffure, they have a rosette medallion in the centre of the forehead and the arms are in a raised position. Suspended from a necklace is a medallion between the small widely spaced breasts. The lower body is columnar.[255] Of those from Meinarti there are two types made in two pieces in a mould and painted, some in pink Aswan fabric, others of Nile silt. A further type is cruder and solid but perhaps also mould-made. The Meinarti female figurines are found in domestic refuse deposits associated with figurines of horses which are directly comparable in method of manufacture, fabric and style of decoration. None of these figurines are obviously ritual or religious objects and, as Petrie suggested for the Egyptian examples, they are probably nothing more than toys.[256] At Ibrim crude dolls were made from crossed sticks, sometimes with the head fashioned from mud. They were clothed with garments made from old rags.[257]

El-Umari says of the inhabitants of Old Dongola that they had a strong inclination for singing, this following the statement that they had a strong inclination to get drunk, although whether the two comments were connected is not made explicit.[258] Certainly in the medieval period from the X-Group onwards there is considerable evidence for the importation of wine and a number of drinking establishments have been identified most notably the *Weinstuben* at Sayala,[259] and the 'tavern' at Qasr Ibrim.[260] Others have been identified at Abd el-Qadir (occupied in the period 600-750) and Mirgissa, where the 'taverns' are much more substantial than the other buildings surrounding them and almost their sole contents were amphorae fragments and drinking cups, of which there were thousands.[261] On the walls of the Ibrim tavern were carved reliefs of an amphora and a bunch of grapes on the vine. If we are to believe the excavator Jebel Adda in the X-Group period catered for a perhaps more clandestine consumption of alcohol. Several deep pits roofed with light poles and straw, subterranean and lightless holes entered only by ladder, contained almost exclusively wine jars and drinking cups. 'In such tiny areas only four or five persons can have sat at any one time, and the only explanation which has occurred to the writer is that they served as clubhouses for men, whether religious or purely social can only be guessed.'[262] However these may well have been nothing more than storage crypts of the type so well represented in contemporary levels at Qasr Ibrim. The drinking goblet is the most characteristic of X-Group pottery vessels, although south of the Third Cataract vessels with a similar function are not common.

It may be erroneous to consider drinking as purely a recreational activity. The ritual significance of drinking wine in a Christian context is clear. Drinking of alcoholic beverages can also have important ritual and ceremonial importance in the interaction between various groups in society as can be documented in many African societies, a practice still to be found today in certain areas. The African roots of medieval Nubian culture may have fostered the importance of beer in this way. It was the arrival of Islam in the region which will have caused a major change with the removal of alcohol from society, at least at an official level.[263]

What life was actually like for the medieval Nubian is difficult to say. Much of Nubia is a harsh land with often limited agricultural potential; the carrying capacity of the land must always have been small. However, traditionally excess population has sought employment outside the region and to those left behind a relatively stable agricultural economy, although sometimes marred by excessive or meagre Nile floods, may have allowed a reasonable standard of living to be maintained. Today Nubians are much better off than their countrymen living away from the Nile. Certainly Arab travellers in the heyday of the medieval kingdoms report a much more prosperous Nubia than that which was observed by the earliest European visitors in the nineteenth century.

CHAPTER 6

Settlements

When looking at the location and nature of settlement in the Middle Nile Valley, the availability of sufficient food resources and/or the potential for the movement of food resources are the most important factors affecting the growth of large population centres. Many other factors determine when, and to what extent, large 'urban' centres develop, but they are all constrained by these parameters.

During the medieval period, as at all other times in the Nile's history, gradual changes in the river itself and in the climate, both of the Middle Nile region and of the regions at the headwaters of the river, must be borne in mind when assessing the viability of a given area for settlement. Although during the last two millennia the climatic conditions which prevail today are relevant, short-term fluctuations occurred throughout. These may have had limited effect on human settlement in the more productive areas, but in the more marginal environments small and short-lived changes may have had a profound impact. Well-established urban settlements may have been more insulated from the adverse effects of these short-term fluctuations as they may not have been directly reliant on local food resources; rural settlements could be very seriously affected. Small variations in the river's course often result in changes in the areas affected by erosion and deposition. Such changes may totally remove, over a relatively short space of time, previously viable agricultural land, forcing a population to move. This is thought to be the explanation for the abandonment of the settlements at Debeira West[1] and at Arminna West, perhaps combined with the loss of agricultural land through the movement of dunes during the medieval period,[2] and may have been an important factor elsewhere.[3]

In an agrarian subsistence economy in a stable environment the ideal settlement pattern is for the farmers to be as close to their agricultural land as possible. On the Middle Nile, where most agricultural land is close to the banks of the river forming a narrow strip, this would favour a dispersed linear settlement pattern. A range of factors could bring about nucleation in many areas, none of which need have a direct economic basis, the inhabitants still being actively reliant on agriculture for their livelihoods. As the needs of the practice of agriculture at subsistence level do not require the concentration of large population groups in specific centres, it is to other causes that we must look to explain the existence of urbanism within the Nubian kingdoms. Agricultural development can be assisted by the development of large centres, but the move from a subsistence economy to the production of a surplus is stimulated by the growth of urban centres and cannot explain that growth itself. Any concentration of population into a village, town or city must imply the existence of other than purely agricultural criteria. Thus to understand the development, nature and impact of centres of population we must examine the factors which led to their existence at a particular time and in a particular place.

Among the statements made in modern studies relating to the growth and function of urban settlements, as opposed to rural settlements where the inhabitants are largely engaged in primary food producing activities, are the following:

The state is a necessary concomitant of urban life.[4]

The growth of cities is a manifestation of the growth of institutions capable of organizing large regions into integrated systems.[5]

The city is a unit of settlement which performs specialized functions in relationship to a broad hinterland.[6]

All these features pertained within the Kingdoms of Nubia, and a number of the settlements fulfil these criteria attaining a sufficient level of complexity to deserve to be considered as towns/cities. In the discussion of settlements, once again we have a pronounced bias in our data towards the extensively investigated regions of Lower Nubia with almost no work having been conducted far to the south. Apart from the excavations at Soba East, and of a church at Jebel Saqadi in the Gezira, no other settlement has been investigated within the kingdom of Alwa, although mounds covered in red-brick fragments are found in some numbers along the banks of the Blue and White Nile and are 'traditionally' dated to the medieval period.

In Lower Nubia several sites have been extensively excavated. At Arminna West, for example, as at many other town sites in Lower Nubia, there is direct continuity from the late Kushite through the X-Group and into the medieval periods, suggesting not only the physical survival of buildings, but also the survival of the structure of society.[7] This also appears to be the case at Meinarti where there was some degree of architectural continuity from the late Kushite into the early X-Group but the site was abandoned for a consider-able period, estimated at 100 years by the excavator, until reoccupied in the late X-Group.[8] The general increase in population in Lower Nubia during the X-Group reflects the change in the status of the region from a periphery to a core area with the establishment of the state of Nobadia.

Centres of population in Nubia in the medieval period differed somewhat from those of the preceding Kushite period. The socio-political factors which saw the rise and continued prominence of the region around Jebel Barkal and of Meroe may no longer have pertained. Certainly no major medieval settlement is known in the vicinity of Meroe, while the very high status burials at el-Hobagi suggest a relocation of the centre of power in that region to the vicinity of the Shendi Basin where the important Kushite towns of Wad ben Naqa and Hosh ben Naqa lay. There is however, no evidence for either of these sites being a major urban complex in the medieval period, although, in the case of Hosh ben Naqa in particular, the lack of fieldwork on that site makes any assessment premature. Around Jebel Barkal we also have little evidence for post-Kushite settlement although the presence of the two important cemeteries at ez-Zuma and Tanqasi demonstrates that there were regional power bases here. According to Bonnet there were extensive remains of a settlement associated with post-Meroitic beer jar sherds at Tanqasi[9] and there are post-Meroitic burials among the ruins of the Kushite temples at Jebel Barkal.[10] At a later date there was a church and settlement at Nuri and the monastery at el-Ghazali lay 16 km up the Wadi Abu Dom.

Old Dongola lay at the southern end of the productive Letti Basin and the large number of medieval communities in this region indicate its importance. The eyewitness Ibn Selim, in the tenth century, noted that within two days journey north of the capital were about thirty villages with beautiful buildings, churches and monasteries, many palm trees, vines, gardens, cultivated fields and broad pastures.[11] The status of the Kerma Basin remains unclear. There was certainly occupation in the medieval period here, and on the nearby Argo Island, but no major urban complex has yet been located. In Lower Nubia Faras lay in a densely populated area and Adams has noted that over half of all the churches known in Nobadia lay within a radius of 60 km from Faras.[12] In many other parts of the Middle Nile Valley, where local conditions were favourable, population density was relatively high, although the need for defence in the later medieval period saw some displacement to more inhospitable but safer areas, particularly in the Batn el-Hajar and

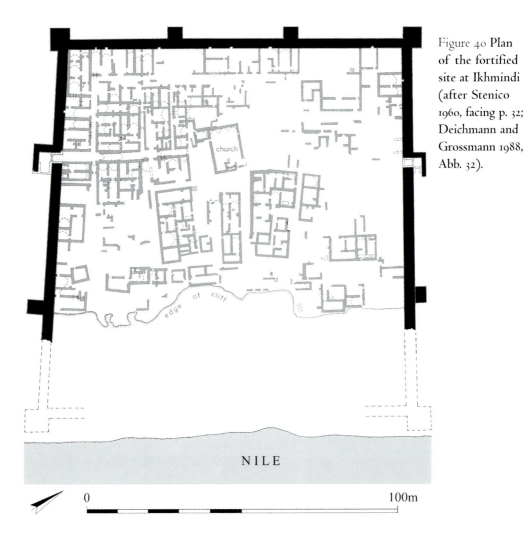

Figure 40 **Plan of the fortified site at Ikhmindi (after Stenico 1960, facing p. 32; Deichmann and Grossmann 1988, Abb. 32).**

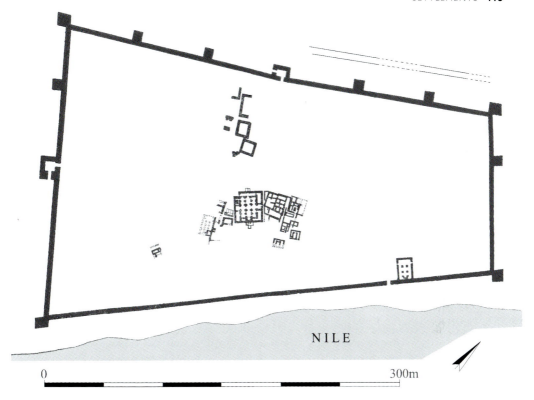

NILE

0   300m

Figure 41 **Faras, plan of the X-Group and Christian remains (after Griffith 1926, pl. XXV;**
Michałowski 1970, fig. 2).

perhaps in the Fourth Cataract.[13] Within the kingdom of Alwa the reduced reliance on the
Nile and its tributaries will have resulted in a more dispersed population, not necessarily
confined to the river's banks.[14]

In few settlements has there been sufficient excavation to allow any meaningful discussion
of town planning. The fortified settlements or forts at Ikhmindi (Fig. 40) and Sheikh
Daud, and perhaps the other sites of that type, are the exception. Orthogonal planning
was not the norm, although some consistency in orientation does occur, partly as a result
of many sites developing along the Nile, the orientation of which influenced the domestic
structures to some extent, and the standardized orientation of churches to either cardinal
or river north. The impact of the Nile on the orientation of structures, it has been
suggested, was responsible for changes in the orientation of the bishop's tombs at Faras
after 802, as though the Nile, on which they were all aligned, was shifting its course.[15]

After the introduction of Christianity in the sixth century the church was a major
feature of many settlements and is frequently the only 'official' building whose function is
known. Churches are often located towards the periphery of settlements, the result,
according to Adams, of their being surrounded by cemeteries[16] although in many cases it
may have been the result of the church being a relatively late arrival in the settlement. There
would have been difficulties in building a large structure in the heart of a pre-existing
conurbation.[17] The earliest churches known, at Old Dongola for example, were built in the

plain to the north of the defended town in the seventh century. Where pre-existing buildings did not have to be respected churches did occupy prominent positions within the urban complexes as at Faras (Fig. 41), Soba East and Tamit for example. A number of very late churches are located at some distance from the communities they were designed to serve. Adams suggests that this may be the result of new liturgical practices within the late Nubian Church.[18] Two very late churches, at Diffinarti and Attiri, are perched on pinnacles, presumably for defence.

The number of churches varied considerably and does not appear to be directly related to the size of the community involved. At Faras West there were ten churches while at Tamit there is a concentration of seven churches in the settlement and another in the adjacent cemetery; a settlement which it has been suggested had a population of no more than two to four hundred souls.[19] Conversely many settlements made do with one church and some had no church at all.[20] Nubian churches, unlike their Coptic counterparts, are almost invariably free-standing structures, except in a monastic context or where they are abutted by palatial buildings, chapels, tombs, or other churches.

A feature of Nubian settlements is the massive amount of rubbish which accumulated within them along with wind-blown sand. A vast build-up of domestic refuse appears to have been a feature particularly of the X-Group and has been noted at Meinarti as well as at other sites.[21] There are many instances where buildings were used over a long period, the inhabitants living above the rubbish, the build-up of which necessitated the raising of thresholds and ultimately the cutting of new doorways at a higher level coupled, in the most extreme cases, with the raising of the walls and the replacing of the roofs.[22]

The metropolises

The presence of particularly rich burials or large tumuli is our main evidence for identifying the centres of political power within the nascent Nubian states. One must exercise caution, however, in locating major settlements, or even metropolises, in close proximity to these cemeteries containing elite graves. In the earlier Kushite period, when the main settlement of the area may have lain close to Jebel Barkal, royal burials continued at el-Kurru 12 km downstream and then at Nuri 7 km upstream, while at a later date, when Meroe, far to the south, appears to have been the principal royal residence, burials continued for a considerable time at Nuri. In the north no large settlements which can be assumed to have been the seat of power are known in the vicinity of the cemeteries at Ballana and Qustul. Likewise in central Sudan no settlement is known which can be associated with the high status burials at el-Hobagi. The other high-ranking cemeteries probably or certainly of this date, at Gemai, Firka, Kosha, Wawa, ez-Zuma, Tanqasi, Khizeinah, Hajar el-Beida and Sururab,[23] also have no known associated settlements. However, in the vicinity of Tanqasi, as noted above, extensive occupation deposits of medieval date have been noted though not investigated in detail.

Both Old Dongola and Soba East were 'new towns' although there is evidence for post-Meroitic burials a little to the north of the former and across the river from the latter site.[24] The contrast with Faras may however, be illusory as we have no direct evidence to indicate that there was continuity of settlement from the late Kushite to the Nobadian town at Faras. The construction of the defensive enceinte over the remains of the Kushite settlement may reflect the desirability of utilizing the important strategic and tactical advantages of the site, as was presumably the case at Old Dongola, rather than demonstrating settlement continuity.

FARAS

Faras had had a long history of occupation and had been the site of a Middle Kingdom fortress and a Kushite settlement, being at one time the 'provincial' capital of the northern part of that state. It must have seemed an obvious choice for the site of the capital of Nobadia. In the tenth century it is described as the capital of Maris,[25] and perhaps anachronistically in the twelfth century, Abu Salih says that it is a well populated city, the capital of Maris where there is a dwelling place of the *eparch*.[26] Defences, enclosing an area of 4.6 hectares, were provided probably early in the history of Nobadia[27] and a mud-brick church, which when originally discovered was thought to date to the fifth century, was probably constructed in the mid sixth. It was succeeded by two further churches built of stone before the cathedral, known as the Church of the Virgin Mary and the Church of St Mary, was built on its site.[28] The construction of the cathedral, possibly by Paulos, the fifth Bishop of Pachoras, may be dated to 707 by two inscriptions, one in Greek, the other in Coptic, which were set in the wall of an adjacent structure 15 m south-east of the main entrance of the building to which they might refer.[29] In the tenth century the cathedral appears to have been damaged by fire in the roof and galleries and the Church on the South Slope of the Kom, dedicated in 930, may have been constructed as a substitute for the cathedral.[30] Within the defensive circuit by the tenth century there were three churches, two palatial structures, a monastery and an industrial complex producing pottery (Fig. 41). Apart from these major buildings little of the rest of the town was investigated. Whether it was densely occupied like the much smaller site at Ikhmindi is unknown. One other monument of especial interest was a large wooden cross which was erected on the highest part of the kom, perhaps to commemorate the conversion of the town to Christianity. A later renovation of this monument consisted of encasing the shaft in a pillar of carved blocks above which the arms protruded.[31]

The demise of the site may have partly been the result of it suffering extensively from a build-up of wind-blown sand. The inhabitants fought a long battle with the sand as can be seen in the cathedral which remained in use even when it was almost totally engulfed. In the thirteenth century the 'Old Monastery' and the 'Palace' were engulfed in sand at a time when the centre of the city may have been largely abandoned. Later in that century there was a renaissance, with the construction of the north monastery with a church at first floor level, over the sanded remains of its predecessor, and the cathedral was rebuilt and renovated.[32] Its continuing ecclesiastical importance is confirmed into the fourteenth century. The latest bishop of Faras known to us was Timotheos, who died in 1372, although it has been suggested that Bishop of Pachorus was largely an honorary title and that he was actually bishop of Qasr Ibrim.[33] The problems caused by wind-blown sand may have been exacerbated when Faras ceased to be an island, which is thought to have occurred during the medieval period,[34] a similar state of affairs to that faced earlier by the inhabitants of the New Kingdom settlement at Amara West. However, the efficacy of an island situation as a protection against wind-blown sand should not be overstated. At Meinarti for example, a small island set in mid stream, only 1 km in length by a maximum of 500 m wide, sand was a chronic problem in the later medieval period, leading on at least one occasion to the abandonment of the village. This occurred in the twelfth century,[35] and the situation at Meinarti, Faras, Abdullah Nirqi and elsewhere may be related to particular climatic conditions pertaining at that time. The sand which caused such a problem at Meinarti appears to have come from a sand bar which was exposed in the river at low water.[36] At Faras, in an attempt to keep the cathedral in use, windows were blocked with *qawadis* (colour plate VIII) and not dissimilar protective measures could be enumerated from many sites. In the late period, when the sand had built up against the cathedral to the level of its windows, a flight of steps was constructed from that ground level down to the north corridor made along the northern facade of the building. The church remained accessible, despite being covered in sand, as late as the reign of King Joel of Dotawo in the later fifteenth century.[37] The Faras cathedral at this time was one of the many churches in late medieval Nubia which were largely subterranean structures.

OLD DONGOLA

Presumably the earliest settlement at Old Dongola was nucleated, making the maximum use of the area within its defended circuit. Unfortunately we know virtually nothing of the original, or indeed of the later, history of the area within the fortifications. Excavations in the last few years have only just penetrated to the level of the wall's construction within the enceinte. Whether the walls were built to enclose a pre-existing settlement remains to be seen although one might expect that such a readily defensible and strategically important site would have been utilized at an earlier period. There is no artefactual evidence at present to indicate that this was so. In the north-west angle of the defences the earliest houses, built directly on the bedrock and contemporary with the enciente, date to the early sixth century. Old Dongola rapidly spread beyond its walls. A substantial red brick structure, Building Y, was built on the lower slope of the hill on which the defended enclosure stood, apparently before the arrival of Christianity, and by the later sixth century two large churches (Old Church and Building X) were constructed.[38] Subsequent events showed this to be an ill-considered development; the churches were extremely vulnerable to attack and one of them was probably destroyed by the invading Arab armies in the mid seventh century. Among the stipulations of the peace treaty drawn up after this conflict was that a mosque be built 'in the courtyard of your capital'. This has not been located. During the seventh to ninth centuries high status dwellings were being constructed 500 m to the north of the ecclesiastical complex, one of which may have belonged to the *eparch* of Nobadia, Petros.[39] Thereafter, the settlement continued to extend to the north and finally covered an area of approximately 2.8 x 0.9 km. Over the whole of this area churches and monastic complexes have been found together with pottery kilns, though how intensively this area was occupied is unknown. By the later eleventh or twelfth century the rich suburb around the house of Petros was in decline, the houses were subdivided and were clearly occupied by people of much humbler status.[40] In the twelfth century Abu Salih describes the city thus 'It is a large city on the banks of the blessed Nile, and contains many churches and large houses and wide streets. The king's house is lofty, with several domes built of red brick …'.[41] The contemporary writer ar-Rumi mentions the 'high, insuperable stone walls.'[42] By contrast el-Masudi is quoted as saying that 'Dongola has no brick houses, except the royal residence of the king; all the rest consists of houses built of reeds.'[43] Although no houses of this type, presumably either circular huts (often referred to incorrectly as *tukl*), or rectilinear *rakuba*, have been excavated on the site, they were probably a very common type of structure in many Nubian towns.

The area within the defences continued to be occupied throughout the medieval period. The earliest houses were demolished and replaced by further houses of at least two stories abutting the wall in the mid seventh century. The excavator suggested that these may have been entered from a circuit street as seen in the fortified settlements at Sabaqura and Ikhmindi. These houses in their turn were abandoned in the tenth century, the whole area was levelled and used for domestic activities associated with the presence of large silos for dry products. In the fourteenth century dwellings were once again constructed and these extended onto the top of the partly destroyed defensive walls. At least one of these structures, it was suggested by the excavator, may have functioned as a guardhouse and its construction was contemporary with a refurbishment of the defences in this area. The adjacent two towers were also crowned by buildings, one of which, the Tower Church, was certainly in use in the fourteenth century.[44] Along the west side of the defences overlooking the river a well-constructed building, which may been palatial, has been discovered very recently.[45]

A number of factors favour the choice of Old Dongola for a major settlement. It is situated at the upstream end of the Letti Basin, one of the few areas on the Middle Nile where natural basin cultivation can be practised and thus its agricultural base was assured. Its defensive capabilities have already been mentioned. It dominates any movement along the east bank of the river which at Old Dongola must leave the river bank and climb across the steep promontory on which the defended settlement lay. It enjoys extensive views across the river over the wide sandy plains to the west. It is also at the point where the Wadi Howar, a palaeochannel of the Nile which extends from northern Darfur and the Chadian border regions, reached the Nile. The importance of this route for trade has been little appreciated but the discovery of a large fortress some 150 km from the Nile suggests that its role may have been greater than formerly considered.[46] Although the fort appears to be of Kushite date the Wadi Howar may have remained an important artery and Old Dongola was ideally placed to control any trade from it.

At Old Dongola the monumental red-brick buildings were extensively robbed for their bricks in the late medieval period. The only possible use for this material would have been to construct other structures but what they may have been is unknown. In the context of the decline of the town one might suggest that the only likely use for this material was the construction or refurbishment of defences although if this was the case no trace remains. However, such walls may themselves have fallen prey to later brick robbers, their bricks being incorporated into the walls of Arab houses, mosques and *qubba*. Although Old Dongola is described by el-Maqrizi as in ruins in the later fourteenth century[47] it once again rose to some degree of prominence but as a post-medieval town, described by Leo Africanus writing in the early sixteenth century, as a town of 10,000 inhabitants occupied by wealthy and civilized people living in miserable houses.[48]

What is particularly noteworthy about Old Dongola, which stands in marked contrast to the evidence so far known from Soba East, is the vitality in church building. Many of the largest and finest churches at Old Dongola appear to have been demolished while still in good condition and replaced by new constructions. Whether the Alwans were constrained by financial considerations, which seems unlikely, or were more conservative, is unknown.

SOBA EAST

Soba appears to have no particular advantages to explain its choice as the site of a major urban centre. It was not a major centre in the pre-medieval nor in the post-medieval periods. It does lie at the mouth of the Wadi Soba, but this is such an ephemeral feature in the landscape as to have offered no obvious topographical advantages to the site of the town. The urban complex covers an area of 2.75 km^2 on the gently undulating plain cut by a number of shallow watercourses. How close it extended towards the river is unclear as irrigation now bounds the site on that side and may have destroyed part of it. Occupation is largely confined to the mounds which dot the site and may always have been separated by wide open areas. The mounds may in part be natural features, being chosen for the site of buildings on account of the protection the additional elevation may have offered from seasonal floods. However, in a number of areas between the mounds evidence for timber structures, both huts and enclosures, has been revealed.[49]

Today the mounds fall into two distinct groups, those covered in fine gravel, and those covered with many fragments of burnt brick which have trapped the wind-blown sand. Trial trenching on the site in the winters of 1981-2 and 1982-3 indicated that the gravel mounds covered the remains of mud-brick buildings which are often well preserved, while the red-brick covered mounds mark the site of buildings constructed of fired brick which have invariably been very extensively robbed. There are a minimum of seventeen, and perhaps a maximum of twenty-nine red-brick covered mounds on the site of which four have been extensively excavated.[50] One covered the remains of three churches, two others concealed the remains of a further two churches, while one covered the remains of a building of uncertain use and another thought to be a temple. Excavations have suggested that the city reached its greatest extent at a very early stage in its development and by the Classic Christian period it occupied a much reduced area, although this may have been the result of the town becoming more nucleated rather than there having been a dramatic fall in population. The several churches known occupy widely spaced locations within the town. Towards the centre is a large complex of buildings which includes at least three churches, two of which are of considerable size (Fig. 35), as well as a large palatial structure, thought to be either a royal or ecclesiastical palace. Small cemeteries have been found in association with many of the churches and have also been located to the east of unexcavated red-brick mounds, suggesting that those also cover the remains of churches. Much too little of the site has been investigated in detail to allow any remarks on the overall town plan. There is no evidence that it ever had a defensive wall, notwithstanding Budge's assertion that he found a stone gateway,[51] and the dispersed nature of the settlement, even when at its most nucleated, would suggest that no defences were ever provided.

In its heyday Soba made a great impression on the few Arab writers who visited it. Ibn Selim describes it thus 'It has fine buildings and large monasteries, churches rich with gold and gardens; there is also a great suburb where many Muslims live.'[52] Although referred to in the sources as Soba it is also named Alwa, Waylula by el-Harrani and Kusa by ed-Dimishqi.[53]

Other major centres

QASR IBRIM

Qasr Ibrim was a site of special status. It had a long history from at least the tenth century BC by which date it already had substantial fortifications (colour plate IV). During the Kushite period it appears to have been a religious centre, ultimately with a total of seven temples apparently laid out to conform to two main axes[54] suggesting substantial control over the planning of the site for a considerable period. In the X-Group there was a changeover to domestic activities with a number of large houses being constructed, although one new temple was built and a number of others remained in use for some time.[55] The site was densely built over, with well constructed and substantial houses.[56] There was clear evidence for animals being stabled within the settlement. In House X9 one room was provided with a rectangular pottery feeding trough and a deep deposit of straw and animal dung had formed on the floor.[57] Many of the houses of this period are devoid of hearths and of food refuse. Plumley and Adams have suggested that they may have been principally used for storage, taking advantage of the defensive nature of the site together with the absence of moisture and of the termite offering protection both from human and natural agents of destruction, and that Ibrim at this time was principally a storage and perhaps also a commercial emporium.[58]

The domestic character of the site is confirmed in the Early Christian period. The temples were destroyed or modified and churches took their place, the high point on the

Figure 42 **The cathedral at Qasr Ibrim.**

site being occupied apparently for the first time by a religious edifice, the cathedral (Fig. 42), which was constructed over the remains of X-Group houses.[59] An official hand in town planning is evident. A number of the earlier houses were demolished and a piazza on two levels was laid out over their remains.[60] The piazza survived into the Classic Christian phase but during Late Christian times it was gradually occupied by dense, irregularly-built stone housing.[61] The site in the Classic Christian Period does not appear to have had a domestic function, those being relegated to the lower town by the river bank. The hilltop was occupied by its churches, large areas of open piazza, a cemetery at the western end of the cathedral and by residences of the *eparch* and of church officials.[62] Abu Salih describes the city with its defensive wall and 'a large and beautiful church, finely planned and named after Our Lady the pure Virgin Mary. Above it is a high dome upon which rises alarge cross.'[63] Elsewhere it is described as a fortress.[64] There were three and possibly four churches within the defences and a late church of Type 4 was also constructed on a small terrace below the eastern wall.[65]

In the immediate aftermath of the Ayyubid invasion led by Shams ed-Dawla, which had rudely shattered the long established peace in the area, the advantages of the defensive potential of the site overcame the inherent disadvantages of the hilltop site high above the only available source of water, the river itself. The whole circuit of the defences was restored at this time after it had been neglected since the Kushite or, at the latest, since the X-Group period. Adams maintains, however, that the site still was not a normal domestic settlement but retained its function as an administrative centre.[66] Although in the Late Christian period dwellings only occupied a part of the hilltop most areas were utilized for storage.[67] Some of these facilities were to be found within ordinary houses but there were also specialized above ground storage facilities. Crypt storage was still practised as it had been at much earlier periods, but Late Christian crypts were usually not within buildings but in the plazas adjoining the occupied dwellings. Some were pits, others utilized earlier rooms dug out at this time specifically for storage use and roofed in a very similar manner to those of X-Group date (see p. 170). By the Terminal Christian period much of the site may have stood empty apart from three massive castle houses close by the western defences.[68] Throughout the history of the site many buildings survived in use for centuries, others went out of use but were on occasion later rebuilt or cleared out and reused afresh.[69]

JEBEL ADDA

This site appears to have risen to prominence in the later Kushite period when it was provided with a mud-brick and stone defensive wall. It enjoyed considerable defensive potential sitting atop a prominent hill (Fig. 100) and Adda is referred to in the Arab sources as a fortress along with Qasr Ibrim.

Although extensively excavated no detailed reports on the work have been published so we know little of its plan. There were several churches, one of which was built on top of the great northern projecting tower of the Kushite defences. This building was destroyed during the medieval period when the north wall of the tower collapsed.[70] In the late medieval period Adda was the capital of the kingdom of Dotawo. Much of the hilltop appears to have been replanned in the thirteenth century and an impressive complex of buildings including a church, an adjacent large building 'of a mansion-like nature', and a palace was constructed. The palatial structure was enlarged in the fourteenth century and continued in use into the fifteenth.[71] The Kushite defences were also refurbished at this period and a new stone-lined gate was constructed.[72]

LOWER-RANKING SETTLEMENTS IN NOBADIA AND IN THE MAKURIAN PROVINCE OF MARIS

Among the lower ranking settlements, that is the settlements of local rather than regional importance, the following have been extensively excavated.

Arminna West

Arminna West appears to have been an important administrative centre in the later Kushite period, a status it apparently lost in the immediately succeeding phase when it suffered a marked decline, presumably because it no longer had a section of its population subsidized by the state or by the region it had administered. However, this trend is not confined to Arminna and suggests a general impoverishment of lower-ranking settlements in Lower Nubia. There was a clear revival in the Classic Christian Period as demonstrated by the architecture. A mud-brick church was constructed and large and finely-built houses reappear although perhaps still occupied by nuclear families. The clustering together of the buildings has been thought to relate to the needs of a highly integrated society rather than to the need for defence, which appears to have been unnecessary at this time. The population may have been between 100 and 200 which may represent the maximum carrying capacity of the area.[73] On the north-west side of the settlement is a 'Public Building'. The fine construction and carefully laid out plan of this structure sets it well apart from houses in the settlement yet it bears no similarity to a church, nor does it appear to be a palatial building.[74] Its function is unknown.

Debeira West

The remains which were excavated date to the period 600 to 1100.[75] The settlement consists of the main nucleus, designated R-8 and outlying sites or suburbs. R-8 is set on a sandstone outcrop immediately to the south of a wadi and contains a substantial rectangular building around which developed a dense concentration of more ephemeral structures forming a maze of interconnecting rooms and courtyards. Beyond this were discrete buildings some separated from their neighbours by streets a few metres in width. There is no church at R-8, the nearest ecclesiastical building is at R-2, a short distance to the north across the wadi and another lies at short distance to the west (R-44). A few hundred metres to the north, at R-60, is another dense concentration of buildings around an early substantial mud-brick building which bears comparison with that at R-8. There appears to have been a hiatus in the occupation of the site some time after 800 following which the town was enlarged with a number of the earlier buildings again brought into use.

Abdullah Nirqi

There were three major periods in the medieval settlement which could be divided into a number of distinct phases. The first settlement was dispersed and consisted of elongated buildings with several rooms separated by thin and often curving walls and constructed of rubble and mud. In the first phase of the second settlement the overall character remained the same, but there was the introduction of a much more substantial barrel-vaulted house type, some of which remained in use until the end of the life of the settlement. According to the excavators, in view of the radical change in the form of the settlement and in the types of buildings constructed within it at the beginning of the second phase, the population of the second settlement was 'living in social and economic conditions entirely different from those of the first settlement'.[76] The second phase, perhaps datable to the eighth century, saw the nucleation of the settlement and the introduction of an entirely new house type, the unit house, well constructed of bricks of a new size, and other multi-roomed houses laid out with streets and passageways between them. In the eleventh or twelfth century the town was provided with a fortified citadel; the defensive wall, incorporating the north-west wall of the church into its line, was provided with projecting towers.[77] The wall was of unusual construction with the lower 1.4 m constructed of stone, the next 1 m of brick and above that again of stone. It was 0.8 m thick and survived to a height of 3.8-4 m.[78] A major destruction of the town by fire might have been a result of Ayyubid military activity in the years 1172-5. Prior to this a number of houses appear to have been already abandoned; the careful blocking of their doorways with brick suggests that the departing owners intended to return.[79] Reoccupation of the site after its destruction may have followed directly and the importance of defence appears to have been a priority; none of the earlier extra-mural buildings were restored. The excavators considered that a number of the new buildings were for military purposes.

Meinarti

This settlement, covering an area 200 x 80 m in size, situated on a small island, was extensively excavated by Bill Adams between 1962 and 1964.[80] Owing to the limited time available it was decided to excavate only one half of the settlement although within the half chosen all periods of occupation were uncovered, a total depth of deposit of 10 m. The substantial buildings and the clear stratigraphy makes this one of the best understood settlements of the medieval period and contributed considerably to Adams' work on defining a chronology for pottery from the Late Kushite to the Late Medieval periods. The site was marked by continuity of settlement throughout most of its history, with what was clearly occupation by the same peoples generation after generation (Fig. 43). The site gradually changed from a Late Kushite settlement, perhaps with some official status to judge from the high status buildings within it, to a pagan Nobadian village. The late Kushite village, partly destroyed by floods, was occupied by people using pottery which was transitional in style between that of the earlier and of the X-Group periods. In the first phase after the disappearance of Kushite artefacts the village was substantially rebuilt, although the central area continued to be occupied by 'public' buildings to which were added 'unit' houses. The substantial buildings were then, perhaps around 450-500, progressively engulfed by 'jerry-built' thin-walled structures although the nature of the artefacts suggest that there was continuity. Adams suggests that these poor-quality houses were constructed when the rural dwellers were forced to move into the village to seek a measure of protection from Nile floods. The architectural condition of the site continued

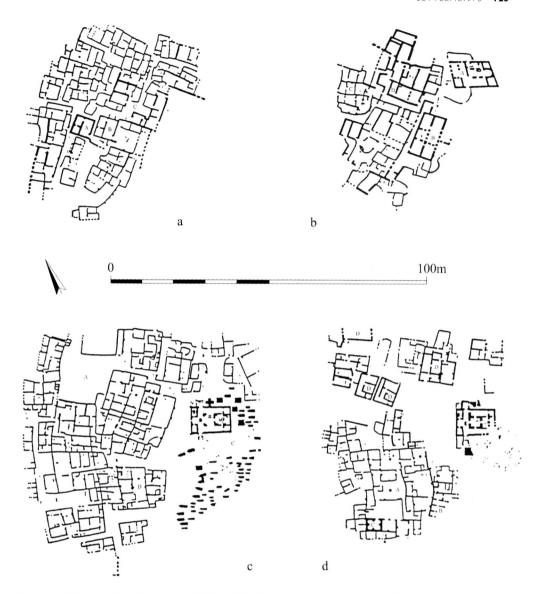

Figure 43 **Phases of settlement at Meinarti (after Adams 2000, figs 3 and 4).**
a. Plan of the X-Group village (level 15b). b. Plan of the Early Christian I village (level 13).
c. Plan of the Classic Christian II village (level 8). d. Plan of the Late Christian I village
(level 5).

to deteriorate, probably culminating in a temporary abandonment of the village. Following
on the destruction of most of the X-Group houses, again the result of flood damage,
there was a major rebuilding and the addition of a church around 660. This phase saw the
revival of massive vaulted architecture with a modification of some of the remaining
earlier houses. There was a trend at this time for house walls to become progressively
thicker, probably an attempt to make them flood-resistant.

Following a major rebuilding of the church the type of housing changed markedly once again, the substantial earlier dwellings being replaced by flimsy structures with very small rooms, which Adams considered to be the foundations of *rakuba*s, a style of architecture adopted as a response to a realization by the inhabitants that they were unable to protect their investment in substantial structures from the destructive high Nile floods prevalent at this time. The artefacts found associated with these levels indicate that the poor-quality housing was not the result of a general impoverishment of the inhabitants. With the end of the period of high Niles the village was rebuilt with an entirely new plan and with quite elaborate houses of a very different type. After the dangers posed by the Nile floods the villagers then faced the problems caused by wind-blown sand, which threatened to engulf their dwellings. Many walls were toppled by the weight of the sand, while sand also began to fill many rooms. To combat the threat walls were strengthened with buttresses, windows and doors were blocked, and long low walls were constructed to impede the progress of the dunes. However, all these efforts were ultimately in vain and the village was again abandoned for a time.

Arab sources mention on a number of occasions a place called 'The Island of Michael' in connection with military activities and it was apparently the residence of the *eparch* on a number of occasions. In the late thirteenth century el-Fariqani, advancing into Nubia, established himself briefly on the Island of Mik'ail 'at the head of the cataract'.[81] According to Abu Salih there was a vast monastery dedicated to SS. Michael and Kosma on the island.[82] In the southern part of the reoccupied village new buildings, many founded on the tops of their sanded up predecessors, may have formed part of Abu Salih's monastic complex, while unit houses were built in the central part of the site with walls uniformly 400 mm thick. Centralized control of much of the village is implicit in the next phase when many of its buildings were decorated with a uniform layer of pale pink plaster. Many of the rooms of the earlier 'monastic' complex went out of use but others survived, among them that identified as the central chapel or refectory, which contained a number of Greek inscriptions. A structure identified as a watchtower was constructed at this period. Over time the 'monastic' complex expanded and traces of a building with elaborate wall paintings was found.

Once again this phase ended with an abandonment of the village. The inhabitants left their homes and many of their valuable possessions neatly stacked on the floors throughout the village, and these gradually disappeared beneath the accumulating sand. This may well be the result of Semamun's order to abandon the region in 1286 in the face of the invasion launched at the behest of the Egyptian ruler Qalawun.[83] When the village was reoccupied, even though many of the buildings were again utilized, no attempt was made to retrieve the objects buried just under the new floors. The watchtower was strengthened and heightened and provided with an internal and external staircase. To the north the unit houses were also strengthened to allow the walls to support vaulted roofs, while some new unit houses, built with thicker walls and vaulted rooms from the first, were constructed. In the mid fourteenth century the island was occupied by desert Arabs for a few years and it was probably they who defaced the murals in the church and in the 'monastery refectory'. They appear to have used the houses to pen their livestock. Following the expulsion of the Arabs the last Christian occupation of the site, continuing

Figure 44 **The South Church at Serra**
(photo Somers Clarke 1899).

to about 1500, was centred on a massive square building, probably a combination of a communal granary and a watchtower.

Serra East

The well-preserved remains of the late medieval town of Ptime Serrah, on the site of the Pharaonic fortress, survived into the 1960s.[84] Within the Pharaonic defences and in the vicinity were thirty separate dwellings of 'unit house' type and there may originally have been twice that number. Although all the houses were independent units at ground level, there was evidence in a number of cases that they were joined at second-floor level with vaults spanning the alleyways between them. Of the four churches, one stood a little to the north of the fortress, one was in the centre of the defended area (Fig. 44), while the other two were built over the sand-filled south ditch. The lack of rubbish material on the site and the absence of evidence for structural modifications in the buildings led the excavator to suggest that the site was only occupied for a period of between 50 and 100 years.

SETTLEMENTS IN MAKURIA

Very little work has been conducted on settlements in the region to the south of the Third Cataract and, as with Alwa, almost all our evidence is biased towards the metropolis. Hambukol remains the exception.

Hambukol

The site occupies a prominent mound, apparently natural, which attains a maximum elevation of 14 m above the surrounding plain, and another smaller mound a little to the north. An 'official building' of unique form, and a few houses have been uncovered on the main mound which was occupied in the eleventh to twelfth centuries and a church has also been identified. Another church, of seventh to ninth century date, possibly with an associated monastic complex dating to the tenth century, on the smaller mound are currently being excavated by a mission from the Royal Ontario Museum.[85] Not enough is known to allow us to discuss the plan and nature of the settlement.

ALWAN SETTLEMENTS

In Alwa we know nothing of the urban centres apart from the capital and it is impossible to even begin to attempt to discuss Alwan settlement patterns and town planning in any meaningful way. The special status of the metropolis makes it extremely hazardous to extrapolate from it to the other settlements within the kingdom. The many settlement mounds covered in red brick along the Blue and White Niles, which are claimed, perhaps in many cases correctly, to be of medieval date, indicate that this ignorance can be addressed in the future by survey and excavation.

Sites away from the river

Cemeteries are known in some numbers away from the river, and often far outside the Nile Valley, but associated settlements are largely unknown. In the Northern Dongola Reach are two cemeteries over 10 km to the east of the river.[86] Why they were located in those areas is unclear. Post-Meroitic and Christian graves are known at Musawwarat es-Sufra. There is, in addition to the evidence for a possible reuse of a Kushite temple as a church, or a newly constructed church, extensive evidence for occupation within the Kushite buildings. Considerable quantities of pottery, described as belonging to 'a post-Meroitic period', were found in the upper layers of rubble commonly associated with fireplaces and hearths.[87] To the north west of the Nile from the modern town of Dongola, in the oasis of el-Laqiya, there are extensive medieval remains including two substantial mud-brick buildings although, as no excavation or detailed survey has been carried out, nothing further can be said about the organization of the site. In the Bayuda there are large numbers of graves of 'medieval type'. The apparent absence of associated settlements suggests that many of the graves could be of individuals from nomadic or transhuming groups. However, the presence of a granite column shaft in a quarry at Bayuda Wells suggests that there was a church, or at least the intention to build a church, in the vicinity. The quarry is much too far from the river to have made the extraction of a column for use in any of the known riverine settlements a viable proposition. It is also a considerable distance from the monastic complex at el-Ghazali, the builders of which will have had much more convenient access to granite quarries immediately upstream of Nuri.[88]

The function of the towns

A detailed discussion of the function of urban centres in Nubia is hampered by the lack of information on their interaction with their hinterlands. In many cases the urban centre is imperfectly known while we have no information whatsoever about the surrounding areas.

In the medieval periods the major urban centres were centres of production of material which was widely disseminated to all levels of society. Pottery, for example, was produced at Faras, Old Dongola and Soba East among other sites. Although other production centres are known the high quality of some of this material does suggest that it was made in a limited number of centres. Other classes of objects were also probably made in the urban centres. By this urban-based production the towns were fulfilling a generative function stimulating the production of a surplus in the rural communities which could then be exchanged in the urban centres for specialized goods. The importance of towns as centres of a market economy, however, is difficult to evaluate. The most important towns were centres of state control and housed the administrative machinery of the state based around the ruler and his officials. Although the locations of the major centres remained stable throughout the medieval period, only in a few cases was there continuity in status from earlier periods and extending after the demise of the Nubian kingdoms. Of prime importance in the early stages of their development may have been an intimate association with the rise to prominence of particular inhabitants who will then have disproportionally favoured their birthplace setting in motion the development of that settlement. Such sites, if relying heavily on their resident elites, were particularly vulnerable to changes at a political level. The Kushite towns at Napata and Meroe and the Alwan capital Soba East may be among the victims of these political changes.

With the lower ranking settlements there may not have been a very clear division between the urban centre and its rural hinterland. Even in the major administrative centres, for example at Qasr Ibrim, there is evidence in the Late Medieval period for the stabling of animals within the town and the presence of domestic animals penned within dwellings at Hambukol and Debeira West has also been noted.[89] Presumably many farmers will have lived in the settlements but have worked in their fields. Nucleation may have been a result of the close family ties existing in those areas and, at certain periods of Nubian history, the necessity to take defensive measures will also have been a determining factor.

Fortified settlements of the early medieval period

The immediate aftermath of the collapse of the Kushite Empire appears to have been one of the few times on the Middle Nile when the needs of defence were a prime consideration. In the north are a series of newly fortified sites at Faras, Sabaqura, Sheikh Daud, Ikhmindi and Kalabsha, some of which were defended at this time, others a little later. These have many features in common both in their plan and style of construction although the enclosure at Faras is considerably larger, perhaps reflecting its importance as the capital of the kingdom of Nobadia. The defences enclose a trapezoidal area, that at Faras with its long axis parallel to the present-day stream of the Nile (Fig. 41).

Within the defences at Ikhmindi (Fig. 40) and Sheikh Daud the plans of the buildings are remarkably regular, reminiscent of the arrangement within the Middle Kingdom fortresses. Ranges of two-roomed apartments back onto the inner face of the defensive wall and are separated by a narrow street from rectangular blocks set within the enclosure. A church occupies the central position, demonstrating that they were built after the conversion of Nobadia to Christianity. Their regular, planned interiors indicate that we do not have here a pre-existing town being provided with defences but purpose-built fortified settlements laid out with reasonable precision. At Ikhmindi a dedicatory inscription records that the enclosure was built 'for the protection of men and beasts' by Tokiltoeton, King of the Nobadae.[90] It has been suggested that at least some of these sites were located near the termini of desert caravan routes and that they may have served as caravanserai.[91] If one takes into account the already existing fortresses at Qasr Ibrim and Jebel Adda they appear to form a regular chain of fortified sites, apart from the long interval between Sheikh Daud and Ikhmindi.

At Faras and Kalabsha in particular the defended enclosure occupied the site of an earlier settlement. However, in neither case can it be shown that earlier buildings remained in use, apart from the Temple of Mandulis at the latter site which was converted for use as a church. There is no evidence for continuity of settlement and the new fortified towns may have been imposed on the pre-existing urban landscape without taking much account of it. The similarities in style of construction, plan, and building techniques indicate that these sites were part of a coherent system, which includes the metropolis of the Nobadian state. Were they administrative centres, the seats of the king and the kinglets of Nobadia?

Table 3. Fortified sites of early(?) medieval date

	Dimensions	Area		Dimensions	Area
Kalabsha	207+ × 147 m+[92]	?	Faras	107-196 × 296-310 m	4.6 ha
Sabaqura	143-148 × 40-68 m	0.8 ha	Old Dongola	350 × 150 m	4.75 ha
Ikhmindi	116-122 × 91 m+	1.1 ha	Sinada	200 × 200 m	4 ha
Sheikh Daud	77.5-104 × 72-99 m	0.7 ha	Bakhit	222-170 × 140 m	2.7 ha

In Makuria there is no similar chain of fortified settlements at this period. There are many walled sites, for example at Old Dongola, Sinada, Selib(?),[93] Estabel, Diffar, Jebel Deiga and Bakhit (Helleila), but these vary considerably in form and do not appear to be a coherent system like the fortified sites provided in Nobadia and Alwa. The defences at Old Dongola were constructed in the early sixth century. Although the defences were extended a little to the north in the aftermath of the invasions in the mid seventh century there is no structural evidence to indicate that they were extended further to enclose the major buildings to the north. The rapid rebuilding of those structures in the latter half of the seventh century, at a time when peace with the Arabs was by no means a foregone conclusion, would have been foolhardy in the extreme if they were unprotected by walls. Ibn el-Faqih, writing around 900, describes Old Dongola as being surrounded by seven walls, the lower parts of which were of stone.[94] Estabel occupies a strong defensive position atop an isolated hill (Fig. 45). Bakhit is one of the most impressive sites of the medieval period in Nubia. On three of the four sides of the trapezoidal enclosure its massive defensive circuit is extremely well preserved (colour plate VI). However there is no trace of a wall along the top of the low cliff alongside the river but, in view of the strength of the defences on the

Figure 45 **The fortress at Estabel.**

other three sides, some additional protection must have been provided, although perhaps a massive wall was not deemed necessary.[95] Pottery collected from the surface suggests that it was occupied from the very earliest Christian period while later Kushite sherds offer the possibility of yet earlier use of the site.[96] The enclosure at Jebel Deiga on the right bank of the Nile across from Korti, has stone walls 5 m thick but encloses a very small area 80 x 60 m in size (c. 0.25 ha).[97]

The internal arrangement of these fortified settlements is little known. At Bakhit a small church is situated within the enceinte and we would expect that a religious monument also occupied a prominent point at Old Dongola, although in this case it may originally have been a temple, perhaps later converted into a church. The large size of the defended area at Bakhit and its rectilinear layout suggests that it is to be dated to the earlier medieval period.[98] No excavation has yet been conducted at Estabel and its date is uncertain. The presence of a granite column indicates that there was probably a church within it. At the lowest part of the interior is a large cistern.

The defences at Old Dongola, enclosing a roughly oval area and with walls strengthened by massive, boldly projecting, round-fronted towers, are in the mainstream of Late Roman civic defences. They can be compared directly with many circuits in the western Roman Empire where the type first makes its appearance in the 3rd century, at Senlis and Dijon in France and Lugo in Spain, and in the fort defences of Pevensey in Britain.[99] The thickness and height of the walls and the dimensions of the towers of the Old Dongola fortifications also fit within the range to be found among Roman fortifications of this period and suggest an awareness of state-of-the-art military architecture in the contemporary Roman world.

The scale of these early defences indicates that the Makurians considered that there was a serious potential threat. They seem too substantial to have been designed to repel small raiding parties descending into the valley from the desert. A further illustration of the seriousness of the perceived threat comes from the provision of outworks in the form of ditches. A single wide flat-bottomed ditch was provided at Faras along the western side of the defences while at Bakhit two rock-cut ditches were dug to protect the more vulnerable curtain which face an uphill slope (colour plate VI). The spacing of these ditches, well in front of the defences suggests that this lay within the effective range of the Nubian's defensive and/or the perceived enemies' offensive weapons.

In the Wadi Abu Dom are four sites which might be classed as forts. The defences at Umm Ruweim 2, Umm Khafur (Fig. 46), and presumably at the nearby Umm Ruweim 1 are entered through tower gates of the same type as seen at Faras.[100] The other site, Umm Kuweib, has a simple opening on one side of the rectangular enclosure. The plan of Umm Ruweim 1 is the most complex. It is a rectangular enclosure with a projecting tower (one containing a gate?) in the middle of each side. Around the inner face of the wall is a continuous range of rooms. Within the enclosure is a smaller rectangle entered by a simple opening from the south east and also with a range of rooms right around the inside. An isolated building, on a markedly different alignment, occupies the northern part of the inner enclosure.[101] The function of these structures is unclear. Umm Kuweib in particular is unlikely to be a military installation, as it lies very close to high ground from which it could have been dominated.

Far to the south, stretching along the river from a little north of Khartoum towards

Figure 46 **The defended enclosure at Umm Khafur.**

Abu Hamed, is a series of fortified sites many of which are very similar in design, suggesting the possibility that they were part of a co-ordinated system. The most southerly is on the summit of Jebel Umm Marrihi, a prominent and isolated hill on the left bank of the river opposite el-Geili. This is a square fort with sides *c.* 83 m long, defended by a stone wall about 3.4 m thick. At each corner is a tower projecting at an angle of 45°, there is also a projecting tower in the middle of three sides, the fourth facing the river having a gateway in the middle, an approach protected by an L-shaped wall, as in the defences at Faras and elsewhere in Nobadia.[102] The very similar fort at Jebel Nakharu, which has a defended annex, is set on the edge of the plateau again on the left bank 40 km to the north of Berber (Fig. 47).[103] At Kurgus a mud-brick fort on the right bank of the Nile is of very similar size and plan.[104] The fourth fort is at Abu Nafisa a few kilometres to the north of Jebel Umm Marrihi. It is set on low ground close to the river but otherwise is similar, although much less well preserved, than that on the nearby *jebel.*[105] Very little work has been conducted at any of these sites but they do not appear to have been densely occupied by buildings. Their date is uncertain. Early medieval pottery has been found at Jebel Nakharu while small-scale excavations at Jebel Umm Marrihi apparently yielded Kushite material.[106]

The fort at Hosh el-Khafir near el-Hobagi is rather different both in plan and situation, as it is located several kilometres to the west of the river. Its regular layout, with its two opposing gateways flanked by 'guard-chambers' and with a centrally-placed building, brings to mind contemporary Roman military installations. Accommodation and workshop facilities were constructed up against the inner face of the defensive wall. A large number of the functional type of archer's loose were found in these rooms together with iron

Figure 47 **The fort and annex at Jebel Nakharu (air photo by C. Downer).**

arrowheads. There was also evidence for iron working and domestic activities. Two other similar sites are known in the region.[107]

Sites fortified in the late medieval period

The late medieval period was marked by a series of long-term conflicts with the Arabs invading from Egypt. Defensive considerations once again became of paramount importance to the inhabitants of much of Nubia and settlements were either provided with defences, and/or relocated to defensible positions, or went into decline. Sites such as Arminna West where no provision was made for defence may already have been in terminal decline. Nucleation of settlement in the late period was another result of the general insecurity.[108] However, some sites are known of the Classic Christian period which were defended, such as Kulb, where the settlement sheltering within its walls was occupied between approximately 800 and 1000 although this may have been a monastic complex.[109]

The changing security situation in the late medieval period is illustrated by the history of Old Dongola's defences. During the Classic Christian period the defences were partly dismantled and elsewhere they were in a state of disrepair. The mud-brick extension wall was still in use during the thirteenth century but was dismantled thereafter. This may have been connected with measures taken in the fourteenth century to refurbish the defences implying a withdrawal to the shortest defensive circuit available.[110]

Among the defended sites constructed at this time may have been that on the hilltop at Jebel Sese close to the New Kingdom town at Sesebi. At Serra a settlement was established within the still serviceable walls of the Pharaonic fortress and a similar situation has been noted elsewhere.[111] The late medieval settlements at Serra, Abkanarti, Kasanarti, Murshid, Kulubnarti and Dal all appear to have occupied sites not settled earlier in the medieval period. Conversely a number of earlier sites were abandoned in the later medieval period[112] although, as noted above, other factors apart from their suitability for defence may account for this. This period was marked by a great upsurge of occupation in the most inhospitable parts of the Nile Valley, in the Batn el-Hajar[113] and perhaps also along the Fourth Cataract.

Several sites have massive fortifications but enclose a very small area sometimes on a

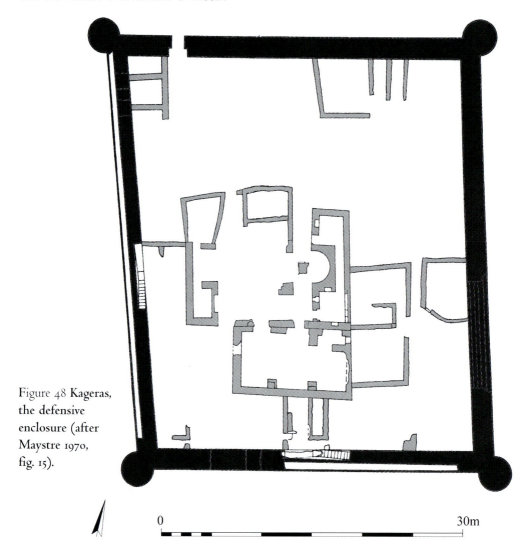

Figure 48 **Kageras, the defensive enclosure** (after Maystre 1970, fig. 15).

0   30m

very steep slope. Two of these in the Third Cataract region at Kassi-Markol and at Shofein opposite Nauri enclose 0.3 ha and c. 370 m² respectively,[114] that at Susinarti (Sunnarti) in the Batn el-Hajar about 0.2 ha.[115] These can hardly be classed as fortified towns but have more the character of heavily defended refuges. The situation of many of them, set on a steep slope, appears to be a compromise between a desire to claim the high ground to facilitate defence and the necessity to enclose part of the alluvial plain by the river to allow secure access to water. The Kassi-Markol fort has a defensive wall built of dry-stone construction 2-3 m thick and still standing to a height of 5-6 m, the wall at Shofein attains a height of 7 m (colour plate V).[116] At Kageras a pre-existing church, dated by Adams to the tenth to eleventh century, was enclosed by a defensive wall in the Late Medieval period (Fig. 48). This wall, although relatively low, 3 m in height of which the upper 0.8 m is parapet, is extremely well preserved with its parapet walk accessed by double stairways mid-way along the south and west walls. At each angle are circular projecting towers about

Figure 49 **The forts at Suweiqi.**

3 m in diameter; close to that at the north-west angle on the north wall is the narrow gateway.[117] Monasteries are often enclosed by a defensive wall but the provision of fortifications around a church is hard to parallel elsewhere in Nubia although on Kisinarti fortifications surround a very small area within which is a church and a few huts.[118] One fortress which is not precisely located, but lay some distance upstream of Old Dongola, was used as a temporary refuge by King David following his defeat at the metropolis in 1276.[119] Among the candidates must be the fortified sites noted above as far upstream as Bakhit and several sites in the Abu Hamed Reach, such as the two forts at Suweiqi by the Fourth Cataract, el-Kab and at Karmel on Mograt Island.

Among the most impressive medieval fortifications are those at Suweiqi where flanking a narrow 'gorge' through which the Nile flows, are two massive forts with walls still standing to a considerable height (Fig. 49).[120] That on the right bank is a roughly trapezoidal enclosure with boldly projecting 'D'-shaped angle and interval towers. The formidable defences are, however, compromised by the presence of several gates, always points of weakness in any defensive system. The fort on the opposite bank is sub-rectangular in shape and divided into two unequal parts by a substantial wall. On its west side it is protected by a rock-cut ditch with a *proteicheisma* on its inner lip (Fig. 50). The presence of such large and strong fortifications in this inhospitable reach of the Nile is surprising. The forts are clearly designed to dominate the river itself yet the river in this region is extremely difficult to navigate on account of the many rocks in its course. This together with the prevailing north wind and the current flowing from north-east to south-west further exacerbates the problems facing riverine transport. It thus remains unclear as to why they were built and indeed who was able to marshal the large manpower resources both to construct and to man them. In their location and in the massiveness of their defences they bear comparison with the Middle Kingdom Pharaonic fortresses at Semna and Kumma in the Batn el-Hajar near the Second Cataract. However, those fortresses were defending the

Figure 50 **Suweiqi Sharq,**
the defences on the west
side with rock-cut ditch
and *proteichisma.*

limits of Pharaonic control, were set on a major trade artery, and at a point where portage
of goods from boats going down and upriver will have been necessary for much of the
year. None of these functions seem appropriate for the Suweiqi forts. Clearly it is our
ignorance of the situation in the region at the time they were built and used which leads
to our failure to understand why they are there. The fort on the right bank may contain
the remains of a late medieval church.

On Shirgondinarti at the Second Cataract there is a complex of walls which run across
wadis. It has been suggested that some of these, the relatively thin walls, were designed to
protect the fields from wild animals although how walls of this sort could have achieved
this is a mystery, as is the identification of these wild animals. Another suggested use was
to slow down rainwater flowing down from the hills but in this extremely arid region such
a provision must have been rather superfluous. They are contrasted with the much thicker
walls further north on the island which also cut across wadis leading to the interior and
were considered to be fortifications. These latter walls will have served to deny easy access,
at least for cavalry, into the centre of the island but their efficacy against even the least
enthusiastic attacker must have been negligible.[121]

Where no collective measures were taken for the defence of the whole community free-
standing fortified houses were built.[122] Many of these occupy hilltop sites and/or are situated
on islands which will have enhanced their defensive capabilities although only against
marauding bands rather than a determined assault. Most of them are placed so as to afford
views upstream whereas one might have expected the major threat to come from the north.
However, apart from the major invasions from Egypt, against which a castle house would
have been ineffective, the continuing maintenance of the kingdom of Dotawo may have
meant that small scale raids were more likely from the south, particularly from the later
fourteenth century with the abandonment of Old Dongola by the Makurian monarchy.

The defensive nature of many of the late medieval sites ensured their survival as
settlements in the turbulent post-medieval period. The major centres at Qasr Ibrim and
Sai were occupied during the sixteenth century by the Ottomans, Old Dongola became the
capital of a local *Mek* under the suzerainity of the Funj sultans of Sennar, while many of
the smaller forts continued in use for centuries. Soba East, which had no defensible
potential, was, on the other hand, abandoned.

CHAPTER 7

Architecture

Monuments of the medieval period were, at least until the progressive extensions of the Aswan reservoir, extremely well preserved in many places (e.g. colour plates VIII and XI). However, as one moves upstream the standard of preservation falls off markedly and within the borders of Alwa there are virtually no upstanding remains. This is not solely the result of population pressure. Many parts of the Nile Valley further north support a dense population in the narrow productive belt alongside the river. Two other factors account for the differing preservation. In the north a number of buildings have been buried, while still in very good condition, by wind-blown sand: the cathedral at Faras and one of the churches at Abdullah Nirqi illustrate this excellently. Also, as one moves southwards towards the area affected by seasonal rainfall, the more monumental buildings tended to be constructed to a greater extent from red brick. Red-brick buildings can productively be demolished and the bricks reused in later constructions, something that is less feasible for mud-brick structures. In addition any mud-brick buildings have, once they fell into disrepair, been at the mercy both of the rainfall and, what is often more damaging, from the effects of standing water at the base of the walls which dissolves their lowest courses causing the walls to fall. It is a combination of these factors that has conspired to force us once again, as in the discussion of so much else relating to medieval Nubia, to rely disproportionately on the evidence from Nobadia and Makuria. Alwa is marginalized in any discussion of architecture.

Nubian monumental architecture predating the arrival of Christianity is extremely rare, although how much this is due to the early monuments being destroyed and overbuilt later in the medieval period is uncertain. Among the most impressive monuments to survive are a series of fortifications which have been discussed in detail in Chapter 6.

Nubian temples

A small number of pre-Christian religious monuments are known, at Qasr Ibrim and Soba East, and perhaps at Old Dongola and Jebel Adda. At Qasr Ibrim Temple 1 sealed a number of rock-cut tombs containing pottery datable to the mid fourth century, and its excavator suggests that it was probably built during the century after c. AD 453.[1] It was constructed throughout of dressed stone and consisted of a single room entered through a pylon. It is clearly within the architectural tradition of the later Kushite period although post-dating the introduction of ceramics associated with the 'X-Group tradition'. It is largely semantics as to whether we call it a late Kushite temple or an early Nubian temple as the earliest 'Nubian' builders and architects may well have been the same people as the latest 'Kushite' builders and architects. At Soba East recent excavations found a very similar scenario. Post-dating the arrival of ceramics clearly produced in a Christian artistic milieu is a building which appears to have much in common with a Kushite temple. It is constructed of red brick and surrounded by an enclosure (*temenos?*) wall built of mud brick and probably dates to the sixth century.[2]

At Old Dongola fragments of a building, designated Building Y, were found beneath a sequence of churches culminating in the Cruciform Church. Little can be said of the plan of the earliest building but it was well-constructed from high quality red bricks.[3] The identification of this building as a temple is entirely hypothetical but, like the Soba East structure, its site was later occupied by a church. At Jebel Adda a temple was found which the excavator considered to be Late Kushite although its date of construction and use could not be closely defined.[4] The building found beneath the Cathedral at Faras, which was originally thought to have been constructed in the fifth century, is now considered to be a church of later date.[5]

The impact of Christianity

The arrival of Christianity had a profound effect on monumental religious architecture. Although the temple and the church are both religious buildings their mode of use was very different and they demanded very different architectural solutions. The temple was the house of the god, designed to contain the god's image and was entered usually only by the priesthood. The church, on the other hand, was a public building, the populace being expected to enter and occupy large parts of it, while the sanctuary, the preserve of the priests, was only a small area at the eastern end. Within the Roman Empire the early church builders had turned to the secular basilica as the model for church architecture, with its axial plan, a long central nave flanked by aisles.[6] It was this basic concept which was introduced into Nubia along with Christianity and there is no continuity between the earlier temple architecture and that of the new places of worship. Some of the earliest churches were constructed within temples, but this was simply an opportunistic reuse of an upstanding monument, which could be modified to suit the needs of the new religion but which, in its spatial arrangement, was usually far from ideal. There was also, of course, the ideological desire to desecrate the old pagan sanctuaries and put them to the service of the Christian god.

The good preservation of churches has been a major attraction to archaeologists who have sought to classify and date the various forms. One of the first attempts was made by Somers Clarke who, in his book, *The Christian Antiquities in the Nile Valley*, divided the churches into three types, basilican buildings with flat roofs, basilican buildings with the necessary modifications to support vaults and domes, and buildings covered by multiple domes which he considered to be of later date.[7] At the same time Geoffrey Mileham (1910) studied Nubian churches, the building techniques etc., and the treatise of Monneret de Villard entitled *La Nubia Medievale*, published between 1935 and 1957, further refined the study. The detailed classification of churches reached its apogee with the publication in 1965 of 'Architectural Evolution of the Nubian Church, 500-1400 A.D.' by Bill Adams.[8] This latter study was based almost exclusively on the evidence from the churches of Lower Nubia of which 118 were known, at the time of writing, between Aswan and Dal. Later studies, particularly by Gartkiewicz, have drawn on the large amount of new material from Upper Nubia where there is a greater range of diversity and from where many of the innovative designs may have sprung.[9]

Architectural layout of a 'typical' Nubian church

The description of Nubian churches which follows is very generalized and is based largely on Adams' study of churches in Lower Nubia, that is in Nobadia, the later Makurian province of Maris. The range of variation from this 'norm' will be discussed later. Churches are typically rectangular with all the rooms contained within the rectangle.

Figure 51 **Reconstruction of a Nubian church (after Somers Clarke 1912, pl. XXV, fig. 5).**

Externally the walls appear to have been provided with little in the way of embellishment. Windows were small and doorways were usually, although not invariably, narrow openings.[10] The most impressive feature of many churches may have been their roofs. Although many, particularly the earlier ones, had flat roofs supported on timbers presumably covered with a layer of mud or mud brick (Fig. 51), others were commonly vaulted or covered with domes. Some of these domes were very prominent and representations of churches on wall paintings (Fig. 52), graffiti (Fig. 53) and actual buildings surviving until recently at several sites, show them as impressive and striking monuments.

Internally churches were divided into three principal areas. The eastern range contained a centrally-placed sanctuary chamber, either of rectangular form or terminating to the east in an apse, which is always, with the exception of Church EDC at Old Dongola (Fig. 54), enclosed within a rectangle and only very rarely projects beyond the building line. It is flanked by one or two rooms to each side. The body of the church had a nave separated, usually by columns or piers, from one or two aisles to each side, while at the west end was either a *narthex* running right across the building, a range consisting of a room in the north-western and the south-western corner with the central space open to the nave, or no special division at all. The liturgical divisions in the early church conformed to that of the

Figure 52 **Nubian churches depicted on wall paintings from Abd el-Qadir (*c.* thirteenth century) and from the cathedral at Faras (*c.* eleventh century) (after Gartkiewicz 1980, fig. 15).**

Figure 53 **Rock drawings of religious buildings at Sabu near the Kajbar rapids.**

Figure 54 **Church EDC at Old Dongola**
(after Dobrowolski 1991, fig. 2).

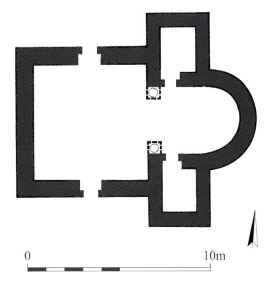

0   10m

architecture. The *bema*, the area reserved for the clergy, included the sanctuary (*haikal*), composed of two parts, an apse and a space in front of it, comparable to the presbytery, and the rooms to either side which are usually equated with the *prothesis,* to the north, and the *diaconicon* to the south on analogy with the Greek Church. The *prothesis* was the more important of the two, being provided with access to the *haikal*, and may have been used for the preparation of the sacred elements for the liturgy.[11] A baptismal font was often placed in the *diaconicon*. The nave and aisles formed the *naos* which was used by the laity while the *narthex* if provided may have been occupied by penitents or those under discipline. Women may have been seated in one of the aisles, relegated to the galleries or, where the north aisle was not big enough to accommodate them, in a side chapel such as was provided at Arminna West.[12] The *haikal* was separated from the *naos* by a symbolic 'triumphal arch' which framed the wide opening between the two. Where rooms were provided at the west end, that to the south was, at least in churches south of Faras, almost invariably occupied by a staircase, although, particularly to the north of Faras, the northern room was sometimes used for this function. The function of the other room is uncertain. Some early churches did not have a stairway as part of the original design, but one was added later to the exterior of the building. In the early churches the altar stood within the sanctuary chamber and doorways frequently led directly from that chamber to the flanking rooms.

    In many of the early churches a tribune, tiers of steps around the inside of the apse, which were occupied by the higher clergy during services, with a special platform in the centre at the top for the 'bishop's cathedra', was introduced and was an integral part of the design of later churches. They were usually constructed of masonry but some were of timber; that at Arminna West consisting of straight steps rather than each step forming a concentric curve within the apse.[13] Where the tribune was added into a pre-existing building the doorways from the apse into the sacristies were blocked and the altar was repositioned in the eastern bay of the nave. Early altars were typically of timber, perhaps with a stone top, although from the eighth century onwards solid masonry structures, *c*. 0.75 x 1 m in size and between 0.6 and 1.25 m high were built. The solid masonry type often had a recess in the back either to house the chalice or to act as a reliquary. The movement of the altar to the west necessitated an extension of the *bema* called the *presbyterium*, a screen (*higab*) being built across the nave and a similar screen dividing off the western end of the north and sometimes of the south aisle, forming a vestibule which allowed the clergy to move unseen from the sacristies to the *haikal*. The triumphal arch now goes out of use and the physical barrier of the *higab* takes its place. In the churches at Arminna and Faras (Rivergate Church), however, there is contemporary provision of a triumphal arch springing from the easternmost piers in the nave and a *higab*. *Higab* are frequently of timber in the early period and of mud brick later, being pierced by a narrow doorway. They vary considerably in form, ranging from a wooden or stone balustrade of open-work,[14] or a low brick wall not higher than 1 m, to a partition wall 3 m high with entrances and windows. The latter type can be equated with the *iconostasis* and is the latest form, only introduced into some churches.[15]

A pulpit, of timber, mud brick, or stone, was almost invariably positioned on the north side of the nave up against the first pier or column from the east. Access onto it was by steps leading up from the west indicating that it was designed for sitting on, in the manner of a Muslim minbar, rather than for standing as is the norm elsewhere in Christendom. The pulpit in the church on Kom E (The Mosaic Church) at Old Dongola preserved the dressed stone slab, 750 mm square, which formed its top.[16] That in Church R-44 at Debeira West is very unusual in having steps leading up to it from the east and the west sides.[17] A feature which has been claimed as uniquely Nubian, and is found in many churches, is the provision of a narrow passage behind the *haikal* linking the north-eastern and south-eastern rooms. Although characteristic of the Classic Nubian church type eastern passages are found elsewhere and examples in Syria, on Lesbos and in Egypt are cited by Gartkiewicz.[18] In late churches, which are of small size, the *bema* extended to fill the whole church, the laity then being relegated to the exterior of the building. This phenomenon is to be seen in many areas in the Middle East, but in Egypt, owing to the actual, or potential, threat of persecution, worship remained behind closed doors.[19]

Adams in his classification of Nubian (Nobadian) churches divides them into converted temples and six other types (Fig. 62).

TYPE T, CONVERTED TEMPLES

Perhaps the earliest church in Nubia was that inserted into the Temple of Taharqo at Qasr Ibrim (Fig. 11). The roughly east-west orientation of the building with the entrance to the west made it ideally suited for reuse as a church and all that was required was to insert an apse into the rectangular sanctuary and to tack on a *narthex* to the west end.[20]

One of the most consistent features of church design was the orientation of the structure with the sanctuary to the east and the long axis running east-west, although river north as often as cardinal north governed the precise orientation. Such an orientation frequently caused problems when a church was inserted into a temple, many of which were orientated very differently. The unhappy nature of these conversions is demonstrated in the reuse of a number of temples. In many of these buildings the only part of the temple of sufficient size to be converted into the *naos* of the church was the courtyard. Within this the church

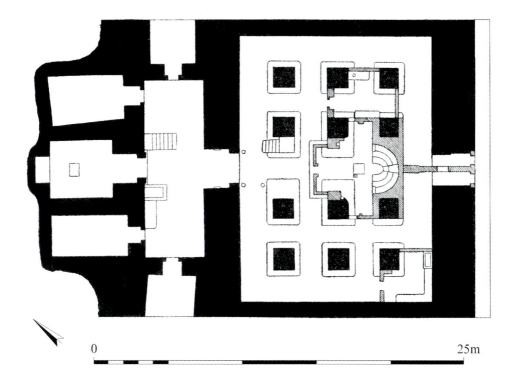

0   25m

Figure 55 **The church at Wadi es-Sebua inserted into a Pharaonic temple (after Monneret de Villard 1935, I, fig. 71).**

was constructed, with the rear wall of its sanctuary towards the main entrance to the temple, as for example at Wadi es-Sebua (Fig. 55). The church here was built in the centre of the court, the large Pharaonic piers forming the angles of the building. A wall extended from the rear of the sanctuary into the entrance of the temple where a twin-portalled arched entrance was inserted.[21] The relatively square proportions of many of these temple courtyards forced the churches to conform and gave them a very unusual shape with the *naos* wider than it was long. The church builders then had to provide a roof over these churches largely independent from the structural elements reused from the earlier temple. It appears in any event that many of the temples were in a state of considerable ruin by the time of their reuse. This was certainly the case at Tabo where the church, built on the site of the first court of the temple probably originally constructed by Taharqo, may date to a period after the total demolition of the temple. The medieval builders usurped the site of the earlier building but were too late to make use of any of its in situ structural features.[22] At Kalabsha greater use was made of the temple structure, the church was inserted into the hypostyle hall which formed the *naos*, the sanctuary chamber and its flanking rooms being added on to the exterior of the west wall of the court. The temple's main entrance then became the 'triumphal arch' flanking the entrance through to the apse. Doorways were pierced through the wall of the court to either side to communicate with the pastafories.[23]

Gartkiewicz has criticized Adams and Monneret de Villard for considering the temple churches as a separate church type. He stresses that, notwithstanding their insertion into pre-existing structures, these churches can be readily compared with contemporary newly-constructed churches elsewhere in Nubia and that they should be integrated into the main-stream of church development. This is particularly clear with the church at Aksha, if Gartkiewicz' reconstruction of the layout of the two main phases is correct. It conforms in the earlier phase to the type exemplified by the Church of the Granite Columns at Old Dongola.[24]

The conversion of the rock-cut shrine built by Horemheb at Abu Oda into a church may have occurred at an early date. Structurally it conforms to the plan of the pre-existing structure; the provision of wall paintings was the main task of the new Christian owners.

THE EARLIEST FREE-STANDING CHURCHES IN NOBADIA

Adams' earliest type, prototype churches, was advanced tentatively. Type 0 is represented by two examples only, from Karanog and Abd el-Qadir South.[25] The former was identified by its excavator as a house; it was designated House 9. Like the other prototype church the most obvious feature to suggest that it is a church is the presence of a pulpit-like structure, although this is extremely small with its upper step measuring only about 500 x 400 mm. There is a partition immediately to the east which is reminiscent of a *higab*, but if it is the entrance through into the sanctuary chamber, which runs the full width of the building, it is narrow and set off axis. This alone should lead one to doubt the identification of the building as a church. It is entered through a doorway in the north-west corner and has a stairway in the south-western room. The Abd el-Qadir structure is perhaps a little more convincing but again an identification as a house appears equally probable.[26]

LATER NOBADIAN CHURCHES

With Type 1 churches we are on firmer ground. These are basically basilican in plan with the sanctuary chamber at the eastern end in the centre, a nave flanked by one or two aisles to each side and, in the larger churches, a *narthex* stretching across the western end of the building. The arrangement of the western end of the building showed some variation at this period. The nave is frequently wider than the sanctuary chamber and is also wider than the aisles, a feature which is later taken to indicate that galleries were provided over the aisles. The earliest of the basilican churches may be the Mud Church at Faras. Little of it was uncovered by excavation but enough to show that it was a rectangular three-aisled church with the three rooms at the eastern end, the central apsed sanctuary chamber directly connected by doorways to the pastafories, and there was a *narthex* at the west end. The use of mud brick in an area with a long tradition of construction in stone may, perhaps, be for liturgical rather than technical reasons, 'the first church built after the Christianization of the country was constructed of the earth of the country in question which nothing had yet sullied.'[27] This tradition may be connected with the later practice of providing a foundation deposit of mud bricks at the corners of religious structures regardless of what materials they were constructed from.[28] The Mud Church was replaced, probably in the second decade of the seventh century, by a rectangular stone structure, a three-aisled basilica, of basically the same plan as that suggested for the Mud Church, with a very wide

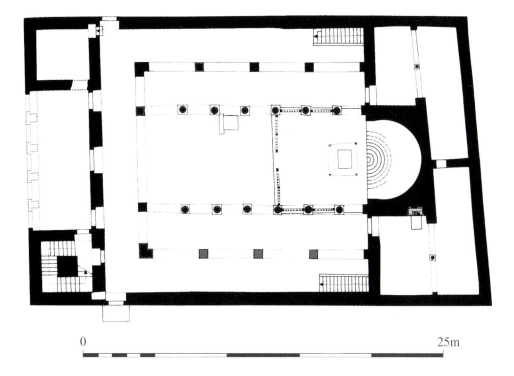

Figure 56 **The cathedral at Qasr Ibrim (after Gartkiewicz 1982c, fig. 4).**

nave separated from the aisles by columns. A tribune was inserted into the apse, possibly during the second half of the seventh century.[29] The use of dressed stone may reflect in part the ready source of reusable material from Kushite structures on the site.

The other major basilican church was constructed at Qasr Ibrim. Of the Old Church very little is known but its successor, probably built in the later half of the seventh century, is still well-preserved (Figs 42, 56 and 102). It is a five-aisled basilica with a wide nave and apse the latter flanked by two pastafories. The west end had an *esonarthex* and a triple-portalled entrance on the main axis through a vestibule flanked by two rooms, the south-western containing the staircase. The northern room appears to have been removed during the medieval period and virtually no trace of it remains. The *haikal* extended along the first three bays of the nave. Behind the apse are two rooms running across the east end of the church, with a wall through which is a narrow door separating them, behind the apse. Beneath these rooms are barrel-vaulted crypts 2 m high entered down two flights of stairs from the north and south outer aisles. Dug into the floor of the crypts are graves, four in the southern crypt and two in the northern crypt. The tribune of stone was an original feature. Like the church at Faras it was built from dressed stone presumably derived from the redundant Kushite religious monuments.[30] The later Kushite Temple 4 may have been totally demolished down to its foundations at this time to provide the required material for the cathedral, the lower 2 m of which is constructed of large blocks taken from the temple. Above that the smaller blocks may have been quarried from nearby on the hilltop.

The nave and aisles were paved in well-fitted stone slabs, two intersecting lines of which in the centre of the building form a cross design. Although described by Abu Salih as having a prominent dome on structural grounds this seems unlikely. The building never seems to have been provided with vaulted roofs, the timber roof either survived intact throughout the life of the building or it was partly unroofed later in its history, as seems most likely in view of the evidence for the collapse of the south arcade during the medieval

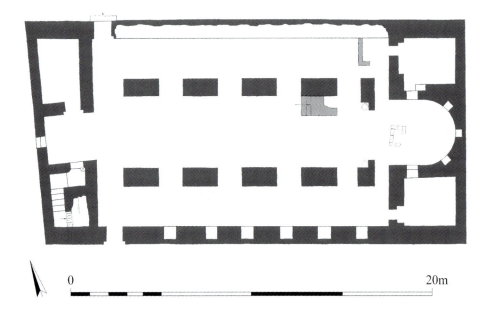

Figure 57 **The Southern Church (Site 40) at Serra East (after Säve-Söderbergh 1970, fig. 22).**

period. This destruction may have been associated with the Ayyubid invasion of the late twelfth century. Thereafter many of the columns were toppled and sealed by a new floor of earth.[31]

Adams includes two variations within Type 2. Type 2a churches (Fig. 57) are so similar in plan, so idiosyncratic in a number of their features, and so restricted in location, as to suggest that they were designed by the same architect. Each has three niches in the apse wall, the sanctuary has doorways communicating with the flanking rooms and is extended well to the west of the sacristies, the whole *haikal* being covered by a vaulted extension of the apse hemidome.[32] The nave is markedly wider, than both the sanctuary and the aisles, and the two western rooms have asymmetrical entrances. The triumphal arch is also distinctive with monolithic columns. Galleries were provided over the aisles and across the western end of the building and the whole structure was roofed with mud-brick vaults. Windows in the external walls of the galleries allowed indirect lighting of the nave. The other sub-type had the same basic plan, but the nave and aisles and the sanctuary are of not dissimilar width and the other details noted above are not present.

In the Classic Christian period churches of Type 3 were the norm. These are divided into three sub-types. Type 3a are earlier churches modified at this time, particularly with

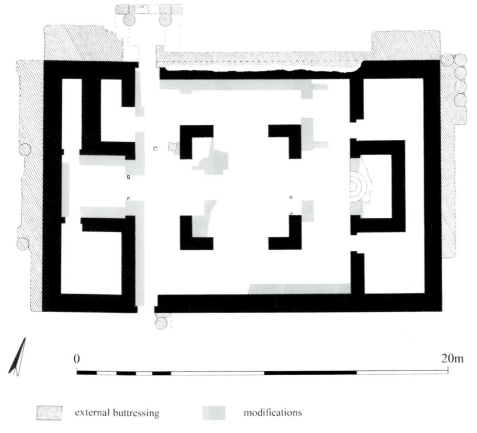

external buttressing   modifications

Figure 58 **An Adams' Type 3b church at Nuri (after Dunham 1955, fig. 216).**

the introduction of the tribune and the modifications to the *bema* that that entailed. Types 3b and 3c are characterized by the presence of the eastern passage although type 3b does not appear to have a tribune. In only one case was an earlier church modified to provide an eastern passage. The central part of the Type 3b (Fig. 58) and 3c churches is frequently crowned by a centrally placed dome.

The Late Christian churches of Type 4 were much smaller than their predecessors, they are much squarer in plan and the centrally placed dome is a diagnostic feature. There is much greater variation in their internal arrangement. Eastern passages are rare, the sanctuary chamber at ground level is rectangular, although perhaps in some cases covered by a hemidome above, there is no tribune and no *presbyterium*. The western rooms are not always present and may be represented by a single stairwell in the south-west corner.[33] Among the best preserved was the South Church at Serra East (Figs 44 and 59). Externally measuring 9.1 x 6.3 m it was a two-storey building with a prominent dome over the eastern bay of the nave.[34] Another church of this type, at Kulubnarti, has a single storey, the roof above the vaults, accessible by the usual stairway, was provided with a parapet 400 mm thick.[35]

Adams cites only two examples for his epitype, Type (?)5, from Diffinarti and Abd el-Qadir. They are extremely small, 'the "aisles" ... are barely wide enough for a man to turn

IV **The fortress at Qasr Ibrim** (*photo W. Y. Adams*).

V **The fortress at Shofein near the Third Cataract.**

I The crypt of archbishop Giorgios in the Monastery of the Holy Trinity at Old Dongola *(photo B. Żurawski)*.

II Tomb of the bishop Petros adjacent to the Church on the South Slope of the Kom, Faras *(courtesy of the SARS Haycock archive)*.

III Christ healing a blind man at the Pool of Siloam. Wall painting in the Monastery of the Holy Trinity at Old Dongola.

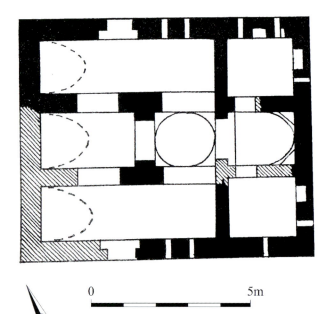

Figure 59 **The South Church at Serra East (after Monneret de Villard 1935, figs 196 and 197).**

0   5m

around', and both have a single room across the whole of the eastern end of the building. Diffinarti has a stairwell in the south-west corner, and a centrally placed western entrance while Abd el-Qadir is entered from the north and south. There are chapels associated with the church at Abd el-Qadir which significantly increased the surface area available within the complex.[36]

In the description of his methodology Adams states that he dated the churches wherever possible directly from epigraphic and archaeological data and used those dates to assign a date range to the types. His basic dating, therefore, for the area covered in detail by his study, still remains valid, and as he notes, the total destruction of virtually all these churches makes further empirical study impossible.

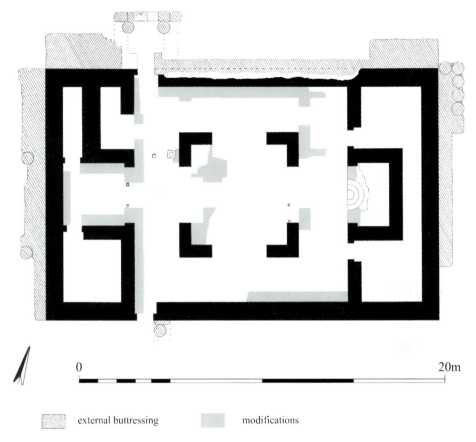

external buttressing   modifications

Figure 58 **An Adams' Type 3b church at Nuri (after Dunham 1955, fig. 216).**

the introduction of the tribune and the modifications to the *bema* that that entailed. Types 3b and 3c are characterized by the presence of the eastern passage although type 3b does not appear to have a tribune. In only one case was an earlier church modified to provide an eastern passage. The central part of the Type 3b (Fig. 58) and 3c churches is frequently crowned by a centrally placed dome.

The Late Christian churches of Type 4 were much smaller than their predecessors, they are much squarer in plan and the centrally placed dome is a diagnostic feature. There is much greater variation in their internal arrangement. Eastern passages are rare, the sanctuary chamber at ground level is rectangular, although perhaps in some cases covered by a hemidome above, there is no tribune and no *presbyterium*. The western rooms are not always present and may be represented by a single stairwell in the south-west corner.[33] Among the best preserved was the South Church at Serra East (Figs 44 and 59). Externally measuring 9.1 x 6.3 m it was a two-storey building with a prominent dome over the eastern bay of the nave.[34] Another church of this type, at Kulubnarti, has a single storey, the roof above the vaults, accessible by the usual stairway, was provided with a parapet 400 mm thick.[35]

Adams cites only two examples for his epitype, Type (?)5, from Diffinarti and Abd el-Qadir. They are extremely small, 'the "aisles" ... are barely wide enough for a man to turn

Table 4. Chronology of Nubian church types as proposed by W.Y. Adams.

Type	Designation	Est. Dates
?0	Prototype	500-650
T	Converted temples	550-1100
1	Basilican	
1a	Great	550-750
1b	Small	550-750
2	Early Nubian	
2a	Fancy	650-800
2b	Simple	650-800
3	Classic Nubian	
3a	Converted	750-1100
3b	Incomplete	750-850
3c	Complete	800-1250
4	Late Nubian	1150-1400
?5	Epitype	1350+

UPPER NUBIAN CHURCHES

Since the end of the Aswan High Dam rescue campaign the focus of archaeological activity has shifted southwards. Qasr Ibrim remains the only archaeological site within the area of the reservoir that survived the inundation and where work on its medieval antiquities, including its churches, is still in progress. Many churches have now been excavated in Makuria[37] and seven in Alwa[38] allowing us to some extent to attempt a much broader view of Nubian ecclesiastical architecture than it was possible for Adams to undertake. On the negative side a small number of buildings in the region of the Fifth Cataract at Gandeisi, el-Koro and el-'Usheir, hitherto considered as churches, can probably now be removed from the discussion.[39]

What is immediately obvious is that what may be the norm for churches within the territory of Nobadia does not necessarily hold good for regions further to the south. The importance of Old Dongola as a major architectural centre and the influence it exerted on Nobadia can be readily demonstrated. The relationship between Alwan and Makurian church architecture remains problematic. We simply do not yet have enough evidence to allow us to assess whether the metropolitan architecture of Old Dongola was a major influence on the architects of Alwa, or indeed, whether it was not the other way round.

MAKURIAN CHURCHES

Excavations begun in 1964 at Old Dongola, and still underway, have revealed the plans of a large number of churches which do not conform to the developmental sequence advanced by Adams for the churches of Lower Nubia. Many of these churches were of large size; they were prestigious buildings which were perhaps in many cases the earliest expression of particular developments which then served to influence architects elsewhere. The earliest church known at Old Dongola is the Old Church, dated to the middle of the sixth century, which was constructed of mud brick, perhaps, like the earliest church at

Faras, for liturgical reasons. It was a three-aisled basilica, with the nave twice as wide as the aisles, and the roof supported on large rectangular piers. The eastern half of the building was widened and had a range of three rooms by the east wall, with a small chamber behind the apse while the western parts of the aisles formed 'dwarf transepts'. To the south-west a stairwell, the entrance to the building, and a chapel filled in the rectangle. The *haikal* extended into the nave and was bounded by a *higab* and the masonry altar stood in front of the apse which was occupied by a tribunal. The *diaconicum* housed a 'walk-through' baptismal font for total immersion. Close by, and of similar date, stood Building X which exhibits many of the features of the typical Nubian Church plan. It was of considerable size, 33.4 x 23.6 m, and was constructed of red brick. There was a range of five rooms across the eastern end, the pastafories linked by an eastern passage. Towards the west end was an *esonarthex* and beyond that were three rooms, with a stairwell occupying the northern room. The central vestibule leading to the main entrance lay on the long axis. It had a clear cross-in-rectangle, centrally-planned *naos*. The nature of the superstructure and of the roofing is unclear although it has been suggested that the cruciform central part of the structure was carried higher than the rest of the building. The presence of two crypts beneath the apse indicate that it is a memorial church.[40] These two churches, the only ones in Makuria so far known which date to the sixth century, exhibit many features which can be paralleled in the Byzantine world but also have a number of features which were to become characteristic of Nubian churches.

In the early seventh century Building X was demolished and replaced by the Church of the Stone Pavement which conformed exactly to the dimensions of the earlier building and the plans of the eastern and western parts of the building remained identical, although the floor of the new building lay 1 m above that of its predecessor. What is of considerable interest is what seems to be the reversal of the trends documented in Nobadian churches by Adams, the change from a centrally-planned structure to one of basilican plan, with five aisles separated by rows of red granite columns. The nave is wider than the aisles and also wider than the apse of the sanctuary chamber which is extended into the first two bays of the nave. The baptistery occupies the room immediately to the south of the apse. Access to the crypts was still maintained. It has been suggested that this building functioned as the cathedral of Old Dongola.[41]

The Church of the Granite Columns (Fig. 60 and colour plate IX) was built in the later seventh century and is one of the finest of Nubian ecclesiastical buildings, probably the model for the best known of Nubian churches, the cathedral at Faras. It was a five-aisled structure, with the nave much wider than the aisles. The apsidal sanctuary chamber dominated the long axis while the short axis also terminated in apses to north and south, the back external walls of which were inset from the building line within wide niches. Flanking these apses were rooms against the external walls, that at the west being a *narthex* running the full width of the building and entered from its south end. The interior has a markedly cruciform aspect, the wide intercolumnation across the nave being mirrored by the columns flanking the short axis between its terminal apses. This cross-in-square plan is readily recognizable in the Faras cathedral and perhaps also in Church B at Soba East (colour plate X and Fig. 35).

Dating probably from the ninth century, and replacing the Church of the Stone

Pavement which was demolished to make way for it, is the Cruciform Church (Fig. 61a). This highly unusual building consists of a central space 14 m square with arms radiating out on each side through two columned porticos. The inner part of each arm is 7.15 m wide, the outer part being reduced to a width of 3.4 m. The north and south arms had entrances leading into them, while the eastern arm, which was longer than the others, may have been a commemorative chapel as it sits directly over the crypts first constructed as a part of Building X. The structure is built of red brick with walls 1.1 m thick surviving to a maximum height of 4 m. Stone architectural fragments found within the building, some in situ, indicate that the lower porticos had elements in grey granite attaining a height of 6.3 m, while the bases, columns and capitals of a second storey approximately 2.7 m high were of red granite. The excavator suggested that the walls of the central part of the building were carried to a height of approximately 14 m and that they supported a dome. In the central area were four additional columns 6.6 m high set on 2.15 m high bases, actually column shafts set deeply into the ground. These do not appear to have had any structural connection with the roofing in the area and it is suggested that they may have supported horizontal beams for the suspension of lamps.[42]

Figure 60 **The Church of the Granite Columns (after Godlewski 1992, fig. 20).**

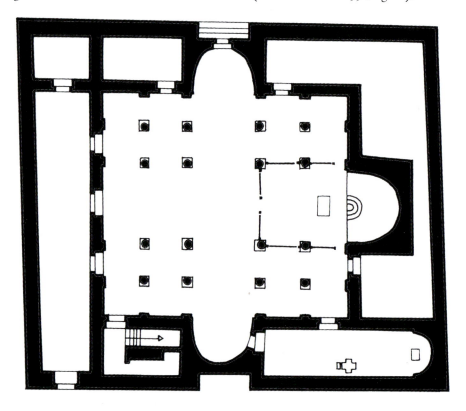

0   25m

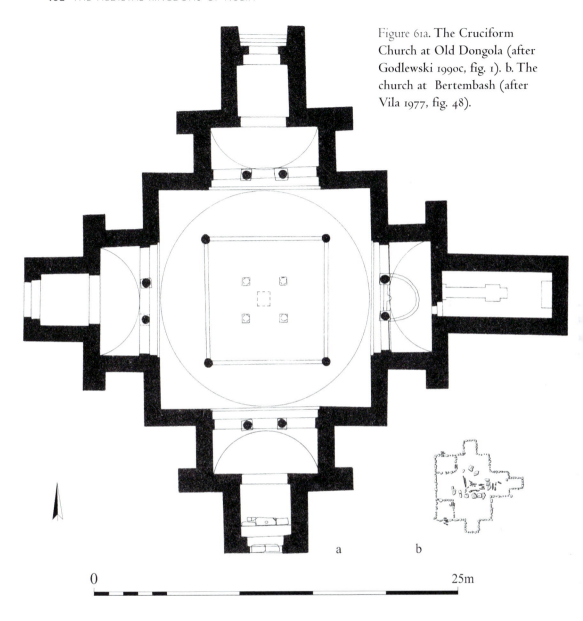

Figure 61a. **The Cruciform Church at Old Dongola** (after Godlewski 1990c, fig. 1). b. The church at Bertembash (after Vila 1977, fig. 48).

a   b

0   25m

  Although the Cruciform Church can be paralleled among martyria in Palestine, Syria and Asia Minor few similar churches are known in Nubia. The closest of these in form, if not in scale, is what must be the strangest of all Nubian churches known, at Bertenbash immediately upstream of the Dal Cataract. The Bertenbash church is small, measuring only 6 x 6 m. The plan is very similar to the Cruciform Church with the three arms to the east, north and south being reduced in size towards their extremities, a feature lacking in the western arm (Fig. 61b). The square spaces between the western arm and those to north and south are enclosed giving the appearance of the tripartite division common to the standard Nubian church design. No evidence remains for the positions of the doorways

which is not surprising as the 'walls' of the church consist of a single row of rough blocks of quartz with maximum dimensions of 300 x 150 mm. The church is nothing more than the plan of a building marked out on the ground by the blocks.[43] Although no other church of this type is known such structures would so easily have been destroyed by later activity. If there were more of this type it may explain why, at some villages, there appears to have been no place of worship.

The Church of the Angels at Tamit, downstream of the Second Cataract,[44] is basically a standard Nubian church but extended on its long and short axes to give a cruciform appearance. The apsidal sanctuary chamber and its contraposed apse in the central area between the two western rooms project boldly within their rectangular casing beyond the building line while the other axis is similarly extended beyond the building line by two rectangular projections which act as vestibules. Internally the spatial effect will have been not dissimilar to that of the Cruciform Church although in plan it also has much in common with the arrangement of such churches as the Church of the Granite Columns. Another church of this basic form is the North-West Church at Old Dongola where both axes terminate in apses contained within rooms projecting beyond the main building line.[45]

Adams' Type 4 is represented at Old Dongola by the Northern Church, built probably in the late thirteenth century. It is 11.5 m square but its thick walls at 1.2 m greatly reduce the internal area of the building. It was crowned by a central dome probably set on a circular drum pierced by windows.[46]

Away from Old Dongola few other Makurian churches are known in detail. However, the monastic church at el-Ghazali, the church at Nuri (Fig. 58) and probably also that at Bakhit are of typical Nubian type as defined by Adams.[47]

ALWAN CHURCHES

The Alwan churches known to us fall into three types although the number of examples assigned to each is pitifully small.[48] Of the 400 churches recorded in the territory of Alwa by Abu Salih[49] most have yet to be located. The church on mound C and Churches A and B at Soba East, are large basilican buildings (Fig. 35) which allow comparison with the largest churches at Old Dongola, Faras and Qasr Ibrim. The Saqadi church was inserted into a pre-existing building the nature of which is uncertain,[50] while Church E at Soba and Temple IIIA at Musawwarat es-Sufra are the only 'normal' churches so far excavated. Building C may have had a special function. The church on mound C is the only Alwan church known to make use of stone columns. What little is recorded of its plan suggests that it may have had a nave with a length of approximately 13.5 m, that is of the same order of magnitude as Churches A and B. Its totally denuded state is good evidence that it was built throughout of red brick.

Churches A and B are of similar size, were constructed of red brick and lie immediately adjacent to each other. In plan, however, they are markedly different and are also, like most of the churches of similar size in Nubia, each unique (Fig. 35). Three main phases were noted in Church A. Of the first phase little survived apart from the barrel-vaulted crypts. In phase II the building was a five-aisled basilica, the inner aisles separated from the nave by large brick piers. The church was entered through a 12.5 m wide, three-portalled entrance in the centre of the west wall which led into a *narthex* which, at least to the south,

was not divided from the southern aisle. The north and south aisle also had entrances 14.5 m wide, the lintels supported on four timber posts of 360 mm square scantling.[51] The sanctuary chamber, flanked by two rooms, extended further to the east and had a semi-circular apse. Across the eastern end of the church were two long rooms to either side of the centrally-placed square room which lay above the crypts. It projected to the east of the building line and was entered from the east by a narrow doorway. Although the timber altar stood in the apse the *haikal* extended into the nave and vestibules were provided at the east end of the inner aisles; the presbytery being delimited by brick walls pierced by doorways from the west. There was no obvious means of communication from the north vestibule to the *haikal*. In the third phase the north and south entrances were suppressed and larger pier bases supported the roof over the nave. The walls dividing off the vestibules were demolished as was the *higab*, the latter being replaced by a *higab* of wood while the whole of the *haikal* was provided with a floor of white and dolomitic marble (colour plate VII).[52]

In almost all cases the foundations of Church B were continued across doorways and wider openings. As a result of this, and of the building having been so heavily robbed, it is impossible to ascertain whether a wall was solid or not. It is hence uncertain whether this was a five-aisled basilica or a three-aisled structure surrounded to the north, south and west by an additional range of rooms. It certainly has a 11.5 m wide three-portalled entrance through the west wall leading into a *narthex* or *exonarthex*. At the east end the central of the five rooms projects a little beyond the building line and was, probably during the construction phase, provided with a small apse projecting still further to the east. The timber altar stood in the centre of the sanctuary chamber and the pulpit occupied the usual position on the north side of the nave. A stairway occupied a room towards the south-west corner. The internal arrangement may have had much in common with the Church of the Granite Columns at Old Dongola and the Faras Cathedral with a clear cruciform shape contained within the centre of the structure by the recessed entrance to the sanctuary chamber, out into the *esonarthex* and the recesses to north and south.[53]

Church C in its first phase had a range of five rooms at the east end, the central one projecting a little to the east. It was similar to the two larger churches but was shorn of its outer aisles. Like them it had a *narthex* with a centrally placed entrance.[54] Church E is of unique plan among Nubian churches but whether it was unusual in an Alwan context is unknown. Like the church at Saqadi it had a brick *higab*.[55] The so-called Temple IIIA at Musawwarat is a slightly skewed rectangular structure 8.63-8.87 x 7.41-7.67 m in size. There is a range of three rooms across the eastern end, the central one with a wide opening from the west where there is a large room with two columns supporting the roof and dividing it into the suggestion of a nave and aisles. It is entered by a centrally-placed doorway and also by doorways to the north and south set well to the west of the centre line of the room.[56] This may actually be a Kushite temple converted into a church, although its form can be paralleled in churches built from scratch, and the presence of the doorways to north and south is a particularly Christian feature. The large number of red bricks, some bearing Christian symbols, derive from a reconstruction of the roof of the temple according to the excavator.[57]

Influences on Nubian Church Architecture

As has been touched upon above Nubian church architecture was open to influences from a number of sources chief among which were Egypt, Syria and Armenia. To these one may add Ethiopia, at least as a potential source. It is clear that not all influences filtered through to Nubia progressively up the Nile. Certainly Egyptian influences were of particular importance at an early period but some of the very earliest churches are more related to ecclesiastical architecture further afield, and their design may have been introduced by the apostles of Nubia along with Christianity itself. The cross-in-rectangle plan as seen in the Church of the Granite Columns at Old Dongola is a Syrian, not an Egyptian, form.[58] Later other Syrian and Armenian influences are found in Nubia which appear not to have made an impact on Egypt. These new architectural styles may have been introduced by the presence of natives of those areas in Nubia or by ideas brought back by Nubians travelling in foreign lands. We should not think of the Nubians as cut off from the Middle East and there was probably a steady flow of knowledge relating to events in the orthodox Christian world to the north. Gartkiewicz considered that on stylistic grounds the small blockwork used in the construction of the cathedral at Qasr Ibrim suggests that it was built by Syrian stoneworkers,[59] and the presence of Byzantine technicians involved in the building of one of Nubia's earliest churches at Ikhmindi is recorded on its building inscription.[60] Gartkiewicz traces a number of sources of inspiration for some of the most important churches at Old Dongola. The Church of the Granite Columns he sees as a fusion of the basilican and Classic Nubian church type, as exemplified in Lower Nubia, with the bi-axial plan with an apse at each end typified by church design in Armenia in the fifth to seventh centuries. Nubian antecedents for the Cruciform Church are not known but its relationship with mausolea and martyria in Syria/Palestine and Greece is clear.[61]

A close relationship between Nubian and Ethiopian ecclesiastical architecture might be expected, but as with much else to do with contacts between the two Christian areas there is little evidence for it. Ethiopian churches show many features common to Aksumite architecture which are totally alien to the architectural traditions on the Middle Nile. A number of features can be paralleled in Nubian and Ethiopian church design but there is an equally large number where there are marked differences. The relationship between the two may be more one connected with their common roots in Byzantine church architecture than of direct links between them.[62] Influences in architecture from the Islamic world, with which the Nubian kingdoms coexisted for many centuries, might be expected. The Nubian churches with the multi-bayed hall arrangement, assumed to have been roofed with a complex of similar domes, may have been influenced by mosque designs and similar buildings are also found in an ecclesiastical context in Egypt.[63]

Nubian churches, functional types

Several different functional church types can be recognized.

COMMUNITY CHURCHES

The most common are those which served the needs of the community; their size was presumably related to that of the local congregation. A number of the smaller settlements

had one or two churches which will fall into this type. Not all communities had a church and therefore some churches may have catered for the needs of a district rather than a single settlement, hence they may be disproportionately large when compared with the community within which they lay.

CATHEDRALS

Of the much larger churches a number can be recognized as the bishop's church, the cathedral of a diocese. Churches of this type include the main church at Qasr Ibrim, the cathedral at Faras, probably the partly upstanding church at Sai and probably one of the known churches at Old Dongola and Soba East. The Faras and Qasr Ibrim cathedrals (Fig. 55) are large five-aisled buildings 24.8 x 22.75 m (564 m²) and *c.* 32-30.7 x 19 m (596 m²) in size respectively. At Old Dongola there are several buildings of similar dimensions but, given the special function of those churches on the site of Building X, it may have been the Old Church, and its successor the Church of the Granite Columns, which was the cathedral church. The Church of the Granite Columns was 29 x 24.4 m in size (697 m²) and was probably the model for the Faras cathedral. The most likely candidate for the cathedral at Soba East is the Church on mound C of which unfortunately so little is known. Its use of columns suggests the possibility that it is earlier than the other large

Figure 62 **Adams' Nubian church types (after Adams 1965b, figs 5-14).**

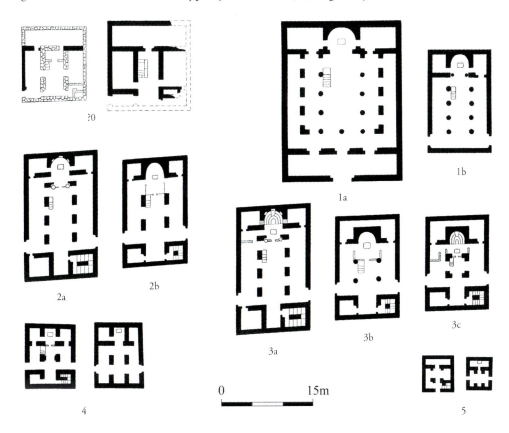

churches at the western end of mound B. Cathedral churches almost invariably have an adjacent smaller church, leading to the suggestion by Adams that the latter were only used by the clergy and he cites the evidence for the absence of *higab* in many of these buildings as a further indication of this.[64]

MONASTIC CHURCHES

A church was an integral part at least in those monastic complexes of coenobic type in Nubia. Churches are known within those complexes at Qasr el-Wizz, at Old Dongola and el-Ghazali and one was almost certainly present at el-Ugal. Where known in detail they do not appear to differ from the style of churches found in many Nubian settlements nor are they of dissimilar size.

MEMORIAL CHURCHES

Some of the largest and most ambitious churches fall into this category. Building X, the Church of the Stone Pavement, and the Cruciform Church, were built successively on the same site. The earliest building was provided with the two crypts under its apse and these were the main focus of the other two buildings. The highly unusual plan and grandiose nature of the Cruciform Church has already been noted and parallels for such structures in the eastern Mediterranean, which are also martyria, are known. Godlewski has suggested that the Cruciform Church may have had a dual function, the central part of the building being devoted to the veneration of the holy cross.[65] The two large churches, A and B at Soba East, one with a prominent crypt, the other with a large tomb to the east of their sanctuary chambers, may also have been erected in honour of the persons buried in or by them.

A much smaller, but probably also a memorial church, built of stone and of unique plan, is Church EDC at Old Dongola. This is the only Nubian church known where the external rounded wall of the apse is visible and projects boldly to the east (Fig. 54). Immediately to the south of the church is a vaulted tomb; both are bounded by the walls of an enclosure forming part of a large complex.[66]

Outside of a metropolis, the church at Debeira may also be a memorial church with a tomb directly below the tribune within the apse.[67] At Tamit and Serra, the superabundance of churches suggest that these had a special function. There is no structural evidence to indicate that they were monastic communities and there seem to be far too many to cater for the local communities. However in the case of Serra, where the late medieval town huddled for protection within the Pharaonic walls, it may be that each church belonged to the people of a separate community which had to be abandoned in the troubled times during the gradual break-up of Makuria.[68] No similar reasoning can be adduced to explain the situation at Tamit.

DOUBLE CATHEDRALS AND CHURCHES

These are not uncommon in the Late Roman and Byzantine world and they appear to have a variety of functions, among them providing accommodation for summer and winter services or association with double dedications, with cults of the martyrs, and of baptism.[69] They can either consist of two contemporary structures or are buildings of differing dates, although often connected physically by a *narthex* or ancillary buildings.[70] The spatial

relationship of the two large churches, A and B, at Soba East is suggestive of the presence of this church type in Nubia (Fig. 35). A similar juxtaposition of churches is to be seen at Tamit where there are two large churches with a smaller church abutting onto the southerly one at the north-east end of the settlement, and two other examples, the Church of St Raphael and its neighbour 2 m to the north-west.[71] A rather different arrangement of what may have been a double church has been observed at Kulubnarti although the extremely poor preservation of this building leads to serious problems regarding its interpretation. The eastern building is certainly a church of standard type. To the west it is abutted by, or abuts, a rectangular building of very similar dimensions which may also be a church.[72]

CHAPELS

Secondary chapels are associated with a number of churches. That abutting the late church at Abd el-Qadir is almost as large as the church itself. A number of rooms identified as chapels have been identified within the monastic complex on Kom H at Old Dongola. One is closely associated with the as yet unexcavated church[73] while others are within the complex of rooms outside the confines of the original monastery to the north-west in what is considered to be a *xenon*. One of these is Room 29 3.5 x 1.6 m in size. There is a square structure against one wall, presumably an altar, the walls are covered with wall paintings among which are representations of Christ and the Twelve Apostles while there is also a large inscription written in ink, part of the liturgy of the Holy Mass.[74]

BAPTISTERIES

The provision of a baptismal font is a very common feature of Nubian churches. In the temple-church at Kalabsha one was inserted into the south-east corner of the hypostyle hall of the temple.[75] In the temple at Wadi es-Sebua the baptistery occupied a similar position in the court but structurally lay outside the church.[76] In purpose-built churches with a range of three rooms at the east end the baptistery almost invariably occupies the south-eastern room. In the larger churches with five rooms it again occupies that immediately to the south of the sanctuary. Other locations for the baptismal font include the south-eastern part of the nave, (possibly) the south-western part of the nave, in an additional room in the south-eastern part of the church (Faras cathedral and Church of the Granite Columns at Old Dongola) or possibly outside the church either to the south or to the north. Such independent baptisteries have been tentatively identified adjacent to the first cathedral at Faras, the monastic church at el-Ghazali and Church A at Soba East.[77]

Early baptismal fonts were designed for total immersion: they have a deep circular basin which could be entered by a flight of steps leading down into them from the east and often also from the west. Godlewski suggests that this type is suited for the baptism of adults and is associated with the earliest phase of Christianity in Nubia. In the Old Church at Old Dongola the font of this type was modified in the second phase when the western steps were separated from the basin by a wall. The later form has a single flight of steps on the west side, again separated from the basin by a wall, presumably indicating that total immersion was no longer practised. Subterranean fonts of cruciform and rectangular form were progressively replaced by stone or ceramic tanks, a fine stone example of late date from the Church of the Granite Columns having a square base tapering cylindrical shaft

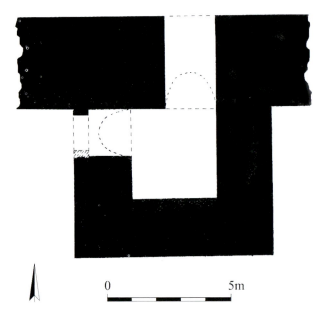

Figure 63 **The north tower-gate at Sabaqura (after Monneret de Villard 1935, fig. 37).**

the gateways the walls are faced with dressed blocks as are the passageways.[86] Approximately 20 m in advance of the west wall is a flat-bottomed ditch, the lower 2 m is vertical and revetted in mud brick with mud plaster rendering, while above that the sides slope at an angle of 60°.[87] The gateway at Sheikh Daud is very similar in many details to the main gates at Faras. Diversity is, however to be found in the materials used, the upper parts of the walls being of coursed rubble.[88] At Kalabsha the whole of the walls are constructed of this coursed rubble and the wall faces are battered to increase stability.[89]

Where examined in detail in the vicinity of the north-west angle, the curtain wall at Old Dongola (Fig. 29) is built of mud brick and is approximately 4.1 m thick at the base with a slightly battered outer face. Along the north side of the circuit and for 15 m along the west wall south of the angle tower the lower 1.5 m is revetted with large stone blocks. Further to the south, where the wall stands atop the very steep slope down to the river, the natural strength of the defences presumably rendered the additional strengthening of the wall with a stone facing unnecessary. The wall still survives to a height of 6 m.[90] At the north-west angle and spaced along the curtain, more closely set along the more tightly curving sections of the walls so that the defenders on the towers were still able to enfilade the intervening curtains, are massive projecting towers with rounded fronts. At the north-west angle tower the stone revetment is carried to a height of 5.1 m and consists of two rows of carefully fitted large stone blocks a total of 1.2-1.5 m in thickness.

Extending to the north of the tower to enclose a triangular area of flat ground immediately beyond the defences was a wall 3.1 m thick constructed of bricks of identical size to those used in the main wall, 435 x 210 x 80 mm. On the west side of this wall and contemporary with it an elaborate substructure was built to provide a terrace on the steep slope down to the river, but unfortunately no trace now remains of the structure it was designed to support. It has been suggested that this must have had a military function but what that might have been is unclear. In the aftermath of the siege of Old Dongola in 652 this mud-brick wall was strengthened by at least two rectangular towers using *spolia* in their foundations (Fig. 30) perhaps indicative of the haste with which they were built.[91]

Estabel is defended by a wall of mud brick and stone. At Bakhit the walls are constructed of undressed stone and mud brick and are strengthened by eighteen boldly projecting semi-circular towers set at intervals of approximately 25-30 m.[92]

and circular basin.[78] A sandstone baptismal font with spouted lip at Arminna West had a hole in the bottom lined with lead which probably connected to a pipe to allow for the draining of the font.[79]

No baptistery has yet been definitely identified in an Alwan church. However, outside and immediately to the south of Church A at Soba East was a rectangular mud-brick structure 6.1 x 5.1 m in size, in the centre of which was a slightly bow-sided tank 2.6 x 2.3 m with its floor 0.5 m below the contemporary ground surface. The tank was divided by a low partition wall and the whole of the floor and the interior face of the walls was rendered in a white lime plaster. If this was a baptistery it is of a unique type. No provision remained to indicate how neophytes may have left the water.[80] A sub-rectangular ceramic tank 972 x 642 mm in size and approximately 320 mm deep was found dumped within a construction pit in Building F. Although the presence of an outlet by the base cannot be paralleled in other baptismal fonts the large cross in relief on its wall suggests that it had a religious function.[81] A not dissimilar ceramic dish 'rather like a bath' was found in the south-eastern room of the church R-44 at Debeira West.[82] As this room is usually used as a baptistery in Nubian churches this dish presumably was the font. Another, bearing an invocation to John the Baptist painted on the rim, a cross in relief within the tank at either end, and two painted pentagrams, was found in the baptistery of the church on the North Kom at Hambukol.[83]

Fortifications

These comprise the largest single building projects undertaken by the medieval Nubians. As so few Kushite fortifications are known it is difficult to assess how much the construction of early Nubian defences owed to earlier local designs.[84] Many of the fortifications of the early medieval period have much in common with the contemporary defences in the Late Roman Empire. The chain of square forts between the confluence of the Niles and Kurgus and the trapezoidal enclosures between Faras and Kalabsha with their projecting angle and interval towers and angled gate-passages can be directly compared to fortifications in Syria and elsewhere.[85]

The curtain wall at Faras is nearly 4 m thick and survived into the 1960s on the west wall to its full height of 11.6 m. The lower 4 m is constructed of small stone blocks, many reused from earlier structures, the south-west tower in particular contains many blocks from a temple of Ramesses II, while above that it was of mud brick. At the angles are substantial square external towers projecting 10 m while, spaced at regular intervals along the curtain, are slightly smaller, approximately 7 m, square to rectangular towers. The lower part of all but one of the towers is solid but there was presumably a chamber above and a narrow passage at one tower leading from a doorway in the rear face of the curtain wall indicates that this was a little over 6 m above ground level. Access to this doorway was presumably by wooden staircase or by ladder of which no trace remained. Two main gates survived in the centre of the south and west walls. These are set within projecting towers a little larger than the interval towers. The gate passage is entered through an arched doorway, springing from moulded imposts, in the side wall and then turns through 90°, through the curtain, into the enclosure (cf. Fig. 63). Another gate on the wall alongside the river is a simple opening 1.25 m wide with no trace of a protecting tower visible. At

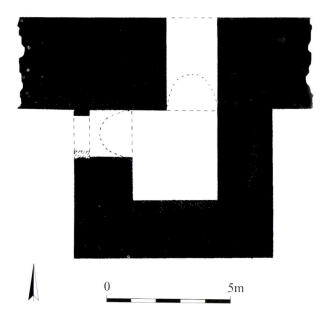

Figure 63 **The north tower-gate at Sabaqura (after Monneret de Villard 1935, fig. 37).**

0   5m

the gateways the walls are faced with dressed blocks as are the passageways.[86] Approximately 20 m in advance of the west wall is a flat-bottomed ditch, the lower 2 m is vertical and revetted in mud brick with mud plaster rendering, while above that the sides slope at an angle of 60°.[87] The gateway at Sheikh Daud is very similar in many details to the main gates at Faras. Diversity is, however to be found in the materials used, the upper parts of the walls being of coursed rubble.[88] At Kalabsha the whole of the walls are constructed of this coursed rubble and the wall faces are battered to increase stability.[89]

Where examined in detail in the vicinity of the north-west angle, the curtain wall at Old Dongola (Fig. 29) is built of mud brick and is approximately 4.1 m thick at the base with a slightly battered outer face. Along the north side of the circuit and for 15 m along the west wall south of the angle tower the lower 1.5 m is revetted with large stone blocks. Further to the south, where the wall stands atop the very steep slope down to the river, the natural strength of the defences presumably rendered the additional strengthening of the wall with a stone facing unnecessary. The wall still survives to a height of 6 m.[90] At the north-west angle and spaced along the curtain, more closely set along the more tightly curving sections of the walls so that the defenders on the towers were still able to enfilade the intervening curtains, are massive projecting towers with rounded fronts. At the north-west angle tower the stone revetment is carried to a height of 5.1 m and consists of two rows of carefully fitted large stone blocks a total of 1.2-1.5 m in thickness.

Extending to the north of the tower to enclose a triangular area of flat ground immediately beyond the defences was a wall 3.1 m thick constructed of bricks of identical size to those used in the main wall, 435 x 210 x 80 mm. On the west side of this wall and contemporary with it an elaborate substructure was built to provide a terrace on the steep slope down to the river, but unfortunately no trace now remains of the structure it was designed to support. It has been suggested that this must have had a military function but what that might have been is unclear. In the aftermath of the siege of Old Dongola in 652 this mud-brick wall was strengthened by at least two rectangular towers using *spolia* in their foundations (Fig. 30) perhaps indicative of the haste with which they were built.[91]

Estabel is defended by a wall of mud brick and stone. At Bakhit the walls are constructed of undressed stone and mud brick and are strengthened by eighteen boldly projecting semi-circular towers set at intervals of approximately 25-30 m.[92]

VI **The fortified enclosure at Bakhit**
(kite photo by B. Żurawski).

VII **Marble floor in the** *haikal*, **and the post-holes of the timber** *higab*, **in Church A at Soba East.**

VIII **The west wall of the cathedral at Faras with the blocked central doorway**
(*photo L. P. Kirwan*).

IX **The Church of the Granite Columns at Old Dongola.**

X Church B at Soba East with the circular tomb monument and apse of the sanctuary chamber in the foreground. The men stand on the pier bases between the nave and aisles.

XI The north church at Faras East *(photo W. Y. Adams)*.

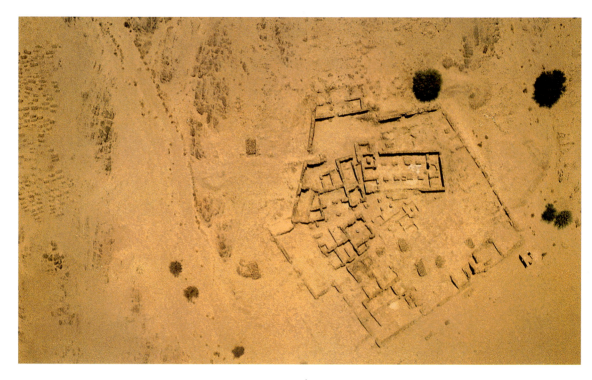

XII **The monastery at el-Ghazali** *(kite photo by B. Żurawski).*

XIII and XIV **Textiles from Qasr Ibrim.** *(photos © The British Museum).*

XIII (far left) **Early Christian;**

XIV (left) **Late Christian.**

XV The Pottery Workshop at Faras during excavation *(photo courtesy of W. Y. Adams)*.

XVI Decorative motifs on Soba Ware.

XVII Wall painting of a king in the Monastery of the
Holy Trinity at Old Dongola.

XVIII (right) Faras, wall painting of a Makurian princess
under the protection of the Madonna and Child
(*photo L. P. Kirwan*).

XIX The north aisle of
the cathedral at Faras
with the wall painting of
the Nativity (*photo courtesy
of S. Jakobielski*).

Of the forts between Kurgus and the Nile confluence, that at Kurgus is built throughout of mud brick, at least at the level visible on the present ground surface, while those at Jebel Nakharu, Abu Nafisa and Jebel Umm Marrihi are of coursed rubble construction. The walls at Kurgus are 5 m thick, those at Jebel Nakharu approximately '11 feet thick' (3.35 m).[93]

'Official' structures

'PALATIAL' BUILDINGS

Substantial mud-brick multi-storeyed buildings are known within the Kushite town at Karanog although their date is far from certain. The best preserved still stood, early last century, to a height of over 8 m and three storeys. Although usually considered to be of Kushite date the presence of wall paintings, which may be of the medieval period, and of artefacts of that date, indicates its continued use.[94] At Faras the so-called Northern and Southern palaces are separated by a narrow alleyway. They are both substantial structures, one almost square, 12.7 x 12.2-13 m, the other rectangular, 14 x 19 m. Both were certainly at least two storeys in height. Although built of mud brick they had carved stone portals and their ground floor rooms are decorated with murals. They date to the seventh century.[95] Two not dissimilar buildings have been excavated at Debeira West on sites R-8 (17 x 9 m) and R-60 (c. 13 x 11 m). The former has two staircases flanking the entrance, one of which is accessed from outside the building. The entrance into the central room was through a stone arched doorway, the only stone construction of this type in the settlement. The building at R-60 originally stood to a height of at least 8 m. Like the buildings at Faras they are of early medieval date.[96] The prominent position of the stairways in these buildings, some of which lay immediately within the main entrance, suggests the importance of the upper storey or storeys.

One of the most famous of medieval Nubian buildings is the mosque at Old Dongola.[97] This building, as the inscription within it records, was utilized as a mosque from 1317. Recent studies have demonstrated that it was probably constructed in the ninth or tenth century and was not a church, as previously assumed, but was perhaps the Throne Hall of the kings of Makuria. It was constructed almost exclusively of mud brick with walls 1.1 m thick. Fired brick was used where additional strength was required while stone was employed very sparingly. The building was of two distinct parts. The ground floor consisted of long and narrow barrel-vaulted rooms of considerable height; the soffit of the vaults is 6.5 m above the internal floor level (Figs 64 and 99). It was probably entered by three doorways, two to the north and one to the south. These rooms have few windows and can only have been suitable for such mundane functions as storage. Their functional separation from the upper floor is demonstrated by the absence of any direct connection between them. On entering the building from the west the doorway led to a monumental staircase winding around a square newel, which gave access to the first floor, consisting of a square hall surrounded by an arcaded loggia on three sides and with additional rooms to the west flanking the stairway. The 'throne hall', 7 m square, had a shallow apse in the centre of its east wall opposite the main doorway and had a coffered timber roof supported on four columns, the central part of which may have been carried up to form a clerestory. Three of the columns, and a few of the original roof beams, still remain in

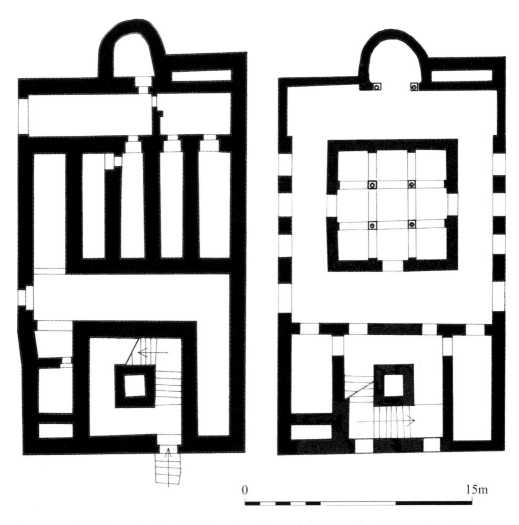

Figure 64 The 'Throne Hall' at Old Dongola, plans of the ground and first floors (after Godlewski 1982, figs 4 and 5).

situ. To the rear of the hall in the east wall of the loggia is an unusual feature, a vertical shaft extending down to ground level where there is an external doorway. The building was probably damaged by an earthquake in the late thirteenth to early fourteenth century and during the subsequent renovation, perhaps directly connected with the conversion of the upper floor to a mosque and the ground floor for use as a caravanserai, a reinforcing revetment extending up to first floor level was added (Fig. 99).

Although much less well preserved, a large mud-brick building at Soba East, 18.6 m wide by at least 46.1 m in length, again has the long narrow rooms at ground floor level, although these have low timber roofs.[98] Like the rooms in the 'Throne Hall' at Old Dongola their main function may have been to elevate the palatial apartments, an arrangement paralleled in the Kushite palace of Queen Amanishakheto at Wad ben Naqa dating to almost a millennium earlier.[99] The thirteenth to fifteenth-century palatial structure at Jebel

Adda, perhaps the residence of the Kings of Dotawo, consisted of several conjoining buildings constructed over a period of time and with a large monumental entrance. It had rooms at ground-floor level which could only be entered from above, a typical feature of domestic architecture in the Late Christian period.[100] Nothing remained to suggest the character of the upper palatial quarters, if indeed the building is correctly identified as a palace.

The substantial mud-brick building designated 'Building One' at Hambukol is unique and there is nothing about its plan, or among the artefacts found within it, to suggest its function. In the absence of specific evidence the excavator suggested that it may have functioned as a public meeting hall. As originally built it was square and was entered by a wide entrance from the south flanked by rooms to either side. The core of the building was a large rectangular hall with two cruciform brick piers supporting the roof. Additional rooms lay to the north and east, one of which was a latrine. Later modifications extended the building to the west and included the addition of a stairtower and the insertion of another latrine. The interior walls were covered in a lime plaster rendering.[101]

Dating from the Late Christian period are several houses at Qasr Ibrim which appear to have been residences of *eparchs*. The earliest, House 763, dates from around 1050 and was occupied for the next 250 years. The two-storey building was constructed throughout of stone up to first-floor level and above that probably in mud brick. The quality of construction was poor and the layout of the building was irregular. There was little to distinguish it from other buildings on the site apart from its size. Its use appears to have been as slovenly as in other less exalted dwellings yet fragments of texts found within it indicate that it was the residence of the *eparch* Isra'il in the twelfth or thirteenth century.[102] Adams suggested that rather than being the official residence of the *eparch* it was a family residence, one of whose members rose to eparchal office, at which time he used his residence for official functions.[103] These *eparchs'* houses are of the same order of magnitude and have a similar number of rooms at ground floor level as the residence of an *eparch* identified at Old Dongola which is several centuries earlier in date.[104]

Two other structures which may fall into the category of palatial are known at ed-Dabayba Um Tobe and Khor Shingawi. Both are isolated, the former is over 3 km to the

Figure 65 **The building at Khor Shingawi.**

west of the river, 35 km to the north of Omdurman and 5 km from the fort at Jebel Umm Marrihi, while the latter is 12.5 km from the river on the left bank of the Nile at the Fourth Cataract. The building at ed-Dabayba Um Tobe has been excavated by the University of Khartoum although no details have been published.[105] It is approximately square, constructed of red brick and is a complex of small rooms. The building at the Khor Shingawi (Fig. 65) is rectangular, is built of stone and is divided into three parts with a total of twenty rooms and corridors. In the centre is a courtyard at ground level with ramps leading up to the rest of the building which is set on a podium approximately 1 m high. Flanking the courtyard to the east is a range of three pairs of rooms aligned across the short axis of the building, to the west a range of three narrow long rooms aligned along the long axis connected by a corridor running along the rear of the courtyard. A suite of several small rooms projects from the back wall of the main complex.

MONASTERIES

Monasteries were among the largest building complexes to be constructed in Nubia. Characteristic buildings were a church, a refectory and accommodation for the monks, although the former may not have been an essential element. A number of groups of buildings have been claimed as monasteries where a church was not an integral part of the complex. Churches, where provided, are of types familiar in other contexts in Nubia. Readily recognizable features of the refectories are the pennanular benches, ranging in diameter between 1.5 and 2 m, on which the monks would sit to eat their meals. Traces of a small podium or stand were found in the centre of two of these in the Old Dongola monastery DM.[106]

At el-Ugal is a large cell-block. In the eastern range two of the cells are 18.9 m^2 and the others are 22.4 m^2, 23 m^2 and 26.6 m^2. The size of this structure, with its 4.5 m-wide central corridor, is comparable to that in the Monastery of St Simeon at Aswan and much larger than that at Qasr el-Wizz.[107] Characteristic of monastic cells are the provision of mastaba lining the walls and of niches, the former for sitting and sleeping, the latter for the storage of goods.[108] El-Ugal also has small barrel-vaulted cells opening off the north side of an east-west corridor to the south-west of the main complex. Other rooms for which a function can be assigned are the kitchens where extensively burnt walls indicate the presence of cooking fires. At el-Ghazali one room had three stands for water jars and was provided with a chimney which may have been designed to cause a draft to assist with the cooling of the water stored in the jars.[109] The el-Ghazali monastery (colour plate XII and Fig. 37) is bounded by an enclosure wall approximately 1 m thick constructed of dry-stone masonry standing in excess of 4 m in height. Entry into the complex was through one main gateway, three smaller gateways and a postern door.[110] A row of cubicles thought to be latrines lay 40 m outside the enclosure.

The monastery currently under excavation on Kom H at Old Dongola, which was called the Monastery of the Holy Trinity, also has a substantial enclosure wall built of mud brick. It subsequently outgrew this, being extended to the west and finally covering an area approximately 120 x 100 m in extent. So far excavation has only revealed a small part of the complex, most notably a domestic service quarter in the north-east angle and two free-standing buildings immediately to the west of the monastery's enclosure wall

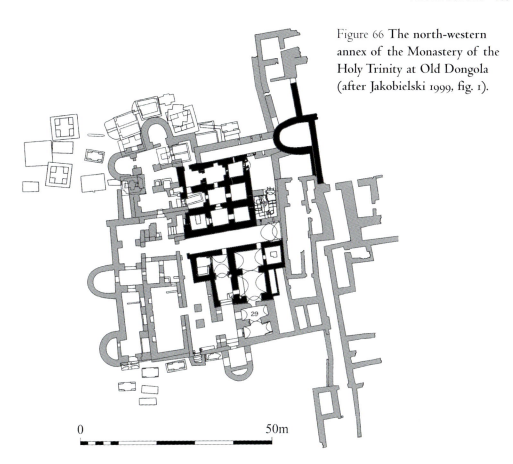

Figure 66 **The north-western annex of the Monastery of the Holy Trinity at Old Dongola** (after Jakobielski 1999, fig. 1).

0   50m

which were subsequently incorporated into a extensive range of rooms that included a series of chapels (Fig. 66).[111] Within the main complex are remains of a large red-brick building assumed to be a church of eighth-century date, perhaps the Church of Great Jesus mentioned on an Old Nubian graffito within the monastery, to which was added a small private chapel in the tenth century.[112]

The north-east angle is thought to have been a service area and consisted of a complex of barrel-vaulted rooms. All the floors were of hardened mud, tiles, mud bricks or were lime plastered. The presence of marble floor tiles, although not found in situ, indicate that some rooms were of greater opulence. Among the installations discovered was a furnace for industrial or domestic use, a well-constructed grain store, and a possible toilet. Up until the mid tenth century domestic refuse was dumped immediately outside the building but this practice had to be abandoned when that area was utilized as a cemetery. Thereafter rubbish was deposited into abandoned rooms within the complex. Perhaps in the twelfth or thirteenth centuries a 'D'-shaped tower was added to the north wall of the complex. It has been suggested that this was to enhance the defensive character of the monastery and similar additions have been noted elsewhere. After the thirteenth century the monastery was extended beyond the defensive wall testifying to the continued vitality of the establishment at that late date. There is, however, no evidence for the continuing use of the complex later than the second half of the fifteenth century.[113] The fourteenth-century building phase was constructed over the filled in remains of the earlier building.[114]

Among other structures claimed as monasteries was a group of buildings in the southern part of the period 6 settlement at Meinarti[115] and a complex of structures designated Site R-60 at Debeira West. Both lack the distinctive features of such complexes. The building at Debeira forming the original nucleus of the complex has already been mentioned. Another building (rooms II-V) within it is highly unusual consisting of a central transverse room off which open two long rooms to the south-east and an internal apsed room to the north-west entered through a small doorway set slightly off centre.[116]

DOMESTIC ARCHITECTURE

There is a considerable range of diversity in domestic architecture and standardized house types are not easy to recognize. One of the most badly-represented house types in the archaeological record, but perhaps also one of the most common, particularly within the Kingdom of Alwa, was the timber hut of circular or rectangular form. Large numbers of timber circular huts have been found dating to the Kerma period at Kerma, and to the early Kushite period at Kerma and at Meroe. To date only two circular timber huts are known dating to the medieval period, at Soba East. These are small, *c.* 4.5 m in diameter and one had a storage jar buried in the floor, the other had a central hearth.[117] Also dating from the early medieval period was extensive evidence for timber enclosures and perhaps for rectilinear timber buildings.[118] Timber structures by their very nature do not survive as upstanding monuments and can only be located through detailed excavation. It may be these factors more than any other which explains their scarcity in the archaeological literature.[119]

Circular huts and shelters of unhewn stone will also have been constructed at all periods as temporary or humble dwellings. How important they were in a rural context in the medieval period is unknown. At Kulubnarti a number of dwellings were excavated which fall between the circular hut and the rectilinear house. Some of these, constructed of undressed stone, are rectilinear, others curvilinear with at least two being two-roomed structures. Rooms rarely exceed 2 m square. They appear to date to the Classic and/or Late Christian Periods.[120] In the Second Cataract region crude stone huts are, at several Late Medieval sites, the only structures within settlements defended by substantial defensive walls.[121] However, throughout Nubia the vast bulk of the medieval houses known are rectilinear structures of mud brick, or much more rarely of stone, varying widely in style and quality of construction, features affected by local traditions and conditions.

At Qasr Ibrim in particular, but also at many other sites, some structures had a very long life in use. Among these at Ibrim are buildings of the early Kushite period which survived into Early Christian times.[122] Of the houses constructed during the fifth and sixth centuries on the site many are substantial buildings. Typical examples are approximately square, between 8 and 10 m each side, constructed with external walls of rough stones set in a mud mortar and 600-800 mm thick. Internal walls were either of stone or mud brick. The walls often have very deep foundations, up to 2 m, a necessary precaution as many of the rooms had subterranean crypts within them. Both internal and external doorways tend to be wide at about 1 m, and had jambs and sills of well-dressed stone or of wood. The exterior and some of the interior entrances had wooden doors. House X8 has four rooms, one with a circular crypt which may be secondary, and a small closet. The adjacent House X7 was much larger containing twelve rooms, some apparently used for storage although one may have been a kitchen and another contained an oven.[123]

The X-Group houses at Arminna West were substantial mud-brick structures and consisted of one or more rooms surrounded by many flimsy structures. The arrangement of rooms in a number of the houses can be compared with late Kushite examples in the region.[124] The two X-Group houses at Meinarti were of almost identical size and plan although the later in date was of rather more massive construction. They were nearly square, entered at the south-east corner and divided to form a larger eastern room and a smaller one to the west which was subdivided to provide two very small square chambers. They were vaulted and had arched doorways, although only the earlier had an internal stairway, later replaced by one outside. Adams noted an absence of domestic fittings within these structures and the presence of enormous quantities of amphorae in one house led him to suggest that it was used as a wine cellar.

Well-built substantial dwellings are often found closely associated with others of a much more ephemeral nature. The latter type is well illustrated by the 'Western Building' at Arminna West dating to the Early Christian period. Only one room was constructed of mud brick, the walls being of one row of headers and were 350 mm thick. To the north-west room 50 had two walls, which formed the external walls of the building, of sandstone slabs set in abundant mud mortar, and of large roughly square sandstone blocks with smaller stones in mud mortar above, originally attaining a height of at least 2 m. The third wall was of similar construction but only 250 mm thick. The walls of the room to the south-east were of mud with a few stones set within it, one wall was 500 mm thick, the others only about 200 mm. The walls were all bent both vertically and horizontally. Other rooms had crude curvilinear walls as thin as 150 mm. This house is typical of those in the contemporary settlement which are markedly cruder than those which preceded them.[125]

At Debeira West the excavators singled out one building which was typical of the better quality dwellings in the settlement. It had two main rooms, an entrance hall and stairs to the roof or perhaps to an upper storey.[126] At Tamit a number of houses were preserved up to first-floor level. House 1 (Fig. 67a) had six small barrel-vaulted rooms at ground level but on the first floor, which occupies the same area, there are only three, the central part of the building being occupied by a large, roughly square room.[127] The earliest house found at Old Dongola was built of mud brick with red bricks used for certain parts of the structure. It appears to have had two storeys with a bathroom on the first floor. The Early Christian houses which replaced it, which still survive to a height of 3.7 m, were certainly of at least two storeys with large arched windows in the upper storey or storeys.[128] A feature of these houses, which is common to the houses excavated beyond the defences, is the presence of a narrow toilet unit by the external wall at the end of one room.[129] Another contemporary house type, at Abdullah Nirqi, typically consisted of two substantial structures usually sharing a party wall, one being longer that the other (Fig. 67b). They were barrel-vaulted and divided by light partitions into a number of smaller rooms. No direct connection existed between the two main parts of the building. Although they continued in use, with modifications, for many centuries another house type appeared, perhaps in the eighth century, the unit house of square plan (Fig. 67c) with one transverse

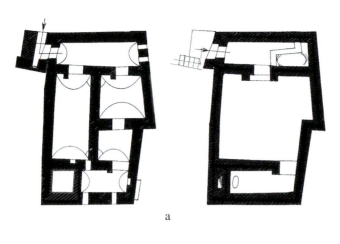

Figure 67 **House types**
a. Tamit, House 1, ground and first floor plans (after Bosticco *et al.* 1967, fig. 7).
b. Double houses, Abdullah Nirqi (after Hajnóczi 1974, fig. 4).
c. Unit house, Abdullah Nirqi (after Hajnóczi 1974, fig. 5).
d. Castle house (House I) at Meinarti (after Adams 1964, 232).

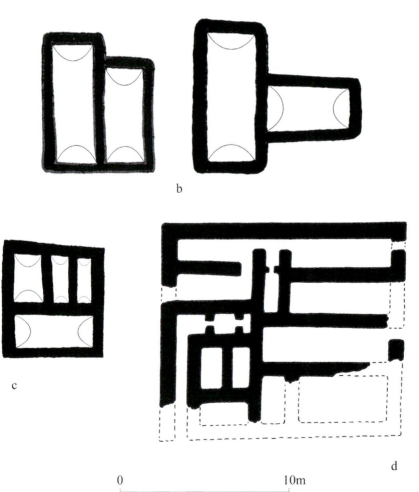

0   10m

room the full width of the building with three rooms at right-angles to it across the back. All were barrel-vaulted.[130]

Late Christian housing at Qasr Ibrim was constructed of stone and was characterized by its lack of homogeneity with regard to size, shape and layout. Many houses were of skewed plan, a feature also noted among contemporary stone-built houses at Kasanarti and Kulubnarti. This contrasts markedly with brick-built structures of the same date on those sites which are much more regular. Adams suggests that this difference indicates that the latter were built by professional builders.[131]

In the late medieval period a special house type was developed between the Third Cataract and Qasr Ibrim, the castle house (Fig. 67d).[132] As the name suggests these were primarily designed as fortified residences. The most characteristic feature is the physical separation of the ground-floor vaulted rooms from the domestic quarters on the first floor. In most of them entry to the building was only at first-floor level and must have been by a removable ladder. The castle house at Meinarti has a very elaborate entrance by way of a narrow angled passage of more than 12 m with two very low doors before one climbed a ladder up a narrow slot into the heart of the building. Trap doors gave access from the first floor down into the ground-floor chambers which were presumably used for storage and the protected storage provided by these buildings may have been an important aspect of their design. Many of them have concealed storage crypts often in the spandrel areas between two of the ground-floor vaults and some of these are entered by ingeniously hidden passages. Even at first-floor level many doorways are extremely low and one would have had to bend nearly double to pass through, making the individual, if he were an intruder, extremely vulnerable to someone waiting on the other side of the door. On average the houses are 9.5 x 8 m in size, and well-preserved examples have been recorded standing to a height of 7 m with a parapet on the flat roof. They are usually constructed throughout of mud brick although some employ stone in the ground floor. Their small size indicates that they were not communal refuges but the dwellings of small nucleated family groups.

What may be a unique type of fortified house was found near Abu Sir and consisted of a circular tower 7 m in diameter, the lower part with a 1 m thick stone wall pierced by a narrow doorway. The ground floor, divided into three rooms, was roofed with vaulting or a dome of mud brick and surmounted by at least one upper storey constructed throughout of mud brick, pierced by at least one narrow embrasure or slot window. Unlike the castle houses it was associated with early medieval pottery.[133]

Only one subterranean dwelling has been recognized, at Debeira West. The building was set within an rectangular pit dug into the bedrock to a depth of over 2 m, the sides of the cut being lined with mud brick covered in a mud plaster rendering. Roofs were mud-brick barrel vaults. An elaborate stairway, its lower treads rock-cut, gave access down into the building from the contemporary ground surface.[134] Many other buildings, for example, the church at Abdullah Nirqi, owing to the build-up of sand became partly subterranean during their use and steps down into them had to be provided.

In the Kingdom of Alwa the only houses to have been investigated are several at Soba East, although none of these have been excavated in their entirety. Some appear to have been substantial largely mud-brick structures but probably with the upper parts of the walls in red brick and with timber roofs.[135]

It is often difficult to assign a function to particular rooms and other enclosed spaces within Nubian houses. Many of the barrel-vaulted ground floor rooms were used for storage and contained mud storage bins, pots set into the floor, or pits covered by stone slabs.[136] At Qasr Ibrim in particular many rooms in the earliest Nubian (X-Group) houses had circular, rectangular or square cellars of considerable size and depth lined with mud brick and/or stone, with mud plaster, or with basketry. They were roofed with timber; one very well-preserved example had six thick branches which supported a layer of palm-leaf ribs placed at 90° carefully tied together with cords, and then covered with palm-leaf matting and pieces of baskets. Entry into the crypts was via a rectilinear aperture, one in House X8 being 550 x 450 mm in size with a raised lip 350 mm high, some were closed by a wooden trap-door.[137] These crypts are often filled with a vast amount of rubbish material, presumably after they had ceased to have their primary storage function.[138] A substantial cellar was found within one house at Debeira West which consisted of a brick-lined and vaulted chamber. When found it was filled with domestic refuse.[139] Another provision for storage of foodstuffs, but also of other items, was by setting large pots into the floors of the rooms, sometimes buried up to their rims. Mud storage bins were also provided, either free-standing circular features or built up against the walls or into the corner of rooms frequently in the kitchen area. At Debeira West the sail-vaults under the first flight of stairs in many houses formed an understair cupboard.[140] Within the similar chamber in the church at Arminna West were found two fragments of parchment bearing Coptic texts and it was suggested that it may have served as a *scriptorium* or storeroom.[141] Broken pottery was apparently stored in this place in the church at Abdullah Nirqi.[142]

At Debeira West many of the well-preserved houses have niches in the walls. The earlier form on that site appear to have been rough circular holes, large enough to have held a lamp. Later they are usually arranged three to a wall and are larger, measuring on average 350 mm long by 250-350 mm deep and are 500 mm high. They are either triangular or arched. In the latest house on the site the niches occur singly or in pairs, are a truncated triangular shape, and some are so shallow as to be merely decorative.[143] One room has cow's horns set into the wall point upwards, above niches; these were presumably used as hooks, perhaps to suspend lamps.[144]

Kitchen areas can often be recognized from the large amounts of domestic refuse within them and by the presence of ovens and storage bins made of mud brick which can be exactly paralleled in modern Nubian houses. Ovens of beehive shape have been excavated at Debeira West and other sites,[145] while hearths of rectangular form delimited by bricks set on edge have been recorded elsewhere. In Building F at Soba East was a number of this type as well as hearths, placed in the corner of two rooms, delimited by a raised lip of mud containing a large amount of ash. No evidence was found to suggest that these had other than a domestic use.[146] At Meinarti in the Classic Christian period few ovens were found in the well-built houses and the cooking appears to have been confined to the open-walled terraces which adjoined them.[147]

Latrines are one of the few rooms within domestic buildings for which a use can be advanced with some confidence. Those in dwellings were usually constructed close to a source of ash which was used to eliminate odours and 'deactivate faeces'.[148] At Debeira West one latrine was provided with a drainage system leading to a room which functioned as a soakaway or as a cesspit. It was 6.5 m in length but only 1.56 m wide and contained a vast amount of pottery sherds in an ashy fill. Another had a small vaulted cesspit with a pipe set vertically through the vault to provide ventilation.[149] One Debeira latrine was provided with a stone slab set in the floor over the drain with a hole in it, another had two stone blocks 'placed conveniently for the feet with a hole between them'.[150] More elaborate toilets are known made of ceramic (Fig. 68) or of stone, including a two seater from Old Dongola.[151] From House PCH.1 came two ceramic seats. One was a ceramic pipe with a collar at the top moulded to form a comfortable seat. The collar is supported by three engaged 'columns crowned with capitals and decorated with impressed decoration and the whole object is red slipped and well fired'. A very similar seat came from the nearby House B.[152] A perfectly preserved example from the Monastery on Kom H has the circular seat atop a vertical pipe set at the narrow end of an egg-shaped basin. A drain hole from the basin allows liquid to flow into the drain at the base of the pipe.[153] In many Nubian houses narrow rooms on the ground floor without any means of entry and with an outlet to the exterior at floor level were cesspits for first-floor latrines.[154] Among the regularly planned houses within the Classic Christian village at Meinarti neighbouring houses were laid out with the latrines placed in a different corner of each house so that all the latrines were close together, thus reducing the area contaminated by these installations.[155] The downside of this arrangement is that in some dwellings the living areas were downwind of the latrine!

In the Monastery of the Holy Trinity at Old Dongola many of the 'D'-shaped projecting towers on the west side of the complex were used as latrines,[156] although this may have been an opportunistic use of the ground floor rooms of these structures rather than their having been designed with this function in mind. In a number of contexts at Old Dongola small bi-conical pieces of clay have been found. Similar objects from the Kerma Classique palace at Kerma and elsewhere at that site have been identified as blanks for sealings.[157] Those at Old Dongola are found associated with latrines and are thought to have had an

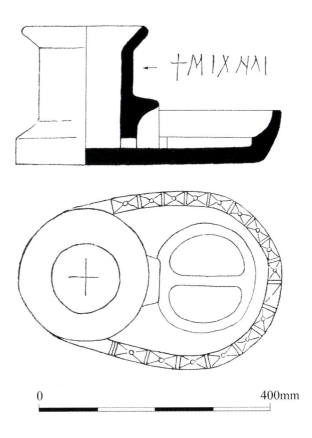

Figure 68 **Ceramic toilet from Meinarti (after Monneret de Villard 1935, fig. 212).**

even more mundane use, being the Nubian equivalent of toilet paper.[158] Certainly pebbles are used, when water is not available, for this purpose in Nubia today (personal observation!).

House A at Old Dongola contained what appears to be an elaborate vaulted bathroom with a stone-flagged floor into which are set two basins which are coated with waterproof plaster, the larger 1.2 x 0.9 m in size and 1.05 m deep, the other 0.8 m deep. A system of pipes fed water from a tank to the small basin. Set vertically in one wall were three ceramic pipes 160 mm in diameter of uncertain function. The walls were decorated with religious paintings including a large image of Christ.[159] At the nearby site of Hambukol a room in what is thought to be the monastic complex had walls that have been repeatedly plastered; it appears to have been subjected to high humidity causing the walls to slump. It is suggested that this may have been a steam bath.[160]

Building construction

It is difficult to make generalizations concerning building techniques across the whole of Nubia. Many local factors such as the availability of particular raw materials in a given area and local building traditions influenced the style of architecture employed. However, there is a trend for a greater use of red brick over mud brick as one moves south into areas of greater rainfall. Red brick is much more expensive to produce but red-brick buildings require much less maintenance. On the other hand, if buildings were well maintained, if the roofs were kept in good repair, and if the rendering of the external faces of the walls was in good condition, there were few disadvantages to the use of mud brick. At Soba East, the most southerly site where we have detailed information on a number of buildings, all the churches are of red brick, yet the palatial structure and all the substantial houses are of mud brick. At Old Dongola, apart from the Old Church, all the later monumental buildings were constructed of red brick while the small churches, the monastery on Kom H and the 'Throne Hall' were built of mud brick.

In Nobadia the largest churches, employing *spolia* from earlier Kushite buildings, are either of stone or, as at Faras, a combination of stone and red brick, presumably because the readily available stone from earlier structures was insufficient to complete the building. Of the relief blocks used in the construction of the cathedral (colour plate VIII) and also in the defensive wall, particularly in the west angle tower, 390 appear to have been taken from the Southern Temple at Buhen while over 140 may have come from the temple built by Ramesses II at Aksha.[161] The extremely haphazard way that reused relief and moulded stones were incorporated into the cathedral will have been entirely masked by the application of the rendering.[162] It is only in the cathedral at Qasr Ibrim that we have evidence for an elegant arcade of dressed and moulded stonework set on slender dressed stone piers (Fig. 102). Structures built of red brick in their entirety are excessively rare, the only church built exclusively of this material was at Faras.[163]

Spolia was also used at Soba East. In Church B a large block bearing a relief of the Kushite goddess Hathor on two faces, perhaps from a capital, was reused in the substructure of the pulpit. In the palatial structure, Building D, in a secondary phase one mudbrick wall was provided with a socle of white sandstone, a number of the reused blocks bearing inscriptions in Greek and Coptic, presumably derived from a Christian structure elsewhere on the site.[164] Damaged column shafts and capitals (Fig. 30), almost certainly from the Church of the Stone Pavement at Old Dongola, which was probably the church destroyed by the Arabs in the invasion of 652, were used in what may have been a hasty attempt to strengthen the defences of the city following the Arab siege.[165] Reuse of much earlier stonework was made in the Church of the Granite Columns when a granite block bearing the name of Taharqo, dating from the seventh century BC, was set up in the baptistery and was probably used as an altar.[166] The finely-dressed stone blocks employed to face the mud-brick walls of the south-western unit in the Monastery of the Holy Trinity[167] were also presumably *spolia* but from where is unknown.

Not available as *spolia*, however, will have been the large numbers of granite columns and capitals which adorned Nubian churches. In two of the major quarries for this and similar hard stones, at Tumbus and Daygeh, the former worked in the New Kingdom and Kushite periods, the latter in the Kushite period alone, there is no evidence for continuing use into the medieval period. At Kitfogga, however, immediately upstream of the Dal Cataract there is a granite quarry with two column drums, presumably of medieval date still on the site (Fig. 69). Other partially disengaged blocks in the quarry demonstrate the methods employed to extract the blocks (Fig. 70) suggesting either that this quarry was used at a much earlier date or that the medieval quarrymen were continuing to use the same techniques as their Kushite predecessors.[168] At Old Dongola a fine granite gneiss, in a dark colour with a greenish olive hue and characteristic white crystalline veins, may have been used because of its marble-like appearance.[169] It has only been found on this site, suggesting that the source was local although geologically this is unlikely.

Although monolithic hard-stone shafts were the preferred material for constructing columns this was not invariably the case. In the Mosaic Church at Old Dongola and in the church on the North Kom at nearby Hambukol the columns were constructed from small, segmental-shaped sandstone blocks, a technique paralleled in Kushite architecture. The columns inserted into the Church of the Granite Columns, although constructed of red brick, were in the same tradition, as were those used in the 'Public Building' at Arminna West.[170]

Mud-brick walls are very vulnerable close to ground level where standing water can readily dissolve the brickwork undermining the walls. The provision of a stone socle was one way of alleviating this problem. However, very rarely there is evidence for this arrangement being reversed as in the 'Stone House' at Debeira West where the lower part of the walls to a height of over 1 m was of mud brick, the upper part of stone slabs.[171]

Figure 69 **Roughed-out column shafts in the quarry at Kitfogga.**

Figure 70 **Wedge holes to extract a block for use as a column in the quarry at Kitfogga.**

Another danger posed particularly to mud-brick walls, but also to those of soft Nubian sandstone, was the strong sand-laden prevailing north wind which has considerable erosive potential, at least close to the ground surface. In the Monastery of the Holy Trinity the external face of the north wall of one room was lined with ceramic paving tiles and plastered over with a hard waterproof lime plaster, probably to combat this problem.[172] The stone revetment on the lower part of the mud-brick defensive walls at Old Dongola may have had a dual purpose, as a protection against the elements and to stop their being undermined by an attacker. Lime-mortar rendering was an important protection for the Nubian sandstone against wind erosion. Particularly in the southern parts of Nubia, where annual rainfall was to be expected, the provision of a render to walls of mud brick was essential. A mud render, if well maintained, could protect mud-brick walls against rainwater damage. Mud rendering was frequently whitened with *jir* made from mudstone.[173] Renders were also provided in the interior of buildings for decorative purposes covered in a white lime/*jir* wash or more carefully prepared as a base for wall paintings. Several kinds of fine lime plasters have been found used in the Church of the Granite Columns at Old Dongola while at Soba East analysis of wall plaster indicated that for wall painting a coarse pink lime mortar was overlain by a layer less than 1 mm thick of *intonaco*.[174]

A few structures are built of stone not derived from earlier monuments. Frequently no attempt was made to dress the stone and the walls are built of rubble although they are often laid roughly in courses. A number of the later medieval fortresses are constructed in this way as are some of those which may be of post-Meroitic date such as Jebel Nakharu. A feature of some of the walls built of this material is the placing of blocks with their long axis vertical, or at an angle forming a rough herringbone pattern, in some parts of the walls. One of the very few ecclesiastical buildings constructed of rubble, Church EDC at Old Dongola, has in the poorly preserved lower parts of the walls two or three horizontal courses alternating with a course of blocks set at an angle.[175] Houses built of stone, with flat timber roofs, have been excavated at Kasanarti and date to the Early Christian period. Around 1100, however, there was a marked change to the use of mud brick. The earlier houses were either modified by the addition of mud brick to raise their walls or the stone dwellings were entirely infilled and new mud-brick structures constructed on top. The new and modified houses were roofed with vaults.[176]

Whatever the material used for construction it would presumably be obtained as close to the building site as possible. For mud-brick buildings there was often suitable mud on the site itself and quarry pits are to be found immediately outside the walls. At Soba East many of the quarry pits associated with the construction of Building F were excavated. In the bottom of one pit finger impressions were preserved and in another the imprint of the basket used to remove the mud. Surprisingly, here many quarry pits had been dug within the building and these large pits were filled on its completion by identical material quarried from outside the building![177] Red bricks were presumably fired in clamps of the type still used today but no trace of these has yet been found.

Buildings, whether of red or mud brick, were often well made with the arrangement of the bricks alternating from one course to another giving a well-bonded construction. A wide range of brick sizes was used and brick dimensions seems to have little or no chronological significance across the whole of Nubia although locally there is sometimes a marked change from one period to another.[178] The churches at the western end of mound B at Soba East illustrate the diversity of brick sizes and wall construction at a single site. The northern church was built of long rectangular bricks, one row of headers and one of stretchers to the course. In the central church two rows of square bricks and one of small bricks laid as stretchers formed a course while in the southern church two rows of headers and a row of stretchers down the centre were employed. Although consistent within each building the brick sizes varied markedly from one to another. All the walls, irrespective of the brick sizes used, were approximately 740 mm in thickness.[179] In the Church of the Granite Columns at Old Dongola three wall thicknesses were employed, 1.05-1.13 m (exceptionally 1.2 m), 0.9-0.96 m and 0.78-0.85 m.[180] The red bricks, 300-340 x 140-155 x 60-75 mm in size, were laid as multiple rows of headers and stretchers to the course, or with bricks laid zigzag fashion in the core of the wall between headers.[181]

Only very rarely was mud and red brick combined in the same wall although such a type of construction is known from the Kushite period, as for example in the outer walls of the palace of Amanishakheto at Wad ben Naqa.[182] The Mosaic Church at Old Dongola has external walls of this type with the more durable red-brick outer facing protecting the more vulnerable mud-brick core and inner face,[183] and the room added onto the eastern side of Church A at Soba is also constructed in this manner but with a foundation entirely of mud brick.[184] Both of these structures date to relatively early in the Christian period.

Mud brick, the preferred material for the construction, at least of most of the domestic buildings that have survived from the medieval period, was ideally suited for ease of modification. The opening of new doorways and windows and the demolition of parts or the whole of walls was easily achieved and many buildings exhibit an almost organic growth and modification often over a very considerable period of time. Buildings were not only extended horizontally and vertically by the addition of new rooms and upper storeys but grew vertically. At many sites when floor levels rose through the deposition of wind-blown sand or domestic rubbish, the roof was removed, the walls were increased in height and the roof replaced. Door and window openings were also re-cut at a higher level as part of this process.

Foundations took a variety of forms. At Soba East the foundations were set in a shallow foundation trench and were the same width as the walls. Frequently the standard brick coursing began at the base of the foundations although the placing of bricks on their edges in the first foundation course was common. Some of the foundations of the Church of the Granite Columns were a little wider than the superstructure but this was not invariably the case.[185] Many buildings were constructed without any foundations at all, the lowest course resting directly on the ground surface. Elsewhere, the tops of walls dating from earlier constructions were used. The North-West Church at Old Dongola was one of those constructed atop a sand dune without foundations but this was compensated for by the builders by the massive construction of the small building with external mud-brick walls 1.6 m thick and internal walls 1.3 m thick.[186] Some walls had additional strengthening with the use of timber lacing. At Qasr Ibrim in the cathedral there was a double frame system with timbers along the outer and inner faces of the walls linked at

Figure 71 **Windows and the positions of the tie beams in the east wall of the cathedral at Qasr Ibrim.**

intervals by tie beams (Fig. 71), while at the Church of the Granite Columns the timbers were only laid along the outer wall face, again with tie beams to bond them into the wall. A variety of complex joints were employed to hold the timbers together, dove tails and splayed indent scarf among them, some were pinned with a small iron nail.[187] Evidence for the use of timber in this manner in Alwan architecture has not survived. However, a 'course' of timber was used in Church A at Soba East in the presumably low walls between the piers which supported the roof over the nave and inner aisles, and one phase of the *higab* was of composite construction, with timber uprights being an integral part of the structure together with the red-brick screen walls.[188] In the Late Christian repairs and rebuilding of the Kushite walls at Qasr Ibrim palm logs served to bond the wall face into the core projecting back 2-3 m into the wall, with the ends visible among the facing stones at slightly irregular intervals of approximately 1 m horizontally and a little more vertically.[189]

Whatever the material used to construct the walls the bonding material was almost invariably mud which often, when used in mud-brick walls, was of a different consistency from that of the bricks themselves. The Mosaic Church at Old Dongola is unusual in that its walls are lime-mortar bonded and a number of lime mixing bins were found within it although these may have been associated with the rendering rather than with the wall construction.[190]

Many mud-brick buildings had substantial walls, those of the palatial structure at Soba East are up to 1.15 m thick, the walls of the 'Throne Hall' at Old Dongola are 1.1 m thick. The style of construction was, at its best, as good as anything found in red-brick buildings. At the other extreme, however, walls could be extremely flimsy with a single row of stretchers to the course.

In the more flimsy structures the roofs must have been of timber, but with the sturdier buildings masonry vaults and domes were a viable option. Although some of the earliest churches may have had vaulted roofs supported on rectangular piers over the nave, there was later a preference for columnar supports, where the greater strength of the stone allowed the roof supports to be much thinner than piers of stone blocks, and of red or mud brick. The use of columns allowed the church architects to achieve a spacious interior design although they were then presumably forced to roof the structures with timber, but these may not necessarily have been simple flat roofs as is generally imagined. At Soba East at least two churches had roofs supported by timber posts set on stone post-pads. One post in Church C, part of the row dividing the nave and the aisles, was 400 x 250 mm in size; the timber posts supporting the lintel over the wide southern entrance into Church A were 360 mm square.[191] A typical development in many churches was for the provision of domes and vaults to take precedence over the open plan afforded by the use of columns. In some churches the earlier columns were removed, as for example at el-Ghazali, while elsewhere the columns were enclosed in brick piers as in the cathedral at Faras. In the Church of the Granite Columns, uniquely, new supports were added to the pre-existing stone columns and the new piers were circular, constructed of red brick (colour plate IX). It is envisaged that both the circular piers and the stone columns were linked by arches and supported domes.[192]

The church at Sahaba appears to preserve evidence for a pitched roof. The cross wall at the west end of the nave slopes in at the top at an angle of about 45° to the ridge line. Apparently this wall was of two phases of construction, the earlier had terminated around the curve of the vaulted nave roof, while the upper part was not, according to the excavators, constructed until after the church had fallen into ruins![193] Why this was done when the building was already in ruins is not explained.

Where timber was used for roofing it was only the main beams that were of that material. As today they were presumably covered with palm fronds, by matting, and then by a layer of mud brick or mud to make them weather-proof. The timber roof of the *narthex* in the Mosaic Church at Old Dongola may have also been covered by thin slabs of ferricrete sandstone.

Arches and more particularly vaults were used extensively in domestic structures. Arches were formed with the voussoirs set radially, perpendicularly ('*par tranches*') or a combination of the two.[194] In vaulted buildings the side walls sometimes stopped at the springing of the vaults while elsewhere the walls were carried up towards the level of the top of the vault, giving a very much more block-like external appearance to the building. The difference may have been largely conditioned by whether or not a flat roof terrace was to be provided. Where vaulted buildings had an upper storey it was common for segmental vaults to span the gaps between the main semi-circular vaults reducing the amount of infill (and its weight) needed to form the level floor for the rooms above. It was these additional vaulted spaces in the castle houses which were then used for storage or as secret chambers.[195] The bricks used in vaults and domes were sometimes curved to the shape of the vault and often have deep finger grooves in their faces to aid bonding. Spans were small, rarely exceeding 5 m, although a dome of a little over 14 m in diameter attaining a height of about 28 m may have covered the central space in the Cruciform Church.[196] According to Abu Salih it was King Raphael who introduced the dome constructed of red brick into Old Dongola in 1002.[197] A small number of late mud-brick churches survived into the twentieth century to a considerable height. The dome in the Central Church at Serra East was constructed of small bricks 260 x 130 x 60 mm presumably to aid in turning the tight curve, in contrast to the bricks used elsewhere in the building which were of the more usual size of 400 x 200 x 70 mm. The transition from the square base to the dome was made by roughly formed pendentives; in the North Church squinches were employed.[198]

The typical Nubian vault had each ring of voussoirs laid back against its neighbour and could be constructed without the aid of centring, although this method frequently resulted in one end of the vault being a little higher than the other.[199] Evidence for the use of centring has been noted at a number of sites including Soba East[200] and will have been necessary in the construction of arches.

It has been suggested that the impetus for the abandonment of timber roofing was the result of the Arab invasion of Egypt cutting off the Nubians from the source of imported Mediterranean timber,[201] something which would have been most keenly felt in Nobadia. Alwa, on the other hand, presumably had access to unlimited supplies of timber in the south of, and beyond, the southern fringes of the state. The latest church in Nobadia known to have been constructed with columnar supports, and a flat timber roof, was the Church on the South Slope of the Kom, built in 930.[202]

Many of the red bricks used at Soba East in the construction and extensions to Building F have marks on them made before firing and a similar feature has been noted at Musawwarat es-Sufra in Temple IIIA. The exact meaning of these marks, which are only found on a small proportion of the bricks, is uncertain.[203] Similar marks on the architectural stone elements at Qasr Ibrim in the cathedral, and in the Church of the Granite Columns at Old Dongola, are masons' marks. It is clear from the study of the Old Dongola material that the base, shaft and capital of each column were identified with a specific letter from the Greek alphabet to ensure their correct matching during the construction.[204]

DOORWAYS

Doorways have flat lintels of either timber or stone, are arched (frontispiece), or, much less commonly, are covered by angled slabs or bricks spanning the opening or with a relieving arch over a flat lintel. Where stone is used, at least in the early medieval period, it is frequently embellished with relief decoration (see pp. 219-21). Well-preserved doorways in the houses at Debeira West are arched, plastered and some of the earlier ones have moulded jambs. Doors where provided, usually in external doorways only, were of wood and pivoted in a stone socket. The earliest example to survive closed the entrance into the X-Group tomb Q.3 at Qustul and was of seven vertical timber planks with a wooden crosspiece at top and bottom secured by nails and with copper-alloy circular plates nailed on to the exterior. It pivoted in a wooden beam at the top beneath the stone lintel and in a socket in the stone threshold.[205] An example from the Monastery of the Holy Trinity at Old Dongola was made of four palm logs bound together with rope and strengthened by the addition of two horizontal beams towards the top and bottom.[206] The extant door to the 'Throne Hall' at the same site, which may date back to the medieval period, is made of thick wooden boards tied together with leather straps. Only the rotating beam is of hardwood.[207] Bolt holes were provided in the jambs and elaborate keys indicate that locks were used. At Qasr Ibrim many finds of parts of lock mechanisms indicate that medieval locks were very similar, if not identical, to the type still used today in Nubia, which are made of acacia and comprise a large housing, stout bolt and several wooden tumblers. Keys are usually also of wood and are a common find at Ibrim but have also been recovered from a number of other sites.[208] Metal keys are also known although these may have been associated with the more complex metal locks found on chests as, for example, those from Jebel Adda, Meinarti and Soba East.[209] The use to which the iron padlock and chain found at Qasr Ibrim was put is unknown.[210]

WINDOWS

At Debeira West all the windows found, both in the domestic and ecclesiastical buildings, were slit windows often arranged in twos or threes in the end walls of vaulted rooms.[211] Very similar windows have been found on many sites as far south as Soba East (Fig. 72).[212] Much larger windows survive, or survived until recently, in a number of churches. At Faras in the cathedral windows on the west wall, which have arched heads, were between 640 and 700 mm in width and were set high in the walls, those with flat lintels on the east wall were 1.78 m high and 740 mm wide.[213] At Qasr Ibrim in the cathedral windows were 3.5 m above ground level with six or more spaced along the side walls.[214] Those in the Church of the Granite Columns at Old Dongola were either rectangular, 510-570 x 750-780 mm and 950-980 x 510-570 mm, or semi-oval 630 x 950 mm.[215] In the 'Throne Hall' arched windows take a variety of forms. Apart from the simple arched type others have a timber transom, with openings above and below while some have a screen wall resting on the timber transom flush with the external wall face forming a blind semi-circular 'tympanum'. They range in size from the large windows 2 x 1 m at first floor level to 1.25 x 0.73 m in the internal windows at ground floor level.[216] Evidence for arched windows, 600 mm wide and 850 mm high, at first floor level has recently been found in the mid seventh century houses on Kom A.[217]

Many windows had elaborate grills made most frequently of ceramic (see p. 221-2). Window glass

Figure 72 **Windows in Building D at Soba East.**

was also used. At Soba East a number of fragments of ceramic grilles have been found with holes 74 mm in diameter with a concentric rebate of 100 mm diameter. Circular glass panes of exactly this size were found close by and presumably were used to glaze frames of this type.[218] Similar window frames have been noted on Kom H at Old Dongola and from the church on the North Kom at Hambukol.[219]

In the Monastery of the Holy Trinity at Old Dongola large numbers of ceramic pipes were found in the service area. It was suggested that they were set into the vaults and were designed to allow light into the rooms where windows could not be provided for defensive reasons, or that they may have been connected with channelling rainwater run-off from the roofs.[220] In the western annex of the monastery two ventilation pipes were set into the vault and were provided with ceramic plugs.[221] Other pipes were set into the enclosure wall at the south-western corner of the monastery to allow for drainage from the courtyard immediately within it.[222] Many similar pipes were found among the rubble in the ruins of Church A at Soba East, presumably derived from the superstructure, but their original location and exact function in that building are uncertain.[223]

FLOORS

In most domestic buildings, as well as in a number of official secular buildings and churches, floors were either of mud or sand and frequently the floor was simply the level within the building at the end of the construction process. In Church R-44 at Debeira West the sandstone bedrock was used.[224] More elaborate floors were however, provided on occasion. Stone floors include those of dressed stone slabs, or 'crazy paving', and of cobbles/pebbles. Red or mud-brick floors were often well laid, the bricks arranged to form a pattern. In Church B at Soba East the floor in the *naos* consisted of single rows of triangular bricks delimited by single rows of rectangular bricks (Fig. 73).[225] Elsewhere in the building bricks were laid in alternating rows of 'headers' and 'stretchers'. In a later phase the *naos* brick floor was sealed by a thick layer of lime plaster. In churches the importance of the *haikal* was enhanced visually by a finer floor, of marble crazy paving at Soba East, Church A (colour plate VII), of pebbles at Debeira West, Church R-2.[226] Mosaic floors formed of different-coloured pebbles are only known within two churches in the Old Dongola region and at Meinarti.

Figure 73 **Floor of triangular and rectangular red bricks in the north aisle of Church B at Soba East.**

Metrology

There is little consistency in brick sizes and it is hazardous to see chronological implications in their dimensions. However, typically medieval bricks are about 70 mm thick while many earlier bricks are thicker, up to 90 mm. At Debeira West medieval mud bricks are on average 310 x 170 x 70 mm in size while those used in one X-Group wall were 410 x 175 x 90 mm. At Soba East the red bricks in the first phase of the northern church on mound B are between 440 and 480 mm in length, in the second phase they are 420 x 220 x 60 mm while the contemporary floor bricks in the *narthex* were 450 x 420 x 70 mm and 470 x 450 x 70 mm. In Church B they are 280 x 280 x 70 mm and 280 x 140 x 70 mm,[227] and in the adjacent Church C they are 320 x 180 x 70 mm. Mud bricks, where made from the same mould, are larger than red bricks as the red bricks shrink by up to 10% during the firing process.[228] In the early defensive walls at Old Dongola mud bricks were 435 x 210 x 80 mm, those in the Old Church were smaller at 316-338 x 157 x 64-76 mm. The earliest red-brick buildings, Buildings Y and X, were constructed of bricks 360 x 160 x 80 mm and 330-360 x 180 x 75-80 mm respectively.[229] This data gives a glimpse of the wide range of diversity possible, which can sometimes be observed among bricks even within the same structure.

Among Nubian structures churches in particular are complex buildings clearly constructed to a pre-determined plan, and presumably some care was taken to mark out the line of the building's walls before construction commenced. Unlike the religious monuments of the Kushite period the system of measurement employed can rarely be ascertained. However, in four buildings, at Soba East and Old Dongola, the use of a module can be postulated. The builders of Church B at the former site appear to have used a module of approximately 716 mm, and many of the rooms are five modules square. The walls are also approximately one module thick. In Church DC at Old Dongola the module of 375 mm has been identified, approximately half the length of that at Soba East. Dobrowolski suggested that the module may be related to the Roman *gradus* (*passus*) and the Greek *bema* which is 2½ short Greek feet, 735-750 mm in length, very similar to the module proposed at Church B and to two modules in Church DC. The square bricks in Church B would thus measure 1 short Greek foot, the rectangular bricks 1 short Greek foot by ½ short Greek foot, and the walls of the three churches at the western end of mound B are one *bema* thick. Attempts to recognize the use of this module in the spatial layout of Churches A and C, however, proved impossible.[230]

The Old Church at Old Dongola was designed using the Greek foot of 308 mm, identical to that used for the Justinianic church of Hagia Sofia in Constantinople. In its successor, the Church of the Granite Columns, two modules have been recognized, the Byzantine foot of 323 mm and another module 316 mm in length.[231] Many Nubian buildings are markedly trapezoidal in shape, presumably owing to inaccuracies in the surveying instruments used, and a similar situation is often seen in Roman surveying. One of the most extreme cases of this is in the earliest church at Meinarti where the angle between the long and transverse walls is almost 20° off a right angle. In a later modification of the building the end walls, and all the transverse partition walls, were rebuilt so that the building assumed a rectangular layout.[232]

There is very little evidence for how buildings were actually laid out on the ground before construction began. However, in Church B at Soba East there is clear evidence to show that shallow grooves were dug in the hard, presumably cleared, ground surface to mark each side of the wall foundation trenches. In the normal course of events all trace of these would be removed during the actual construction of the building, but at Soba what may have been a change of plan resulted in one foundation line with its grooves being preserved under the building's floors (Fig. 74).[233]

While there is considerable continuity in domestic architecture from the Kushite through the medieval period, and indeed in many cases into the present, the monumental

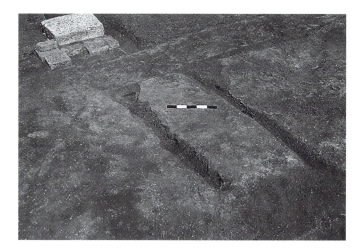

Figure 74 **Setting-out lines for the foundations of Church B at Soba East.**

architecture differs markedly. A major change is the move from construction with dressed stone blocks to mud brick and red brick construction. This is partly a response to developing artistic conventions. Kushite temples were frequently decorated with reliefs and for these smoothly dressed stone was necessary. In the medieval period wall painting was the preferred method of artistic expression executed on a mud or lime rendering. The material used to form the walls was, therefore, no longer constrained by their artistic embellishment, allowing the use of the much cheaper mud and red brick. The distinction between the two periods is, however, even with monumental buildings far from clear cut, as a number of Kushite temples also bore painted decoration applied to a render and were constructed of mud brick.

CHAPTER 8

The Economy

Agriculture

Agriculture was the mainstay of the Nubian local economy, augmented to some extent by animal husbandry and by hunting and fishing. Almost all the foodstuffs available to the Nubians were locally produced. The presence of agricultural land capable of growing sufficient crops to sustain the local settlements was essential. The Nile Valley in Egypt is renowned for its fertility, the agricultural land being replenished by the silt deposited during the annual floods. To the south of the First Cataract, however, only very rarely is there a similar agricultural potential. In Nubia the river generally flows between high banks above which it does not usually flood. The areas which are inundated in a good year along the river banks and on the islands, known as *seluka* land, are of limited extent. In Lower Nubia, as well as further upstream between the Second and Third Cataracts, attempts may have been made to increase this all important *seluka* land. A number of spur walls have been observed extending into the river which, it has been suggested, were designed to collect silt during the flood season, thereby increasing the amount of *seluka* available later in the year. These have been claimed to be of Pharaonic date although a medieval date has also been proposed.[1] In the Second Cataract and throughout the Batn el-Hajar, associated with many of the Late Medieval settlements are stoutly built walls, 1 m or more thick, running across the river channels flooded at high water and on the alluvium close to the river, presumably designed as soil-retaining walls[2] analogous to the wadi walls systems viable in areas of greater rainfall.

It is interesting to observe the location of the major centres over time, Kerma in the productive Kerma/Seleim Basin, Old Dongola close to the Letti Basin, and Napata also close to an extensive basin. In each case these centres are adjacent to substantial areas which may have been watered directly by the river in a good year. However the Nile flood has always been variable and this renders much of the basin land unsuitable for agriculture. In the recent past the areas watered by Nile floods have varied in the Shendi and Dongola reaches between 109,280 *feddans* (45,898 ha) and 10,730 *feddans* (4507 ha).[3] The cities of Meroe and Soba East, well to the south, could draw on the increasingly productive hinterland to help feed their populations. Recent observations in the Keraba after the wet year of 1988 when the whole of the Wadi el-Hawad and the Wadi el-Sawad were brought under cultivation by the agricultural population usually resident on the Nile banks,[4] indicates the potential productivity, albeit on an irregular basis, for agriculture and presumably more frequently for pastoral activities, of this hinterland.

High Niles have been postulated in the period between 600 and 1100[5] which may well have been a time of plenty, although such high Niles cause considerable destruction of settlements and can greatly effect the topography along the river banks.[6] The basins will have been more reliable as pasture and the importance of the Northern Dongola Reach for horse breeding must have been based on the use of the Kerma/Seleim Basin.

Some irrigation was possible of the land immediately above that inundated by the river. The primitive *shaduf*, a counterweighted lifting device had been in use for millennia, but this could only effectively raise water a maximum of 3 m and in limited amounts. It has been estimated that it is only suitable for the irrigation of areas of one half to two thirds of a *feddan* (0.21-0.28 hectares).[7]

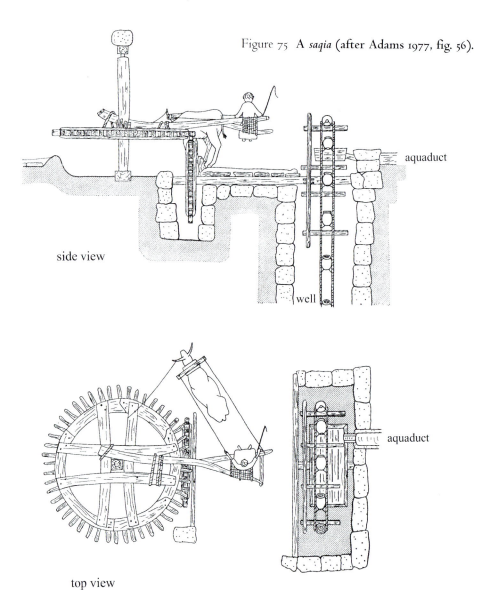

Figure 75 A *saqia* (after Adams 1977, fig. 56).

side view

aquaduct

well

top view

aquaduct

Perhaps late in the Kushite period, but certainly soon thereafter, the much more efficient *saqia*, was introduced into Nubia.[8] The *saqia* (Fig. 75) is a wooden wheel which carries two endless parallel ropes to which are attached pots. It is rotated through a series of gears by a draught animal, the pots filling with water as they are submerged and emptying that water at a higher lever into an aqueduct.[9] The utilization of the *saqia* can usually be demonstrated archaeologically by the presence or absence of the distinctive pots known in Arabic as *qadus* (pl. *qawadis*) which have a cordon below the neck and a small button base to assist with their attachment to the ropes. The arrival of the *saqia* is considered to have brought about an agricultural revolution only surpassed by the introduction of mechanized water pumps in the twentieth century. The *saqia* is certainly much more efficient that the *shaduf*, allowing a lift of between 3 and 8 m, and will have allowed a considerable increase in the amount of land available for agriculture and increased the duration of that availability as the flood waters began to recede. However, part of the increased efficiency of the *saqia* is offset by the need to grow fodder for the draught animals, usually oxen, needed to drive it.[10] The contribution of the *saqia* even for the agriculture in the region around Soba East is illustrated by a passage in Ibn Hawqal, 'The most prosperous part of the country [Nubia] is the territory of Alwa, which has a continuous chain of villages and a continuous strip of cultivated lands, so that a traveller may in one day pass through many villages, one joining the next, supplied with waters drawn from the Nile by means of *saqias*.'[11]

In southern Nubia there is sufficient rainfall in a normal to good year to allow rain-fed agriculture particularly where run-off from a large catchment area is channelled into a restricted zone so that the water moistens the soil sufficiently to allow the crops to grow to maturity. Such conditions occur particularly in the Keraba to the east of Shendi and especially along the Wadi Awateib. The wide wadi floors where they debouch onto the plain are suitable for agriculture and sizeable areas can be farmed for several months of the year. There is however, virtually no evidence for water management schemes which could have increased the potential of these areas although at least some of the Kushite *hafirs* may still have been functioning.[12]

CROPS

Many of the crops which are familiar in Nubia today flourished in the medieval period. According to el-Mas'udi, writing in the tenth century, Nubia produced palm trees, vines, dhurra, bananas, wheat and big citrus to which ar-Rumi adds the dom palm and 'a kind of thorny tree' and el-Qazwini mentions barley.[13] El-Maqrizi referring to events in the later thirteenth century records that in the north of Nubia cotton was grown, and cotton-growing in the area between Sai and the Third Cataract was mentioned by Ibn Selim in the tenth century.[14] Palm trees were rarer in the Kingdom of Alwa than further north according to Ibn Selim and this is also the case today where the increased rainfall and humidity in the Khartoum region is less conducive to the production of high-quality dates.[15] The staple grain was dhurra/sorghum (*Sorghum bicolor* ssp. *bicolor*) and it is a common find throughout Nubia in medieval contexts. At Qasr Ibrim a storage basket full of dhurra heads has been found in a Late Christian context,[16] and another, an intermediate race between dhurra and bicolor, has been radiocarbon dated to the period AD 420-640 (95% probability).[17] At least by the Late Medieval period race dhurra of cultivated sorghum was being grown alongside race bicolor. A large shallow basket thought to have been used for winnowing was also recovered from this site.[18] The grain was harvested using iron sickles[19] and prepared using simple saddle querns or the more technologically advanced rotary quern.[20] One of the uses of dhurra was to produce a beer known as *mizr* which may have been an important component of the diet, as the processes which are used to produce it do not involve the cooking of the dhurra and hence the *mizr* (*marisa*) retains high levels of essential vitamins of the B complex and vitamin C.[21] Apparently the inhabitants of Old Dongola were not always moderate in their intake; el-Umari remarks that they 'are strongly inclined to get drunk with wheat alcohol'.[22] Although emmer wheat continued to be grown until the Early Christian period two new types of wheat are first seen at Qasr Ibrim in the late Kushite period. One is a free-threshing tetraploid, the other a hexaploid, both types known in Egypt since the Ptolemaic period. Neither type seems to have been an important crop in the Ibrim area.[23]

At Soba East bulrush millet (*Pennisetum glaucum*) and hulled barley (*Hordeum* sp.) are also represented[24] and foxtail millet (*Seteria italiaca*) was found in a Late Christian pilgrim jar at Hambukol.[25] *Pennisetum typhoides* appears in the archaeological record at Qasr Ibrim in the mid X-Group period and was presumably an introduced species from the south.[26] Some of the grain was used to make the flat unleavened bread called *kisra*. This was made by pouring the mixture of flour and water onto the smooth burnished surface of a special large flat pot called a *doka* on which oil from a castor oil seed has been rubbed. *Doka* are a common find on medieval sites throughout Nubia and at Debeira West and Qasr Ibrim the castor oil seeds were also found.[27] On an *ostracon* from Debeira is written 'lentils, 13 artabae; 8 modii'.[28] Pulses have also been found at Soba East[29] and there is evidence for the appearance of termis bean (*Lupinus albus*) and the pea (*Pisum sativum*) at Qasr Ibrim from the mid X-Group period along with the continued production of lentils. The date of introduction of the cowpea (*Vigna unguiculata*) is uncertain but it is found regularly in late medieval contexts.[30] Sesame (*Sesamun indicum*), known in Egypt earlier, is also found at Ibrim at this time and is recorded as a crop of the part of Nubia within which Ibrim lies by Ibn Selim.[31] Debeira furnished cucumber seeds (*Vicinas communas*) and ground nuts (*Arachis hypgea*) as well as great quantities of date stones, which were found throughout the settlement suggesting that the date was as important then as it is now in the local economy. It may also have been one of the few agricultural products exported to Egypt. Until recently the annual departure of the date fleet from the Mahas and Sukkot regions was still a major event.[32] The discovery of amphorae full of dates suggests that they were also used to produce an alcoholic beverage.[33] Among the other edible fruits are dom palm nuts, an example of which, from an X-Group grave at Debeira, was used to form the handle for an iron pin. Fig seeds have been recovered from Soba East along with grape pips although whether these latter were imported, perhaps as raisins, or were grown locally is unclear. Certainly the climate in central Sudan is not ideal for growing this Mediterranean species and Ibn Selim noted that vineyards were less frequent in the Kingdom of Alwa than in the areas further to the north.[34] Vineyards in the region around Old Dongola and elsewhere in Makuria are recorded by several Arab writers. A number of amphora, which appear to be of local manufacture, have been found in late seventh/early eighth century deposits on Kom A, as have mud bungs with impressions of vine leaves on their lower surface.[35] Some of the amphorae from Old Dongola were resinated on the interior and had clearly been used for the transportation of liquids.[36] According to a number of Arab sources vines were grown mainly in the southern part of Lower Nubia, in Makuria. It has been suggested that the impetus for the local wine industry was a direct response to the interruption of the supply of wine from Egypt in the mid eighth century.

Apart from the physical remains of the vine and its grapes there is other archaeological evidence in Nubia for the local production of wine in the form of grape-pressing installations, of which twelve are known between Ikhmindi and Meinarti.[37] These however, have been dated to the late Kushite period. None appear to have continued in use for long and no similar installations of medieval date are known.

Another typically Mediterranean crop, the olive was, according to Ibn Selim, grown in the region between Sai and the Kajbar rapids,[38] and what was considered to be an oil press was excavated at Debeira West.[39] There were also desiccated remains at Soba East of the fruits of the Christ's thorn (*Ziziphus spina-christi*) and *Capparis decidua*.[40]

It has been suggested that there was something of an agricultural revolution at some time between the first and the mid sixth centuries. The evidence from Qasr Ibrim is for the introduction of a number of new crop species both from the north and the south which must have had an important impact on the agricultural potential of the area. The bringing together of winter crops from the north and summer crops from the south will have greatly increased the potential for year-round crop production and the arrival of the *saqia* within this same period will have made this year-round cultivation a practical proposition.[41]

ANIMAL HUSBANDRY

Domesticated animals were utilized for meat but, as today, they may only have formed a major part of the diet on special occasions. At Debeira bones of sheep, goats, cattle and pigs were found in domestic contexts and it was noted that the ratio of pig bones was high.[42] At Soba East cattle bones are by far the most common followed by those of caprines. Of the latter over 80% appear to have been sheep. No evidence for domesticated pig was noted at Soba East or on Kom H at Old Dongola but at the nearby site of Hambukol pig bones were found in an animal pen associated with House C-One.[43] The Soba East cattle have an estimated stature of 1.4 m to the withers. The greatest number were killed between the ages of twenty and thirty-six months although many older animals, between thirty-six and forty-eight months, were eaten. The sheep appear to have been tall animals, characteristic of those of subtropical regions. The majority of the caprines were slaughtered between the ages of seventeen and forty-one months, suggesting that these animals were reared primarily for meat.[44] El-Idrisi says that at Old Dongola the inhabitants ate camel meat, both fresh and sun-dried, which they ground and boiled in camel's milk.[45] El-Umari describes one of their most exquisite dishes: lubiya beans (*Dolichos lablab* Linn.) soaked in a meat broth dressed with the beans and meat together with unspecified leaves and roots.[46] The domestic chicken was probably present at Soba East[47] and has been noted at Qasr Ibrim in the late fifth or early sixth century.[48] Dovecotes, the inhabitants of which were presumably reared for their meat, were a feature of the region a little north of Old Dongola, as they still are today.[49]

El-Mas'udi records that the Nubians had fine camels, sheep and cattle. Their kings rode pure-bred horses but the people had only small packhorses.[50] A number of travellers in the eighteenth and nineteenth centuries commented on the very fine horses in Sudan, renowned throughout the Middle East, which were from the Dongola Reach.[51] James Bruce, who travelled along the Nile to Sennar and Ethiopia in the 1770s, noted that Dongola and the dry area near it was 'a centre of excellence for this noble animal'.[52] Presumably this was the source of the Makurian kings' fine-bred horses in the medieval period.

Livestock will have been the mainstay of the nomadic economy. The importance of the nomadic element in the population of Nubia is difficult to assess. These peoples are by the nature of their lifestyle very difficult to recognize archaeologically. Their dwellings are of a very ephemeral nature and their artefacts tend to be few in number, many are made of organic materials which only survive in the most favourable of conditions. We would expect that, in a response to the increasing rainfall as one moves upstream offering much greater potential for occupation outside the Nile Valley, the proportion of the population made up of nomads will have increased. They were presumably therefore, much more important in Alwa than in the northern kingdoms.

There is even less evidence available for nomads in the medieval period that in the preceding Kushite Kingdom when the presence of *hafirs* associated with temples indicates an attempt to control the nomadic component of the population. The Arab sources mention a large number of tribes, particularly to the east of the Nile, who were progressively converted to Islam and some of which acknowledged the suzerainty of the Alwan king. These were perforce largely nomadic. Close to the river there will have been, as in the recent past, a symbiotic relationship between the nomads and the sedentary farmer with perhaps a considerable overlap between the two groups in an attempt to make the optimum use of the resources available.[53] Even in the most arid of regions, in Lower Nubia, in the early nineteenth century, Burckhardt records people who dwelt for a part of the year by the river, during the cultivation season, and spent the rest of the year with their families in the desert[54] and such a lifestyle was presumably equally feasible in the medieval period.

FISHING AND HUNTING

Almost all Nubian settlements that have been investigated archaeologically lie close to the river and one would expect that fish would have formed a readily available food source. El-Maqrizi records that, in the inhospitable Batn el-Hajar where there is very little agricultural land, the staple food of the inhabitants was fish and that they also used fish oil to anoint themselves.[55] The plentiful fish in the region around Old Dongola are mentioned by el-Idrisi.[56] Fish bones survive less well than those of the large mammals and may hence be poorly represented in the archaeological record. However, bearing this in mind the contribution of fish to the diet of the medieval Nubians appears to have been small. At Debeira West the only evidence for the eating of fish was vertebrae of Nile Perch and a spine of *synodontism*.[57] Fishing also appears to have been a minor activity at Soba East.[58] Iron-barbed fish hooks have been recovered from Qasr Ibrim along with a fragment of a cotton and flax netting, perhaps from a fishing net.[59] Both at Debeira West and Soba East hunting made a very minor contribution to the medieval diet. However, the evidence from the service area of the monastery on Kom H at Old Dongola indicates that the main source of meat there came from the gazelle and that domesticated species were less well represented.[60]

Manufacturing

TEXTILES

An extensive collection of equipment associated with spinning, weaving and sewing has been found at Qasr Ibrim leading to the suggestion that it was a major cloth manufacturing centre.[61] Much of this is of wood which is rarely well preserved at other sites, therefore how typical or otherwise Ibrim may have been in this respect is uncertain. Whereas at most medieval sites pot-sherds, roughly circular with a central hole, were used to form spindle whorls at Ibrim they formed less than 9% of the whorls, with 1.5% being of stone (a single example) and the rest of wood.[62] In pre-Christian levels on that site mud loom weights were extremely common but the use of the warp-weighted loom does not appear to have continued later. Evidence was found for card weaving in the form of a number of the wooden tablets. Vast quantities of textile are also preserved on the site; 23,432 pieces being discovered in one season alone (colour plates XIII and XIV).[63] Cotton, wool, silk and linen were represented. Whereas the silk cloth was all imported from Egypt, elsewhere in the Middle East or even China, much of the rest may have been of local manufacture. All were coloured with the use of only four dyes, madder (*rubia tinctoria*) for shades of red and orange, indigo (*indigofera tinctoria*) for blues; and weld and Persian berries, both used to produce shades of yellow. Other colours were made by overlaying two of those just noted. A blanket recently discovered within a grave at Kassinger Bahri near the Fourth Cataract is made from wool of a natural yellow colour. In this case the blue was produced from indigo or woad (*isatis tinctoria*) and red from a mixture of madder and indigo.[64]

Ibn Selim records that the Nubians downstream of the Third Cataract produced a rough material from the locally grown cotton.[65] Wool was derived not only from caprines but also from the camel. A study of the textiles found on the right bank of the Nile between Faras and Gemai showed that the use of camel wool was extremely common whereas sheep's wool was found only in a few cases.[66] Only at Kulubnarti has evidence been found for the use of human hair to make mats, string, cord and braid.[67]

POTTERY

Pottery is one of the most common artefacts found on archaeological sites in the Nile Valley from the Mesolithic onwards. The medieval period is no exception and at some periods the profligate manner in which still usable vessels were discarded, particularly in the X-Group, indicates that even the relatively fine pottery was both plentiful and cheap. However, at other times shortages are apparent, the reduced availability caused either by financial stringency on the part of the owner or as a result of particular pottery types going out of production. In those cases we find attempts to prolong the life of vessels by repairing them with thongs passed through holes drilled to either side of the break. It has been estimated that, if each family broke 3 pots per year in a settlement of 100 families, that might result in the deposition of 6,000 sherds per year, 600,000 per century, and the amount of pottery discovered on medieval sites makes such an estimate appear plausible.

The rate of breakage is by no means uniform. Prized table wares would be used less frequently and with greater care, coarse storage jars buried in the ground would be well protected, while cooking pots, exposed to all the rigours of heating and cooling, will have been at great risk. *Qawadis*, of which at least forty were needed per *saqia*, were prone to breakage and also probably had a short life in use.

The technology of pottery production has shown considerable continuity and conservatism over many millennia. This is particularly true of the hand-made wares which are traditionally associated both with local manufacture for use in the household and with production by women. Whether either of these generalizations are correct for the situation is medieval Nubia is open to debate. In northern Nubia the hand-made wares exhibit a high degree of standardization from one region to another over a distance of at least 1,000 km, which would suggest that they were produced at one or a few closely related centres. On the other hand, the relatively poor quality of the vessels would made long-distance transport of them difficult, and their low unit cost, it might be suggested, would make such movement uneconomic. However, at least from the Debba bend to Aswan, apart from at the cataracts at low water, transportation by river was feasible and, as all the settlements lay in very close proximity to the waterway, even given the fragility of the vessels and their low value such long distance transportation may still have been viable. Adams after weighing the evidence favours local production of these wares with one notable exception. In the very late medieval period, *c.* 1500-1600, with the demise of the wheel-made wares, a range of hand-made vessels were produced which were clearly designed to fill the gap in the market. The forms approximate to those previously confined to wheel-made vessels and a wider range of vessels bear painted decoration.[68]

There is no evidence for the production of hand-made wares in complex kilns. At least some of the hand-made wares were presumably fired in bonfires in which the pots were packed around and covered with combustible material which was then set alight, or were placed in small pits over which the combustible material was heaped. This method of production is still employed with some degree of sophistication in Western Sudan, but is usually confined to small-scale production. This need not always have been the case and there is evidence from elsewhere for major industries with extensive trading networks relying entirely on pots fired in this way.[69] There is some evidence that pit kilns were also utilized for wheel-made wares.[70] By these means only low temperatures, in the region of 600-700°c, could be attained and hence the relative softness of the fabric of the hand-made wares.[71]

The typical medieval kiln for the firing of wheel-made wares, which can be closely paralleled in a Kushite context,[72] is a two-chambered cylindrical structure, usually with the lower part of the kiln dug approximately 1 m into the ground, access into it being provided by a stoke-hole usually facing away from the prevailing north wind. In many cases the subterranean pit is lined with mud brick and the superstructure is constructed of the same material which, owing to the heat generated during the firing, has burnt to the consistency of red brick and is often also vitrified on the surface owing to the excessive heat, which was so deleterious to the structural integrity of the kiln and necessitated numerous repairs. The furnace chamber was usually about 1.35 m high and was roofed by a floor supported on two arched ribs springing from engaged piers. The firing floor was pierced, allowing the heat to rise from the lower chamber and circulate around the pots before exiting through the upper part of the kiln, which was never, as far as we know, vaulted, but was presumably covered with some material such as the caked cow dung which is still used today for this purpose in Egypt. By experimentation it has been determined that a temperature of approximately 850°c may have been attained, and ethnographic parallels suggest a firing time of about 4 hours. The fuel used was presumably the locally available timber, tamarisk and acacia, although dhurra stalks and animal dung may have been used in the smaller establishments and for firing hand-made pottery. To maximize fuel efficiency kilns were presumably only fired when fully loaded, and it is clear that a kiln load could consist of a wide range of forms closely packed together in the firing chamber. The bulk of the kilns known in Nobadia are between 1.2 and 1.7 m in internal diameter; a much larger example at Faras may have been inefficient and seems to have been superseded by two smaller installations. At Old Dongola, however, several kilns with diameters between 2.4 and 3 m have been excavated.[73] There are also a number of much smaller kilns, as little as 400 mm in diameter, which may have been designed to fire special pots, although this cannot be demonstrated by the available evidence. One of the kilns at Old Dongola has, on its northern side, a brick structure interpreted by the excavator as a chimney.[74]

The essential raw material for pottery production, clay, was available virtually everywhere in the Nile Valley. All the hand-made wares, and the bulk of the wheel-made pots, were fashioned from the Nile mud although some of the finer pottery types were made from fossil clays, found along the desert margins. A wide range of temper was added to the clay and the nature of this material, the type of clay employed, together with the forms of the pottery and the styles of decoration can be used to suggest the location of the production centres. Hand-made pottery is generally coarse and little trace of its manufacture has been found. Ethnographic data suggests that the pottery was made from one lump, the vessel walls being extruded by 'pinching' rather than by using the coil method. A turntable of some sort to allow the pot to be rotated is commonly used.[75] The most simple method is to rest the pot on a mat sat on the floor and many Nubian pots exhibit mat impressions around the base from just such a method of manufacture. To produce uniform vessels a fast wheel is an essential requirement for all but the most skilled potters. The wheel probably used in Nubia was the kick wheel, where the rotary motion is imparted by the feet on a stone affixed to the bottom of the vertical axle, at the top of which the turntable is mounted.

The location of pottery manufacturing on a large, 'industrial' scale will have been affected by the availability of fuel on the one hand and of ease of access to the market on the other. As already noted, the availability, in most areas, of riverborne transport will have allowed a wide range of localities to have access to the market. Perhaps for these reasons no single manufactory seems to have remained in use for more than a few hundred years. The earliest evidence for medieval pottery production comes from Debeira East where several kilns have been excavated along with adjacent small enclosures, delimited by walls perhaps never any higher than 400 mm, which may have been used as drying areas for the pots prior to them being placed in the kiln. The very high level of standardization of X-Group ceramics suggests that all the examples of particular types were made in the same centre, although there may have been more than one centre, each specializing in a range of forms. The Debeira kilns were producing what Adams calls Classic X-Group red ware

(Ware R1) and a coarse, unslipped, reddish-brown, utility product (Ware U1), confined almost exclusively to *qawadis* and ceramic pipes. The final products at the site show influences from imported Byzantine pottery and may date to the period around the arrival of Christianity.

Recent work at Old Dongola is demonstrating that it had an industrial complex commensurate with its status as the capital of the Kingdom of Makuria. Indications, revealed through a magnetometer survey, which is an ideal method of picking up anomalies caused by the effects of the heat generated by kilns and furnaces, for a large number of kilns have been noted in the area 500 m to the north of the original walled city. In contrast to many other sites the pottery quarter at Old Dongola was used for many centuries and kilns have been found dating to between the Transitional and the Late Christian periods. The Transitional period wares being produced here have been found in pagan graves, but bear decoration inspired by Christian ideology.[76] Of the post-Classic kilns, dated 1100-1200, kiln R2 was emptied before it was abandoned unlike the adjacent kiln R1 where the contents of the last firing remained within it.[77] Among the products of these kilns were a number bearing the painted signatures of the pot painters,[78] and four different marks taken to be signatures of painters have been noted on a number of vessels recovered in House PCH.1.[79]

The best preserved installations have been excavated at Faras and appear to have been in use from the early eighth until into the tenth century (colour plate XV).[80] A pre-existing building with an occupation spanning two phases was modified, initially with the addition of one small kiln. This was followed by three further phases and the construction of several large kilns and ancillary installations which included bins for mixing the clay; a great deal of mud from this activity was found splashed onto the lower parts of the surrounding walls. A common feature of all the intensively used kiln sites was the massive amount of debris generated. At Faras deposits adjacent to the kilns indicated that each time a furnace was cleaned out a deposit 50-150 mm thick of ash and pottery sherds was deposited. The steady build-up of the surrounding ground level necessitated the continual rebuilding of features at a higher level and sometimes, when the stoke-hole became too difficult of access, the kiln was extended vertically and reused at a higher level. At Faras by the date of the abandonment of the kiln complex there had been a build-up of 50

Figure 76 **Waster dumps and ash layers by the pottery kilns at Old Dongola.**

layers of debris, 3 m in thickness, and similar situation has been observed at Old Dongola (Fig. 76).[81]

We know very little about the organization of pottery production. In X-Group Nobadia the kilns at Debeira East were only used in the latter part of that period and not all the forms of pottery then current were produced there. Unfired vessels in a white ware have been found at Qasr Ibrim, which was presumably another production centre, but where the early red wares were produced is unknown. In the Early Christian period there appear to have been many centres in Nobadia, as is indicated by the great diversity in wares. Among the kilns in operation at that time were those at Debeira, Serra and Faras. In the united kingdoms of Nobadia and Makuria, Faras and Old Dongola were clearly major production centres and another has been claimed at el-Ghazali in the Wadi Abu Dom although no installations have yet been found there. It is clear that there were at least two centres in Classic Christian Makuria producing closely-related yet different pottery, that from the southern centre being of slightly better quality than the Faras products. Old Dongola must be considered as a serious candidate for the site of this southern production centre. A stamp used to produce the central roundels of bowls of this type has been found in the service area of the monastery on Kom H,[82] but the significance of such a find is uncertain as similar stamps have been noted at a number of other sites where there is no obvious direct connection with fine pottery manufacture.[83] At Faras and elsewhere utility pottery was often fired within the same kilns as the finer table wares. For some time at Faras there was the production only of amphorae of an unusual form by the whole factory.

The installations at Faras appear to have been abandoned in a hurry, the potters leaving large numbers of vessels in all stages of manufacture on the site, and this during the period of greatest prosperity for the Kingdom of Makuria. Economic factors do not seem to have been to blame, as the demise of the Faras production resulted in a severe shortage of similar pottery types which was only filled later by the large-scale importation of pottery from Aswan. This expansion of the Aswan market was clearly a result of, not a cause of, the collapse of the Faras potteries.

It was only around 1100 that a Nubian successor to the Faras potteries emerged, and gradually over the next century came to dominate the market, at least in the area between the First and the Fourth Cataracts. These products are remarkably uniform suggesting that they were produced at one centre which must have been even larger and longer-lived than the Faras industry. Old Dongola has been suggested as the site of this industry. The Terminal Christian period saw a return to many smaller scale production centres probably reflecting the unsettled nature of the times when long-distance trade may have been hazardous if not impossible. There is little evidence for continuity into the post-medieval period; the wheel-made industries disappear except for the local production of *qawadis* although even some of these were then made by hand.[84] Why the production of wheel-made pottery ceased is unclear. It was presumably not a direct response to a general impoverishment of the potential consumers as, at least for a time, decorated hand-made pottery was made instead. The worsening economic condition of Nubia in the face of long periods of insecurity and the influx of new people into the region must have made the maintenance of a large-scale industry increasingly more difficult and less viable. The potters producing hand-made vessels, with their lack of permanent installations, will have had much more mobility and hence greater flexibility in reacting to the changing situation, and this must have given them an advantage.

There are also other kiln sites which may have produced more local wares, and *qawadis* in particular were presumably made at many centres. At Soba East the only kiln so far excavated within the Kingdom of Alwa was being used for *qawadis* production.[85] Within a domestic structure at Arminna West was a rectangular chamber 2 x 1.85 m in size which had three brick piers 1.15 m high against its north and south walls. The walls were heavily burned, leading to the suggestion that this was a pottery kiln, perhaps used for the production of domestic wares on a small scale by the women of the village.[86] No evidence, however, was noted for how the floor separating the furnace and firing chambers was constructed. Many other kilns in the smaller settlements, catering for local consumption, have been excavated in Lower Nubia, even some which do not appear to be associated with any habitations.

In Egypt there is evidence for pottery production for internal consumption, but also for retail, by monasteries and a similar relationship may have existed in Nubia. Certainly at Faras the pottery developed within a pre-existing building which was of such a size and complexity as to suggest that it may have been monastic. The large amounts of Classic Christian pottery at the monastery at el-Ghazali likewise may reflect monastic pottery production at that site. Monasteries and kilns are known at Old Dongola but so far there is no clear evidence for a link between the two. Adams draws attention to the inspiration for the designs painted on Classic Christian pottery, from Coptic manuscript illumination, which would have been familiar to monks and would have been ready accessible to them.

The only Alwan kiln known lies immediately adjacent to a palatial building which may have been associated with the Church.

In Nubia, unlike Egypt, pottery decoration was an art form and its wide popularity suggests that it was appreciated as such.[87] Among the most prized pottery may have been the Islamic glazed wares imported especially from Fustat but also from other centres. The forms are of limited utility and extremely fragile yet they are found as far upstream as Soba East.[88] Even more surprising is the, albeit rare, appearance of Chinese porcelain in the Nile Valley.[89] The only possible evidence for local production of glazed wares in Nubia is at Soba East where a small

Figure 77 **Glazed aquamanile from Soba East.**

group of highly distinctive vessels with a very poor quality glaze have been found. The quality of the glaze and the form of the vessels (Fig. 77) which, although copying Persian *aquamanile*, do so in such a way as to have lost the functional aspects of the originals, suggest the possibility that they were idiosyncratic local products by a potter who was familiar in general terms with the very fine lustre ware examples which were made in Iran, but neither fully understood their form nor was competent enough to produce a proper glaze.[90] The *aquamanile* from Hambukol is of rather different form and the style of decoration is much less alien to Nubian tradition.[91]

MINERAL RESOURCES AND METALWORK

Evidence for the production of iron as opposed to its use is rare. A little to the north of the defences of Old Dongola two small circular furnaces less than 1 m in diameter have been located. The better preserved is formed of mud bricks set on end surviving to a height of 400 mm. An opening 120 mm wide by 145 mm high has a 400 mm channel hollowed out of the bedrock leading to it. Within were found alternating layers of iron ore and charcoal and a radiocarbon dating of the latter material suggested that the furnace was abandoned in the early sixth century.[92] Two oval pits within Building F at Soba East may also have been used for smelting. They showed evidence for intense heat but no metalworking debris was recovered.[93] Five hundred metres to the east of the monastery at el-Ghazali are extensive mounds of slag with a number of what may be beehive-shaped furnaces. The appearance of the slag was said to be like that produced in the course of smelting by the 'blooming' process.[94] Though not certainly of medieval date the association of these with the monastery seems likely although the post-Meroitic defended enclosures at Umm Ruweim 1 and 2, Umm Khafur and Umm Kuweib, for which no satisfactory function has been suggested, lie not far away upstream.

In Tomb B.95 at Ballana were found 5 iron ingots with an average length of 340 mm and 31 with an average length of 380 mm came from Tomb B.80.[95] Iron was used extensively for weaponry and large numbers of arrows in particular have been found in post-Meroitic graves.[96] Tools of iron are also common and a range of knives, hoes (*toria*), adzes, axe and hammer heads, blades from a bow saw, tongs, chisels and metal cutters were found in the royal tombs at Ballana and many of similar types have been found on occupation sites. At the nearby settlement of Jebel Adda an early X-Group blacksmith was buried along with his hammer, tongs and trimming file.[97] Iron was also used to make bindings for strengthening boxes and chests.

Copper alloy was widely used for a range of items including needles, vessels of varying forms and weaponry.[98] The bulk of the material has been recovered from pagan graves, particularly from the royal and elite burials. Many of the finer pieces from Lower Nubia are of foreign manufacture. Those locally made include vessels formed on a lathe with cast elements soldered in place. The finely decorated bowls from el-Hobagi are thought by their excavator to represent a continuation of production in the Kushite style into the later fourth century although an alternative view is that they were recovered from earlier Kushite graves and re-interred at that time.[99] On a number of occasions a single arrowhead of copper alloy was interred in graves along with large numbers of iron heads, the copper-alloy heads perhaps having had an amuletic value to increase the power of the iron-tipped arrows.[100]

Metal utensils were not common. Cutlery was not utilized in food consumption with the possible exception of the spoon, wooden examples of which have been found. For food preparation wooden spoons and ladles and iron knives were available. The rarity of metal containers may partly be the result of the reusable nature of the raw material and its intrinsic value as scrap.

Although during the medieval period the gold mines in the Eastern Desert lay beyond the area usually controlled by the Nubian states small-scale extraction may still have been possible within the valley itself, and gold from the Upper Blue Nile is mentioned in some of the sources (discussed in more detail below). A small unworked ingot of silver was recovered from a cache below the floor of a house at Meinarti, suggesting that the raw material, which is not available in Nubia, was imported to be worked up locally into finished objects.[101]

GLASS

No unambiguous evidence for the manufacture of glass has yet been found in Nubia although a wide range of glass vessels, many imported as containers, as well as window glass, is known. However, from a few sites, among them Debeira West and Soba East, large lumps of unworked glass have been recovered.[102]

JEWELLERY

Some of the finest jewellery is that recovered from early medieval pagan graves, particularly those at Qustul and Ballana. Among the finds are very heavy anklets with terminals in the form of lion heads, anklets of large beads, elaborate bracelets, earrings, finger and toe rings and a profusion of necklaces with beads in a very wide range of materials including semi-precious stones, silver and gold.[103] The most common ornaments worn by medieval Nubians were strings of beads made from a wide variety of materials. Continuing a very ancient tradition many of these were of ostrich eggshell. At Ibrim the most common were

Figure 78 **Stone finger rings from Soba East (after Allason-Jones 1991, fig. 71).**

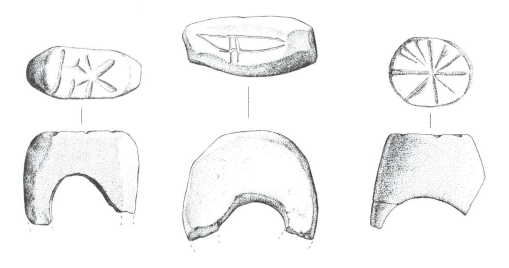

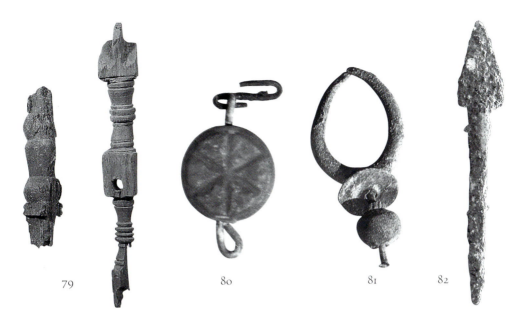

79   80   81   82

Figures 79-82 **Wooden furniture elements (79), earring (80), an iron finger ring (81) and a copper-alloy arrowhead (82) from Soba East.**

of glass, with blue beads being the most frequent, perhaps to ward off the evil eye. Beads from that site were also found of shell, pottery or faience, stone, wood, bone and cowrie shell and were probably worn as bracelets, used as part of earrings or as decorative ornaments on objects.[104] An adult male buried in a grave at Kassinger Bahri near the Fourth Cataract wore blue and white faience beads as a diadem.[105] At Soba East there appears to have been a liking for large and rather unattractive beads, either of ceramic or of unfired mud, some of which may have come from rosaries.[106]

Rings were made from a wide variety of materials, sometimes with a decorated bezel, and designed for use as signet rings or as amulets, such as that from Qasr Ibrim bearing the cryptogram ΧΠΘ, the abbreviation for the archangel Michael.[107] Rings worn on the thumb are an attribute of status and some of the Makurian kings are shown wearing them on wall paintings. The crude rings of stone from Soba East (Fig. 78) are unusual.[108]

Jewellery was made from a wide range of materials, often with more than one material used in an item (Figs 79-82). Some of the material used to make jewellery appears rather unsuitable both from an aesthetic and practical point of view. Among these objects must be mentioned the mud finger ring with decorated bezel from the monastery on Kom H.[109] At Soba East there appears to have been a penchant for the use of iron for jewellery.[110] Although jewellery was certainly made locally the discovery of a slate mould at Soba East, designed for casting finger rings, and a medallion inscribed in Arabic, underlines the possibilities for the manufacture of items by itinerant craftsmen.[111]

BASKETRY, MATS, CORDAGE, GOURDS AND WOODWORK

Objects made from all these materials only survive where conditions are extremely favourable. Moisture and termites are the most destructive agents, and at many sites one or both of these have conspired to denude the archaeological record of these categories of finds. Wood in particular could be used as fuel or could be reshaped and reused. Good timber was always a relatively scarce commodity in Nubia and little will have gone to waste. It is only at a few sites, Qasr Ibrim in particular, where preservation of all types of material is excellent, that the importance of the organic component in the Nubian cultural assemblage can be appreciated.[112] There is no reason to assume that Qasr Ibrim was unusual in this heavy reliance on organic material for the production of a wide range of artefacts.

Alongside pottery, basketry and gourds were extensively used as containers; some of the latter are decorated.[113] Baskets and mats were made from dom and date palm leaves and from the halfa grass, while cordage was made from the stringy fibres on the palm trunk. Two-handled baskets, of identical form to the modern *guffa*, have been found at Qasr Ibrim and the impression of what may be a similar basket was found at Soba East, where it had been used to carry the mud used as mortar in the construction of Building F.[114] Basketry was also used to fashion lids, stoppers, and smaller bags often with the use of leather as a strengthening component.[115] Small bags were also made from a variety of textiles. Matting was used as a structural element in flat roof construction and reused to line storage pits at Qasr Ibrim. Mats were presumably also used on the floor for sitting on, as today at mealtimes when the Nubians sit around a communal bowl to eat, or for sleeping upon. An Ibrim example may have been used as a mattress complete with padding.[116] Although the mats themselves frequently do not survive their impression is preserved on the lower parts of pottery vessels which were formed on a mat, as was a terracotta *stela* from Arminna which preserves the mat impression on its rear face.[117] Mats and basketry were very rare at Meinarti even though, in many levels, the conditions were suitable for their survival.[118] Wooden bowls were also widely used.

Nubian houses today have little in the way of furniture and medieval Nubian dwellings may have been similar. Portable furniture will have included wooden chests, remains of which have been found on a number of sites, and beds, of which the *angareeb* still used today has a very long history; almost identical examples to modern *angareebs* have been found in 3,500-year-old Kerma graves. At Qasr Ibrim, where conditions for preservation are ideal, there is still a great rarity of furniture although the odd bed or chair leg and small elements from larger items have been recovered. Among the small elements are many lathe-turned objects (Figs 79 and 80) which may be balusters from chairs of benches or from wooden screens or doors.[119] Beds, some well preserved, have been found in early Nubian burials before the introduction of Christianity but are very rare in a funerary context thereafter.[120]

Among the finest wooden objects from X-Group graves are chests. One from Jebel Adda was inlaid with carved ivory figures of deities. Although the lock had been smashed and the contents plundered a few traces of beads indicate the type of objects it had contained.[121] A very fine inlaid chest with four legs came from Tomb Q.14 at Qustul. The front is elaborately decorated with ivory and panels painted red and green. It had iron hinges and a copper-alloy lock with two hasps ending in seated lions. In this case the hasps had been cut and the contents removed, the excavators considered by the workmen who constructed the tumulus over the tomb.[122]

FOOTWARE AND LEATHER GOODS

Discarded footwear is well represented at Qasr Ibrim and the Late Christian material has been published in detail.[123] Among the simplest types of footwear were sandals made from palm leaves of a design familiar from the modern plastic flip-flop which today is worn extensively by the people along the Middle Nile. Many of the palm-leaf sandals show little evidence for wear and their use may have been restricted to the house. Palm-rope sandals

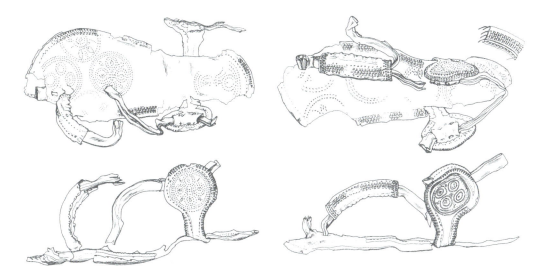

Figure 83 **Leather sandals from Soba East (after Wills 1998, fig. 113).**

are also known; at Ibrim they appear to be an Early and Classic Christian sandal type. A more elaborate type, common in the X-Group at Qasr Ibrim, has an outer sole made of dom palm leaf and an insole of date palm fibre. The uppers are made from a seventeen-strand plait of date palm leaf and the 'Y'-shaped strapping is of dom palm leaf.[124] The most common footwear at Ibrim for everyday use was the leather sandal made of cow hide and often of simple design, each a single piece of leather with straps attached. Much more elaborate footwear, however, was available made from leather. A particularly fine pair of leather sandals was found in situ on the feet of a 25-35-year-old lady at Soba East (Fig. 83). These had a four-ply sole, the top layer, the insole, being highly decorated with stitched or punched roundel designs, three containing a cruciform pattern along the long axis of each sole with two partial roundels at the widest part of the sole. On the straps by the ankle were two further roundels bearing the same type of decoration. They may well be of local manufacture.[125] A single example of a knee-length riding boot was found at Ibrim in an *eparch*'s house and was made of fine leather or pigskin. Shoes were of light construction more akin to a modern slipper and did not withstand wear well; many at Qasr Ibrim show evidence of excessive wear. One or two-ply soles were used with uppers of fine and soft leather. From Soba East comes a randed turn-shoe which is probably one of the earliest examples known.[126] Some fine examples of shoes, with patterns in gilt, can be seen on wall paintings at Faras mostly on the feet of women.[127]

Leather was used for belts and one of these from Qasr el-Wizz, 43 mm wide, was heavily decorated with stamped and tooled designs, as was another from Old Dongola which was tied around the shroud of an individual buried in one of the graves on Kom H.[128] Quivers are among the most elaborate leather objects made. Finds are almost totally confined to the X-Group, reflecting funerary practices rather than that they were not used at a later date. Very fine examples have been found at Jebel Adda where they form the panoply of archers buried in their graves along with bows and archer's looses. Some graves of single individuals contained several quivers. The quivers are of cut and stained leather and decorated with tassels.[129] Large numbers have also been recovered from graves at Qustul and Ballana.[130]

CLOTHING AND OTHER TEXTILES

The many depictions of the upper echelons of Makurian society on wall paintings show them attired in rich robes. Large amounts of textile have been found particularly in graves but also in domestic rubbish deposits at Qasr Ibrim. Two fine collections of apparel come from graves, one presumably of an important civil dignitary, the other that of a bishop. The civil dignitary, Gapoiapa, was buried in all his finery at Jebel Adda in the late thirteenth century. A long coat of red and yellow patterned damask of Mameluke origin lay folded over the body which was clothed in a pair of plain cotton trousers of long and baggy cut under the shroud. A pair of red leather slippers with turned-up toes lay at the foot of the coffin which was made from a hollowed log. The body was wrapped in enormous pieces of gold-brocaded striped silk bearing stamps of Egyptian government offices. The excavator suggested that Gapoiapa was attired in a variant of the upper-class fashion prevalent throughout the Middle East in his time.[131] The clothing belonging to the Bishop of Pachoras, Timotheos, found at Qasr Ibrim was extremely well-preserved. His outer garment was a voluminous bell-shaped hooded cloak of fine dark blue wool embellished with silk and with a lining of red-brown cotton. Around the head was wrapped a turquoise-blue fine cotton veil. His main garments were of the *jellabiya* type described below, and trousers beneath which was a narrow cotton body-belt stitched with white silk. A fine linen *mappa* was tucked into the front of his cloak.[132]

At Old Dongola the possible royal individual buried in clothing made from fine textiles, some with gold thread, in a crypt beneath the Monastery on Kom H has already been mentioned (see p. 39). Among the other items of clothing is a colourful knitted woollen belt from a burial beneath the floor of the chapel Room S1, of a type depicted on wall paintings of monks in the monastery.[133]

Within the Kingdom of Alwa remains of fine clothing have only been recovered from Soba East. A number of individuals buried to the east of Church A had been interred with fabrics, including some with gold thread interwoven among the flax fibres. Both flax and cotton were found, probably from garments, and also a knitted cap. It was suggested that the flax items were imported as ready-made garments from Egypt. Textiles from other graves at Soba were all very poorly preserved but may be from items of clothing and from shrouds.[134]

Figures 84 and 85 **The *jellabiya* and trousers belonging to Bishop Timotheos from Qasr Ibrim (photo The British Museum).**

In the nineteenth century, and as late as the beginning of last century, many Nubians went naked, and el-Qazwini, writing in the thirteenth century, noted that the inhabitants of Old Dongola went naked except that they were wrapped with skins.[135] However, there is considerable evidence, from Qasr Ibrim in particular, that garments were extremely common and were presumably worn by all sections of society. At Ibrim the medieval Nubian male was usually dressed in a long loose gown of cotton or linen of similar type to the *jellabiya* worn by his descendants today. A round opening admitted the head and this was sewn around with another, often contrasting, fabric. The addition of a square underarm gusset to allow greater freedom of movement only appears commonly in the Terminal Christian period, perhaps under the influence of Islamic dress. It was most commonly of undyed cotton but some garments were in solid blue or had blue and white stripes. The only undergarments worn may have been trousers, a very baggy garment probably extending to immediately below the knee and tied with a cord at the waist (Figs 84 and 85). Wool was used for heavy mantles or wraps, in the natural brown colour or in a variety of brightly coloured hues.[136] Loin cloths have been found in graves at Kulubnarti and elsewhere. These are of trapezoid form woven to the required shape on the loom rather than being cut or hemmed.[137]

Trade

PROBLEMS OF INTERPRETING THE DATA

The interpretation of the literary, and particularly the archaeological, evidence for trade can be extremely problematical. One difficulty is the result of the nature of trade itself. In the Oxford English Dictionary trade is defined as the 'Exchange of commodities for money or other commodities, commerce; business done with a specific class or at a specific time; a transaction.'

The meaning of the word commodity in the context of trade is extremely wide and not only encompasses physical goods but less tangible things like goodwill, the promise of a favour in the future, or simply an undertaking to desist from some potentially harmful pursuit on the part of one party to another. One cannot, therefore, assume that the presence of artefacts which are clearly imported indicates an equal and opposite trade in some other commodity which can be sought in the archaeological record.

Among the problems affecting the correct interpretation of the data are those posed by the reuse of artefacts involving their secondary transportation, by the copying of exotic objects by local craftsmen, by the movement of the craftsmen, and by the longevity of certain types of artefacts, both the longevity of their production run and the longevity of their survival in use.

TYPES OF TRADE

Various types of trade have been defined and it is essential to understand the range of trading mechanisms before one attempts to draw conclusions from the evidence for trade. This is particularly the case with the evidence for trade recovered from the archaeological record where objects are found, but where there is often no clear evidence as to how they came to be there.

Polanyi (1968) was the first to characterize trade under the three headings of reciprocity, redistribution and exchange.

> Reciprocity – used to describe the movement of goods and services between symmetrical groups.
> Redistribution – the gathering in of goods by a central organization or individual and their
>   dissemination back to the masses.
> Exchange – the movement of goods back and forth in a market system.

Each of these types of trade can be observed in the historical record in Nubia. All three types of trade can result in the movement of goods from one place to another. The exchange in all cases can be an equal or unequal transaction. It can be influenced by coercion, as when the powerless peasant is forced to pay taxes to an elite or conquering group, or it can reflect the differing perceptions of the value of certain objects between different societies or individuals. The early European contacts with West Africa, where relatively worthless goods (to the Europeans) were traded for valuable products is a good example. Trade does not always involve the movement of goods both ways as goods are frequently traded for favours or services. It must also be borne in mind that goods can move through other mechanisms unrelated to trade. Goods can be given as gifts although this is rarely totally altruistic and is usually a reciprocal arrangement of some sort. However, goods do move with individuals as personal possessions and the interpretation of the presence of such objects can distort our perception of trade, particularly where the volume of evidence is small.

Redistribution is frequently connected with taxation, the state collects goods or services from its subjects and these are redistributed in the form of further goods or services. This can be manifest in the collection and redistribution of foodstuffs from central granaries, but also it can be a trade between food and services on the one hand and the maintenance of peace and the infrastructure of the state on the other, or a combination of these. One feature of redistribution systems is that the party in charge of the system is usually able to maintain a reasonable profit margin if it so desires, returning less than it takes. Such a system is essential to the maintenance of an elite, although it can be cloaked in a different form by such legal fictions as the state ownership of land whereby the subjects are seen to be paying a rent rather than a tax. There is some evidence to indicate that the inhabitants of Makuria were, under the law, the slaves of the king[138] and that all their produce, therefore, legally belonged to the state.

Throughout the medieval period such a redistribution mechanism based on some form of taxation was presumably in force. Two non-food-producing elites were maintained in medieval Nubia, the religious elite and the civil elite, except perhaps in the immediately post-Meroitic period when there is little evidence for a grandiose religious establishment. The Church in the medieval period presumably filled the same niche in society and had similar economic demands as had the temple in earlier times. Another 'parasitic' group on the primary food producers may have been the military, although we know little or nothing about the army of the Nubian kings.

There was one further redistribution system which was widespread in Nubia up to the time of its conversion to Christianity, the result of the practice of burying objects, often of great value, with the dead. As Adams notes 'the adoption of Christian beliefs ... put an end to the clandestine industry of grave robbing, which for centuries had functioned as a rough-and-ready redistribution system in Nubia.'[139]

For market exchange one needs a production surplus, access to a market where the exchange can take place, and a means of transporting the goods to and from the market. On a local scale market exchange needs the minimum of facilities but for more long-distance exchange a peaceful and stable environment greatly facilitates the process, which can be severely handicapped by political and social unrest.

Another essential is a means of assessing the value of the commodities to be traded. In Upper Nubia throughout the medieval period, as in most other periods of its history, there was no currency and, therefore, all trade was achieved by barter. Ibn Selim notes that neither the *dinar* nor the *dirham* are of any use and that all transactions are carried out by the exchange of slaves, cattle, camels, iron tools and grains.[140] This is not an ideal way to trade low value bulky goods over long distances, owing to the necessity of physically taking one's goods to the owner of the commodities one wishes to acquire. In Lower Nubia however, Islamic coinage did circulate. Coins are a rare find in the archaeological record although *dirhem* are referred to in a number of Old Nubian texts from Qasr Ibrim. From that site have been found several Islamic coins and a few coin weights, one inscribed in Old Nubian '*Eparch* of Nobadia'.[141]

TRANSPORT

The feasibility of trade is directly related to the transportation facilities available. In the ancient and medieval Mediterranean world transport by water was vastly cheaper than by land. The availability of water transport, therefore, affected the viability of trade particularly in bulky, heavy or low value goods. There is no reason to doubt that similar cost factors pertained in medieval Nubia.

The suitability of the Nile for transport varies along its course. In the reach from Abu Hamed to ed-Debba, where the direction of the current and the prevailing wind coincide, movement upstream is virtually impossible for vessels under sail. Elsewhere boats were able to float downstream with the current or sail upstream before the north wind which blows virtually all the year round. Local movement of people and goods in the favourable reaches of the river must have occurred and at high water sailing through some of the cataracts was possible. Owing to the problems posed by the riverine conditions and the circuitous course of the river itself, land transport, by donkey and especially by camel, was always an important alternative for the movement of certain types of goods.

SOURCES OF INFORMATION

There are two main sources of information for trade in Nubia, the direct evidence of the written record and the indirect evidence derived from archaeology where the implication of the recovery of objects and materials from particular locations suggests the movement of those goods from their place of origin.

Literature

References to trade between medieval Nubia and the outside world come almost exclusively from Egyptian sources, either Byzantine or Islamic, or from information gleaned in Egypt. This information may well be biased, is often ill-informed and may be selective. It is extremely difficult to evaluate the shortcomings of the literary evidence and it must be used with some caution.

The Byzantine historians speak at some length on the export of the Christian ideology to the south,[142] but tell us little of the material objects of trade, although when the Makurians sent an embassy to the Emperor Justin in 573 they came bearing traditional African gifts, elephant's tusks and a giraffe.[143] With the arrival of the Arabs in Egypt trade takes a prominent position in the relations between Egypt and Nubia and was formalized in the *Baqt* treaty of 652. This is a peace treaty and not primarily a trade agreement. It does not reflect an agreement for the mutual benefit of the signatories but presumably reflects the relative positions of strength of the two parties.[144] There are varying views on the relative worth of the goods stipulated in the *Baqt* but it may well be that it was the Makurians who were disadvantaged as a result of it. However, it did endure largely unchanged for several centuries and, therefore, may not be as inequitable as has been thought. By enumerating the quantity and range of goods which were to be moved both ways across the frontier it provides us with the first literary evidence on which to base an estimate both of the trade surpluses of the two states and of their import needs. Many of the commodities noted are familiar from earlier sources. The main items may be summarised thus: from south to north – 400 slaves; from north to south – 1000 *ardebs* of wheat, 1000 *ardebs* of millet, 1000 vessels of wine, two horses and cloaks and other textiles.[145]

At a later date a number of new items were added including wild animals for display in Egypt, particularly under the Fatimids.[146] The goods sought from Nubia were those that had been sourced there for millennia and the trade goods may be compared with those listed in *The Annals of Thutmose III* of the tribute from Wawat, the northern part of the

Egyptian domains in Nubia and from Kush lying to the south, which includes cattle, gold, slaves, ivory, ebony and harvests.[147]

Trade along the Nile appears to have been rigidly controlled. The major point of exchange of goods brought by river between the Nubians and the Muslims was at Philae where the Nubian boats offloaded their cargoes and where the Muslim boats moored.[148] Around 1300 the Sultan el-Malik en-Nasir, according to et-Taghribirdi, abolished the taxes levied on every slave on the boats of the Nubians at the point of transhipment.[149] Aswan, where there was a large population of Nubians, was the terminus of Nubian caravans.[150] The Nubian/Egyptian frontier was not preclusive and Muslim traders were able to enter the northern part of Makuria as far south as Baqwa at the downstream end of the Second Cataract where the cataract and official sanction halted further progress. Only those with express royal permission were allowed to travel further.[151] In the twelfth century Abu Salih speaks of Upper Maqs, at the upstream end of the Batn el-Hajar, as the major customs post where all were searched on pain of death, including the king.[152] It was there that a lively trade in goods from the north and south was carried on.[153] The increasing power of the Muslims in Lower Nubia may have led to the move of the customs post upstream to a less vulnerable locality.

There is a hint of the use of another route, which may have left the Nile near Sai, and passing through Selima Oasis, reached Kharqa, which is mentioned as a place where people coming from Nubia pass through on their way to Middle Egypt.[154]

Some of the most valuable evidence for Nubia's trade comes from letters and official documents discovered at Qasr Ibrim. These are firsthand accounts of trade contacts and provide fascinating details of how trade was actually organized. Qasr Ibrim appears to have been an important centre of trade via the port of Aidhab on the Red Sea coast, documenting a conduit for trade which bypassed Egypt although that trade was still under Muslim control, the Muslims acting as middlemen.[155] The *eparch* was facilitating trade on behalf of the Makurian king according to letters from Ibrim. Dating from the twelfth century are several letters between the *eparch* and an official at the Fatimid court who owned ships at Aidhab and had a trading business based at Qoz. The Muslim official appears to have acted as an agent for the Makurian ruler dispatching goods to him and selling slaves on his behalf. On his death or retirement his brother continued the correspondence.[156] Rather more surprising is the evidence contained in another letter indicating that the *eparch* also had a similar arrangement with the Alwan king.[157]

Archaeology

The study of the archaeological evidence for trade has certain advantages. The element of human bias is largely removed from the data, although the competence and the personal interests of the excavators can have some effect on the recovery of data. However, every effort should be, and in most cases is, made to remove this bias. In theory archaeology should be able to provide evidence relating to all periods and is not reliant on the interest of some literate society on the processes of trade to and from Nubia. One great disadvantage is that artefacts are difficult to date, hence it is not easy to tie in the data we glean from archaeology with what we know of political activities from the literary sources. This is much to be regretted, as the influence of political events on the pattern and scale of trade can be very significant. The material found in the archaeological record is, unfortunately, biased by a number of factors beyond human control: the differential survival of artefacts and other trade goods, influenced on the one hand by the materials themselves and on the other by the climatic and local environment in which they were deposited.

Ceramic material is in many ways the least susceptible to the bias of survival and it has a number of other advantages from an archaeological point of view. In the medieval period it is a common material, often embarrassingly so when one has to process it from excavation. It was clearly cheap to produce and purchase yet it is easily broken, difficult to repair and rarely reusable.[158] It is produced from a plastic material which can be moulded and decorated in an infinite variation of styles, features which can often be allocated to particular cultures and time periods. This allows it to be dated, to some extent, and to be used as an indicator of particular phases of a culture. Its frequently distinctive nature further allows one to recognize it wherever it is found. The raw material is abundant, of low value and, therefore, usually uneconomical to transport, so that one can be confident that the pottery was made close to the source of the clay and that it was the finished product rather than the raw material which was exported. Hence the typological characteristics will relate to the area around the source of the clay.

A range of scientific techniques are available which can be used to attempt to locate the source of the raw material, but their use in the Nile Valley is problematical. All the techniques seek to define the minerals and/or trace elements which form a distinctive feature of the clays from a particular area and can be used to distinguish clays from different sources. Much of the pottery in the Nile Valley, particularly, but not invariably, the coarser wares, is made from the silt which is brought down the river in large quantities. The silt is a mixture of material from all the areas from the river's source to the point at which it is found. Owing to the differing characters of the White and Blue Niles, the latter with its rapid flow is responsible for the movement of the bulk of the silt found downstream from Khartoum. The geology of much of the valley is not distinctive, and this, coupled with the mixing of the minerals in the silt, makes precise identification of the original source of the analysed material extremely difficult if not impossible. In a recent study of a number of ceramics recovered from the excavations at Soba East[159] the mineral signature of almost all the ceramics was not sufficiently distinctive to suggest a more precise source than in the Nile Valley. Only in one case did the presence of muscovite mica, a mineral not found upstream of the Fifth to Fourth Cataract area, suggest a more localized source. Pottery is the only material we have from Nubia which can assist in our attempt to assess the scale and nature of Nubia's internal trade, which will be discussed in more detail below.

Other artefacts with a good rate of survival include objects of stone, of glass and of metalwork. Stone and glass, like pottery, are virtually indestructible. However, stone is less easily worked and many objects made from it are not distinctive in design, hence not closely assignable to a particular culture, source or date. Scientific techniques can be used in an attempt to locate the source, but this is only useful when the stone is itself uncommon. In Nubia the stone used may have been drawn from a wide range of areas. By its nature stone, particularly large stone elements, tends to be quarried as close to its place of ultimate use as possible, but this is by no means invariably the case. Glass has a wide range of form and decoration, but is a much higher value product than pottery and hence by no means as common. The raw material from which it is made is ubiquitous and less susceptible to being tied down to a particular area. Some metals survive well in certain conditions, gold survives well in all environments. However, the precious metals have frequently been removed during the quest for loot, they were never common and great pains would have been taken to recover them should they have been lost by accident. In the medieval period they may have had a very long life in use being passed from one generation to another. Other metals are subject to decay in certain environmental conditions although their survival rate in Nubia, with its arid climate, is generally high. Metals are a relatively high value product and they are frequently moved as a raw material and worked up into artefacts far from their source. They can also be consigned to scrap and reworked, factors which can add an element of confusion when we try to assess their movement through trade. Their stylistic characteristics need not reflect their original source.

Usually the source of artefacts has to be ascertained by a study of the form and techniques used in manufacture related to the known distribution of similar artefacts. It is generally the case that artefacts from a given source are commoner the closer one approaches that source. However, this is not always the case particularly when objects are produced principally for export. The Egyptian potters of the medieval period at Aswan seem to have produced types of pottery specifically designed for the Nubian market which were rather different from the normal Egyptian wares.[160] Where the manufactory is known, e.g., with pottery where the kiln is known, a source for the material can on occasion be ascertained precisely. The objects themselves are almost always mute as to the mechanisms by which they have arrived in a particular context. Only extremely rarely do they preserve written data which explicitly states from whence they came. Some of the best examples of this are the amphorae which bear *dipinti* – painted inscriptions with the names of the owners of the estates on which the amphorae were made, where they were filled, and often a description of the contents. They are also on occasion dated. Such a practice may have been more widespread than is now apparent, but the nature of the painted inscriptions means that, except in the most favourable of circumstances, no trace of them has survived. However, the *dipinti* on the amphorae from Qustul and Ballana do not give the origin of the amphorae or of their contents. These inscriptions, in red and black ink, most frequently appear to indicate that the amphorae held dry goods, corn or barley was suggested. They also bear names, which may be those of the merchants who supplied them, followed by numbers, perhaps batch numbers.[161]

In Nubia a number of vessels bear graffiti which may relate to their movement as trade items. However, it has not so far proved possible to ascertain the meaning of the symbols noted. They may refer to the potter who made the vessel, to the owner of the vessel or of its contents, to the contents themselves, or to the recipient amongst other interpretations. Recent finds of amphorae of local manufacture at Old Dongola bear inscriptions which have been interpreted as addresses for delivery. These mention a bishop Maria[kudda?] and the *archpresbyter* Michael Psate.[162] Some vessels were sealed with mud bungs (stoppers) which are often bear stamp impressions (Fig. 86).[163] These presumably are not there for decorative but for functional reasons. The wide range of stamp impressions, and the relatively small

Figure 86 **A selection of stamps on mud bungs from Soba East** (after Allason-Jones 1991, fig. 79).

database at present available for study, has so far made it impossible to ascertain the precise meaning and function of the symbols, so we have little idea of the source of the commodities and of the mechanisms for their movement, whether via the market economy or as a result of redistribution (i.e., taxation). Stamps have been found at a number of sites; those from Debeira West were thought to have been used to stamp bread although their use on bungs seems equally plausible.[164]

During the medieval period some pottery was traded over considerable distances. The Aswan wares are extremely common in the region between the First and Second Cataracts, much less common in the Batn el-Hajar and extremely rare further south, although they do reach as far upstream as Soba East.[165] Faras products have a distribution along the river of at least 250 km while in the Late Christian period the market extends for over 650 km along the valley. The market was dynamic and the ebb and flow of one industry was dependent on the level of competition from another. The Aswan potters seem to have filled the gap in the market caused by the demise of the Faras potteries in the tenth century only to face increasingly stiff competition from the development of the Late Christian Nubian industry which dominated the ceramic supply later. Some of the finest ceramic products, the Islamic glazed wares in particular, never faced any competition from local Nubian products and, although found in relatively small amounts, are distributed throughout Nubia. Adams suggests that the trade in pottery was not organized by the producers but by merchants who purchased wares at the factory and then organized their transport by river wherever possible.[166] The economic viability of trade in low-value pottery may have been influenced by the trade in other commodities and we may expect cargoes to be made up of a wide range of goods, the movement of high value goods making it feasible to move very low value goods from place to place. Pottery may also have been traded at very favourable rates as return cargoes, ships moving Aswan products upstream to their markets may well have taken on local products which would then be sold downstream and vice versa.[167]

Organic products are frequently very poorly represented in the archaeological record. In extremely damp conditions where there is an shortage of oxygen they can survive very well and in extremely dry conditions survival is equally impressive. Between these two extremes survival varies considerably. In Nubia survival falls off as one moves south into the rain belt. The chemical composition of the burial medium can also have a very adverse affect on survival particularly of bone. Another factor is the activity of certain insects, particularly termites which are voracious consumers of most organic morsels and no respecters of antiquities. Among the organic products which leave little or no trace in the archaeological record are the human and animal commodities which were often traded 'on the hoof'. At all periods for which we have literary evidence central Africa has been a source of slaves. Although we may assume that this trade was of considerable scale it cannot be documented archaeologically. Slavery is specifically mentioned in the *Baqt* and in earlier documents. Occasional finds of shackles have been noted, but never in sufficient quantity in any single location to allow one to suggest that they were associated with the trading of slaves and a number of other interpretations for their use could be suggested. Under the Fatimids the Egyptian army contained very large numbers of Nubian slaves, many more than could have been supplied by the *Baqt*. Many of these must have been obtained by trade.[168]

The nature and direction of the trade in animal products is likewise difficult to document. Into the late antique period many of the animals which we now consider to be central African species were found over a much greater range in the Middle East and North Africa. The recovery of such materials as ivory and ostrich eggshell does not allow us to suggest whence that material may have come and by what routes. A single tusk found beneath the central church on mound B at Soba East[169] may have come from an animal killed in the vicinity, although Soba is now far to the north of the present range of the elephant. In the twelfth century elephants, along with giraffe and gazelle, are described as living in the vicinity of Old Dongola.[170] In the next century leopards and giraffe were still common in the region.[171] In the late thirteenth century the Makurian king Shekanda, as recompense for Muslim support, undertook to supply annually three elephants, three giraffe and five she-leopards, along with domestic animals to the Sultan.[172] The import of sheep from Nubia by the Sultan Nasir in 1340 was for breeding purposes[173] and does not indicate that these were normally an international trade item. Skins very rarely survive yet may also have been a major item of trade.

Other natural products include hard woods, which are mentioned by Ibn Selim. During the floods ebony,[174] logwood, frankincense, a timber called in Arabic *el-qana*, and one which smells like the olibanum floated down the river and were, presumably, 'harvested' by the Alwans. The large logs were used to form the helms of boats.[175]

Cotton was exported to the north in the later Kushite period. Archaeological evidence from Qasr Ibrim indicates trade in cotton in the first four centuries AD after which the introduction of the plant to the area presumably brought about the trade's demise.[176]

Trade in certain food items may have been extensive. Ceramics may have played a significant role in the movement of edible commodities. They frequently only had a value as containers of a commodity which is often unknown. However, they are by no means the only types of containers that may have been available. Containers of wood, skins and cloth sacks may have been equally or more common. When recovered from the archaeological record pottery containers are found where they have been discarded after their more precious contents have been removed. This was observed at Soba East, where, in one room of the mud-brick palatial structure, Building D, were found many thousands of sherds of large canteen-shaped pots which are generally referred to as pilgrim flasks. These, two complete examples of which had a capacity of 7.35 and 5.9 litres,[177] were presumably traded as containers for a liquid of unknown type. The contents were presumably emptied when the containers arrived at their destination and the flasks promptly discarded, just as today we would discard an empty tin of baked beans. Elsewhere in the building a different approach was adopted. Over 1,000 mud bungs were found in large dumps within and immediately adjacent to the building.[178] It was clear that these had been used to seal the mouths of the large jars traditionally known as 'beer jars'. The jars themselves were not recovered in quantity on mound B suggesting that they still had a function after the contents were removed: presumably they were returned to whence they came to be refilled. The different treatment of the pilgrim flasks and the 'beer jars' may relate in part to the distance from their source to their destination. The pilgrim flasks were made in the area of the Fifth to Fourth Cataract or further downstream (source at Old Dongola?) and hence it was presumably more economical to dump them than return them as empties. The source of the 'beer jars' is unknown but may have been local. Very large numbers of bungs were also found in the nave and sacristies in the Central Church at Abdullah Nirqi. These were also stamped and covered with a red wash.[179]

From the evidence of the pottery vessels, amphorae, used to transport wine, it would appear that the heyday of trade in this commodity from Egypt to Nubia occurred in the Early Christian period. The sources of the pottery, and presumably of the wine, were, mainly, Aswan and the Theban area, and amphorae are found throughout Lower Nubia. The Ballana 6 type amphorae even travelled as far upstream as Soba East.[180] Around 750, however, the trade abruptly ceased, perhaps to be connected with the Abbasid persecutions of Christians at that time and the destruction of monasteries, the main producers of the wine.[181] Amphorae and kegs were not exclusively used to transport wine and it has been suggested that some of those entering Nubia may have contained honey and oil from Egypt as well as dry goods as noted above.[182]

THE SOURCES AND VOLUME OF NUBIA'S INTERNATIONAL TRADE

Archaeology by its very nature can tell us little of the organization of trade; it illustrates the final destination of particular commodities but rarely does it tell us how they got there. The evidence for Nubian trade is no exception although the recovery of papyri and parchment from Qasr Ibrim, and possibly from other sites in the future, may open up a new and valuable source of information. Trade in Nubia, as documented at present by the literary and archaeological sources, seems to be totally confined to trade with Egypt at all periods. The volume of trade is often considerable and often in high value goods. We can, without any difficulty, see the attractions to the people of Nubia of the goods being offered by the Egyptian merchants. Certainly not all the goods entering Nubia came initially from Egypt, but we have insufficient evidence at present to evaluate how much arrived without passing through Egypt, i.e., via the Red Sea.

Apart, perhaps from the time of the raids into Egypt during the late Roman period few objects seem to have entered Nubia as loot. Throughout history the relations between Egypt and Nubia were generally friendly, or it was the Egyptians who were in a position to loot and pillage. In the light of this most of the objects which were imported into Nubia must have been acquired as a result of trade. The value of imported goods was often high, as only expensive objects or much sought after commodities such as wine could command a sufficient price to make their transport viable over the long distances involved.

However, low value goods brought by Muslim traders from Egypt included, according to Nasir-l-Khusraw writing around 1050, beads, combs and coral.[183]

The big question is, what were the people of Nubia able to give in return? As noted above the literary sources refer principally to slaves, gold and animal products as the exports of Nubia. In the Late Roman period the military prowess of the Nubians on the one hand and the weakness of the Roman forces in Egypt on the other allowed the Nubians to trade peace for subsidies, as the reference in Procopius makes clear,[184] and this is presumably the explanation for the wealth of imported objects in the royal tombs at Qustul and Ballana.[185]

It is extremely difficult to quantify what proportion of the economic activity of Nubia the attested imports and exports represent. Nubia, like Egypt, has always had a principally agricultural economy which supports a largely self-sufficient sedentary population. The growth of large urban centres will have resulted in the presence of a sizeable group of non-food producers, but bulk trade in foodstuffs was probably exceptional (although see below). The presence of the urban centres will have fuelled trade in foodstuffs, but it would be very surprising if this trade was over long distances.

Most staple foods are bulky, are required in quantity and not usually able to command a high price in the market place. They were, prior to the advent of modern transport, uneconomical to move over long distances. It is more likely that the population would gravitate towards an area of sufficient food resources than food would be brought to the people. Food is hence unlikely to have formed a major item in international trade except in certain favourable circumstances. Ibn Selim notes that the provisions of the people of Alwa were brought to Soba by boat from a considerable distance, presumably to the south,[186] and the bulk food requirements of the inhabitants of Old Dongola were supplied from the especially fertile regions of the Northern Dongola Reach,[187] presumably from the Kerma, Seleim and Letti Basins. High value foodstuffs were traded over long distances, the most obvious being wine, but this was a trade from north to south, a trade in a luxury commodity which could not, owing to the climatic conditions, be produced on a large scale locally (however, note the short-lived attempts to practice viticulture in Nubia[188] and the Arab sources recording the growing of vines quoted above). Late Roman amphorae have been found dating from the fifth or sixth century as far south as Soba East.

Of the international trade goods gold was available in northern Nubia and had been extensively worked since New Kingdom times.[189] Elsewhere in Sudan gold is not at all common. Our perception of the importance of gold in Nubian trade may be influenced by its undoubted importance at the time of the Ancient Egyptians. Ibn Selim records that gold is plentiful in Alwa while Ibn Hawqal has the curious statement that, although the Alwans control gold mines, 'no one among the people care for it'.[190] Kirwan has suggested that the gold mining area around Fazugli (Famaka), to which the Aksumite kings sent expeditions,[191] lay under Alwan control. The Nuba were also said to collect gold from the Tuta Mountains, also known as the Gold Mountains,[192] although the location of these is unclear. In the recent past gold was exploited on a small scale in the Red Sea hills, Northern Province, south of Wadi Halfa, Southern Funj and in Equatoria.[193] The rich gold fields in the Eastern Desert lay beyond Nubian control, being exploited by the Blemmyes/Beja and later by the Muslims.

The supply of slaves in the north must have always been sparse, particularly when the whole of the Nile Valley from Sennar to the First Cataract lay within the bounds of the medieval kingdoms which generally peacefully coexisted. Raids out into the hinterland of the Nile Valley may have yielded some 'merchandise' but the pickings must have been slim. Throughout the nineteenth century southern Sudan proved a mecca for slave traders from the north and there is no reason to doubt that the resources of human and animal merchandise were not just as easily available at an earlier date. The south of Sudan is the obvious source for the international trade items for which Nubia was famed. However, as noted above, this merchandise is precisely that which is not recognizable in the archaeological record.

On a local level, where it was possible to bring bulk commodities to the market place, trade by barter was not a problem. However, with long distance trade, and especially international trade, only certain commodities could be traded practically. For this trade, probably largely confined to the Nubian elites, the most suitable exports were small high value material and slaves, the latter being exported 'under their own steam'. To purchase foreign luxury items, commodities which were of high value to the vendor were essential. The importance of the luxury trade will have been in the generation of the excess wealth which in turn contributed to the development of urbanism. One of the prerequisites for the development of urbanism is the existence of groups within society who exist without recourse to agricultural endeavour. At the pinnacle of these groups are those in positions of political or religious power, a position either bestowed upon them by their fellow citizens or seized by force of personality or force of arms. By their special status these groups tend to amass wealth by controlling wealth-producing activities and/or by taking to themselves in the form of tax the produce of others. In Nubia with its relatively low agricultural potential, dominance of the agricultural base would not have been an ideal source for amassing wealth and the power that accrues from it. For generating a surplus of wealth from trade, however, Nubia was ideally placed. In Nubia, and increasingly as one moves to the south, was a vast reservoir of resources much sought after by the wealthy classes and royalty in Egypt. As middlemen in this trade the Nubians, or at least a certain sector of the Nubian population, was able to amass wealth. The development of this trade will have required an administrative machinery to manage it and this, together with the wealth generated, will have created a suitable environment for the rise of urban centres. Those with surplus wealth tend to be consumers, using their wealth to purchase non-essential goods which require skilled craftsmen and artisans to produce them, be they fine objects, grandiose buildings or tombs. Thus the wealth allows the growth of a further class who service the elite.

How much the elite relied on trade and on agriculture for their wealth is difficult to access and will presumably have fluctuated over time, trade in particular being much affected by the contemporary international situation. The Nubian elite's control of agriculture and, perhaps in some cases, the control of such essential agricultural equipment as the production of the *qawadis* for use on the *saqia*, may also have been of considerable importance. At Soba East, a kiln producing *qawadis* (and *doka*) was located by the major ecclesiastical complex on mound B, possibly indicating some official control over production.

The medieval inhabitants of Nubia have left few records of their own trade so we are in most cases denied information on their trade networks from their own hands. Ibn Selim[194] records that at Soba East there was a large colony of Muslims. If these were merchants, as seems likely (elsewhere Ibn Selim mentions Muslim merchants in Alwa),[195] one can be sure that there was something to trade. The presence of Muslims at Soba is interesting for another reason. The kingdom of Makuria to the north, which shared a border with Egypt, had very restrictive laws designed to keep Muslim traders out of Upper Nubia. As noted above they were allowed to trade freely in Lower Nubia but, except with the specific permission of the king, they were forbidden to pass south of Baqwa at the downstream end of the Second Cataract into Upper Nubia.[196] The presence of Muslims at Soba indicates that there must have been direct access between the kingdom of Alwa either to Egypt or, conceivably, to one of the Red Sea ports. El-Idrisi also records that the Alwans traded with Egypt.[197] However, Alwan trade contacts with Aidhab via Qasr Ibrim have already been mentioned.

Routes, probably from the kingdom of Alwa, perhaps from the important later entrepot at Berber, to the Red Sea ports of Badi, Dahlak and Sawakin are mentioned by Ibn Selim.[198] The use of the Korosko Road by the Nubians is noted by el-Maqrizi, although in the tenth century its southern terminus on the Nile close to Abu Hamed, lay under Makurian control except during the brief occupation of that region by el-Omari.[199] El-Yaqubi in the ninth century indicates that Muslims did use the route from the Wadi el-Allaqi direct to Alwa at that time.[200] Islamic goods certainly did reach Soba, as can be seen from the fine glassware, including table wares and containers for perfume and other products, and the small quantities of glazed wares recovered by excavation.[201] A glass jeton of the Egyptian caliph el-Zahir, dated 1020-35, was also recovered along with a stone mould for casting a medallion and finger rings, the former bearing an Arabic inscription.[202] A few pieces of Chinese porcelain of twelfth to thirteenth-century date have even been recovered from the site.[203] The discovery of the mould at Soba highlights the difficulty of interpreting the significance of the presence of an object in the archaeological record. The itinerant craftsman would have been able to produce at Soba, or anywhere else for that matter, presumably with the minimum of facilities, objects designed in an artistic milieu far removed from the place of manufacture, yet such objects will have been locally produced, perhaps from local raw materials. This offers a glimpse of the movement of the producer rather than the movement of the goods he was producing. Clearly one man could traverse vast distances within his working life but his presence in a particular place may have no connection with trade routes. This has important implications for the spread of artistic influences, technology and for assessments of trading networks.

Trade between Alwa and Makuria presumably used a route across the Bayuda perhaps following the Wadi Muqaddam direct from the confluence of the Niles towards the Nile bend near ed-Debba, or the old Kushite route from the region of Meroe towards the upper reaches of the Wadi Abu Dom and then rejoining the Nile past the monastery of el-Ghazali at modern Merowe.[204]

It is highly unlikely that long-distance trade was conducted by individual settlements, rather that trade of this sort was organized in larger administrative centres serving as headquarters for the trade. Inter-village trade may, however, have been important in staple foodstuffs,[205] although how the poorer regions raised the means to pay for this trade must be considered. Trade between Egypt and the major trade centres in Nubia was reciprocal, between those centres and the villages it may have been largely of a redistributive nature. In northern Nubia Qasr Ibrim and Jebel Adda functioned as major administrative and trade centres. Ibrim was the seat of the *eparch*, the chief official in the area charged specifically with the conduct of relations with the Muslims. As already noted documents found at Ibrim indicate that the *eparch* was acting on behalf of the rulers of Makuria in trade dealings with the Muslims both forwarding goods to them and selling slaves on their behalf.[206] The presence of other administrative centres is implied by Abu Salih, who records that there were thirteen kings in Nubia ruling under the supremacy of the Great King,[207] presumably he who resided at Old Dongola. None of these centres can be identified with certainty.

TRADE WITH SOUTHERN SUDAN, KORDOFAN, DARFUR AND THE ETHIOPIAN HIGHLANDS

In the present state of our knowledge we have little or no evidence on which to base a discussion of trade or any other contacts between the civilizations on the Middle and Lower Nile and the tribal societies to the south, although we can appreciate the potential wealth that could accrue from the exploitation of southern Sudan. Virtually no objects of Nubian manufacture have been found south of Sennar of any period prior to the Turko-Egyptian conquest of Sudan in 1819-20, although it is not entirely clear how much this relates to the absence of archaeological investigations in those areas. The boundary between the two areas marks the boundary, prior to the nineteenth century, between the literate and prehistoric societies and still today marks a boundary between an area of archaeological investigation and one where archaeological work has been virtually non-existent. These factors conspire to highlight the lack of contacts between these areas, where all reasonable considerations indicate that there must have been a considerable amount of interaction. The Nubian states on the Middle Nile may not have traded with the south at all, but have raided it and built some of their prosperity on its exploitation much as the pharaohs of the Old and Middle Kingdom did in Wawat and Kush in Northern Nubia. If this is the case then the description of Nubia as a cul-de-sac, rather than as a corridor to Africa, seems more appropriate.[208] Nubian influence on the south of Sudan may have been negligible or entirely destructive. It would appear that the southern limit of the spread of Mediterranean and Egyptian culture lay on the southern borders of Alwa, probably in a very similar location to the southern borders of the Kushite Empire.

The location of the Makurian capital at the point where the Wadi Howar meets the Nile may not be entirely fortuitous. The discovery of a fortress 150 km to the west of Old Dongola in the Wadi Howar, albeit probably of Kushite date, suggests that the wadi was used as a route to the west. In the nineteenth century the town of ed-Debba, 30 km upstream from Old Dongola, was a major centre for trade with Kordofan and Darfur.[209] However, actual evidence for trade with these areas has yet to be identified.[210]

There is very little evidence for contacts between the states on the Middle Nile and the Ethiopian highlands. The foray by the Aksumites into the Nile Valley and their possible capture of Meroe in the mid fourth century AD is well known,[211] but any artefacts suggesting trade contacts are virtually unknown.[212] In *The Periplus of the Erythraean Sea*, dated to the second or third century AD, there is reference to trade in ivory from 'beyond the Nile' through Aksum to Egypt via the Red Sea, and this route was certainly a means of bringing the produce of Black Africa to the Ancient Mediterranean world. What proportion of the trade from southern Sudan and beyond went by this route rather than along the Nile Valley is difficult to say. A presumed shift in the trade routes from the Nile to the Red Sea has been advanced as one of the reasons for the decline of Kushite power.[213] In the sixth century AD Cosmas Indicopleustes records the Aksumite trade expeditions into the Blue Nile Valley in Sudan, an area which one may have expected to lie within the sphere of influence of the Kings of Alwa.[214]

A confusing passage of el-Idrisi's recounts how Bilaq, a town of the Nuba, lying between two arms of the Nile, is the point where merchants from Nubia and Ethiopia gather together with those from Egypt. Although part of his description suggests that Philae is the town referred to, he explicitly states that it is in the land watered by the Nile and 'by that river which comes from the country of the Habashah [Ethiopia]'.[215] He also states that it was a distance of ten days by land from Alwa and less than that by river. If by Alwa the capital at Soba is meant, and in the preceding passage el-Idrisi used Alwa to designate the city of Soba, then this estimate of journey time between Soba and the mouth of the Atbara is not far off the mark, for a journey even from the furthest northerly frontier of the Kingdom of Alwa to Philae it is very wide of the mark. It has been suggested that there were two towns named Bilaq, one of which stood at the confluence of the Nile and Atbara, and Vantini provides some additional information to support this.[216]

CHAPTER 9

Art, language and literacy

The art of the medieval period, as it survives in the archaeological record, contrasts markedly from that which preceded it. There is an almost total absence of sculpture in the round. Not a single statue of a Nubian ruler survives. Decorative relief sculpture is rare, and there are no narrative figurative reliefs comparable to those of the Pharaonic and Kushite periods. Commemorative monumental art is confined exclusively to wall paintings, a type of decoration by no means unknown, although rarely extensively preserved, at earlier periods at, for example, Kerma, el-Kurru and Meroe.

In the modern literature, owing to the much greater amount of archaeological work in Makuria, particularly at Old Dongola, it is assumed that Old Dongola was the artistic centre of Nubia, influences radiating out from it to the north, which at least by the early eighth century was a part of Makuria, but also to the south into Alwa. Although there is insufficient evidence to contest this hypothesis it must be remembered that the subservient cultural position of Alwa may be illusory.

Art

CONTINUITY IN ARTISTIC EXPRESSION

As with many other aspects of culture it is difficult to trace the development of art from the late Kushite into the medieval period. As will be noted in more detail below, there appears to be a marked break between the Kushite and medieval traditions. In some cases this is the result of there being a hiatus in the use of a particular type of item, be it architectural stonework in Makuria and Alwa or fine pottery in Central Sudan. With the re-emergence of the fashion for the use of these categories of object in the early medieval period their character is very different. More continuity is to be expected in Nobadia where there was a much greater continuity of settlement. However, it is difficult, for example, to discuss pre-Christian Nobadian stone carving as there is considerable uncertainty as to whether the pieces of architectural stonework used were carved at that time or were reused from earlier Kushite structures. The artistic achievements of the Kushite pot-painters seems to have exerted little influence on the fine ceramics in Nobadia of the fifth and sixth centuries. It is only with the arrival of Christian-inspired motifs, and, in the case of architectural decoration, with the renewed desire to construct lavish religious monuments, that we can recognize a renaissance on the part of the artists working with many media.

ARCHITECTURAL SCULPTURE

Whether there was an uninterrupted production of architectural sculpture from the Late Kushite into the early medieval period is unclear, the result of the rarity of buildings of sufficient status to have been so embellished that can be firmly dated to the period of the pagan Nubian kingdoms. The relief-decorated architectural elements used in the elite and royal burials at Qustul and Ballana which certainly date to this time may have been reused from earlier Kushite monuments and such reuse continued for centuries. The fine lintel decorated with a winged disc and *uraei* over the doorway into Room 3 of Tomb 95 at Ballana, erected in the fifth century is paralleled by the reuse of another lintel with a winged disc surmounted by a frieze of *uraei* over the main doorway into the cathedral at nearby Faras, erected over two centuries later.[1] Temple 1 at Qasr Ibrim, firmly dated to the pagan phase of medieval Nubia, does not bear any decoration on its door lintel apart from a simple cavetto moulding.[2]

With the arrival of Christian motifs and the construction of churches contemporary architectural sculpture can be readily recognized. Sculpture in an architectural context is a feature of the earlier phases of the medieval kingdoms, from the sixth to the early eighth century. The use of stone architectural and timber elements in the trabeate architecture of the early period favoured the embellishment of monuments with sculpture of which the main elements were column and pilaster capitals, lintels, door jambs, balusters and screens and window grills. In Nobadia direct continuity of stone cutting from the later Kushite period through into the medieval period can be observed, particularly at Faras where the tradition of working the soft Nubian sandstone and of using many of the same decorative motifs survives. Some of the motifs were modified and the cross was introduced as a major element along with a number of influences from the Coptic Christian art of Egypt. In Makuria there is much less continuity, at least in the production of some architectural elements, especially of capitals. Much of the relief carving was painted although little trace of this usually survives.[3]

Bases, columns and capitals

The monolithic hard-stone shafts used in Nubian churches usually have a simple collar at the lower end, a collar or grooves towards the upper end and occasionally have crosses in relief part way up the shaft.[4] The standard of workmanship employed on the shafts is poor, they are frequently not of regular shape and the decoration is roughly worked. Hard-stone bases are of simple form with a rectangular or cuboid lower part with a markedly tapering short shaft above terminating at a diameter the same as that of the column to be supported. They do not bear any decoration.[5]

The capitals fall into two main groups depending on the type of stone from which they are carved. The sandstone capitals in Nobadia show strong links with the classical world and many of the elements of Graeco-Roman Corinthian and Composite capitals are readily discernible. They also exhibit similarities to later Kushite sandstone capitals and capitals of local manufacture pre-dating the arrival of Christianity, as found at Faras and Sahaba.[6] In Makuria, south of the Third Cataract, sandstone capitals are excessively rare and none are known from Alwa. A number of early examples, dating probably from the sixth century, have however, been found in the church on Kom E at Old Dongola. They are distinct from the Nobadian examples, having an unusual leaf form, a combination between the classical acanthus and the local ribbed palm frond. The style finds parallels in Egypt and also on the Kushite kiosk at Naqa.[7] The other group, prevalent throughout Makuria and known also from Alwa, was of hard stone. The Makurian and Alwan style of capital was much simpler, the decoration being carved in low relief. There is a development of these capitals from the earlier, more heavily decorated examples, an attempt to replicate the style of the sandstone capital on the more intractable hard stone,[8] to a simplified version, which is much more block-like in shape (Fig. 87). It represents a move away from intri-

Figure 87 **Capitals from the Church of the Granite Columns at Old Dongola.**

cately decorated items towards an emphasis on the monumentality of the architectural whole in which the massive granite columns and block capitals played a significant part. The small marble capitals from Faras, decorated with the acanthus leaf, were probably imported from Egypt.[9]

It is unclear why the Makurian and Alwan stone masons and/or architects chose to use hard stone for capitals. During the Kushite period sandstone was the major medium for architectural elements throughout the whole empire, hard stone being sometimes employed for door sills but chiefly for altars and statues although the use of sandstone became accepted even for these elements in the later Kushite period.

The cross was used on most of the hard-stone capitals, even among those of the earlier period at a time when the sandstone capitals, sporting all the other motifs, almost invariably eschew the use of the cross in this decorative context.[10] The later capitals of Makuria and Alwa display influences derived from Byzantine and Armenian art, with their basket-like form and their use of the cross-in-wreath motif and of monograms as decorative elements.[11]

Around the end of the seventh century granite capitals of the simplified form appear in Nobadia, by then the northern province of the Kingdom of Makuria, and totally replace the sandstone type. However, it must be noted that, earlier in the seventh century, the cathedral at Qasr Ibrim was provided with granite capitals, of rather more varied form and decoration that the type later introduced from the south.[12] What is surprising, particularly with the granite capitals, is the range of diversity in their design. There are often significant differences between the individual face of each capital and a lack of any attempt to make 'sets' of capitals reflecting 'the disappearance of any fixed rules whatsoever in column and capital systems'.[13]

Lintels, arches and jambs

To span openings, whether over doors, or windows or between piers and columns, flat lintels or arches were employed. In later Nubian architecture the greater reliance on brick architecture, whether of fired or mud brick, led to a reduced role for stone voussoirs and for timber and stone lintels. At an earlier period it was these elements which were often carved and formed an important part of the decorative scheme, particularly within churches.[14] Discoveries of similar decorated items in profane architecture are much rarer. The tradition of working and carving sandstone in Nobadia extended to the decoration of these elements. In Makuria items of this type are much rarer and none are yet known from Alwa.[15] A wide range of decorated door and window lintels, door jambs and voussoirs are known particularly from Nobadia. One of the most common motifs used to decorate these is the Maltese cross within a roundel and the plainer lintels are decorated solely with a centrally placed motif of this type, or with the central cross flanked by two others. Another very common motif is a rosette, of eight petals or more, circumscribed by a circular border and this is found centrally placed as the sole ornament on lintels or as part of the trilogy of motifs. Much more elaborate decoration does occur, as for example on a lintel from Faras with a central 'rosette' motif within a circular border with a guilloche frieze along the upper part of the lintel and the areas to either side divided into three fields occupied by rosettes (Fig. 88).[16] Among the rich repertoire of the stone carver can be

Figure 88
Sandstone lintels from the Rivergate Church at Faras (after Griffith 1926b, pl. LIII).

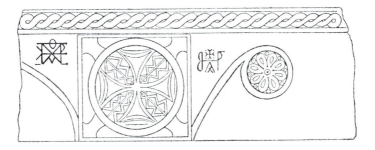

seen influences from the earlier Kushite period and from Hellenistic Egypt apparent both in Kushite and Coptic art, particularly of the Thebaid.[17] Nubian pieces can, however, generally be distinguished from contemporary Coptic items owing to their simplicity of style and an equilibrium between symmetry and harmony. The repertoire is largely confined to geometric and floral motifs.

The vine, either with or without bunches of grapes, with its important iconographic significance,[18] is widespread. As with many other motifs there is a marked stylization which is apparent in the representation of the vine leaves. There is a range of types including the undulating stem with leaves, with alternating leaves and bunches of grapes and solely with grapes. Two types, where there are alternately two leaves and two bunches of grapes within each meander of the stem, and where a leaf and a bunch of grapes occur together in each meander, do not occur later than the seventh century as may also be the case with motifs derived from Kushite art, apart from the lotus which continued to be popular. Zoomorphic motifs are not common but include the eagle, fish, cock and lion. Few timber lintels survive but a well-preserved example spanning a window was preserved in the cathedral at Faras. It is decorated with rosettes, examples with smooth and grooved petals alternating.[19] The timber framing in the walls of the cathedral at Ibrim, which was carried across the window openings forming their sills and lintels, was also decorated.[20]

Embellishment of doorways also included, on occasion, the provision of stone jambs or stone pilasters, with or without a carved stone lintel. Some of these are very elaborately decorated. A fine pilaster, perhaps originally flanking a doorway in the church within the monastic complex at Qasr el-Wizz, has a Maltese cross towards the base, and a guilloche pattern up the shaft above, which is an eagle shown *en face* and a palm capital above.[21] Among the doorways decorated with stone jambs and lintels some have the decoration on all three elements designed as a unit, whereas elsewhere the decoration of the matching jambs contrasts with the very different decoration of the lintel.

Within the Church of St Raphael at Tamit two arches survived constructed of stone voussoirs of which the front face of the keystone and two other voussoirs symmetrically placed to either side are decorated. On one arch the keystone bears a monogram of the patron of the church, on the other a complex cross motif. The other four voussoirs bear a four-petal motif.[22] Two of the voussoirs from the cathedral at Faras have monograms of the bishops Pilatos and of Paulos.[23] A fine series of decorated voussoirs are known from Qasr Ibrim. No trace of wall plaster has been found in the cathedral here[24] and for embellishment it may have always relied on carved stonework and woodwork and on the well-dressed stone from which it was constructed.[25] Among the rare examples of sandstone carving from Makuria is a voussoir decorated with a monogram, later reused in the west arm of the Cruciform Church[26] and another bearing a cross within the monastic church at el-Ghazali (frontispiece).[27] The third voussoir in the arch over the west gate of the enceinte at Faras bears a carving of a lion in relief, and what may have been the keystone bore a cross. Another voussoir found close by, and probably from the same arch, was decorated with a rosette.[28] This is a very rare example of a decorated arch in a non-religious context.[29] The lion-headed spout in a water tank at Aksha, thought to be of medieval date,[30] is reminiscent of the lion-headed spouts in the late Kushite wine presses, although the style is very different.

The influence of Islamic architectural decoration on Nubia can rarely be documented. However, the recent excavations in the monastery on Kom H at Old Dongola have uncovered a doorway covered by a scalloped arch and flanked by very slender engaged columns with simple capitals, constructed of brick, rendered and whitewashed. The arch and the capitals find ready parallels in an Islamic context in the tenth century and, particularly, in the twelfth and thirteenth centuries, and are so far unique in Nubia.[31]

Balusters and screens

In a number of churches the *higab*, the screen between the *haikal* and the *naos*, was constructed of stone or wooden uprights with screens between. A number of the stone elements have survived and many are elaborately decorated. A particularly fine sandstone example was discovered in the church on Kom E a little to the north of Old Dongola. It is decorated with plaitwork; an entwined two-band ribbon extending from each corner to a square motif in the centre, the whole bordered with a deeply moulded frame. The carving, in high relief, is carefully executed. Close parallels to the motif are to be found at Philae.[32] From the monastic complex at el-Ugal came a square-sectioned baluster 1.26 m high which has a monogram in raised relief within a sunken panel, the whole thing being covered in a thin lime wash.[33] Examples of timber screens rarely survive, but fragments from that in the cathedral at Qasr Ibrim indicates that these could also be heavily decorated.[34] An unusual, but extremely fine, group of ceramic screens from the Monastery of the Holy Trinity are decorated on one side in paint while on the other the same decoration is executed in relief and then painted in several colours. The whole decoration is set within a decorated border of a continuous guilloche or other motifs. Although fragmentary, one screen clearly depicts a leaning figure wearing a turban (or coif), part of a sword and galligaskins. They appear to be part of a set and to date to the late period. They reveal strong Islamic influence.[35]

Window grills

Window grills were made either from stone or from terracotta and took a wide variety of forms. The most highly decorated combine relief and painted decoration. The earliest examples were in stone and followed traditional models with mainly geometric and floral motifs. The close links they exhibit with Coptic work, particularly in Upper Egypt are evident.[36] Of the large numbers that must have originally adorned the Church of the Granite Columns at Old Dongola, the decorative scheme of six can be restored in their entirety, five from rectangular and one from an arched or, more correctly, a semi-oval window. Among the decorative elements are Maltese crosses, diamonds, roundels and four-pointed stars (Fig. 89). The only zoomorphic form is the fish, used in combination with roundels to form cross motifs, both highly symbolic in a Christian religious context. A similar combination of fish-shaped lozenges forming a cross can be seen on Nubian fine painted pottery. On one face the window grills were painted in a cream slip.[37] One of the best preserved from a domestic context came from House A.106. This ceramic grill, designed for an arched window, has a diamond lattice in a rectangular field with half of a petal motif in the semi-circular field above.[38] Another, from a window of the same shape, has been recovered from the monastic complex on Kom H. The semi-circular field at the

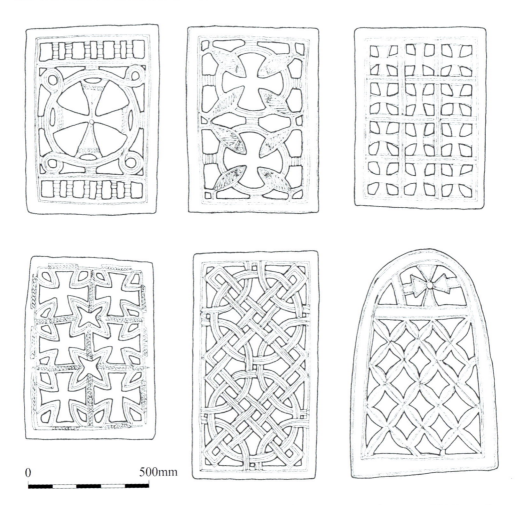

Figure 89 **Ceramic window grills from the Church of the Granite Columns at Old Dongola** (after Gartkiewicz 1990, fig. 117).

top is occupied by a cross in a roundel, while the decoration below is unfortunately too badly destroyed to be reconstructed. It has been dated to the seventh century.[39]

Friezes
One of the finest friezes was used to decorate the apse of the first cathedral at Faras. It consisted of twenty-four eagles with outstretched wings and with a cross on their heads, standing before an altar (Fig. 90). Each eagle faces towards the centre of the apse and is flanked by engaged columns.[40] Another frieze of this type decorated the cathedral at Qasr Ibrim. Traces of paint on this indicate that the ground was painted blue.[41] A sandstone door-jamb from Serra East bears very similar motifs, with the two eagles preserved facing one to the left, the other to the right. In the restricted space available the columns are dispensed with, the eagles and altars being enclosed by a vertical raised border.[42] In the later cathedral at Faras there was a similar frieze but in this case painted rather than in relief.[43]

TOMBSTONES

Although most Christian Nubian tombstones simply bear an inscription embellished by little more than crosses there are a few that are much more elaborate. A fine series of bishops' tombstones from Qasr Ibrim, five of which date to between 1037 and 1132, are of stone and are finely decorated indicating the survival of a stone-working tradition at Ibrim. Two motifs were used, representations of the rays of the rising sun or domes crowned by crosses. The former motif is widespread in the Nubia and Egypt, the latter may be confined to Ibrim where these tombstones were presumably carved. The decoration may have been inspired by the roofing of the cathedral on the site, which at the time of the invasion of Shams ed-Dawla had a dome surmounted by a cross. The carved decoration was enhanced with bright colours and the letters of the inscriptions below were also highlighted in colour.[44]

SCULPTURE IN THE ROUND

Sculpture is extremely rare in medieval Nubia. No large-scale pieces are known comparable with the royal statues and those of deities from the Kushite period and the ba-birds from Kushite cemeteries in Lower Nubia. Statuettes of animals and humans, which are often very crude, are found and many of these follow a tradition documented in Nubia for millennia.

MOSAIC

The use of this decorative technique is only known at Old Dongola, in its immediate vicinity, and at Meinarti. The reconstructed Church of the Stone Pavement dating to the

Figure 90 **A section of the sandstone frieze from the first cathedral at Faras (photo The British Museum).**

aftermath of the Arab invasion of 652 has a mosaic, set in a Nile silt matrix, laid in the *haikal*, with local desert stones set on a soft lime mortar to form a rhomboidal pattern.[45] The mosaic in the church on Kom E in the nave has a geometric pattern made from white and dark pebbles contemporary with the sandstone paving in the *haikal*. Later a cross-shape was cut into this pavement and filled with another geometric pebble mosaic. Another mosaic was added in the later *narthex*, set in a hard lime plaster. At a much later date the mosaic was relaid, the geometric patterns augmented by curvilinear, perhaps floral, motifs. The survival of mosaic in the *narthex* is the direct result of a section of it having been enclosed by a brick screen.[46] Another has recently been found in the church at Hambukol and consists of black and white pebbles.[47]

The Meinarti mosaic, dating from the earliest church on the site (600-700) is made of dark-coloured cobbles with lighter cobbles forming a cross in the centre of the nave. On the reconstruction of the church in the next century the mosaic was covered by a floor of mud.[48]

WALL PAINTING

The earliest reference to Nubian wall paintings in the literature to have come down to us is in the writings of Abu Salih in the twelfth century, who describes paintings of the Makurian king Giorgios, son of Zacharias, and of the governor, in an elegant church, and also the paintings in the Temple of Mandulis, which had been converted to a church by this date.[49] Early modern travellers were also attracted by the wall paintings, the first being Norden in 1738 while describing the church within the Pharaonic temple at Amada (Fig. 91).[50] The artistic quality of the paintings was not, however, always appreciated. Somers Clarke wrote 'The interior surfaces [within churches] were covered with whitewash and this again was liberally ornamented with paintings, in earth colours, of a grim byzantine type. The few pieces that are left make us regret profoundly that we have lost so much. Archaic, conventional, as the fragments are, there is often an impressive dignity about the simple workmanship that is very striking.'[51]

It was the discovery of the extensive series of paintings in the cathedral at Faras in the early 1960s which formed the basis for a detailed study of this ubiquitous Nubian artistic expression. Early descriptions, drawings and later photographs, of wall paintings are extremely useful as many have been destroyed in the not too distant past, sometimes by the over-zealous activities of archaeologists, particularly in the case of converted temples where the 'decadent' traces of the churches were removed, with little regard to their

Figure 91 **The temple at Amada with the dome constructed on its conversion into a church, drawn by Henry Beechey in 1818-19 (courtesy of The Bankes Collection, The National Trust).**

Figure 92 **Wall painting in the converted temple at Wadi es-Sebua drawn in 1818-19 possibly by Alessandro Ricci (courtesy of The Bankes Collection, The National Trust).**

importance, to allow the original Pharaonic or Kushite buildings to be investigated (Fig. 92). Even where direct human activity has not destroyed paintings the passage of time has caused many to greatly deteriorate.

A close study of the painting techniques is currently underway in the monastery on Kom H at Old Dongola. Although related to the techniques used in the Eastern Mediterranean at this time the extreme heat and aridity of northern Sudan, coupled with the need to apply the paint usually onto mud-brick walls with an absorbent and soft mud render, resulted in some novel solutions. Firstly the wall surface was prepared with the addition of an equal mixture of clay and sand bound with milk of lime, between 2 and 10 mm in thickness. This was smoothed either with pumice stones, examples of which have been recovered from the monastery, or by hand. To stabilize the surface a 1:1 mixture of silt and white kaolin was applied in a semi-liquid state and it was on this smoothed and damp surface that the paint was applied. First the outline was sketched in dilute yellow ochre and infilled with a priming layer of pure kaolin. The outline was then reinforced with undiluted ochre and the other colours then added, moving from the lighter to the darker tones. Most of the pigments used were available locally, although some, such as blue derived from azurite, had to be imported.[52]

Most Nubian buildings were dark, with small windows designed to keep out the blinding sun and the heat. In many rooms of the Kom H monastery this was taken to extremes and the only light that can have been available to view the vast numbers of paintings was that of an oil lamp. The compositions are often very large yet the space available for viewing them was severely limited and this coupled with the small area illuminated by the flickering flame of the lamp will have given an altogether different impression of the mural art than that we have today, when the paintings are viewed on site over fallen walls and through collapsed vaults, or on the pages of excavation reports. The naivety of the paintings and the bold colours when viewed as a whole under bright light will have been invisible to the viewer looking at the paintings as they were intended to be viewed and in the same conditions of light and space under which they were conceived and executed.[53]

In churches

The earliest wall paintings to survive from medieval Nubia date to the second half of the seventh century although those at Abu Oda may possibly be even earlier. These appear to have coexisted with the use of relief decoration as, for example, in the apse of the first cathedral at Faras where the eagle frieze may have been surmounted, on the *intrados* of the hemi-dome, by a painting of Christ in glory.[54] The rarity of early wall paintings may largely be the result of the rebuilding and refurbishment of many early churches. Whereas stone architectural elements from these buildings survive to be reused time and again, painted wall-plaster from demolished walls survives only as small fragments or not at all. With the greater use of mud and red brick, particularly in ecclesiastical structures, the use of relief decoration was dramatically reduced and wall painting dominated the decorative programme.

The paintings at Abu Oda are very different from those of any of the paintings in Nubia which followed them. Three of the paintings, on the 'vaults' of this rock-cut structure are unique both from the point of view of their iconography and of their position within the church. They are the only vault paintings preserved in situ although this may largely be the result of vagaries of survival.[55] The paintings are very naturalistic in style and the figures were probably portrayed in a landscape setting. The closest parallels come from Sinai. Among the early paintings in the church at Naqa el-Oqba, the composition in the apse can be closely paralleled in the churches at Bawit and Sakkara while another apse composition from Debeira also shows the strong influence of Coptic art at this early period. At this period the lower parts of the walls were probably decorated either with architectural ornament, painting imitating marble veneer, or with small panneaux. The repertoire of Christ in glory and paintings of the apostles were to remain important in later Nubian church decoration.[56]

Owing to the very poor state of preservation of the earliest churches at Old Dongola it is unclear whether painted decoration was used. However, in the baptismal fonts in the sixth-century Old Church and in the early seventh-century Church of the Stone Pavement the plaster rendering is painted to imitate marble veneer.[57]

Wall paintings of the later seventh and early eighth century are only known at Faras, Wadi es-Sebua and Abdullah Nirqi and probably Abu Oda where two paintings of angels seem to be additions to the mural art of this church. They show a homogeneity of style and much similarity in iconography, particularly at the former two sites. By far the best collection of paintings of this period, as of most other periods, comes from the cathedral at Faras (colour plates XVIII and XIX). All the paintings on the walls of the original building were executed by the same school and some of them set the iconographical norm which was followed throughout the history of the building, surviving all subsequent repaintings and modifications. Such was the composition in the sanctuary apse which uniquely was divided into three registers. Interestingly the lower register is a frieze of eagles (or doves) with spread wings and surmounted by a rosette, facing each other under an arcade supported on columns, clearly a painted version of the carved sandstone frieze that had occupied this position in the first church on this site.[58] Above was a representation of the Madonna standing among the apostles while the *intrados* of the hemi-dome was covered with a representation of Christ in glory (*Maiestas Domini*) in the midst of the four apocalyptical beings. Among the other subjects were numerous paintings of the Madonna and Child, archangels, saints, a massive nativity scene and the only image derived from an Old Testament story, The Three Youths in the Fiery Furnace. The only rooms not decorated with wall paintings were the southern vestry and one of the northern rooms. Portraits of bishops, perhaps kings or *eparchs*, and a princess, do not appear to date to the initial decoration of the building. None of the paintings are set within a landscape, a clear break with the earlier traditions of Nubian wall painters. Bishops and secular officials are depicted with brown faces while the faces of cult images are in white.[59]

As a rule all the paintings were set at least 2 m above floor level and were devoid of any frame or border, nor was any decorative dado apparent, although decorative painted friezes were probably provided immediately below the level of the flat timber roofs. As a general rule certain compositions were painted in a particular part of the church. Flanking the apse, the decoration of which was noted above, the east end of the north aisle would usually bear a scene of the Nativity, to the south The Three Youths in the Fiery Furnace, while the west end of the nave had a large figure of Christ or the Virgin with Child.[60] Archangels are depicted by the entrances into the churches as doorkeepers.[61] The area devoted to particular painting types however, as can been seen in the Faras cathedral, varied over time and it is often impossible to suggest a connection between the subject of a painting and its location. Considering bishop's portraits, for example, the earliest are painted in the south aisle; in the ninth century the south chapel was used; in the tenth century it was this room and the baptistery; the eleventh century paintings occupied the whole of the south-eastern part of the church; while the latest paintings were confined to the area of the *haikal*.[62] The large number of paintings of bishops at Faras indicates that the tradition of painting the portrait of a newly ordained bishop, as recorded by John of Ephesus, was standard practice, at least from the eighth century onwards. At Faras this tradition seems to have been rigorously followed.[63]

The development of Nubian wall painting from the early eighth century onwards can be charted in the cathedral at Faras with the many refurbishments of the decorative programme into the fifteenth century.[64] This provides a sequence into which other, generally much less complete, paintings from other sites can be slotted. Using a combination of stratigraphic, architectural and epigraphic evidence, as well as artistic criteria, the paintings at Faras were divided into styles and dates assigned to the use of each. This work is now being supplemented by the large corpus of paintings still being unearthed from the monastic complex on Kom H at Old Dongola.

The following styles of painting were defined at Faras:

Plaster layer	Style	Date range
Earliest layer	Violet style / "A"	eigth century
	Late Violet style / "B"	first half of ninth century
	Intermediate style / "C"	mid ninth century
	White style / "D"	second half of ninth to early tenth century
Second layer	Yellow-red style / "E"	early tenth century
Third layer	Multicoloured I style / "F"	late tenth to early eleventh century
	Multicoloured II style / "G"	eleventh century
	Multicoloured III style / "H"	twelth century
Latest layer	Late style / "I"	thirteenth century onwards

It should be noted that the names of the styles are not always an accurate indicator of the prevalence of one particular colour, nor necessarily represent the predilection of artists of a particular period for one colour. They are derived from the initial impressions gained by the archaeologists when the paintings at Faras were first unearthed. The paintings considered to belong to the White Style, for example, do so because most of the subject matter at that time consisted of paintings of apostles, who were customarily shown dressed in white robes.[65]

There was only one major redecoration programme affecting the whole building, carried out around the turn of the ninth century. At that time all the internal walls were replastered and redecorated in the Multicoloured style with forty-eight representations, all by one workshop, during the episcopates of Petros I, Ioannes III and the first years of Marianos.[66] Later, although new plaster was applied where necessary to repair badly damaged areas or to cover new architectural features, usually a new coat of whitewash was applied. While new compositions were added to the Cathedral many older paintings were renovated by being retouched or repainted to conform with current artistic styles.[67] In the apse three phases of modifications to the original painted scheme have been identified, spanning several centuries. The Nubians seem to have had little appreciation for fine and/or old works of art, setting more store on keeping up with the current fashions, even when this meant overpainting a masterpiece with something which fell far short of it, at least in our eyes.[68]

In the late period, that is from the end of the eleventh century until the fourteenth or fifteenth century, there is a progressive abandonment of the iconographic and stylistic rules adhered to earlier, making the close dating of the new compositions difficult.[69] The general trend is to move from complex multicoloured compositions to more schematic and less colourful paintings. This is not to say that all late paintings are of poor quality; some may even be classed as masterpieces.[70] Although the patterns used are as rich as in earlier paintings they are of different types, as is the choice of colours. Grey is used frequently, and the contrasting use of green and red is a feature of late art, never seen in the classical period. The most detailed painting is in the rendering of the robes of officials and the changes in the painting of these could reflect changes in style of the ornamentation used on the actual clothing. Another characteristic of late painting is the display of emotion, which has a dramatic effect and yet is achieved by the simplest of means, the inclination of the head of one figure to another, for example, highlighting their relationship. The majority of late paintings are, however, very inferior. The figures are static, usually depicted *en face* and are frequently out of proportion, with small heads but large hands and feet. They eschew classical realism and exhibit linearism and schematicism, which culminates in the so-called 'dynamic phase' with its exaggerated decorativeness and mannerism. The contrasting colours give the impression of coloured drawings rather than paintings, with 'lack of proportion, primitivism, linearality and schematism underlining the decline of pictorial art'. This style can be closely related to contemporary art in Byzantium, in the period of the Comnenian and Palaeologian dynasties and indicates direct influence from Byzantium on Makurian art.[71]

Many local painters seem to have been active at this period and the recognition of particular styles is difficult. However, a close scrutiny of iconographic types and of secondary stylistic features does allow paintings to be grouped, and the recognition that there were artistic trends still followed throughout Nubia allows paintings at some sites to be dated largely on analogy with the paintings from the cathedral at Faras and with the very large and still expanding corpus of late paintings currently being excavated at Old Dongola. Similar compositions were used in the late period to the earlier and they were arranged in the same way on the walls of churches and in similar positions.

One scene introduced in the late period was a variation of those seen earlier where Christ, the Virgin, archangels or saints are shown offering protection to religious or secular dignitaries. The earlier compositions with the larger figure of the protector behind the dignitary, or with the protector standing next to the dignitary, continue, but are supplemented by the protector shown as a small-scale half or three-quarter figure appearing from behind clouds. The new type is known from Faras, Abd el-Qadir and also from the monastery on Kom H at Old Dongola.[72] Another of these late modifications of an earlier image was the representation of the Holy Trinity with a single body topped by three heads, a type of representation forbidden by the Council of Trent. Two representations of this type are known from the church at Abd el-Qadir; the figure sits on a simple stool unlike the earlier Trinity paintings where an elaborate throne is provided.

It is clear from looking at the cathedral at Faras, but also from many other churches, that the mural decoration was frequently renewed; up to four layers of plaster decorated with paintings were preserved at Faras. Although the main compositions, as noted above, will have been dictated by the established traditions of the Church, many of the other paintings were individual donations. Below a number of the murals of early eleventh-century date in the north aisle of the Faras cathedral are inscriptions written in Greek recording the name or names of the person who commissioned the work and requesting assistance. One such inscription runs 'Lord Jesus Christ (and) Mary guard, protect, strengthen, help thy servant Mariame, daughter of Mariata. So be it. Amen.'[73] On other occasions where an individual, whether a churchman, a member of the royal family or a high official, is depicted with the protector, they may also have been the donor. At Wadi es-Sebua the small figure adjacent to the archangel may be the donor of that particular mural.[74]

In monasteries and other religious structures
In one room of a structure at Faras, which may be a monastery, wall paintings survived dating from the Early Christian period. The impost level of the vault projected a little and was painted white. On this band is a long painted inscription, which appears to consist of the palindrome *sator arepo tenet opera rotas*, and extending above it were crosses at intervals, one of which was of large size, in white paint edged in red. A painted inscription in Coptic which can be read as 'I, Al...' may be the signature of the painter and there is another 'I, Yopshenka ...' elsewhere in the room.[75] The current excavations of the Monastery of the Holy Trinity at Old Dongola are continuing to yield a vast range of wall paintings dating to the period from the mid eleventh to the fourteenth centuries. The paintings, associated with the use of the north-western annexes as a commemorative complex, comprise most of the repertoire of iconographical subjects usually found in a church suggesting that the presence of a chapel within this complex may have dictated the style of decoration of the

whole complex.[76] In Room 29, the east wall is decorated with a composition the nearest iconographical parallel for which comes from the apse decoration of the cathedral at Faras, supporting the identification of this room as a chapel for liturgical ceremonies or perhaps even for the celebration of mass.[77] Also comparable with the cathedral at Faras, for example, are the paintings in Room 31 where local bishops are shown protected by archangels.[78]

Among these paintings are some of the greatest masterpieces known from Nubian mural art. One of these is a painting of a king under the protection of the Holy Trinity (colour plate XVII). The king wears a robe decorated with medallions each containing an eagle. His raised right hand supports a cross, while in his left hand he holds a tiara-shaped crown topped by a cross against his chest. In the clouds above him sufficient remains to indicate that the three busts of the Holy Trinity were depicted, the central figure *en face*, the flanking figures turned inwards. The figure on the right rests one hand on the king's shoulder, the central one crowns the ruler with the heavenly crown and the figure on the left holds the cross of the king's earthly crown. Each holds a book in the left hand.[79] This painting is also of particular interest from a technical point of view as it clearly demonstrates that the artist made use of a stencil. The heads and halos of the Trinity are identical in regard to shape and size apart from the changes necessary to allow the flanking figures to look towards the centre of the composition. In Room 29 the artists used two stencils to produce the heads of the twelve apostles, one for the heads of the old men, the other for the heads of the young men. Furthermore stencils appear to have been used by artists working in different media. The same stencil was used for laying out painted floral motifs on the monastery walls and on a ceramic window grill.[80]

Almost all the paintings in a religious context are either individual figural compositions or are representations of the cross. One room however, in the Monastery on Kom H, is rather different and appears to show eleven scenes depicting perhaps consecutive episodes, either in the lives of the monks in the monastery or of the archimandrite, culminating in a *prothesis* scene, a lying-in-state of the deceased.[81] One of the few purely decorative schemes is in the Anchorite's Grotto at Faras where the east wall was painted in its lower part with a register of adjacent diamonds, within which, and in the interstices between which, were single heart-shaped leaves.[82]

Not all painting in a religious context is of high standard. In what has been identified as a chapel within a monastic complex at Meinarti are some extremely crude paintings including 'a stick figure of Christ with single lines for the trunk, arms and legs'.[83]

In secular buildings
Although most of the known wall paintings come from churches and monasteries, other types of building were decorated in the same way. The Royal 'Throne Hall' at Old Dongola retains traces of painting on the walls of the main stairway, preserved as a result of their being covered by whitewash when the building was converted into a mosque in the late medieval period.[84] On the first landing is a representation of a 'Warrior Saint' while on the south wall of the third flight is a Saint Rider'.[85] In the 'Throne Hall' itself are traces of three periods of painted decoration, one of the first period compositions being of a cross with a bust of Christ in a central roundel flanked by roundels in the arms containing winged figures,[86] while on the west wall is part of the representation of a bishop. Running

around the room on the upper parts of the walls was a decorative band consisting of a stylized floral elements.[87]

Small fragments of paintings of seventh-century date are known from the Southern Palace at Faras and are among the few examples of painted decoration surviving from public buildings.[88] No contemporary paintings are known in Makuria and Alwa. However, the painting dating to the end of the eighth or very early in the ninth century from House A at Old Dongola, of the victorious Christ trampling a serpent, a lion and a basilisk, an image drawn from Psalm 90,[89] suggests that it is a development of early Nobadian mural art of a so-far unknown but similar Makurian style which has not been preserved. All the rooms of the house are decorated, with floral and geometric murals, the figurative scenes being confined to the room with the bathing installations.[90] At the nearby site of Hambukol in Building B-1 were many fragments of painted plaster and one well-preserved scene of the upper part of a naked man encompassed by flames. An inscription in Old Nubian beneath it suggests that this is inspired by the destruction of Nineveh in the Book of Jonah.[91]

One of the most unusual paintings in a domestic context is that from a dwelling in site R-8 at Debeira West where there is a representation of a boat within which are human and animal figures including a prancing horse and birds, depicted in black, red and yellow. The probably contemporary writing of the names of Adam and Eve in Arabic suggested to the excavators that this was a Muslim representation of Noah's Ark although it is firmly dated to the medieval period.[92]

Almost all Nubian figurative paintings, whether in a secular or ecclesiastical context, have a religious inspiration. A notable exception to this is recorded by the fourteenth-century writer en-Nuwayri when describing the Muslim occupation of Old Dongola in 1276. Within a new quarter of the town built by the Makurian king David and named by him Aidhab to commemorate his capture of that town, were paintings depicting Muslims captured at Aidhab and others killed at Aswan.[93] Military propaganda of this type is well known in the Middle Nile Valley on reliefs of the Pharaonic and Kushite periods. Whether the instance described by en-Nuwayri is actually unique is unknown. The Muslims destroyed these paintings in 1276 and it is not clear whether they were wall paintings or were on a different background which would be much less likely to survive.

Virtually nothing is known of Alwan wall painting. Fragments of painted plaster have been recovered at Soba East from within Church E, from the infill of the ground floor of the palatial building, Building D, and on mound P.[94] All are very small, and although they provide evidence for polychromatic decoration little can be said about the decorative programmes of which they formed a part. There is no reason to doubt that the churches at Soba were as profusely decorated as those of Makuria and Nobadia but the very extensive destruction of the buildings has robbed us of the evidence.

There is an adequate corpus of material from Nobadia which is sufficiently homogenous for us to talk of a Nubian painting school which, after drawing its inspiration principally from Egypt, Palestine, Syria, Byzantium and perhaps Ethiopia, utilized distinctive artistic conventions and developed a clear artistic and iconographic character of its own.[95] Foreign influences did, however, continue to influence Nubian art at later periods as has been noted above. Whether these were direct contacts or transmitted via Egypt or elsewhere is unknown.[96] The large number of paintings from the Monastery of the Holy Trinity at Old Dongola, already a substantial body of material and likely to expand considerably as a result of the on-going excavations, is allowing a detailed assessment to be made of the artistic links between the metropolis and the province of Maris at least in the later phases of Nubian Christianity.

PORTABLE WORKS OF ART AND MANUSCRIPT ILLUSTRATIONS

Almost all paintings known to us were executed on the walls of buildings. However a few portable paintings have been found and identified as icons although at least one of these may be part of a book cover.[97] Icons are also known carved on wood and ivory.[98]

A number of illustrated manuscripts have survived. Among these is a fine illustration of St Menas which accompanied an Old Nubian text describing the Miracle of St Menas, now in the British Library. The saint is depicted on horseback dressed in military garb with a shield and spear while beneath is the naked boatman.[99] Another, opposite the first page of text on a manuscript dating to 973, preserves the lower part of a standing figure,[100] probably a representation of the man who paid for the production of the manuscript, recorded on the colophon as Neshshadena, Sonoj[101] of Adda. The attitude of the figure and the richly decorated robes can be closely paralleled on wall paintings of *eparchs* at Faras.[102] Other illustrated manuscripts have designs of geometric panels.

POTTERY DECORATION

Heavily decorated pottery, mainly with painted motifs but, especially within the kingdom of Alwa, also with incised decoration, is extremely common in medieval Nubia. There is very little continuity from the equally fine and abundant later Kushite wares. The 'abrupt and total abandonment of the traditional Kushite vessel forms and designs and their replacement by almost exact replicas of the contemporary pottery of Roman Egypt' has led Bill Adams to concluded that there must have been an influx of potters from the north at the beginning of the X-Group.[103] Thereafter, there was a gradual divergence in style between Egyptian and Nubian pottery, the latter showing more variation and inventiveness together with a more precise and formal execution. The classic X-Group style is very distinctive and, owing to the continued practice of burying pots with the dead, large numbers of complete examples are known. The commonest motif is a teardrop-shaped blob of paint, usually in white, black or red, arranged in registers around the upper part of the beakers (Fig. 6) but vertical slashes and pendant festoons are also unique to this style.[104]

To the south of the Third Cataract pottery of the post-Meroitic period[105] is similar in style throughout the whole of Makuria and Alwa (Fig. 10). Decoration is both painted and incised, but a large proportion of the vessels are devoid of any decoration. Some of the 'chalices' with painted decoration have complex designs in white paint on the red surface, over the whole of the exterior surface and sometimes on the interior.[106] Where the 'beer' jars are decorated it is usually with red slip applied to the neck and sometimes with other decoration on the upper body, among the motifs being red slipped zigzags and horizontal bands. Among the incised decorations are a few rare examples of animal motifs, an antelope-like animal from el-Hobagi and stylized snakes on vessels from Shendi and

Soba East,[107] very much in the late Kushite tradition. Zigzag motifs, four of which are regularly spaced around the vessel on top of the flat rims of black burnished bowls, are known from a number of sites[108] while other common decoration is made by pressing a pointed object into the clay frequently forming zigzag resisters around the neck of the pot or triangles and diamonds on the body.[109] Sometimes this style of decoration is infilled with red, white or yellow pigment as at Soba East and Saqadi. The presence of identical decoration at Abu Geili which is usually dated to the late Kushite period suggests that this was a type of decoration coming into fashion in the late Kushite period and extending into the post-Meroitic, as does its presence at el-Hobagi.[110]

Whereas in the north the fine late Kushite ceramics are replaced by fine X-Group vessels in quantity, fine painted wares appear to be less common south of the Third Cataract. Some of this material which, as with the X-Group pottery is an entirely new type, was certainly made at Old Dongola. Many of these vessels, usually small bowls, have a red surface often decorated with a black rim stripe with pendant decorative motifs, circles, rectangles, triangles and crosses, frequently infilled with a black lattice on a white ground. A variation is to be seen in some bowls which have a red collar containing the decorative motifs while the lower part of the exterior is covered in a white slip. Others have a black painted band a little below the rim on which decoration in white translucent paint is applied. This material, like the contemporary X-Group pottery to the north, is clearly influenced in design by Romano-Egyptian styles.[111] Very similar decoration is found at Soba East but the motifs there are more varied and rarely abut the rim stripe (Fig. 93). Crosses are a common motif.[112] The relative rarity of this material at Soba East suggests

Figure 93 **Black and White style motifs on pottery from Soba East (after Welsby 1998, figs 74 and 75).**

that it may be imported, although whether from Old Dongola or from elsewhere is unknown. Similar pottery has been found in post-Meroitic graves at Firka and Gabati and has been dated to the fifth to seventh centuries.[113]

The highly distinctive Soba Ware decoration is very different from that found in the rest of Nubia. There is a very wide range of motifs, applied usually over the black to brown slip on the exterior or on the exterior and interior. The simplest decoration consists of a single register of individual cross motifs around the exterior while the most complex cover the whole surface (colour plate XVI, Fig. 94).[114] Almost 500 motifs have been published,

Figure 94 **Painted decorative motifs on Soba Ware (after Welsby 1998, figs 79, 80, 85, 86, 89, 91 and 95).**

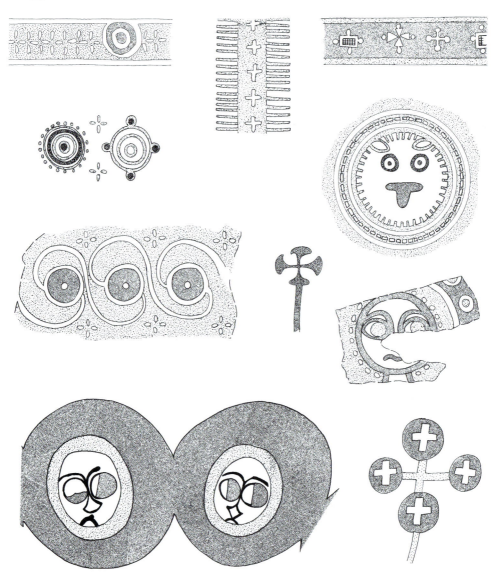

almost all of them geometric or curvilinear patters or combinations of patterns. There are, however, a small number of representations of the human face and of animals including types of antelope, lions, birds and a frog.[115] The decoration is polychrome, and principally involves the use of white, red and yellow. The inspiration for much of this decoration is clear. A wide range of the small motifs can be almost directly paralleled on wall paintings, especially those published from Faras. Among the typical ornaments published by Martens-Czarnecka dating to the Violet Style in the eighth century, five of the seven linear registers are extremely similar to decorative registers on Soba Ware as are some of the motifs of the later styles.[116] What we do not know is how the pot painters came to use this repertoire. Were they copying from the painted murals within the churches at Soba East, were they using the same pattern books as those used by the wall painters, or were they one and the same as the wall painters? The human faces, set within roundels representing halos(?), also have many features in common with those depicted on murals. The animal representations, however, hark back to Kushite tradition, particularly the depiction of the frog. The roundels, often partly in relief, of stylized animal heads have no known antecedents.[117]

By the Classic Christian period Soba Ware had disappeared from the scene and the type of fine decorated wares was much more standardized, at least within Nobadia and Makuria. The decoration, applied usually over the cream slipped and polished surface, was in brown or black and consisted of a wide range of stylized, often floral, motifs. Animals do figure in the repertoire, particularly birds, although human figures are entirely absent. The change in decorative style was dramatic and Adams considers that it was introduced by a new group of pot decorators, either Nubian or foreign, who were now drawing their inspiration not from the decoration on earlier pottery but from Coptic manuscript illumination. Among the motifs borrowed the guilloche, connected leaf friezes, rinceau, interlace, zoomorphic designs and elaborate representations of the cross can be recognized, as can the distinctive plume-like elements considered by Adams to be adapted from Coptic paragraph marks.[118] The suggestion of pottery production in a monastic context at Faras and el-Ghazali may explain how these influences were readily available to the pot decorators. Once established these styles of decoration remained in use, although gradually evolving and displaying a tendency to become more and more ornate until around 1300, after which there is a counter trend towards simpler, more boldly executed, designs, a process documented in detail by Adams.[119]

A small number of the utility wares also bore painted decoration; some of the most elaborate are on the so-called pilgrim bottles. These are large canteen-shaped vessels with two ring handles flanking the neck and are decorated on the slightly domed sides and/or around the edge.[120] Many of the pilgrim bottles found at Soba East have a distinctive style of decoration. The area to be decorated is first painted in red, then the black painted motifs are overlaid on that ground. Sometimes the end result is for the black motif to appear red infilled but elsewhere the motif does not cover the whole of the red background.[121]

Apart from the small number of imported fine wares from Makuria and beyond, no locally produced fine ware took the place of Soba Ware.[122] However, in contrast to much of the pottery further north the Alwans maintained an important tradition of black and

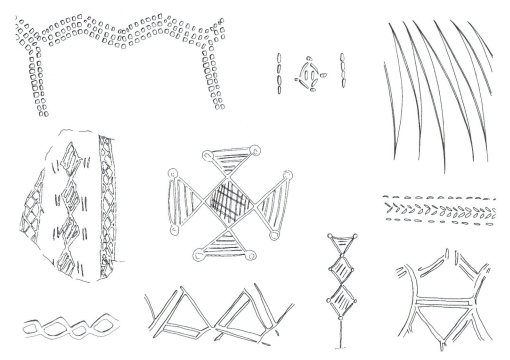

Figure 95 **Incised decorative motifs on medieval pottery from Soba East (after Welsby and Daniels 1991, figs 123, 126 and 128; Welsby 1998, figs 59, 64, 68, 71 and 72).**

red burnished pottery with incised decoration (Fig. 95). Black burnishing is much more common than red burnishing but very similar forms with similar decoration are found in either colour. One of the longest lived motifs is the saw-tooth or wolf's-tooth decoration which bears close similarities to decoration found on pottery of the Neolithic period some 5000 years earlier.[123] 'Modern' motifs were not, however, neglected and the cross in a wide variety of forms is used to decorate pottery, both by the potters themselves and later scratched on as graffiti.[124] The later 'beer' jars at Soba have incised decoration, usually to be found immediately below the rim on the interior or exterior, and a number of motifs are largely confined to vessels of that type.[125]

Adams considers, in the light of the continuity in Nubian pottery forms and decorative styles from the Classic Christian periods onwards, and the lack of subsequent borrowings of artistic forms from their major competitors in Egypt, that Nubian pottery was a genuine art form. 'Styles seem to have been adopted, and at times copied, for no other reason than that the potters admired them.'[126]

Language

As we have seen as late as the end of the fourth or the beginning of the fifth century Meroitic was still a written language although how many people by that date could read it is uncertain. In northern Nubia Greek was well established and it took over from Meroitic as the language of official inscriptions during the fifth century. Alongside it, and used for royal inscriptions and letters during the fifth century, as well as later for religious, administrative and commercial matters, was Coptic, a language derived directly from the ancient Egyptian vernacular language, Demotic.[127] Greek and Coptic were used during the medieval period throughout Nubia for inscriptions of all types from royal tombstones to graffiti on walls and on pottery and must have been widely understood.[128] From the eighth century onwards they were joined by the written form of a language known as Old Nubian to distinguish it from the living language of Nubian still spoken, but not written, in northern Sudan and southern Egypt today.[129] Old Nubian as a spoken language may have been of considerable antiquity and has been thought to have been the language of at least some dwellers along the Middle Nile in the second millennium BC. In the medieval period it was the spoken language in Nubia and was used in a wide range of written correspondence of both a private and an official nature.

The level of at least some degree of literacy in these three languages appears to have been high.[130] A strong desire to be commemorated by an inscription, often with a Greek text, is evident on tombstones, even if such formulaic usage says little about the level of

Figure 96 **Pottery marked with the names of their owners and sometimes with the cryptogram for Michael from the Monastery of the Holy Trinity at Old Dongola (after Pluskota 1997, figs 3 and 4).**

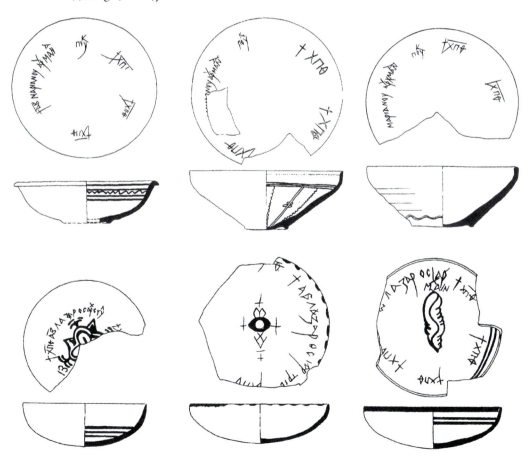

understanding and use of that language by the stone carver or the inscriber of ceramic tombstones, or indeed of their clients. The tombstones are most frequently inscribed with a prayer for the dead derived from the *Euchologion Mega* and are found throughout Nubia not only in the large metropolises.

Perhaps the best indicator of the level of literacy is the prevalence of graffiti, particularly on pottery (Figs 28 and 96) from a wide range of sites and associated with many types of buildings, from churches to humble dwellings. Graffiti is extremely useful in assessing the level of knowledge of the languages used in Nubia as in many cases there can be little doubt that the writer is a native Nubian not a visitor from countries where there was a greater use of Greek, Coptic or Arabic. Of the large numbers of graffiti carved on the walls of the cathedral at Faras, those which employ Greek, often intermixed with Old Nubian, have been described thus, 'the number of mistakes made in this category of inscriptions is practically unlimited'.[131] An examination of the various inscriptions and documents in Greek indicates that there is no linear progression from a sound knowledge of Greek in the early medieval period to the use of appalling ungrammatical Greek towards the end. Hägg singles out the letter dated to the mid fifth century between the Blemmyan and Nobadian kings as an example of just how bad Greek can get, suggesting that this is a literal transcription of the pidgin Greek used by the two rulers, at least in their written correspondence; it was their *lingua franca*.[132] He cautions however, against a comparison of the Greek used in Nubia with that of Classical Athens or even of the educated inhabitants of the Roman Empire. Nubian Greek has to be viewed in context where at least some of its peculiarities are common to the usage of the language elsewhere in the Greek-speaking world.[133] Greek and Coptic continued in use into the late medieval period and it has been suggested that Greek was still spoken as a living language as late as the eleventh century, but was certainly also written later.[134] A graffito in the Monastery of St Simeon at Aswan, dated to 1322, is written in the Old Nubian script but the language is debased Greek.[135] On the scroll of Bishop Timotheos, dating to the late fourteenth century, most of the text is in Coptic, while the greetings to the congregation at Faras at the beginning are in Greek.[136] Among the very latest Greek texts known from Old Dongola is an *ostracon,* bearing the beginning of Psalm 26, which dates to the late thirteenth or early fourteenth century. The text exhibits a dependence on Old Nubian.[137]

The three medieval languages are represented throughout Nubia and coexisted with Arabic. However, the use of Coptic, in particular, at the monastery at el-Ghazali may be associated with the presence there of Coptic monks. By contrast the official written language at Old Dongola was Greek[138] and the small number of *stelae* from the region at the mouth of the Wadi Abu Dom, a little over 10 km downstream from el-Ghazali, are likewise in Greek.[139] The provision of dedicatory inscriptions on the construction of a building (the cathedral?) at Faras by Paulos in 707, in both Greek and Coptic, strongly suggests that both languages had an official status at that time.[140] Certainly in the earlier medieval period Greek was the official language of the Nubian Church but Ibn Selim in the tenth century, referring to the Kingdom of Alwa, noted that 'their [religious] books are in Greek ... they translate these into their own language'.[141] At least at Qasr Ibrim the use of Greek does not appear to have continued after the third quarter of the twelfth century.[142] Evidence for the teaching of Coptic in Nubia has been found. At Faras a Coptic alphabet was written in black ink on a decorated stone block reused in the wall of the cathedral,[143] while the Coptic alphabet was also found on an *ostracon* from Debeira West.[144]

The Old Nubian alphabet is largely borrowed from Coptic, itself derived from Greek, retaining three of the Coptic special characters with the addition of a few extra letters derived from Meroitic such as h̄ñ and w.[145] Two at least of these not only derive their form from Meroitic but have the same value and this indicates that there must have been a time when people could both read and speak Meroitic and wrote in Old Nubian. Millet has guessed that this may have been around 600,[146] although we do have a gap in the written record between the latest inscription in Meroitic, thought to date to the later fourth century and the earliest in Old Nubian thought to date to the eighth century. Old Nubian continued to be written as late as 1485.[147] Old Nubian is one of the Eastern Sudanic family of languages of Nilo-Saharan stock and is fairly closely related to a number of tribal languages of southern Sudan and Uganda. The Old Nubian language, as known to us from the epigraphic material, is an ancestor of the modern Nubian dialect of Mahasi, one of the three dialects to survive on the Middle Nile where Nubian is still spoken by the local population. However, modern Nubian does not have a written form. Although Old Nubian as a written language is homogenous, at least in the territory of Makuria which includes Nobadia, it has been suggested that the spoken dialects differed. Mahasi may have been used in the northern province of Makuria and Dongolawi in the heartlands of Makuria. Among the texts in Old Nubian from Soba East the alphabet used differs somewhat from that current in the north, according to Griffith, who noted that all the non-Greek letters are peculiar and that there are no letters borrowed from Coptic.[148] There is the possibility that one or more additional Nubian languages were used in medieval Alwa.

A late linguistic arrival in the region was Arabic. As the language of Nubia's powerful northern neighbour its introduction into the far north is readily understandable and it was widely used in commercial and diplomatic correspondence.[149] There was also considerable movement of Arab traders and diplomats within the Nubian kingdoms which will have helped to foster a knowledge of the language. The penetration of the language on a large scale, however, was a direct result of the colonisation of Nubia by Arab speakers from Egypt, and via the eastern desert into the Nile Valley.

Much of our evidence for the written languages comes from inscriptions, particularly funerary inscriptions on *stelae* of stone or terracotta. The inscriptions on *stelae* tend to be formulaic, usually beginning with an invocation and ending with the date of death. Although the titles of the deceased are frequently given there are few details of the individuals, of their ancestors and descendants. The royal tombstone of David, King of Alwa conforms to the standard style (Fig. 97). More common are *stelae* of ecclesiastical dignitaries, of which a series is known from Faras and from Old Dongola (see Chapter 3). This data adds considerably to the prosopography of medieval Nubia, and, where dated and associated with structures or artefacts, provides invaluable chronological pegs from which to reconstruct the history and cultural development of Nubia from the archaeological sources. Of especial importance in this context was the list of bishops written on the wall of a niche in the south-eastern room of the Faras cathedral. This contained the names of twenty-seven bishops with a gap for another. The first fifteen were all in one hand and had

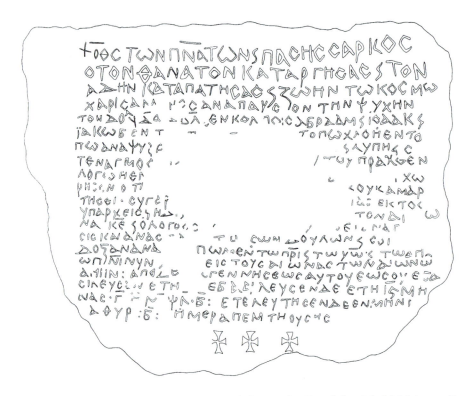

Figure 97 **Tombstone of the Alwan King David from Soba East (after Jakobielski 1991, fig. 153).**

presumably been copied from an earlier document. Each entry consisted of the name of the bishop, the word for years, the year of the episcopate, the month and the day of death. In the latter half of the list an additional column occasionally contains the word 'died'. It can be correlated with wall paintings, executed on behalf of the individual named or of that individual, and also sometimes with the funerary *stelae*. Another list, unfortunately largely illegible, may have contained the names of *eparchs* or the kings of Makuria. Two other lists are of priest and deacons.[150]

Building inscriptions are rare but have been found recording the construction of the fortress at Ikhmindi, of churches at Faras and of the conversion of temples to churches at Debod and Taifa. The graffiti on pottery, along with those carved on buildings and rock outcrops, tend to be short, often only a single letter or a monogram. The marks on pottery made after firing are often presumably owners' marks. At Old Dongola personal services have been found belonging to five monks, among them *archiepiscopos* and *archimandrites* of the Monastery of the Holy Trinity. They bear inscriptions scratched on their interiors. Many have the sign of the cross followed by AB, the abbreviation for ABBA, and the name of the monk (Fig. 96). Some then have the monk's title, the name of the monastery and the cryptogram for Michael, XΠΘ, several times.[151] Among the more interesting graffiti carved on buildings, which have important historical implications, are those of Joel, King of Dotawo, within the cathedral at Faras and of Giorgiou, Christ loving king, on a lintel at Soba East.[152]

Our perception of the prevalence of written material in Nubia is dramatically altered by the evidence from Qasr Ibrim. The ultra-dry conditions and the absence of termites on that site, which has contributed to the excellent preservation of organic materials, allows us to glimpse the wealth of written material on papyrus, parchment and paper. On the site are preserved thousands of documents in Meroitic, Latin, Greek, Coptic, Old Nubian, Arabic and Turkish. The perfect preservation meant that stray pieces of writing material could be picked up after many centuries and reused, hence we get documents written in one language on one side and in a different language on the other. Although knowledge of the written word appears to have been widespread the command of a given language often leaves much to be desired.

Papyrus was used for the earlier texts during the Kushite and Ptolemaic periods but continued in use in the medieval period.[153] Thereafter parchment[154] makes an appearance. Paper, which was introduced into Egypt in the late eighth or early ninth century,[155] was used in Nubia during the Classic Christian period and in Late Christian times and, at least at Qasr Ibrim, almost entirely replaced other writing materials.[156] Books with pages of both parchment and paper(?) have been found at Ibrim and book covers have survived elsewhere. One of the best preserved books was discovered at Serra East in the winter of 1963/4. The text is written on twenty-four numbered pages of parchment, varying a little in size, but approximately 270 x 180 mm, and provided with a leather cover. It is a translation into Old Nubian from the original Greek of a sermon contained in the writings of John Chrysostom, probably dating to the eleventh or twelfth century.[157]

Lengthy texts were also written on potsherds. Although the potsherds themselves usually survive in good condition the writing upon them usually fares much less well. However, *ostraca* have been recovered from a number of sites where the organic writing materials have completely vanished. The only documents to survive from Alwa are on three large and one small *ostraca* from Soba East: one a magical text, another may have been a letter, a third containing short invocations which may be a writing exercise, and the fourth has a fragment of a religious text on one side and a drawing of a church on the other. Where identifiable the texts were in Greek or a mixture of Greek and Old Nubian.[158]

CHAPTER 10

The collapse of the Nubian kingdoms

The sources for the late thirteenth century

The events of the later thirteenth century are recorded in great detail by a number of sources. Here, as with many of the Muslim accounts of events in Nubia, the detail provided and the precise dates given suggest the veracity of the sources, but how are we to reconcile the contradictions, not only between the various sources for the same events, but also within individual accounts? If David, as recounted below, for example, attacked Aidhab after the start of the Muslim year 674, beginning on 24 June 1275, how was he able to undertake the extensive building projects with which he is credited after the capture of Aidhab, before the Muslims advanced against him in January 1276, reaching Meinarti by March of that year and advancing directly on towards Old Dongola, dates and events described by en-Nuwayri?[1] Other sources recount that the attack on Aidhab took place on 18 August 1272, within which year also falls the attack on Aswan and the execution of the *eparch*.[2] If the attacks by David are dated to 1272 David seems to have got off very lightly, and escaped retaliation until the well-documented invasion of Makuria in 1275 which, both logically and according to many of the sources, followed on directly from David's attack on Aswan. Further confusion is sown by en-Nuwayri. If the peace treaty of 1276 between Shekanda and the Muslims involved the partition of Makuria, the northern part thereafter coming under the direct rule of the Sultan, how can en-Nuwayri describe the invasion of 1287[3] as the first stage in the conquest of Makuria, all preceding invasions being just raids. In addition many of the descriptions, apparently of different events, appear very similar in detail. This may be the result of the Muslim invasions following a tried and tested pattern with an inevitable sequence of defensive actions on the part of the Makurian king, or of a confusion in the sources, with different personalities and different dates being attached to the same event.

The account given below seeks to reconcile the major discrepancies, but other interpretations of the evidence are possible.

Table 5. Summary of the relations between the Makurians and Muslims in the later thirteenth and fourteenth centuries.

1265   Raid into Makuria, as far as Old Dongola, by the *wali* of Qoz.
1275   The Makurian king David attacks Aidhab and Aswan.
1276   Muslim advance into Makuria.
        Defeat at Old Dongola of King David, who flees to el-Abwab but is handed over to the Muslims.

1276   Shekanda installed on the Makurian throne.

        King David arrives as a prisoner in Cairo.

1286   Muslim invasion of Makuria, the Makurian king orders the evacuation of the country.

        Defeat of King Semamun at Old Dongola, installation of a new king by the Muslims.

1288   Return of the Muslim army to Cairo.

        Semamun re-occupies the Makurian throne.

1289   Dispatch of another Muslim army to oust Semamun.

        Old Dongola, evacuated by the Makurians, falls into the hands of the Muslims.

1290   Muslim garrison at Old Dongola, the rest of the army returns to Cairo.

        Semamun recaptures Old Dongola, executes the Muslim appointee, and re-establishes his control of the kingdom.

1304   King Ayay of Makuria travels to Cairo to request Muslim military support.

1305-6 Muslim army operating in Makuria on behalf of King Ayay.

1315   Attack on King Kerenbes by a Muslim army. The king fled to el-Abwab but was handed over to the Muslims.

        Abdallah Barshanbu placed on the Makurian throne.

        Kanz ed-Dawla, nephew of Kerenbes, escapes from Cairo, defeats the Makurian king at Old Dongola and reigns on behalf of his uncle.

1317   The 'Throne Hall' of the Makurian kings converted to a mosque.

1323   Muslim army re-installs Kerenbes on the Makurian throne.

        Kerenbes ousted by Kanz ed-Dawla after the Muslim army withdrew. Kanz ed-Dawla the first Muslim ruler of Makuria.

1365   Alliance of a Makurian pretender with the desert Arabs, defeat of the king at Old Dongola.

        Old Dongola abandoned, capital transferred to Daw.

        Dispatch of a Muslim army to Makuria to aid the Makurians, relief of Daw which was being besieged by the Arabs.

A Muslim invasion in 1265

El-Maqrizi describes an attack on Makuria in 1265 by the *wali* of Qoz who, marching from Aswan, advanced to near Old Dongola, 'killed many people, took prisoners and then returned'.[4]

Makurian aggression and Muslim retaliation, David and Shekanda 1275-6

According to Ibn Khaldun, around 1276 the Makurian king (Mintashkil) came to Cairo to seek the sultan Baybars' help against his nephew David who had seized power.[5] This individual is very confusingly given a variety of different names by historians, Meshked, Shekanda, Mertashkar? and Marqashenkuz, although Shekanda is most commonly used. He may have been of the Makurian royal house residing in Cairo rather than being the ousted king himself. What is certain is that a Makurian king called David attacked Aidhab on the Red Sea and 'committed hideous actions' and then advanced on Aswan burning the *saqias*. This was a very impressive undertaking as the distances involved across the harsh Eastern Desert must have presented formidable obstacles. According to Nasir-I-Khusraw, who travelled in a small party from Aswan to Aidhab in the eleventh century, the journey took fifteeen days with one stretch of five days between wells.[6] The Arab sources give no reasons for this aggressive act which must have been seen by the Makurian king as an extremely risky operation. For the rationale behind David's action we need to look at the developing situation in the Eastern Desert at this time. Arab infiltration into that region had been dramatically increased after the defeat of the Beja in the ninth century. By the end of the twelfth century Aidhab had become one of the most important ports in the Muslim world and through it passed much of the trade from India, East Africa, Yemen and Jeddah to Egypt. The dangers posed by the Crusaders to the Hajj route across the Sinai caused movement of that route to the south, through Aidhab. To protect this trade Egypt had showed increasing interest in security in the Eastern Desert and Baybars extended his control along the whole of the Red Sea littoral as far south as Sawakin. The Makurians must have viewed this with alarm as it threatened to isolate them from access to Red Sea trade and place control of all Nubian international trade in the hands of the Egyptian ruler, whether trade down the Nile or via the Red Sea.[7] David's action may, therefore, have been a desperate attempt to break this stranglehold; an attempt which was doomed to failure.

The son of the sister of the king whose throne had been usurped by David, Shekanda, accompanied the Muslim army led by the *wali* of Qoz sent to avenge these attacks. The Muslims left for Nubia on 20 January 1276 but were attacked by the Nubians on camels before they could cross the frontier. The Makurians were defeated and the *wali* went on to take the fortress at Daw, capturing many prisoners, among them the *eparch*, who was sent to Cairo where he was executed by being sawn in two. The *emir* Shams ed-Din, bringing up the rearguard, wrought destruction and exterminated any who had survived the initial onslaught, advanced against the king and defeated his new *eparch* then residing at Daw. The Muslims then moved on to the Island of Mikhail (Meinarti) at the downstream end of the Second Cataract and the *eparch* who had replaced the executed previous incumbent of that office swore allegiance to the Muslim appointee Shekanda. The Muslims finally caught up with King David at Old Dongola which they reached on 31 March 1276 and defeated him. David fled to seek sanctuary with the King of el-Abwab, but was handed over by Adur to the Muslims, reaching the Sultan's court in June 1276. During their seventeen-day occupation of Old Dongola the Muslims burnt down the church of Sus. David had also constructed a palace he called Aidhab, a complex of churches and houses, and a square, decorated with paintings of his victories at Aidhab and Aswan, which were destroyed by the Muslims.

The price for the Muslims support for Shekanda was heavy. After they installed him on the throne of Makuria they offered the Makurians the choice of embracing Islam, of paying the *jizya* (tax on the infidel) or of being killed. Not surprisingly they avoided the last option and apparently also the first, and agreed to pay the *jizya* of one dinar per head. The Makurian king was seen as the representative of the sultan and it was in that capacity that his subjects swore allegiance to him. One half of all the revenues of Makuria were to belong to the sultan and the Makurian king also agreed to provide every year 3 elephants, 3 giraffes, 5 female panthers, 100 camels and 400 oxen. The most important clause was that which began the dismemberment of the state, with the districts of el-Ali and el-Jabal being placed under the personal control of the sultan. Within those provinces all the dates and cotton were to be handed over to the sultan as well as any other goods which by tradition had been reserved for the Makurian kings.[8] El-Furat Mufaddal, writing in the early fourteenth century, was probably in error when he noted that the citadels of Qasr Ibrim and Jebel Adda were also the private property of the sultan.[9]

Semamun and the invasions of 1286-90

The reason for the beginning of hostilities is unclear. El-Zahir records details of a complaint made by the king of el-Abwab to the sultan about the mistreatment of envoys between them by the king of Dongola.[10] Whatever the cause the Muslims attacked in strength. Two armies were involved, one under the *emir* Alam ed-Din Sanjar el-Masruri, the *mutawalli* of Cairo and one under the *emir* Izz ed-Din el-Kurani, the governor of Qoz, with regular troops, Mamelukes and Bedouin. The armies advanced along both banks of the Nile and, in the face of this invasion, the Makurian king Semamun ordered the country to be evacuated, his *eparch* Jorays[11] withdrawing from Daw (Jebel Adda), the Island of Mikhail, and the other centres as the Muslims approached. Semamun concentrated his forces at Old Dongola but was defeated by the army of Izz ed-Din and pursued upstream for fifteen days, during which Jorays was captured along with one described as 'a cousin of the regent of Dongola'. The son of the sister of the king was placed on the throne by Izz ed-Din and Jorays was confirmed as *eparch* under the new ruler. The Muslim armies returned, laden with booty including slaves, horses, camels, oxen and clothes, arriving at the sultan's court in August 1288.

What followed was to be repeated several times over the next century. Immediately the Muslim army withdrew, Semamun returned to Old Dongola, vanquished his enemies in the city, and regained control of the country. The Muslim royal appointee, Jorays, and the garrison which had been left in Old Dongola, fled to the sultan's court. Another large army was rapidly assembled under the command of the *emir* 'Izz ed-Din Aybek el-Afram, which left Cairo in October 1289,[12] the troops being accompanied by grenade boats (used to carry inflammable war materials) and large and small boats carrying provisions, coats of mail and other equipment, a total of more than 500 vessels. On arriving at Aswan the Makurian king died and another puppet, the son of the sister of king David who was at the sultan's court, was dispatched to join the army. As in the earlier invasion the army was split into two, one half advancing along each bank with the *eparch* being sent ahead through the region under his control, from Daw to the Island of Mikhail, to reassure the natives, to protect them, and to prepare the halting places for the army. South of Meinarti the populace had been evacuated and the Muslims rampaged right up to Old Dongola putting any who had remained behind to the sword and burning houses and *saqias*. Old Dongola was also evacuated and the king fled upstream a journey of fifteen days to an island, which is probably to be identified as Mograt, at the head of the great Nile bend. The *emir* with his army pursued the king but the boats were unable to follow through the Fourth Cataract. After the Muslim army had been encamped on the Nile bank across from Mograt for three days the Makurian king, after refusing to swear allegiance to the sultan and fearing the arrival of the Muslim boats, fled upstream to the Kingdom of el-Abwab, where apparently he did not suffer the fate of his predecessor David, who had been arrested and handed over to the sultan's forces. However, the royal princes, officials and priest abandoned on Mograt made their peace with the Muslims, swore allegiance to them, and handed over the Makurian crown and other royal regalia, before the army returned to Old Dongola.

After a parade of the army in full war apparel on both banks of the river, and with the grenade boats in mid stream, a great banquet was held in the largest of Old Dongola's churches and the royal appointee from the sultan's court was enthroned, swore loyalty to the sultan and was required to pay the *Baqt*. Leaving a garrison behind in Old Dongola the Muslim army returned to Cairo, arriving there in May 1290. Once again as soon as the main Muslim force had retired Semamun returned to Old Dongola and, supported by many princes and the army, he arrested the king in the palace and gave safe passage to the Muslim garrison which withdrew to Qoz. He executed the sultan's king in a rather gruesome way, and also the *eparch* Jorays. Semamun then set about strengthening his position by writing to the sultan and offering gifts as well as requesting a pardon and agreeing to contribute the *Baqt* every year. The sultan, with other problems on his mind, left Semamun alone.

King Ayay

Several sources[13] record the arrival in Cairo in 1304 of the Makurian king Ayay bearing rich gifts, slaves, camels, cattle, leopards, vitriol (elsewhere alum) and emery stone (elsewhere whetstones)[14] and that he requested military aid from the sultan. An army was duly dispatched and, accompanied by Ayay, marched into Nubia. We are not told what stimulated the request nor what the result of the campaign was. The army returned in 1306 after a nine-month absence having suffered many hardships in the war against the blacks and also because of shortage of provisions.

A visit by an unnamed Makurian king to Cairo, again bearing gifts, is mentioned by Ibn Iyas but without further details.[15]

It was at this time that the Venetian, Marin Sanudo, drew up a plan, which he submitted to the pope in 1310, with the hypothetical scenario of an attack by the Nubians on Egypt from the south. He modified his plan in 1320, when he clearly had some knowledge of the realities of the situation. He added that the military strength of the Nubians was very low, if it existed at all, and that they would need western troops to assist in such an attack. Vantini suggests that he received his information from Genoese merchants who had been authorized by the Sultan Qalawun, from 1289 onwards, to travel to Old Dongola for trade purposes.[16] Needless to say no action was taken by western Christendom and Makuria's protracted decline continued.

King Kerenbes

El-Maqrizi is our only source for the journey of Kerenbes to Cairo(?) to pay a fine imposed on him for killing his brother.[17] By late 1315 Kerenbes had fallen from favour, at least in the eyes of the sultan, and was attacked by another Muslim army bringing another son of the sister of King David, Abdallah Barshanbu, from the sultan's court to be placed on the Makurian throne.[18] In an attempt to forestall the invasion Kerenbes dispatched the son of his sister, Kanz ed-Dawla, who was a Muslim and his legitimate successor, to the sultan asking that he be placed on the Makurian throne, but he was detained in Cairo and the expedition went ahead. As the Muslim army approached Old Dongola the king and his brother Abram fled to el-Abwab, like kings David and Semamun before them, in the hope of obtaining asylum, but they were detained by the king of that country who informed the Muslim general that the king was under arrest. They were then handed over to the Muslims and sent in chains to the sultan.

Abdallah Barshanbu was installed on the Makurian throne but did not enjoy that exalted position for long. By his proud manner, his rude and cruel treatment of his subjects, and the changes he made to the laws of the state, he rapidly alienated the populace. After the return of the Muslim army from Old Dongola, Kanz ed-Dawla, still resident in Cairo, requested permission to go to Aswan to raise funds from *saqias* belonging to him there, which he should pay as tribute to the sultan. However, on being granted permission to travel to Aswan he crossed the frontier into Nubia and at Daw was received by the populace with respect and they hailed him as king. He then advanced on Old Dongola and defeated and killed Abdallah Barshanbu in battle. Although Kanz ed-Dawla reigned over Makuria he did not accept the crown out of deference to the legitimate king, his uncle Kerenbes. The sultan then sent Abram, the brother of Kerenbes, to Nubia to arrest his nephew, Kanz ed-Dawla and send him back to the sultan. If this were achieved the sultan promised to free both Abram and Kerenbes and to reinstate Kerenbes on the throne of Makuria. Abram duly made his way to Old Dongola, was well received by Kanz ed-Dawla, who handed over the kingdom to him, and the two then proceeded on a tour of the country to allay the fears of the populace. However, at Daw Abram put Kanz ed-Dawla in chains and was determined to send him to the sultan but, on Abram's untimely death, Kanz ed-Dawla was again accepted as king and this time was crowned. He then began to gather support from the desert Arabs to face the inevitable retaliation from Egypt.

El-Maqrizi recounts details of an amazing expedition against the Arabs of Aidhab, 500 horsemen led by the *emir* Alauddin Moghaltay setting out from Qoz in March 1317 on the orders of the sultan.[19] This was not directed against the Nubians, but the force, after advancing across the desert towards Aidhab, moved along the Red Sea coast, passed by Sawakin, and then returned to Egypt by first traversing the desert to el-Abwab and then, presumably, following the Nile (Old Dongola is specifically mentioned), arriving in Cairo in August after an absence of eight months. That such a journey was feasible with horses and in such a short timescale is surprising as is the absence of any mention of hostilities between the expedition and Kanz ed-Dawla who had recently thwarted the wishes of the sultan yet again.

Kanz ed-Dawla was the first Muslim ruler of Makuria although this does not seem to have particularly endeared him to the Muslim Egyptians, nor to have signalled a rapid Islamization of the kingdom. However, it is during his reign that we have the first concrete evidence for the presence of a mosque at Old Dongola. An inscription in Arabic on a piece of stone, still visible and set into the wall of the audience room of the Makurian king's throne hall, records that 'This blessed door for religion (i.e., Islam) was opened by the hands of Seif ed-Din Abdullahi el-Nasir in the year 717 on the 16th of the month Rabia the first' (1 June 1317) (Fig. 98).[20] The mosque (Fig. 99) remained in continuous use until 1969. It is presumably this mosque which is described by the early fourteenth-century writer el-Umari as 'a great mosque where travellers can stay'.[21] It is around this time that Ibn Khaldun records that the Nuba ceased to pay the *jizya* because they had embraced Islam.[22]

Figure 98 **The dedicatory inscription of the mosque at Old Dongola.**

Figure 99 **The 'Throne Hall' at Old Dongola with the revetment added perhaps during the modifications associated with its conversion to a mosque and caravanserai in the fourteenth century.**

The narrative picks up several years later when on 1 December 1323 a force of 500 horsemen set out for Nubia accompanied by Kerenbes, although a graffito in the Monastery of St Simeon at Aswan mentioning the king is dated to 7 April 1322.[23] Arriving at Old Dongola, Kerenbes wrested power from Kanz ed-Dawla who fled while Kerenbes once again ascended the Makurian throne, only to be attacked and ousted by Kanz ed-Dawla after the Muslim forces had withdrawn. Kerenbes was still waiting in Aswan in 1326 for another chance to recover his throne but this never came and Kanz ed-Dawla remained firmly in control.[24]

An unsuccessful Muslim invasion

The year 1348 saw another Muslim refugee try his luck in Nubia. The *wali* of Qoz, Ismail el-Wafidi fled from the town and, accompanied by a group of followers, attempted to seize the kingdom of Makuria, only to be defeated and killed along with all his men by the Makurians.[25]

The Makurians and their allies, the Mamelukes against the desert Arabs

Running parallel with the constant warfare between the Muslims and the Makurians were Muslim attacks against their brethren, the desert Arabs, the term presumably used in the sources at this time for the Beja. Notwithstanding the disastrous policy adopted by claimants of the Makurian throne of requesting assistance from the sultan of Egypt, around 1365 a claimant, the usual son of the king's sister, allied himself with the Arab tribe of the Bani Ja'd and fought a fierce battle against the king at Old Dongola, emerging victorious and killing the king. While the loyalists supported the claim of the brother of the late king to rule the kingdom and withdrew to Daw in the north to continue resistance to the usurper, the victor of the battle of Dongola was crowned king at Old Dongola and held a feast to celebrate the occasion. The nobles of his allies, the Bani Ja'd, were invited to the feast, trapped within the banqueting hall, and murdered. The king then went on to dispatch the Arab army, stripped the town of all its stores and fled to Daw, making peace with the loyalist forces on condition that he be made *eparch*. The king and the new *eparch* then appealed to the sultan to help them reconquer the rest of the kingdom and undertook to bring a tribute to Egypt each year, presumably a resumption of the *Baqt*.

The sultan's army of 3,000 cavalry left for Nubia on 8 December 1365, the stores and weapons being brought by boat. After these had been portered around the First Cataract and the unladen boats brought through, the stores were once again loaded and the army and fleet moved southwards. After one day's journey the advancing army was informed by messengers from the Makurian king that the Arabs were besieging Daw. Leaving the remainder of the army and the stores, it was presumably the Muslim cavalry that pressed on in haste, overnighting at Qasr Ibrim where the Muslim commander seized the leaders of the Arabs through treachery. The headquarters of the Arabs on the Island of Mikhail was captured, bringing the hostilities to a close. An agreement was signed whereby Daw became the seat of the Makurian king, Old Dongola being in ruins and also, it was feared, too vulnerable to an Arab counter-attack. The *eparch* took up residence at Ibrim and the Egyptian army withdrew.

Thus is the sequence of events as recounted by el-Maqrizi.[26] It highlights the self-destructive nature of the Makurian dynastic squabbles. As a result of this particular episode the legitimate successor of the king ended up as *eparch* of a rump state, the metropolis of Old Dongola lay in ruins and the enmity of the powerful desert Arabs was assured. The tales of treachery committed by the usurper against his allies, and by the Muslims and the King of Makuria against their enemies, are salutary as is the apparent ability of the brother of the king to forgive the nephew who had murdered his brother and caused such devastation to the state; not only to forgive him, but also to associate with him at the highest levels in his government.

Ibn Khaldun describes the mechanism that brought about the collapse of the Makurian state referring to events in the fourteenth century. According to him the spread of the Juhanya Arabs throughout Makuria made it a place of pillage and disorder. The Nubian kings, presumably a number of kinglets, at first tried to restore their authority but were then forced to make alliances with the invaders, giving their daughters in marriage to them. Following the Nubian principle of matrilineal succession the end result was that control of Makuria rapidly passed into the hands of the Arab nomads who, by their lack of discipline and selfishness, were unable to continue monarchic rule and the whole area degenerated into anarchy without any trace of centralized authority.[27]

Once Old Dongola ceased to be the seat of the Makurian kings it disappears from the historical record only to reappear as an important centre in the Funj period when it was the capital of the northernmost province of the Funj Sultanate.[28]

The kingdom of Dotawo

With the abandonment of Old Dongola as the capital of northern Nubia the kingdom of Makuria may be said to have come to an end. Although not mentioned by the Arab sources a number of contemporary documents and graffiti refer to the kingdom of Dotawo.[29] At Qasr Ibrim, where most of the documents have been found, the earliest reference to this kingdom dates from the twelfth century when there is no doubt that Ibrim lay within the kingdom of Makuria, and other manuscripts from that site record the presence of the *eparch*, who was a Makurian official in a senior position, in the area. At an

Figure 100 **The cemetery at Jebel Adda with the fortress beyond (courtesy of the SARS Kirwan Archive).**

international level, as the Arab sources indicate, it was the king of Makuria and his *eparch* who was of importance while on the local level the *eparch* and the king of Dotawo were of more importance. There is only one mention among the documents from Ibrim published so far of the king of Makuria. The documentation relating to the *eparch* at Ibrim is more common than that of the kings of Dotawo and there is every reason to accept that Ibrim was the residence of the *eparch* but was probably not where the kings of Dotawo resided. The kings of Dotawo are usually assumed to have been based at Jebel Adda (Fig. 100), the medieval name of which was Addo, the Daw of the Arabic sources.[30] Adams has drawn attention to the meaning of the suffix *-tawo* in modern Nubian, 'under' or 'below', and suggests that Dotawo meant 'the country below Do' or perhaps 'the principality ruled from Do'.[31] The excavator of Jebel Adda uncovered a large complex of buildings which he claimed was one of the palaces of the peripatetic kings of Dotawo.[32]

Two documents of 1331 from Edfu in Upper Egypt refer to Siti, King of Dotawo.[33] Carved on the wall of the rock-cut shrine of Horemheb, close to Jebel Adda, which was converted into a church, was a graffito of fourteen lines which begins 'In the name of the Father and of the Son and of the Spirit: I, Joel, King of Kings of Dotawo, for whom this inscription was written in the grotto of Epimaco ...'.[34] Other graffiti in the grotto mention King Koudlaniel whose kingdom is not stated and King Tienossi of Ilenat.[35] Joel is also mentioned in a letter written on fine leather discovered at Jebel Adda together with a list of court and ecclesiastical officials among them Bishop Merki of Qasr Ibrim.[36] The letter is dated to 1484.[37] At Faras in the cathedral there is a graffito recording King Joel; he is mentioned on a dedicatory inscription from within the Church of St Raphael at Tamit and possibly also at Sai.[38] In 1155 a bishop of Selim is mentioned in a document from Qasr Ibrim along with the king of Dotawo; the kingdom presumably included the bishoprics of Ibrim and Selim.[39] Mention is also made of the Bishop of Kurte in Dotawo.[40]

Although it has been suggested that the kings of Dotawo and of Makuria are one and the same, and occasionally the independent Arab sources and documentary sources from Ibrim record kings of the same name at about the same time on the two thrones, on other occasions the individuals were certainly not the same. In addition, the activities engaged in by the kings of Dotawo, local matters relating to Ibrim and its region, seem entirely inappropriate to have been dealt with personally by the Makurian king. As already noted the Arab sources record that the Makurian king was the Great King under whom were a number of lesser kings. At least up until 1365-6 we should see the kings of Dotawo as local rulers under the suzerainty of the king of Makuria. Although the material from Ibrim relates to activities both of the *eparch* and the Dotawan kings there is little direct evidence of how jurisdiction was divided between the two offices. The *eparch* does appear however, to have been charged with international relations and contacts with the Muslim inhabitants of the region while the local king dealt with civil and legal matters of local import.

As recounted above, in 1365-6 Old Dongola was abandoned as the seat of the Makurian monarch and the court moved to Daw. If Daw is correctly identified with Jebel Adda how do we reconcile the same town being both the capital and seat of the Makurian king and, as we assume, the capital and seat of the king of Dotawo? The most obvious solution is that, from that date, the rump of the Makurian state was focused on the Kingdom of Dotawo and held sway, at least in the mid fifteenth century, from Qasr Ibrim to Faras. After 1366 there is no mention of a king of Makuria, nor, it must be admitted, is there any mention of the kings of Dotawo. The replacement of the vassal king of Dotawo by the royal family from Makuria[41] finds some support in the titles of Joel, King of Kings of Dotawo, directly comparable to the title of the Makurian kings, 'Great King, ruling over 13 lesser kings'.

THE ARCHAEOLOGICAL EVIDENCE FOR LATE MEDIEVAL MAKURIA AND DOTAWO

In the early fourteenth century the 'Throne Hall' of the Makurian kings at Old Dongola was extensively damaged, probably by the earthquake which is known to have struck north-eastern Africa at this time, and it may have been this, rather than enemy action, which was responsible for the destruction observed both in the Church of the Granite Columns and the Cruciform Church.[42] Following on an initial period of abandonment of the Church of the Granite Columns (Church of the Brick Pillars) indicated by a deposit of wind-blown sand covering the floors, sealed by rubble, presumably from the collapse of the vaults or perhaps a partial demolition of the building, it was reused. The upper surface of the rubble was levelled over the whole of the interior and the roof may have been repaired using timber and palm matting. After these roof repairs were destroyed by fire the building was finally abandoned.[43] The Northern Church appears to have continued as a place of worship well into the fourteenth century, perhaps being abandoned while still in good condition in the later half of that century. It was then used to house storage vessels before the ceramic floor tiles were removed and the central dome collapsed.[44]

Although in some cases we can see evidence for the abandonment of churches as places of worship we are often unclear what significance this may have had. At Arminna West squatters occupied the church probably in the late twelfth century, but as other evidence from the site suggest that the settlement was largely abandoned at this time[45] the church may have been superfluous to requirements. This seems more likely than that the local population had already embraced Islam. At Soba East there was a phase during the use of Church C when the building was either demolished or in an advanced state of disrepair, during which time timber structures were built on its site. It was subsequently rebuilt on the same scale as the original building and functioned as a church.[46] The presence of squatters within Church A marked the end of the use of that building for worship. Its fate and the temporary abandonment of Church C, in the heart of the metropolis of Alwa, should be significant and the Church A evidence perhaps indicates that the fortunes of Alwa were already at a low ebb by the twelfth century. The disuse of Church A, and the desecration of the tombs to the east of the building, may perhaps be related to the presence of non-Christian burials in the cemetery to the east of Building G although, in the absence of dating evidence for the latter, this is incapable of proof.[47] Evidence for what has been interpreted as a decline in the fortunes of the city at Old Dongola, dating from the twelfth if not the later eleventh century, have also been observed.[48]

We have some literary evidence for the destruction of churches by the Muslims in the late thirteenth century including one at a place called Sus. This church had been constructed by Muslim prisoners of war that King David had captured in his campaigns against Aidhab and Aswan.[49] The, as it turned out, temporary, conversion of the cathedral at Ibrim into a mosque in 1173 has already been mentioned. The location of the burial of Bishop Timotheos, which occurred in 1372, suggests that at that time the Cathedral at Qasr Ibrim was still in a reasonable state of repair although the crypts had become filled with earth.[50] The date of the conversion of Church Four at Jebel Adda into a mosque, whether in the later medieval or the post-medieval periods, is unknown.[51] The church, structure 9651, situated on the plateau 500 m from the fortress at Ibrim, was converted into a mosque in the sixteenth century.[52]

Church Seven at Jebel Adda was probably constructed, according to the excavator, in the fourteenth century. The abandonment of churches does not directly correlate with the abandonment of the Christian faith in the communities in which those churches stood. The Adda Church Seven had gone out of use before the end of the medieval period; it was used as a dwelling by a Christian family before its final abandonment.[53] Similarly at Meinarti the only church known in the settlement may have been abandoned around 1365 at the time of the occupation of the village by the Beni Kanz and the Beni Ikrima, yet there is clear evidence for continued occupation of the site by people still professing the Christian religion.[54]

In the region between Qasr Ibrim and the Third Cataract increasing insecurity accounts

Figure 101 **Castle house, House C1, in the settlement 21-S-2 at Kulubnarti.**

for the appearance between 1100 and 1500 of a new house type, called by Adams the castle house. Examples at Kulubnarti date to between 1100 and 1300 (Fig. 101), that at Meinarti is not earlier than the late fourteenth century.[55] At Meinarti, in an attempt to provide greater protection the inhabitants reinforced most of the houses by strengthening the walls, replacing the flat timber roofs with vaults and making the access from outside much more difficult. What may have been a look-out tower was built at the southern edge of the village.[56] Although many castle houses remained in use for several centuries, well beyond the medieval period, the presence of inscriptions in Greek, and the content of those inscriptions which appear to be invocations meant to confer protection on the building, indicate that their original builders were Christians. These structures are a local response which further upstream is manifest in the development of large fortresses, and elsewhere by the relocation of settlements into more defensible and more inhospitable areas.

At Kasanarti, Abu Sir and Meinarti, as noted above, there are watchtowers which are so placed as to command the river upstream, suggesting that a significant threat was for a time expected from the south. Such a situation presumably relates to activities by the desert Arabs infiltrating into the heartlands of Makuria rather than to major invading armies advancing from Egypt, against which, in any event, the local defensive measures can have offered little protection.[57]

The disappearance of Dotawo

For over a century after the establishment of Daw as the capital of the independent state of Dotawo it appears to have avoided the depredations of its Muslim neighbours, the area it occupied no longer being of strategic significance. Left to their own devices the kings of Dotawo continued to profess Christianity and acted as patrons and protectors of the Church.[58]

The cathedral at Faras was still in use, or at least accessible and visited as a place of pilgrimage, in the latter half of the fifteenth century.[59] At Qasr Ibrim, while the documentary evidence indicates that the hilltop remained the administrative centre both for temporal and heavenly affairs, remaining the residence of the *eparch*, the *domestikos* and the bishop, who dwelt in the three substantial structures within its walls, most of the old stone-built houses were either abandoned or had been demolished. However by the end of the fifteenth century all vestiges of authority had ceased and the hilltop stood unoccupied until entered by the Ottomans.[60]

Ibn Iyas preserves what may be the latest mention of hostilities between the Muslims and the Nubians. In 1518 the *emir* Ali b. Umar attacked the 'Lord of Nubia'.[61] Already the rulers of Egypt were on the defensive. In 1517 the Ottoman Turkish armies of Selim had entered Egypt and under Suleiman the Magnificent a Turkish garrison was established at Qasr Ibrim, in the 1560s, and at Sai.[62] The kingdom of Dotawo seems to have vanished from history in the intervening period.

At the time of the Ottoman occupation of Ibrim the cathedral lay in ruins. Possibly as a result of an earthquake all but one of the twelve columns in the nave had fallen and the whole of the north arcade had collapsed. The Turkish traveller Evliya Çelebi, who visited Ibrim in the first half of the seventeenth century, records that the mosque which was built within the cathedral was constructed by Suleiman and, therefore, must date to the 1560s or soon thereafter.[63] Already by that date over one metre of debris had accumulated within the cathedral[64] suggesting that it had been out of use for some time. Çelebi also states that in Suleiman's time Ibrim had fallen into the hands of the kings of Funjistan and Berberistan, although we may doubt that the Funj actually advanced so far north.

The fate of Alwa

In stark contrast to the blow-by-blow account preserved by the written sources of the disintegration of Makuria in the thirteenth and fourteenth centuries, almost nothing is recorded of the demise of Alwa. In the accounts of the invasions of Makuria in 1276 we hear for the first time of what appears to be an independent kingdom of el-Abwab, the earlier northern province of Alwa.[65] The king of el-Abwab is also recorded in 1286 and 1287 without any mention being made of Alwa.[66] We have no details of how this area broke away from central Alwan control, nor of its relations with Alwa thereafter. Its king usually takes the side of the Muslims in Muslim/Makurian conflicts, perhaps indicating both el-Abwab's hostility to Makuria as well as a pragmatic approach to the potential threat of aggression from the powerful Muslim forces encamped on its northern frontier. The only king of el-Abwab known to us by name, Adur, sent an embassy to the sultan in 1286 bringing a present of an elephant and a giraffe and professing obedience to, and friendship with, the sultan.[67] The transportation of these gifts must have posed a major problem if the Nile route through Makuria was closed but no details are given of the mission's journey to Egypt. The devastation caused in Makuria by the actions of king Adur is one of the reasons cited by the Makurian king for the 'utter destruction' of his country in 1290.[68]

The ruler of el-Abwab is described as one of the kings of the Nubians and was said to control vast territories.[69] In 1290 Adur was also engaged in a campaign against king Any who had fled apparently from Makuria to the land of the Anaj in 1289.[70] Who Any was is far from clear.

In a list of the foreign rulers with whom the Muslims corresponded is one Junayd, sheikh of the Jawabra, described as a branch of the Hakariyya, in the territory of el-Abwab. He is described as a new correspondent, the first letter dating to 1367.[71]

The kingdom of Alwa, spared the depredations of the Muslim armies from Egypt, fell to the Funj invaders from the south, or to the Abdallab Arabs. The Funj, a people of uncertain origin but possibly from central or southern Sudan (an association with the Shilluk has been suggested),[72] were established on the Blue Nile by the beginning of the sixteenth century. According to Tabaqat Dayfallah, writing about 1700, the capital at Sennar was founded by the Funj ruler Umarah Dunqas after the Funj overcame the Nuba in 1504-5.[73] An earlier, presumably Funj, town had been founded thirty years before at Arbagi only 60 km from Soba up the Blue Nile. The Funj Chronicle, written in its present form around 1870, records how the Funj ruler, while resident at Jebel Moya in collaboration with a number of Arab tribes, determined to make war upon the kings of Soba and el-Qerri and that it was decided that Umarah Dunqas should be make king in place of the king of Alwa.[74] Abdallab tradition, however, maintained that it was Abdallah Jamma who took from the Christian kingdoms in the south 'the bejewelled crown of the Anaj kings'.[75] At an earlier date the Anaj had been described as subject to the kings of Alwa, although the equation of the Anaj and Alwa in this context is only supposition.

Alwa seems to have declined into a condition where it could be snuffed out without opposition.[76] The collapse of Alwa may, however, not have been as painless as it appears. It presumably was preyed upon over a considerable period by the desert Arabs from the east and by the Funj from the south. The archaeological evidence suggests that by the time the *coup de grâce* was administered in 1504 Soba was already largely in ruins. Two of its fine churches, excavated between 1982 and 1986, may already have been in ruins by the early thirteenth century and the fine tombs, presumably of ecclesiastical dignitaries, some with clothes decorated with gold thread, had been pillaged by that date.[77] On the south-eastern extremity of the city, on mound Z, a group of burials, clearly of an intrusive, non-Christian group, were found within an earlier Christian cemetery.[78] Unfortunately these individuals, buried without grave goods, could not be dated and their origin is unclear. They were buried in a variety of attitudes from dorsally extended to tightly crouched burials orientated to all points of the compass. One grave contained two flexed individuals. They do not appear to respect either Christian or Muslim burial traditions. Similar burials have also been noted elsewhere on the site.[79] The presence of these burials on mound Z suggests on the one hand, a continuing acknowledgement of the sanctity of that area, but on the other a total disregard for Christian mortuary practices. Were these people resident at Soba with the approval of the Christian inhabitants, or were they invaders occupying by military might the former capital of the Alwan kingdom?

In 1523 the Jewish traveller David Reubeni passed through Soba on his way north from Sennar and described it as a city in ruins, the inhabitants living in wooden dwellings.[80] The once fine buildings of the metropolis of the kingdom of Alwa, the richest and most powerful of the Nubian kingdoms, had long ceased to exist.

CHAPTER II

Postscript

By the time of the arrival of the Ottoman Turks in northern Nubia in the early sixteenth century the medieval Nubian states had disappeared from history. The succeeding period, into the early nineteenth century, is little known. Few sources refer to the situation within Nubia and virtually no archaeological work has been undertaken on sites of that period with the notable exception of Qasr Ibrim and, to a much lesser extent, Sai and Old Dongola. However, the political extinction of the Nubian states did not apparently bring about a total and immediate collapse of Christianity. The support of the State will have been lost, at least in Makuria, with the presence of a Muslim incumbent on the throne from 1323 and the continuing hostilities between Nubia and Egypt will have made contacts between the Alexandrian Patriarch and his flock more difficult. As early as 1235 the patriarch refused to send bishops to Nubia on account of the disturbed political situation in the region although, as the evidence of Timotheos makes clear, this prohibition was not upheld by all his successors.[1] In 1540 a delegation of Nubians requested that the Abyssinian ruler dispatch priests and monks to instruct them but no assistance was forthcoming and the absence of a clergy will have had a serious effect on the continuance of Christian worship.[2] Notwithstanding this, as late as the eighteenth century there were rumours of people still adhering to the old religion. In a letter written by Father Giacomo Rzimarz of Cremsir to Cardinal Belluga on 23 January 1742 he mentions that he was informed by a Berberine that in that man's village called Tangos which is on a island in the Nile, there are still some Christians.[3] Well into the eighteenth century the king of the small Nubian Kingdom of Kokka was recognized as being a Christian.[4] When western Christian missionaries arrived in the nineteenth century the practice of Christianity had vanished from Nubia and missionaries in the recent past have concentrated their activities in Southern Sudan, well beyond the areas which came under the writ of the medieval Nubian kings.

Continuity

There was no distinct break between the medieval Christian and the post-medieval Islamic periods. Many of the people along the Middle Nile came from families who had occupied the area for centuries, if not for millennia. Although the profession of the faith of their forefathers may have lapsed through lack of an organized clergy to provide guidance,[5] and from the clear earthly benefits of converting to Islam, there must have been considerable continuity in their everyday lives.

As at the end of the pagan period some of the old religious monuments were put to

Figure 102 **The arcade of the eastern aisle and the mihrab cut into the east wall of the cathedral at Qasr Ibrim.**

the service of the new religion. However, only a small number of churches were converted for use as mosques, among them the Church on the Point at Qasr Ibrim[6] and the cathedral within the fortress there (Fig. 102). Many of the larger churches which would have been suitable for conversion may have been extensively destroyed before the arrival of Muslims in sufficient numbers to make such a conversion viable. The Church of the Granite Columns at Old Dongola was already in an advanced state of decay, having been extensively demolished and its floors covered by between 1.5 and 2.5 m of rubble before the earliest post-medieval housing was constructed on its site.[7] Late medieval churches were generally so small as to have been of little use as mosques. The 'Throne Room' at Old Dongola is a special case, as the inscription within it makes it clear that it was converted into a mosque during the medieval period.

A number of sites retained their sanctity after the Christian period. Cemeteries remained in use and Christian tombs were reused in the Muslim period or attributed to Muslim saints as at Kulubnarti and Sahaba.[8]

Many late medieval buildings, particularly the substantial castle houses, survived for centuries in a usable condition and were modified by their new occupants, or by the Muslim descendants of the original Christian owners. Two of the late houses at Jebel Adda were utilized by the Mamelukes, evidenced by the presence of coins, and then by the Ottomans.[9] At Ibrim the early X-Group temple was in use as a dwelling over 1,000 years after it was built and its Ottoman inhabitants modified it.[10]

There is not only continuity in the physical manifestations of medieval Nubian culture.

A number of practices which are clearly Christian in origin today still play a part in Nubian popular religion. Into the 1960s in the Nubian settlement at Kulb, on the west bank of the Nile opposite Aksha, women in labour invoked assistance from the Virgin Mary and the angels. Elsewhere there is practised a form of baptism which involves a ritual ablution in the Nile followed by marking the sign of the cross on house walls, and a number of other survivals could be cited.[11] However, among many of the people there is no sense of respect for their Christian ancestors. They are, for example, perfectly happy to assist archaeologists to excavate the graves of Christians, something totally forbidden for graves of Muslims.

Perhaps the most significant survival from medieval Nubia is the use of the Nubian language. Although most Nubians speak Arabic, the three dialects of modern Nubian, Kenzi, Mahāsi and Dongolawi are widely used. Indeed the importance of the Nubian language is stressed by it being one of the defining features of modern Nubia. Although the spoken language survives, it is no longer written, Arabic having supplanted it as the only written language in Northern Sudan.

The dominance of the medieval Nubian kingdoms for almost 1,000 years has done much to shape the modern Middle Nile Valley. The Nubians' success in holding the forces of Islam at bay for so long has resulted in a fiercely independent quasi-national identity, not totally engulfed by Islamic culture as were the inhabitants of many other regions of the Sudan. The survival of their distinct cultural identity in the region between ed-Debba and the First Cataract may have been aided by their homeland being for much of the post-medieval period on the periphery of the two major states in the region, the Ottoman and Funj sultanates. Certainly the regions further to the south, those which had lain within the Nubian Kingdom of Alwa, lost much of their Nubian traditions along with the use of the Nubian language.

Today archaeology is once again revealing the splendours of the X-Group and post-Meroitic rulers and the impressive architecture, fine ceramics and incomparable mural art of the vibrant Christian culture which followed on their conversion in the sixth century. In every respect the cultural achievements of the medieval Nubians stands on a par with those of the other great civilizations on the Middle Nile, Kerma and the Kushites.

Kings of the Blemmyan and Nubian kingdoms in the Nile Valley

There are many gaps in the king lists and of those individuals known few are precisely dated. There is considerable confusion caused by the Arab sources where many different names are used for what are thought to be the same individual. The information below is drawn largely from Munro-Hay's detailed discussion of the evidence published in 1982/3 with additions from *Fontes Historia Nubiorum* for the early period and from a number of other sources for individual details. For a number of other undated kings see Munro-Hay 1982/3, 131-2, 134.

Kings of the Blemmyes

Tamal	
Isemne	
Degou	
Phonen	*c.* 450

Kings of Nobadia

Kharamadoye	*c.* 410/20	
Silko	*c.* 450	
Aburni	*c.* 450	
Eirpanome	- 559/574 -	
Tokiltoeton	*c.* 577	
WRPYWL	*c.* 580	nephew and successor of Tokiltoeton(?), variations on the name include Awarfiula and Orfiulo.
Zacharias	*c.* 645-55	son of Barky. Whether this individual was actually a king is uncertain.

Kings of the Makuria

Qalidurut	- 651/2 -	
Mercurios	696-710 - ?	
Simon		
Abraham		
Mark		reigned for six months

Cyriacus	- 747-68 -	
Chael or Michael	*c.* 785/94 - 804/13	
Johannes	*c.* 850? or before 822?	
Zacharias I	- 835 - 856/859/866?	
Giorgios I	856/859/866 ?	before June 887[1]
Zacharias II	920 - 930+ ?	
Kabil, Surur's son	*c.* 943	
Giorgios II	- 969 - before or until 1002	
Raphael son of Raphael	- 1000 - *c.* 1006	
Stephanos	*c.* 1027	King of Makuria?
Solomon	- 1077 - 1079/80	abdicated
Giorgios III	1079/80 -	
Basil I	- 1089 -	
Giorgios IV	1130 - 1158	is recorded on a funerary inscription found within a monastery in the Wadi en-Natrun in Egypt. Although written in Old Nubian it does not state over which kingdom he ruled.[2]
Moses Giorgios	1158 -	If a different individual than Moses/ Moses Giorgios, King of Dotawo
Murtashkar	- 1268?	
David I	- 1268 - 1272 (or 1275/6)[3]	
Shakanda	1276 -	
Barak	- 1279 ?	
Semamun	1286 -1287/8	
Semamun' nephew	1287/8 - 1288	
Semamun	1288 - 1289	
David's nephew (Budamma?)	1289 - 1290	
Semamun	1290 - 1295 - ?	
Amay	- 1304/5 -	
Kernabes	1311 - 1316	
Barshanbu	1316 - 1317 (or 1318/19)	
Kanz ed-Dawla	1317 (or 1318/19) - 1323	includes the very short rule of Abraham (in 1317?)
Kernabes	1323 - 1324	
Kanz ed-Dawla	1324 -	
al-Amir Abi Abdallah Kanz el-Dawla	1333	

death of king ?	1365/6	killed by his rebel nephew
rebel nephew	1365/6	on the throne at Dongola
brother of the murdered king	1365/6 -	on the throne at Jebel Adda
Taanengo	perhaps between	
	750 – 1000	a king of Makuria or a kinglet? Controlled the Jebel Adda region at least

Kings of Alwa

Giorgios	?	recorded on an inscription from Soba East
Asabiyus (Eusebios)	c. 938 - c. 955	son of Juti
Astabanus (Stephanos)	c. 955 -	son of Giorgios who was Asabiyus' brother
David	999 - 1015	
? Basil	12th century	recorded on a letter in Arabic from Qasr Ibrim
? Paul	12th century	recorded on a letter in Arabic from Qasr Ibrim

Kings of el-Abwab

Adur	- 1286 - 1292 -	

Kings of Dotawo[4]

David		
Moses Giorgios (?)	1144 - 1199 ?	The kings Moses and Giorgios may or may not be the same individual as Moses Giorgios
Basil	- 1199 -	
Elite	later 12th century	thought to be the name of a king by Griffith,[5] but the word Eil may actually be the definite article.[6]
Paul or Piarl	- 1281 -	
Giorgios Simon	- 1287 -	
Siti	c. 1300 - 1334 -	
Joel	- 1464 - 1484 -	

Kings or vassal kings of Dotawo

Koudlanie		
Tienossi		King of Ilenat

Notes

Chapter 1
1 OS, 52
2 OS, 71
3 OS, 130
4 OS, 457, 459
5 For an entirely contrary view see Spaulding 1974, 25ff. For an attempt to define the limits of medieval Nubia see Salih 1982, 72.
6 Annual precipitation of 3 mm for Wadi Halfa, near the Second Cataract, can be contrasted with the Khartoum region at 164 mm and with Wad Medani on the Blue Nile between Khartoum and Sennar at 373 mm (Sudan Almanac 1964, 59-61).
7 Burckhardt 1819, 448ff.
8 Griffith 1928, 118
9 Łajtar 1997, 114
10 Griffith 1913, 61
11 Łajtar 1991, 161-2
12 trans. Łajtar 1997, 124
13 Monneret de Villard 1938, 119
14 Griffith 1928, 131
15 Switsur 1991, 350
16 Tanqasi culture and Aloa ware, terms once used to describe the pottery of that culture, are now no longer generally employed.
17 Adams 1964, 241-7
18 E.g. Adams 1999, 6

Chapter 2
1 Török 1989, 113, figs. 300-312
2 Strabo XVII.C.1§2
3 Pliny VI.35
4 Priese 1973
5 Behrens 1986; Bechhaus-Gerst 1991
6 See Kirwan 1974, 47.
7 Procopius 1.19.29
8 FHN, 1181
9 FHN, 1188ff.
10 Török 1980, 85
11 Török has recently suggested that a territorially intact Kushite state may have been taken over by a post-Meroitic ruler, but broke up in the early fifth century (1999, 153).
12 FHN, 1120
13 FHN, 1127-8; cf. Török 1987, 224
14 This term was applied to the river valley for a distance of 12 schoinoi upstream of the First Cataract, as far as Maharaqa which was the border between Rome and Kush from the first to the third century.
15 Török 1987, 225; FHN, 1137
16 Cf. Papadopoullos 1966, 20
17 FHN, 1165
18 See Millet 1973.
19 FHN, 1105ff.
20 FHN, 1150, fn 778
21 FHN, 1158ff.
22 OS, 8
23 FHN, 1190-1
24 FHN, 1128
25 FHN, 1137
26 FHN, 1150, fn.777, 1153. For the suggestion that some of the grave goods in the earlier tombs at Ballana may be booty see Török 1987, 227.
27 Blockley 1985
28 FHN, 1140; Kirwan 1974, 48
29 For a specific example, a reliquary, cited by Török see FHN, 1141 with references.
30 Jordanes FHN, 1193-4
31 Priscus FHN 1153ff.
32 Two scrolls found at Qasr Ibrim and dating to the mid eighth century clearly indicate that the Blemmyes and the Beja were the same people (Plumley 1983, 160).
33 Kirwan 1972, 171
34 See Plumley 1975b, 25-26. For doubts expressed about a Blemmyan presence at Ibrim see Török 1987, 224.
35 Strouhal 1986, 189; Strouhal and Jungwirth 1971, 18. A distinctive type of pottery has been noted in Lower Nubia which is broadly contemporary with the presence of the Blemmyes in the Nile Valley. However, the restricted distribution of this material, which is not found throughout the area known to have been under Blemmyan control, suggests that it is not a Blemmyan leitmotiv (see Strouhal 1978; 1984, 157ff.). Conversely, not dissimilar pottery has been recorded in the Eastern Desert.
36 Based on the absence of royal regalia. However, Patrice Lenoble suggests such high value objects may have been removed by tomb robbers (pers. comm., June 2000).
37 Török 1986, 192
38 FHN, 1105-6
39 FHN, 1105
40 Lenoble has suggested, from a consideration of the abundant grave-goods in Tomb B.80 at Ballana, many of which he identifies as the symbols of imperium, that that tomb may be the resting place of Silko (1997, 149).
41 Török 1986, 193
42 See, for example, Lenoble 1999.
43 Bates and Dunham 1927; Kirwan 1939
44 FHN, 1169. Török has suggested that there were several distinct political entities among the people known as the Nobades and that some of these may have been allied with Rome while others fought against the Empire (1987, 230-1).
45 Lenoble 1992, 11; 1996, 83
46 Alexander 1999, 59
47 Millet 1967, 55-57; 1984, 118
48 Welsby 1998, 277
49 Plumley 1975b, 16-17; see also Horton 1991, 272-3
50 See Driskell et al. 1989, 28-29
51 FHN, 1155-6
52 Török 1999, 153.
53 Trigger 1967, 65, 67, 80
54 Ibid. 81
55 Junker 1925b, 85; translation in Trigger 1967, 80
56 For a discussion of the literary sources for the location of the frontiers of the Nubian kingdoms see p. 83
57 Eisa and Welsby 1996, 135
58 See, for example, the topographical arguments in Kirwan 1987, 129ff. where the writer is arguing that the Alwan capital in 580 must have lain at Meroe rather than at Soba East.
59 FHN, 1151, 1152
60 Soba East was first recorded as the capital by el-Yaqubi in 891-2.
61 Adams 1986, I, 51
62 Trigger 1967, 83; Adams 1977, 402
63 For the evidence for the latest occupation of the settlement at Meroe, found during Garstang's excavations, see Török 1997, 39. There is also at least one iron furnace of post-Meroitic date (pers. comm. J. Anderson, 2000).
64 Bradley 1984, 210-11; Shinnie and Robertson 1993, 897

Chapter 3
1 FHN, 1165
2 FHN, 1175
3 Procopius 1.19.1
4 Vantini 1981, 36-7
5 Kirwan 1937, 289
6 See Kirwan 1982, 142-3 for an alternative view which doubts the existence of any Melkite mission to Nobatia. Other scholars believe that the Melkite mission may have been more successful than John of Ephesus was prepared to admit (Monneret de Villard, 1938, 65).
7 OS, 8
8 This is recounted by John of Ephesus who was present during the audience between Julian and the Empress Theodora on the missionaries' return to Constantinople (OS, 11).
9 Kirwan 1937, 292
10 OS, 27-8
11 See, for example, Kirwan 1980, 136; 1982, 143-4, for a restatement of the traditional view see Godlewski (forth.).
12 See the reference in John of Ephesus to the delegations sent to the Alwans by the Nobadian kings while his uncle was king, and in the time of his uncle's predecessors (OS, 22-3).
13 FHN, 1180; Godlewski 1992, 281, 284.
14 OS, 14
15 OS, 17
16 Malek 1984, 48 with references.
17 Vantini 1981, 49
18 Godlewski 1991b, 87
19 Jakobielski 1972, 143-5
20 E.g. Kirwan 1982, 143; Edwards 2001
21 Nautin 1967; FHN 1175. For the structural evidence for the conversion of the temple into a church see Grossmann 1987.
22 FHN, 1178

23 Plumley 1975b, 19-20; Adams 1996, 69. See also Griffith 1926b, 51; Kirwan 1937b, 96
24 For Taifa see Kirwan 1987, 131; for Tabo pers. comm. C. Bonnet.
25 Kirwan 1987, 121
26 *FHN*, 1195
27 Monneret de Villard 1938, 85; *FHN*, 1194
28 Kirwan 1987, 131
29 Godlewski 1992, 282
30 Donadoni 1959
31 Godlewski 1992, 278
32 Welsby and Daniels 1991, 34
33 Welsby 1998, 272, 277
34 Kirwan 1966, 126
35 Millet in Kirwan 1987, 123
36 Mills 1982, 48, pl. LII
37 Edwards 1994, 177
38 Sjöström and Welsby 1991, pl. IIIb
39 Welsby and Daniels 1991, 324ff.; Welsby 1998, 272
40 Zurawski 1994, 322
41 Kirwan 1987, 132
42 Geus 1991, 57
43 Zurawski 1999, 229. For the textiles see Zurawski 1999b, figs. 32-34.
44 Welsby and Daniels 1991, 62; Vogelsang-Eastwood 1991, 307-8
45 Edwards 1994, 176
46 Zurawski and el-Tayeb 1994, 302-3
47 Ibid., 301-2
48 Lenoble 1995
49 Lenoble 1997
50 Kirwan 1963, 70
51 Emery 1965, 87
52 Lenoble 1996, 67
53 See Lenoble 1991; 1994
54 Williams 1991, 26
55 Kirwan 1939, 3ff.
56 Bates and Dunham 1927
57 Lenoble 1994, 115
58 Edwards 1994, 164
59 Lenoble 1991
60 Jacquet-Gordon and Bonnet 1971-2, 78
61 Edwards 1994, 172-3
62 Cf. Woolley and Randall-MacIver 1910, pl. 114
63 Kirwan 1939, 16. The identification of this object as a bed may be in error. The excavator noted that it may have been a coffin and the presence of iron brackets at the corners suggests that this latter identification may be more likely. In another burial Kirwan found evidence for what he considered to be a funerary couch with circular poles supporting a canopy (1939, 5, pl. XV, A.11/15).
64 W. Y. Adams 1999b, 31, 43
65 Kolodziejczyk 1982, figs. 6 and 7
66 Łajtar has suggested that the monastery may actually have been called the Monastery of the Great Antonius (1995, 53).
67 Zurawski 1997b, 205; see also

references to grave goods elsewhere in Zurawski 1999b, 235. The grave goods from the crypts beneath the western annex on Kom H at Old Dongola are illustrated in Zurawski 1999b, figs 6-16.
68 Zurawski 1986, 414-5
69 Zurawski 1997b, 205-6
70 Welsby and Daniels 1991, 62. The lamp was of type 6S, the bowl over it of type 135N and the other bowl of type 196N (ibid., figs. 118, 111 and 113).
71 Anderson 1997, 172
72 Zurawski 1997b, 206
73 Ibid., 207
74 W. Y. Adams 1999b, 17. A similar situation has been observed in much earlier Nubian graves as in the Kerma Ancien graves at site P37 in the Northern Dongola Reach (Welsby 2001, 209, 212).
75 Török 1997, 273
76 Török 1997, figs 145-7. For this type elsewhere see Lenoble 1991, at Berber; Anderson and Ahmed (forth.), at el-Fereikha; et-Tayeb (pers. comm.), at Hamur/ Bukibul.
77 In Török 1988, 197
78 Fuller 1999, 205
79 Ricke 1967; Strouhal 1984
80 Strouhal 1984
81 Millet 1963, 154; Fuller 1999, 207
82 Török 1988, 81ff.
83 Emery and Kirwan 1938, fig. 8
84 Edwards 1998; Garstang *et al.* 1911, 35
85 Bates and Dunham 1927, 74
86 Kirwan 1939
87 Ibid., 29, pl. VI.3
88 Lenoble 1989, 97
89 Shinnie 1954, 68ff.
90 Ibid., 70ff.
91 There is no direct correlation observable across Nubia between the type of grave, the placing of the body and the tomb monument (see discussion in W.Y. Adams 1998, 33). Hence little can be said about funerary practices of the Christian medieval period from observations of surface remains.
92 W. Y. Adams 1999b, 10; Welsby 1998, 47
93 Edwards 1998, 208
94 Welsby 1998, 51 [grave (Z3)163]
95 Welsby *et al.* 1994; Lenoble 1987; Edwards 1988, 208; Caneva 1988, 209 – 65% of the burials at el-Geili have the head to the east.
96 Caneva 1988, 212
97 Welsby 1998, 59
98 W. Y. Adams 1998, 28; 1999b, 42
99 W. Y. Adams 1999b, 17
100 Welsby and Daniels 1991, 122; Welsby 1998, 51, 54-5
101 For example at Sai, Geus *et al.* 1995, pl. IX.

102 See W. Y. Adams 1999b, 45
103 For a very well preserved example from Sai see Geus *et al.* 1995, 121, fig. 17.
104 N. K. Adams 1999, 52, 61, 69
105 Wills 1998
106 Welsby and Daniels 1991, 62; Vogelsang-Eastwood 1991, 307
107 Plumley 1975c, 3, pl. II
108 Cartwright 1998, 267
109 Welsby 1998, 53; Allason-Jones 1998, 79
110 For example grave 33 at Jebel Ghaddar North (Zurawski and et-Tayeb 1994, fig. 11).
111 In grave (Z3)96/180 at Soba the ledges were constructed of mud bricks (Welsby 1998, 49). The absence of stones implies that timber had been used here instead. Evidence for timber used in this way has been found at el-Geili (Caneva 1988, 209).
112 W. Y. Adams 1999b, 39
113 Zurawski 1999b, 244
114 Zurawski 1997b, 196
115 W. Y. Adams 1999b, 10-11
116 W. Y. Adams 1998, 27
117 E.g. at Gabati, Edwards 1998, 92, 99
118 Zurawski 1997b, 197
119 Steindorff 1935, Tafel 6
120 W. Y. Adams 1998, 27. See also the bishop's burials at Qasr Ibrim noted below.
121 Welsby 1998, pls. 27 and 28. For a similar grave at Old Dongola see Zurawski 1997b, fig. 4.
122 Zurawski 1985, 413
123 Welsby 1998, 56-9, Filer 1998, 231; Abdul Rahman Ali Mohamed 2000
124 Zurawski 1999b, 252
125 Jakobielski 1986, 303-4, figs. 8 and 9; Godlewski 1992, 281
126 W. Y. Adams 1996, 82-3
127 Shinnie and Shinnie 1978, 32
128 Jakobielski 1978, 134-6
129 Godlewski 1992, 279
130 Dzierzykray-Rogalski and Promińska 1978
131 Welsby and Daniels 1991, 42
132 For the Byzantine churches see Mathews 1971, 77.
133 W. Y. Adams 1996, 75-7
134 Scanlon 1970, 45-6, plan 1
135 Shinnie and Shinnie 1978, 17
136 Mileham 1910, 29
137 Säve-Söderbergh 1970, 225
138 Mileham 1910, 32
139 Promińska 1978, 243
140 Dzierzykray-Rogalski and Jakobielski 1975
141 Millet 1967, 59
142 Zurawski 1999b, 222ff.
143 Millet 1963, 159
144 Junker 1925b, 158; W. Y. Adams 1965, 170
145 For cairns thought to cover Christian graves at Gabati see Edwards 1998, 71ff. For well-built, tall, cylindrical cairns at Wadi Qitna and Kalabsha South see Strouhal 1984.

146 Lenoble 1989, 93-120
147 Hakem 1979, 152; Lepsius 1853, 212-3
148 Emery and Kirwan 1938, 78 and 91
149 Edwards 1994; Kirwan 1939, 3, 24
150 Millet 1963, 150
151 Jacquet-Gordon and Bonnet 1971-2, 78
152 For an example in the Wadi el-Tereif see Welsby 2000, pl. 2.
153 Millet 1963, 163
154 Millet 1964, 8; see also Welsby 1998, 275-7.
155 Fuller 1999, 206. For a photo of one of these structures, see Simpson 1964, pl. X, 3.
156 For the chapels see Williams 1991, 26-7.
157 Ibid., 27
158 Jacquet-Gordon and Bonnet 1971-2, 78
159 W. Y. Adams 1998, fig. 2. For a general discussion of monument types in the restricted area between the First Cataract and Missiminia see ibid. 19-24.
160 Noted in cemeteries near the Fourth Cataract (Welsby forth.)
161 Welsby (forth.)
162 Welsby 1998, 49ff. Wooden poles were also probably used as grave markers in the Kushite period at Karanog, see Woolley and Randall-MacIver 1910, 7.
163 Discussed and illustrated by Monneret de Villard 1935-1957, 71-2, fig. 60.
164 Zurawski and et-Tayeb 1994, 308
165 W. Y. Adams 1965, pl. XXXVIIb
166 Kákosy 1975, fig. 1, tombs 9 and 50, pl. IV/2
167 Zurawski 1987, 276. Perhaps to be assigned to this general type are those monuments at Qasr Ibrim noted by Monneret de Villard 1935, fig. 96, A, described as Cross-topped *qubbas* by W. Y. Adams 1998, 23.
168 This type is seen elsewhere for example on the North Kom at Hambukol (pers. comm. J. Anderson).
169 Gartkiewicz 1990, 303
170 W. Y. Adams 1986, 170. One visible in Adams 1965, fig. 4 immediately north of the church.
171 Fanfoni 1979, tav. 6, 7
172 Zurawski and et-Tayeb 1994, 308
173 W. Y. Adams 1998, 24
174 Zurawski 1997, 175
175 W. Y. Adams 1999b, 38
176 W. Y. Adams 1999b, 10, 24
177 Welsby 1998, 54; see also Grave (Z3)174 for a slightly more elaborate monument of this same general type (ibid. 51).
178 See Welsby 2001, pls 3.27-3.31. For graves of this type near the Fourth Cataract (Welsby forth.)

179 Żurawski 1986, 413-4
180 Michałowski 1965, 49ff.
181 Cf. W. Y. Adams 1987, 333
182 Millet 1963, pl. XLV, fig. 1;
Shinnie and Shinnie 1978, 32;
Trigger 1967, 24; Jakobielski *et al.* 1993, 296; Żurawski 1999b,
221. What is probably a tomb
monument of this type was later
incorporated into the suite of
rooms added to the south-west
corner of the Monastery of the
Holy Trinity at Old Dongola
where it was used as a vestibule
(see Żurawski 1999b, pl. III,
room R3).
183 Millet 1963, 156
184 See Michałowski 1970, pl.
11; Hajnóczi 1974, 366ff.
185 Barnard 1994, 56. See also
for Qasr Ibrim, Monneret de
Villard 1935, 112-3; for Jebel
Adda, ibid., 180.
186 W. Y. Adams 1965, 170,
pl. XXXVIIc; see also
W. Y. Adams 1998, 23.
187 W. Y. Adams 1998, 23
188 Welsby and Daniels 1991,
91-2
189 This type of monument is
unknown elsewhere in Nubia
but can be readily paralleled in
Byzantine funerary architecture
(Żurawski 1987, 275-6).
190 Żurawski 1997b, 204
191 Ibid., 200
192 The tumuli were in Site
NE-45-F/3-O-1, the box graves
in NE 45-F/3-N-302 (Welsby
forth.).
193 Strouhal 1990.
194 N. K. Adams 1999, 68
195 Junker 1925
196 Łajtar 1997, 109; Hägg
1982, 55-62
197 Łajtar 1997, 109
198 Jakobielski 1991, 275. For
comments on this translation and
suggested minor emendations see
Hägg 1998, 114-5. The reading
of the date for the king's death
has been called into question by
Łajtar (pers. comm. March 1999)
199 Simpson in Trigger 1967, 14
200 Łajtar 1991, 158
201 See Filer 2001.
202 Shinnie and Shinnie 1978,
107
203 Trigger 1967, 33
204 Blackman 1927, 101
205 Barnard 1994, 52-3
206 W. Y. Adams 1999b, 17
207 Edwards 1998, 197
208 As at Jebel Adda see Millet
1963, 150.
209 Żurawski 1997b, 200;
1999b, 213
210 W. Y. Adams 1965, 169
211 Gartkiewicz 1990, 300. For
Hammam el-Farki see Monneret
de Villard 1935, III, 20; for
Hambukol see Anderson 1999,
74, pl. XXXVI; for Soba East
see Jakobielski 1991, 274.
212 Żurawski and et-Tayeb 1994,
305

213 Petrie 1937, 5
214 Żurawski and el-Tayeb 1994,
310; Żurawski 1997b, 200
215 Griffith 1927, 69, 80,
pls LIX, LX
216 Żurawski 1997b, 200
217 Żurawski and el-Tayeb 1994,
314
218 See Rostkowska 1982b.
219 See Żurawski 1999b, 209.
220 Żurawski 1997b, 200
221 Żurawski 1999b, 208-9 with
references. The Mis Island
example was discovered by the
SARS survey mission in 1999.
222 Shinnie and Chittick 1961, 23
223 Żurawski 1987, 275-6
224 For a discussion of the
iconography of the Cross in
medieval Nubia see Dinkler
1975. Van Moorsel (1972)
distinguished seven types of
crosses.
225 Published by Budge 1915,
519-20
226 For numerical cryptograms
see Plumley 1982c.
227 Pluskota 1997, 237. On the
rationale behind the use of the
name Michael see also Anderson
1998, 185.
228 Żurawski 1986, 416
229 Ibid., 416
230 Żurawski 1987, 276
231 Millet 1967, 60
232 Żurawski 1987, 277 with
references.
233 Żurawski 1997b, 206;
1999b, 222ff.
234 W. Y. Adams 1996, 241-2
235 Vercoutter 1970, 156,
pl. 129
236 Grzymski 1990, 148; Hägg
1993. Hägg notes that the texts
on these bowls are not related to
Coptic usage but can be closely
paralleled in Sassanian Babylon
probably dating to the sixth and
seventh centuries. He suggests
that the bowls were designed as
traps for demons (ibid., 393-4).
237 Żurawski 1994b, 212; pers.
comm. J. Anderson.
238 Ibid. 155. There were also
numerous pots buried beneath
the floors and in the corners of
the house. These were probably
associated with burials of
afterbirth and/or foetuses or
were personal body smoking pots
rather than foundation deposits
(pers. comm. J. Anderson).
239 Hughes 1963, 126,
pl. XXXb
240 Knudstad 1966, 167, fn. 4.
See also Żurawski 1992 for a
general discussion of the
magical use of ceramics.
241 W. Y. Adams 1965, 173
242 Millet 1967, 61
243 Godlewski 1991, 93
244 Jakobielski and Medeksza
1990, 197
245 Żurawski 1994b
246 Welsby 1998, 33
247 Żurawski 1994b, 216

Chapter 4
1 El-Mas'udi *OS*, 128
2 Glubb 1978, 46ff.
3 El-Waquidi in *OS*, 48. It was
entirely appropriate that
Aristulis should seek the aid of
the *foederati* Beja and Nubians to
help ward off the Muslim attack.
4 *OS*, 95; also el-Baladhuri *OS*, 80.
5 *OS*, 639, see also 638, fn. 43.
6 Munro-Hay 1982/3, 96, 135
7 Ibn Hawqal, reference in
Christides 1992, 344.
8 The use of artillery by the
Arabs at the siege of Old
Dongola, it has been suggested
by Vantini, is anachronistic, such
machines having no place in the
highly mobile armies of early
Islam (1981, 65).
9 El-Baladhuri *OS*, 80-1
10 Godlewski 1991c, 108-9
11 On the relative value of the
goods mentioned in the *Baqt* see
p. 204.
12 See el-Khordadhbeh *OS*, 69.
13 See Christides 1992, 345.
14 *OS*, 132-3
15 *OS*, 57, 59 fn. 5, 74, 106, 316
16 Ibn el-Khordadhbeh *OS*, 69;
el-Baladhuri *OS*, 82; el-Mas'udi
OS, 128; el-Maqrizi *OS*, 650
17 *OS*, 241
18 *OS*, 640
19 Vantini 1975, 640, fn. 45
20 Plumley 1983, 159
21 Az-Zahir *OS*, 430
22 El-Mas'udi *OS*, 132
23 El-Baladhuri *OS*, 81
24 Michael the Syrian *OS*, 320.
These events are recorded by
several sources among them
Severus *OS*, 193ff.; Abu Salih
OS, 330-1; Barhebraeus *OS*,
420ff.; el-Maqrizi *OS*, 644ff.
Some sources appear to record a
second journey by Giorgios to
Baghdad, as a prisoner along
with the King of the Beja in
852-3. For a discussion of the
evidence see Vantini 1970b.
25 El-Baladhuri *OS*, 82;
el-Baghdadi *OS*, 106
26 In el-Maqrizi *OS*, 646.
27 En-Nuwayri *OS*, 476
28 John the Deacon *OS*, 43-4.
W. Y. Adams considers this whole
campaign to be legendary, an
example of Christian Egyptian
propaganda (1977, 454), but to
discount a contemporary
Egyptian source, however partisan
it may have been, which
describes in detail an event, the
veracity or otherwise of which
would have been so obvious to
the readership, seems unjustified.
29 Jakobielski 1972, 52
30 *OS*, 180ff.
31 *OS*, 727ff.
32 *OS*, 158
33 See Vantini 1970b.
34 *OS*, 708-18
35 En-Nuwayri *OS*, 476
36 In el-Maqrizi *OS*, 635. The
fifteenth century historian et-

Taghribirdi may be referring to
these events when he records
that 'The king of Nubia
marched on Aswan and beyond,
down to Akhmim, killing and
plundering, taking prisoners and
setting fire to villages' after events
in Syria dated to 963 (*OS*, 735).
See Monneret de Villard 1938,
122; cf. W. Y. Adams 1977, 456.
37 W. Y. Adams 1968, 189, fn. 16
38 Plumley 1983, 161
39 Abu Salih *OS*, 328; el-Makin
OS, 377; el-Intaki *OS*, 386;
el-Maqrizi *OS*, 634
40 En-Nuwayri *OS*, 476
41 *OS*, 358
42 Quoted by Plumley, 1983, 162.
43 Plumley 1983, 163
44 Michałowski 1964, 205
45 Jakobielski 1972, 165, fn. 28
46 Information on these events is
to be found in several sources
among them Abu Salih (*OS*,
328), el-Athir (*OS*, 358), Abu
Shama (*OS*, 368ff.) and
el-Maqrizi (*OS*, 673-4).
47 Rostkowska 1982b
48 Sources quoted by Crowfoot
1927, 148-9.
49 Ed-Dinawari *OS*, 65
50 Ibn Qalanisi *OS*, 285; el-Athir
OS, 354-5
51 Severus *OS*, 214
52 Ibn Iyas *OS*, 782
53 *OS*, 170
54 *OS*, 131
55 Abu l Fida quoting from a
book by Ibn Sa'id *OS*, 463.
56 El-Wardi *OS*, 725
57 El-Andalusi *OS*, 412
58 Az-Zahir *OS*, 431
59 Severus *OS*, 205-7
60 For the similarity in cross
forms see Ratynski 1982,
249-50, 255.
61 Williams 1991, 84
62 Millet 1963, 153
63 Lenoble 1997, 140
64 Millet 1963, 153, 159, fig. 7;
Williams 1991, 77ff., 90ff.
65 For arrows and spear-heads
from Soba East thought to be
used for hunting see Allason-
Jones 1991, 132, nos 97-103,
fig. 63 and 64; 1998, 62-3, nos
51-68, fig. 27. For archer's
looses from Soba see Shinnie
1955, 58, pl. XXa; Allason-
Jones 1991, 147-8; 1998, 76
nos. 215-230, fig. 31.
66 Martens-Czarnecka 1992, 368
67 For the Qustul and Ballana
examples see Emery and Kirwan
1938, 221ff.
68 For the Qustul and Ballana
examples see Emery and Kirwan
1938, fig. 85; Török 1988, 95.
69 Emery and Kirwan 1938,
219-21
70 Plumley 1975b, 24, pl. XIV.3
71 Emery and Kirwan 1938,
149-50
72 Williams 1991, 87
73 Emery and Kirwan 1938,
249-50

74 Millet 1963, 153
75 Allason-Jones 1991, 135 no. 108-10, 160, fig. 65
76 OS, 400
77 John the Deacon OS, 43
78 El-Hakam OS, 57
79 Allason-Jones 1991, 128, fig. 60
80 Steinborn 1982, 312
81 Emery and Kirwan 1938, 254
82 A caparison of some sort is almost invariably depicted on wall paintings (Steinborn 1982, 338).
83 Steinborn 1982, 311, 317, 339, 342
84 Et-Taghribirdi OS, 730. For examples of these bells see Emery and Kirwan 1938, fig. 94.
85 Kirwan 1939, 3
86 Emery and Kirwan 1938, 259ff.
87 In el-Maqrizi OS, 613.
88 Ibn Selim in el-Maqrizi OS, 603-4.
89 Hägg 1990, 161; see also Chapter 5.
90 Plumley 1983, 163

Chapter 5
1 In el-Maqrizi OS, 613.
2 OS, 162
3 OS, 601
4 OS, 637
5 OS, 153
6 OS, 643
7 Kirwan has a radically differing view of this unification arguing that it was the Kingdom of Nobadia, el-Nuba to the Arabs, which took over Makuria. The *Baqt* was a treaty not with the King of Makuria (el-Maqurra) but with the king of el-Nuba. The transfer of the capital of the united kingdom, from Faras to Old Dongola, he suggests was a result of the greater security offered by the location of the latter far from the Egyptian border (1980, 135-7).
8 Munro-Hay 1982/3, 98; Monneret de Villard 1938, 78ff. where he quotes from *The Life of the Patriarch Isaac*, 'It happened that in that time the king of Makouria sent delegates to the archbishop (patriarch) with some letters, informing him of how the (number) of bishops of his country (*chora*) had diminished, because of the length of the journey, because they were unable to pass [by the shorter road] by order of the king of Maurotania, because peace had not been concluded with him. There were two kings in that country [Nubia]: both were Christian, but they were not at peace. Because the king of Maurotania was at peace with the king of the Saracens, the other one, the one of the great country of Makouria, was not at peace with the king of the

Saracens.'
9 Monneret de Villard 1938, 81-3. See also Godlewski 1991c, 121 who suggests a date in the later seventh century and quotes other relevant references.
10 OS, 40
11 Török 1988, 149ff.
12 Plumley 1978, 236
13 OS, 165-6
14 The small fortified settlement crowning Jebel Wahaba contains stone buildings and others of mud brick, the latter perhaps of later date. Preliminary survey suggests that the extant remains date to the Late Medieval and Islamic periods (Salih and Edwards 1992, 77).
15 OS, 605. Several different readings of the village's name are possible, among them Yastu (Salih 1982, 77, fn. 20).
16 Crawford 1951, 30
17 OS, 481
18 OS, 482, 688
19 A number of modern scholars have suggested that the frontier of Alwa lay much further upstream, e.g., Crawford 1947, 14. This region does appear to have been a border zone during the New Kingdom with boundary *stelae* of the Egyptian pharaohs, Thutmose I and III, inscribed on the rock at the Hajar el-Merwa at Kurgus, 40 km upstream from Abu Hamed (see Davies and Welsby Sjöström 1998).
20 Griffith 1928, 132
21 In el-Maqrizi OS, 609
22 OS, 165
23 OS, 171
24 OS, 165
25 Balfour Paul 1952; Edwards 1991
26 Eisa and Welsby 1996
27 Balfour Paul 1952
28 Addison 1951; Welsby 1999a
29 For an attempt to draw the borders of Makuria and Alwa based on a consideration of the archaeological and literary sources see Salih 1982, fig. 2.
30 Krump 1710, 214. For other references see Hinkel 1979, 93-6.
31 For an alternative location, at el-Ghazali, see Anderson 1999, 71, fn. 1 with references.
32 OS, 174; Vantini 1982, 39-40. For a discussion of sites with Christian links to the east, west and south of the Nubian kingdoms see Vantini 1999.
33 Bonnet 1991, 19
34 Referred to by Gleichen 1905, I, 204.
35 Kuper 1988; Welsby 1999b, 165
36 El-Idrisi OS, 266
37 In *The Life of the Patriarch Joseph*, OS, 194.
38 Chittick 1955, 91-2; Mallinson 1998, 44. For graffiti in Greek or Coptic at Jebel

Audun(?) 80 km south east of Korti see Crowfoot 1920, 293.
39 See Chittick 1955, 88-90; Welsby 1996b, 48-50
40 Edmonds 1940. Other sites which may be of medieval date and be along cross-desert trade routes have been recorded in the south Libyan desert and in the Bayuda.
41 OS, 165
42 El-Andalusi OS, 404
43 Arkell 1951
44 Shaw 1936
45 Penn 1931; Addison in Penn 1931, 184
46 Arkell 1961, 191ff.
47 Arkell 1936; 1959
48 Monneret de Villard 1938, 194ff.; Żurawski 1999, 226. For suggested Christian Nubian influences in Chad see Arkell 1963.
49 Török 1974
50 Ibn Selim in el-Maqrizi OS, 610.
51 Monneret de Villard 1935, 275; Fattovich 1987, 97
52 OS, 164
53 Fattovich 1984; 1987, 97-8
54 OS, 612
55 OS, 773
56 Spaulding 1971, 61-2
57 Ibn Hawqal OS, 163
58 OS, 333
59 John the Deacon OS, 40-43
60 Michael the Syrian OS, 317
61 Severus OS, 215; Abu Salih OS, 331-2
62 El-Idrisi OS, 274; ar-Rumi OS, 346
63 Dzierżykray-Rogalski and Jakobielski 1975, 44-5
64 This is probably not the name of the king but an Arabic rendering of a Nubian or Greek name, or of a title (OS, 130, fn. 11).
65 OS, 130
66 OS, 166
67 Vantini 1981, 117
68 Jakobielski 1991, 276
69 Griffith 1928, 127
70 Jakobielski 1978b, 148; Łajtar and van der Vliet 1998, 47
71 Griffith 1928, 121ff.
72 OS, 127
73 Török 1988, 169-75
74 Török discusses the origin of the crowns and notes that the craftsmen, whom he considers to be Egyptian, had a limited grasp of the iconographic niceties (1988, 174).
75 Török 1988, 223
76 OS, 319
77 Ibn Selim in el-Maqrizi OS, 614.
78 Martens-Czarnecka 1982, 71.
79 Ibid. 73; Innemée 1995, 284.
80 Cf. Bonnet 1982, 15ff.
81 Lenoble 1997, 146
82 Ibid., 146-7
83 Żurawski 1999, 227. Żurawski also discusses the practise of the ceremonial shaving of the head

during the coronation, a tradition known from Ethiopia, and associated with the investiture of *mekks* in the post-medieval period on the Middle Nile, ibid., 227.
84 El-Mas'udi OS, 370
85 Martens-Czarnecka 1982a, 68-9, 96-99
86 OS, 614
87 El-Mas'udi OS, 134
88 Ibid. OS, 134-5. For taboos surrounding the king see Żurawski 1993, 33-35.
89 OS, 44-5; 333. See also Plumley 1978, 239.
90 In Millet 1964, 14.
91 Griffith 1913, 166
92 Hägg 1990, 159
93 W. Y. Adams 1996, 245 with references to Browne.
94 OS, 603
95 John the Deacon OS, 43
96 OS, 602
97 El-Furat OS, 532
98 Jakobielski 1987, 233
99 Munro-Hay 1982/3, 98
100 Jakobielski 1972, 96
101 Godlewski 1991b, 86
102 Dzierżykray-Rogalski and Jakobielski 1975, 44; Munro-Hay 1982/3, 106
103 Plumley 1978, 241
104 Łajtar and van der Vliet 1998, 37
105 OS, 323
106 An *anteparchos* (deputy *eparch*) is attested at Jebel Adda perhaps in the early eleventh century (Millet 1967, 59).
107 El-Nuwayri OS, 470, 471, 478
108 Cf. W. Y. Adams 1996, 42ff., 217-8
109 Martens-Czarnecka 1992, fig. 3
110 Michałowski 1967, pl. 92; Martens-Czarnecka 1986, 100-1
111 Martens-Czarnecka 1992, 312-3
112 Żurawski 1997b, 132-3
113 OS, 603
114 Ibn Selim in el-Maqrizi OS, 604
115 Pers. comm. J. Anderson.
116 In W. Y. Adams 1996, 226-7
117 Ibid., 227
118 Ibid., 225, 226
119 Plumley 1978, 241
120 In W. Y. Adams 1996, 225, 245
121 Ibid., 245
122 Abu Salih OS, 324
123 Cf. Papadopoullos 1966, 20
124 *FHN*, 1165
125 Hägg 1990, 160
126 Griffith 1928, 132
127 Hägg 1982, 56-59
128 Łajtar 1998
129 Anderson 1999, 74. Although the title *tetrarchos* may suggest that he was one of four officials Łajtar has noted the earlier use of the term to refer to a ruler of lower status than a king. Mariankouda may have

been a direct deputy of the king like the *eparch* of Nobadia (pers. comm. May 2000).
130 W. Y. Adams 1996, 225
131 Listed in W. Y. Adams 1996, 247-8.
132 W. Y. Adams 1994, 37
133 Translated as 'Queen mother' by W. Y. Adams 1996, 247.
134 Plumley 1978, 239
135 Hägg 1990, 161
136 Cf. W. Y. Adams 1977, 509-10; 1994, 35, 37.
137 *OS*, 609
138 W. Y. Adams 1977, 534
139 Abu Salih *OS*, 333
140 John the Deacon *OS*, 41
141 Plumley 1975c
142 Plumley 1975, 101
143 Säve-Söderbergh 1964, 38-9
144 *OS*, 214-5
145 *OS*, 340
146 Jakobielski 1972, 26ff.
147 Ibid., 86
148 Monneret de Villard 1938, 159
149 Cf. Jakobielski 1972, 27 with references.
150 This passage is quoted in Crawford 1951, 26. See also Monneret de Villard 1938, 156.
151 *OS*, 249
152 Gartkiewicz 1980, 149
153 Godlewski 1992, 279
154 Gartkiewicz 1990
155 Clarke 1912, 34-8; Shinnie 1955, 25ff.
156 Jakobielski 1972, 27
157 Innemée 1990
158 Ibid.
159 Jakobielski 1972, 166
160 W. Y. Adams 1996, 252
161 Łajtar and van der Vliet 1998, 40ff., 48
162 W. Y. Adams 1965b, 121
163 *OS*, 375; also reported by the later thirteenth to early fourteenth-century writer el-Qalqashandi *OS*, 575-6.
164 Munro-Hay 1982/3, 98; see Monneret de Villard 1932, 309-16 in support of this evidence; also Kubińska 1974, 71-2.
165 See Van Moorsel 1970.
166 *OS*, 321. See also comments in Säve-Söderbergh 1970, 238-9. W. Y. Adams (1965b, 116) suggested that the introduction of the tribune and the segregated *haikal* may be connected with the change from Melkite to Monophysite Christianity, but this seems unlikely in view of the fact that these features were introduced into many churches in Nobadia, which according to our sources was always Monophysite.
167 Innemée 1992b, 166
168 Vantini 1981, 147ff.
169 Plumley 1983, 161
170 Jakobielski 1998, 163
171 Ibid., 166
172 Martens-Czarnecka 1998, 88-90.

173 Plumley 1983, 161
174 Severus *OS*, 195
175 Frend 1991. However, according to Ratynski (1982, 223) in Nubian theology the gospel according to St John appears to have been held in a higher regard than the Synoptic Gospels. All quotations from the Bible on the walls of the cathedral at Faras are taken from the Gospel according to St John.
176 Ratynski 1982, 223-4
177 See for example the crosses depicted on wall paintings at Faras (Ratynski 1982, 256ff.), and on pottery at Soba East (Welsby 1998, figs. 80 and 81).
178 Ratynski 1982, 239
179 Allason-Jones 1991, 128
180 Ratynski 1982, 258, 260
181 Godlewski 1990c, 136. For sepulchral crosses and cruciform mastaba see pp. 58, 63
182 W. Y. Adams 1996, 186, pl. 54
183 El-Maqrizi *OS*, 681
184 Browne 1991, 74
185 Müller 1970
186 Millet 1974, 56-7; Anderson 1999, 82
187 Millet 1974, 57
188 *OS*, 613
189 *OS*, 326
190 *OS*, 324, 335
191 Scanlon 1972, 7; W. Y. Adams 1986, I, 17
192 Zurawski 1994, 323; Jakobielski *et al.* 1993, 289
193 Shinnie and Chittick 1961, 15, 25
194 Jakobielski 1997, 161; for the commemorative complex see Zurawski 1999b, 251ff.
195 Jakobielski 1997, 163
196 Jakobielski 1998, 163
197 Zurawski 1999c
198 Jakobielski 1999, 145
199 Jakobielski 1997, 167
200 These are listed in Anderson 1999, 71-2, fn. 4.
201 Hirschfeld 1992, 33
202 Ibid., 31-3
203 W. Y. Adams 1977, 479
204 See Anderson 1999, 81-2
205 Scanlon 1972, 21
206 Anderson 1999, 78ff.
207 For a list of anchorite cells with references see Anderson 1999, 71. For wall paintings of anchorites in the cathedral at Faras see Łukaszewicz 1990.
208 1927, 83-91
209 In Jakobielski 1972, 66.
210 Jakobielski 1972, 115
211 Edwards 1996
212 El-Mas'udi *OS*, 134
213 *OS*, 613
214 *OS*, 608. Are these people the population of el-Abwab?
215 Severus *OS*, 213
216 Millet 1967, 59
217 Adams 1964, 248; 1965, 172, 174
218 Säve-Söderberg 1964, 39 and

pl. VII
219 Millet 1964, 10; 1967, 59; see also Monneret de Villard 1938, 118; Säve-Söderbergh 1982, 52-5
220 Caneva 1988, 214, 400. The radiocarbon date was 360±60 bp, calibrated to AD 1520 ± 90.
221 Shinnie and Shinnie 1978, 6, 9, 11, pl. Xib
222 Trigger 1967, 13
223 In el-Maqrizi *OS*, 601
224 In el-Maqrizi *OS*, 721-2
225 W. Y. Adams 1996, 227
226 Ibid., 223
227 Plumley 1975, 107
228 Glidden 1954. The dating of the oldest of these to a century earlier by Monneret de Villard was, according to Glidden, the result of a misreading of the Arabic.
229 Hasan 1967, 27-8
230 W. Y. Adams suggests that the many anomalous features of the cemetery at Sakinya, particularly the 314 tombstones in Coptic, suggests that it was an expatriate community of Egyptian Christians (1998, 21, fn. 1).
231 Arkell 1963, 320
232 Christides 1992, 349; Dzierżykray-Rogalski 1985, 258-9
233 Michael the Syrian *OS*, 316
234 In Hrbek 1977, 70.
235 Severus *OS*, 205; 668, fn. 66
236 Vantini 1981, 158
237 Quoted by ar-Rumi *OS*, 346.
238 *OS*, 240
239 El-Idrisi *OS*, 267
240 Armelagos 1977, 82
241 For similar conditions among the Alwan population see Filer 1998, 222-3.
242 Dzierżykray-Rogalski 1985, 254ff.
243 Armelagos 1977, 80, 82-3
244 Van Gerven and Greene 1999
245 Trigger 1970, 358; Michael the Syrian *OS*, 311
246 Cartwright 1998, 261
247 El-Faqih *OS*, 91; el-Idrisi *OS*, 267. The fourteenth century Jacob of Verona noted that circumcision was one of the three baptisms practised by the Nubians, the others being baptism by water and the branding of a cross on the forehead (quoted by Rostkowska 1982b, fn. 11).
248 Geus *et al.* 1995, 122, pl. Xb
249 Edwards 1998, pl. IV
250 W. Y. Adams 1996, 181, pl. 50, a and b
251 In the church at Meinarti and in the cathedral at Faras (W. Y. Adams 1999c, 9, pl. 3; Michałowski 1967, 105, pls 23-5).
252 Godlewski 1991b, 95; Shinnie and Shinnie 1978, 78
253 W. Y. Adams 1996, 198, pl. 60

254 Emery and Kirwan 1938, 344-47; W. Y. Adams 1996, 200
255 For examples found in Nubia see for example Shinnie and Shinnie 1978, pl. XLIV.b; Adams 2000, fig. 30.
256 Petrie 1927, 60; W. Y. Adams 2000, 93
257 W. Y. Adams 1996, 200
258 *OS*, 511
259 Török identifies this as an 'assembly house of cult associations' (1999, 149 fn. 138). It was dated to the Roman period by its excavator (Kromer 1967, 114-1) although Adams has suggested on the pottery evidence that its use falls within the X-Group period (1977, 363).
260 Plumley and W. Y. Adams 1974, 217-19. The tavern (House X-4) was thought to have been constructed in the late Kushite period on account of the style of the stonework used in the lower courses of its walls and the presence of Kushite pottery in the lowest levels. However the pottery associated with its earliest use was of X-Group type.
261 W. Y. Adams and Nordström 1963, 39, fig. 6b; W. Y. Adams 1966, 281-2
262 Millet 1967, 58
263 See Edwards 1996b, 1999b.

Chapter 6
1 Shinnie and Shinnie 1978, 107
2 Trigger 1967, 78-9
3 W. Y. Adams 1968, 188-8
4 Trigger 1972, 576
5 Blanton 1981, 393
6 Trigger 1972, 577. For further references to the complex questions concerning the growth and function of urbanism see Sinclair *et al.* 1993, 21ff.
7 Weeks 1967, 5
8 W. Y. Adams 2000, 9
9 See discussion of Lenoble's paper in Welsby (ed.) 1999c, 184.
10 Dunham 1970, pl. LIX
11 In el-Maqrizi *OS*, 606
12 Adams 1965b, 88
13 It should be noted than many of the sites in this latter region were occupied earlier in the medieval period. Evidence to support the theory of immigration in the late medieval period is at present not available.
14 For discussions of the location of agricultural land as a background to the location of settlements see among others Trigger 1965, 13-14; Edwards 1996, 70ff. – primarily a discussion of the location of Kushite settlement but equally valid for the medieval period.
15 Zurawski 1986, 417, fn. 9
16 W. Y. Adams 1965b, 88ff.
17 At Qasr Ibrim the cathedral was constructed on the highest

part of the site over the remains of X-Group houses although these may have been demolished long before the cathedral was constructed. The pottery sealed beneath the cathedral was almost exclusively of X-Group date (Plumley and Adams 1974, 214).

18 W. Y. Adams 1996, 81-2
19 W. Y. Adams 1977, 488, 743 fn. 112
20 W. Y. Adams 1965b, 90
21 W. Y. Adams 2000, 11
22 E.g., Debeira West, Shinnie and Shinnie 1978, 6; Meinarti, Adams 2000, 10.
23 Lenoble 1992, 11
24 Mahmoud el-Tayeb 1999
25 Ibn Selim in el-Maqrizi OS, 602.
26 OS, 323
27 For the suggested dating of these defences to the Late Kushite period see Griffith 1926, 25. In view of the similarity to other defended enclosures in Lower Nubia, some of which are certainly of medieval date a similar date for the Faras defences seems likely (see below; also Karkowski 1986, 314).
28 Godlewski 1992b, 112-3; Jakobielski 1972, 180-1, 189
29 Jakobielski 1972, 37ff. Although these inscriptions are usually assumed to refer to the cathedral there is no good reason to accept this. They are set into the wall of another building which appears, from the scant traces of it which survive, to have been an important and impressive structure. Taking the evidence at face value the inscriptions should relate to the construction of that edifice.
30 Jakobielski 1972, 111, 114
31 Michałowski 1964, 196; Jakobielski 1972, 24, 29
32 Jakobielski 1972, 167-8
33 Ibid., 168
34 Trigger 1965, 33
35 W. Y. Adams 1965, 161
36 W. Y. Adams 2000, 6
37 Ratynski 1982, 250-1
38 Godlewski 1992, 278
39 Godlewski 1991b, 79ff.
40 Ibid., 91
41 OS, 326
42 OS, 343
43 In Abu Shama OS, 370.
44 Godlewski 1998, 171-9
45 Pers. comm. W. Godlewski.
46 Kuper 1988
47 OS, 701; cf. Jakobielski and Ostrasz 1967, 140
48 OS, 772
49 Welsby and Daniels 1991, 12 – (AE4), 21 – (MN8); Welsby 1998, 22-3
50 Welsby and Daniels 1991, 29
51 Budge 1907, I, 325
52 In el-Maqrizi OS, 613.
53 OS, 447, 457
54 Horton 1991, fig. 5

55 Driskell et al. 1989; Alexander 1999
56 Plumley 1975b, fig. 2
57 Ibid., 9
58 Plumley and W. Y. Adams 1974, 224
59 W. Y. Adams 1996, 74
60 Plumley 1975b, 8
61 W. Y. Adams 1996, 31
62 Ibid., 89
63 OS, 327
64 Ibn Selim in el-Maqrizi OS, 602.
65 W. Y. Adams 1996, 79-81
66 Ibid., 34, 89
67 Ibid., 62ff.
68 Ibid., 31
69 W. Y. Adams 1996, 41ff.; Plumley 1975b
70 Millet 1964, 10
71 Millet 1967, 61-2
72 Ibid., 62
73 Weeks 1967, 6
74 Ibid., 28
75 Shinnie and Shinnie 1978
76 Barkóczi and Salamon 1974, 333
77 Schneider 1970, 89, 95
78 Barkóczi and Salamon 1974, 326
79 Ibid., 335
80 W. Y. Adams 1964; 1965; 2000; 2001
81 El-Maqrizi OS, 649
82 OS, 324. Although the Island of Michael is generally identified with Meinarti this is not certain; see Łajtar and van der Vliet 1998, 37. For the possible remains of the monastery here see W. Y. Adams 1999c, 10ff.
83 En-Nuwayri OS, 479; el-Furat OS, 540; el-Maqrizi OS, 684
84 Knudstad 1966, 166ff.
85 Grzymski 1993; Grzymski and Anderson 1994; Anderson 1999. For the dating J. Anderson, pers. comm.
86 Welsby 2001, 20-1, 597-8
87 Hintze 1963, 224-5; 1967-8, 294-6; Török 1974. Note the inscription in Greek recording a king and others in Old Nubian published by Hintze (1959, 181-2).
88 For mention of a church 160 km south of ed-Debba see Shinnie and Chittick 1961, 25.
89 W. Y. Adams 1996, 101; Grzymski 1990, 155; Shinnie and Shinnie 1978
90 Donadoni 1969, 26-30
91 Trigger 1965, 146. A medieval caravanserai has also been identified at Mirgissa (Vercoutter 1970, 157).
92 The extent of these defences are far from clear and some of the area they enclose is very steeply sloping and will have been unsuitable for settlement (see Curto et al. 1965).
93 Sinada is an early Christian fortification midway between Old Dongola and ed-Debba. For it see Grzymski 1987, 11

and Żurawski 1999c, 160; for Selib see Żurawski 1999c, 159.
94 OS, 92
95 Note the trace of a linear feature along the river side of the enclosure on the kite photograph published in Żurawski 1999c, fig. 1.
96 Żurawski 1999c, 150-2
97 Żurawski 1999c, 152. It is dated by Żurawski to the seventh to eighth century (pers. comm. May 2000). Its small size and location can be compared with the later forts in the Third Cataract and elsewhere noted below.
98 For the plan see Lepsius 1913, 252; for aerial photographs see Żurawski 1998, pl. XLVII; 1999c, fig. 1.
99 For these sites and a general discussion of Late Roman fortifications in the western Roman Empire see Johnson 1983 wherein are plans of Senlis fig. 31, Dijon fig. 26, Lugo fig. 48, Pevensey fig. 80.
100 Chittick 1955, figs 2-4
101 For a photograph see Welsby 1996, fig. 16.
102 Crawford 1953, 39-40
103 Ibid., 18
104 Sjöström 1998b, 32-3
105 See Arkell 1953 where it is visible on plate 3
106 Hakem 1979, 155. The rarity of Christian pottery in the vicinity of Jebel Nakharu and the presence of only one small Christian cemetery suggests that the fort does not date to the Christian period (pers. comm. J. Anderson, October 2000). For other not dissimilar fortifications, but of uncertain date, at the Fifth Cataract see El-Amin and Edwards 2000, figs. 4 and 9.
107 A centrally placed building, set within a bastioned enclosure, was a feature of the installation at Hosh el-Kab (pers. comm. P. Lenoble, June 2000).
108 W. Y. Adams 1965c, 175-6
109 Dinkler 1970b, 267ff.
110 Jakobielski et al. 1993, 301; Godlewski 1997, 186; 1998, 179
111 For the reuse of the fortress at Sahaba see Säve-Söderbergh 1970, 232.
112 W. Y. Adams 1994, 21
113 W. Y. Adams 1977, 513
114 The area given here is for the main fortified area. Extending towards the river from the south-west angle is a spur wall which may have enclosed a small annex.
115 Chittick 1957, fig. 2; Dinkler 1970b, fig. 36
116 Edwards and Salih 1994, 40-2, 47-50
117 Chittick 1957, 42-4; Maystre 1970, fig. 15
118 Adams and Nordström

1963, 38. The suffix –arti is a Nubian word meaning island.
119 El-Mufaddal OS, 498
120 Titherington 1939; Donadoni 1997, 19. The latter writer mentions late Christian pottery in these forts. However, earlier material has been noted by the Gdansk Archaeological Mission (pers. comm. Z. Borcowski and B. Żurawski).
121 See Säve-Söderbergh 1970, 236; Gardberg 1970, 51
122 W. Y. Adams 1977, 514; 1994

Chapter 7
1 Alexander 1994, 22; 1999, 59
2 Welsby 1998, 272-3
3 Godlewski 1992, 278
4 Millet 1967, 55-7
5 Godlewski 1992, 282
6 Krautheimer 1975, 41ff.
7 Clarke 1912, 31-2
8 Restated in W. Y. Adams 1992.
9 Gartkiewicz 1975; 1980; 1982; 1982b; 1987. See also Grossmann 1985; 1990.
10 W. Y. Adams noted that in the church at Kulubnarti there was no evidence for the external doorways ever having been provided with doors (1994b, 149).
11 To be associated with this function are the chalices found close to the altar in this room in the Northern Church at Old Dongola, a rare find in Nubian churches (Godlewski 1990b, 53).
12 W. Y. Adams 1965b, 94; Adams in Trigger 1967, 13.
13 Trigger 1967, 14
14 At Arminna West a higab was built of upright sandstone slabs (Trigger 1967, 13).
15 Gartkiewicz 1982, 53, fn. 31
16 Żurawski 1997c, 184
17 Shinnie and Shinnie 1978, 31
18 Gartkiewicz 1980, fig. 14. For an example in Israel at Tabgha see Crowfoot 1941, fig. 15.
19 W. Y. Adams 1965b, 118
20 Plumley 1975b, 19-20
21 Godlewski 1982b, fig. 3.1
22 C. Bonnet pers. comm.
23 Monneret de Villard 1935, I, fig. 30
24 See Gartkiewicz 1980, fig. 22.
25 W. Y. Adams 1965b, fig. 5
26 For the plan see Adams and Nordström 1963, 36, fig. 6c.
27 Godlewski 1992, 278
28 Ibid., 282. See also Żurawski 1999b, 212ff.
29 Godlewski 1992, 284
30 Plumley 1975b, 17
31 W. Y. Adams 1996, 74ff.
32 W. Y. Adams 1965b, 107; Godlewski 1992, 283
33 The church at Naga el-Oqba which Adams assigns to this type, has been dated to the seventh century by Godlewski (1992, 285) while that at Sonqi Tino, an Adams Type 4?, has

been dated to the earlier tenth century (Godlewski 1990b, 50).
34 Mileham 1910, 41-2; Monneret de Villard 1935, 204, figs. 193-5; Knudstad 1966, 168
35 W. Y. Adams 1994b, 149
36 Clarke 1912, 54, fig. I
37 Tabo; Hambukol, North Kom; Old Dongola – Old Church, Building X, Church of the Stone Pavement, Church of the Granite Columns (Church of the Brick Pillars), Cruciform Church, Northern Church, Church EDC, Church DC, North-West Church, Tower Church, Pillar Church, Mosaic Church; Nuri; el-Ghazali.
38 Musawwarat es-Sufra; Soba East – church on mound C, Churches A, B, C and E; Saqadi.
39 Welsby 1996, 189-90
40 Godlewski 1992, 278-9
41 Ibid., 280
42 Godlewski 1990c
43 Vila 1977, 108-10
44 Bosticco et al. 1967, fig. 20
45 Jakobielski and Medeksza 1990
46 Godlewski 1990
47 Shinnie and Chittick 1961, fig. 2; Dunham 1955, fig. 216; Lepsius 1913, 252; Adams 1965b
48 Welsby 1996, fig. 4
49 OS, 326
50 No structural remains survived of the church thought to have been inserted into the temple, building G, at Soba East (Welsby 1998, 44).
51 The provision of wide entrances in the north and south walls is a unique feature among the large churches in Nubia but may be paralleled in the Church in the Desert at Adindan which has two two-portalled entrances through its north and south walls (Clarke 1912, 70, pl. 17).
52 Welsby and Daniels 1991, 37ff.
53 Ibid., 70ff.
54 Ibid., 85ff.
55 Welsby 1998, 29ff.
56 Török 1974
57 Hintze 1962, 195. Although it was claimed by the excavators that the so-called Temple of Isis, M 600 at Meroe was converted for use as a church what evidence was available to support this is unknown, see Garstang et al. 1911, 17; Kirwan 1988, 300; Török 1997, 170.
58 W. Y. Adams 1965b, 108
59 For the evidence for the use of foreign workers to construct a church and a monastery in Egypt see references in Gartkiewicz 1982, 68, fn. 67.
60 Donadoni 1959
61 Gartkiewicz 1975, figs. 4 and 6; 1982, 81
62 Cf. W. Y. Adams 1965b, 124
63 Gartkiewicz 1987, 243

64 W. Y. Adams 1996, 81
65 Godlewski 1990c, 136
66 Dobrowolski 1991
67 Shinnie and Shinnie 1978, 17
68 J. Anderson suggests that they could also have belonged to different extended family groups (pers. comm. October 2000).
69 Krautheimer 1969, 163ff.; Sodini and Kolokotsos 1984, 307-12
70 Krautheimer 1969, 178
71 Bosticco et al. 1967, fig. 2
72 W. Y. Adams 1994b, 268ff.
73 Jakobielski et al. 1993, 296-7
74 Jakobielski 1998, 162ff.
75 Godlewski 1982b, 136
76 Ibid., fig. 3.1
77 Godlewski 1979, 27-8; Welsby and Daniels 1991, 62, 66-7
78 For a detailed discussion of Nubian baptisteries see Godlewski 1979. The different phases of the Old Church baptisteries are documented by figures 58-61, the font in the Church of the Granite Columns is illustrated in fig. 86.
79 Trigger 1967, 11
80 Welsby and Daniels 1991, 62, 66-7
81 Welsby 1998, 174
82 Shinnie and Shinnie 1978, 31
83 Anderson 1999, 75
84 For Kushite fortifications see Welsby 1999b, 165.
85 Monneret de Villard 1957, figs. 77-9, 88; Stenico 1960, 67ff.
86 Griffith 1926, 25-28
87 Mileham 1910, 23
88 Presedo Velo 1964, 14, Lám I
89 Curto et al. 1965, 30ff.
90 Godlewski 1997, 179; 1997b
91 Godlewski 1991c
92 Lepsius 1913, 252. I am grateful to Bogdan Żurawski for details of the building materials employed at Estabel and Bakhit.
93 Sjöström 1998b, 32; Crawford 1953, 39
94 Woolley 1911, 15-25
95 Godlewski 1992, 286-7
96 Shinnie and Shinnie 1978, 3-6, 33-37
97 Godlewski and Medeksza 1987
98 Welsby and Daniels 1991, 93ff.
99 Vercoutter 1962
100 Millet 1967, 62
101 Grzymski 1989
102 W. Y. Adams 1996, 42ff.
103 Ibid., 47
104 Godlewski 1991b
105 Hakem 1979, 155
106 Jeuté 1994, 72
107 Welsby 2001, 21-5; Scanlon 1972, 16
108 Anderson 1999, 80
109 Shinnie and Chittick 1961, 20
110 Ibid., 22
111 Jakobielski 1998b, 55; 1999, 142. The northern of these free-

standing buildings NW-N was 9 x 9.3 m in size, had nine barrel- vaulted rooms, originally with flat roofs supported on timber beams, at ground level with probably an upper storey. Although it stands outside the monastery it has been described by Jakobielski as the Keep of the Monastery.
112 Jakobielski et al. 1993, 295, 296
113 Żurawski 1994
114 Jakobielski 1998b, 57
115 W. Y. Adams 1964, 228; 1999c, 10
116 Shinnie and Shinnie 1978, 34
117 Welsby 1998, 23
118 Welsby and Daniels 1991, 66-70, 81-84; Welsby 1998, 24ff.
119 For the suggested extensive use of light dwellings of timber, straw and matting in the Second Cataract and Batn-el-Hajar in the Late Medieval period see Adams and Nordström 1963, 43.
120 W. Y. Adams 1994b, 267; see also Adams and Nordström 1963, 42-3.
121 Adams and Nordström 1963, 38
122 Plumley 1975b, 15
123 Plumley and Adams 1974, 215, fig. 1; Plumley 1975b, 8, 10-11, fig. 2. Note the suggestion that these buildings were not actually designed as houses but were principally for storage (Plumley and Adams 1974, 224).
124 Trigger 1967, 79
125 Ibid., 26-28
126 Shinnie and Shinnie 1978, 10
127 Bosticco et al. 1964, fig. 7
128 Godlewski 1998, 171-5
129 Godlewski 1997, 186-7
130 Hajnóczi 1974, 349ff.
131 W. Y. Adams 1996, 35
132 W. Y. Adams 1994. Adams considered that the type was not found upstream of Firka but the range has now been extended to the Third Cataract (see Edwards and Salih 2000, 64-5).
133 Adams and Nordström 1963, 38-9, fig. 6d
134 Shinnie and Shinnie 1978,11-13
135 Shinnie 1955, 18-23
136 E.g., at Debeira West, Shinnie and Shinnie 1978, 6.
137 Plumley 1975b, 8, 11; Plumley and Adams 1974, pl. XLV.1
138 Plumley and Adams 1974, 221
139 Shinnie and Shinnie 1978, 17
140 Ibid., 106
141 Trigger 1967, 12
142 Schneider 1970, 92
143 Shinnie and Shinnie 1978, 105-6
144 Ibid., 11, pl. XIVc
145 Ibid., 106; for examples from

Old Dongola see Godlewski 1991b, 92.
146 Welsby 1998, fig. 14.1-5 and 5
147 Adams 1965, 159, 161
148 Żurawski 1994, 336, fn. 32
149 Shinnie and Shinnie 1978, 10-11
150 Ibid. 10, 12
151 Ibid. 106; Żurawski 1997, 169
152 Godlewski 1991b, 92-3, pl. 1
153 Pluskota 1997, fig. 1
154 E.g., at Old Dongola Godlewski 1991b, 93; in castle houses W. Y. Adams 1994, 19.
155 W. Y. Adams 1965, 159
156 Jakobielski 1997, 163; Żurawski 1997, 175, 178
157 Gratien 1993, pl. 2
158 Żurawski 1994, 333
159 Jakobielski 1979
160 Anderson 1999, 80
161 Karkowski 1981, 30ff; 1986, 311
162 Gartkiewicz 1986, 248
163 W. Y. Adams 1965b, 90
164 Welsby and Daniels 1991, 97; Jakobielski 1991, 276-7
165 Godlewski 1991c, 109
166 Godlewski 1979, 114
167 Żurawski 1997, 171
168 Vila 1976, 72-3; cf. Harrell 1999. Hard-stone monolithic columns are not a feature of Pharaonic and Kushite architecture in Nubia. In the light of this it is probable that many if not all the workings at Kitfogga are of medieval date. For another granite quarry at Bayuda Wells, probably worked in the medieval period, see Jackson 1926, 30.
169 Gartkiewicz 1990, 120
170 Weeks 1967, fig. 12
171 Shinnie and Shinnie 1978, 16. A not dissimilar situation has been noted at Soba East in the dwelling excavated on mound A where the lower courses were of mud brick and the upper of red brick, the latter providing a greater protection against rainfall (Shinnie 1955, 18).
172 Jakobielski et al. 1993, 294
173 Gartkiewicz 1982, 70, fn. 75
174 Maddox 1991; Morgan 1998. For a discussion of the preparation of walls for painting see pp. 224-6. Chapter 7
175 Dobrowolski 1991, 29
176 W. Y. Adams 1964, 221
177 Welsby 1998, 35, 38
178 E.g., at Debeira West, see Shinnie and Shinnie 1978, 104.
179 Welsby and Daniels 1991, fig. 13
180 Gartkiewicz 1990, 143
181 Ibid., 118, fig. 72
182 Vercoutter 1962
183 Żurawski 1997c, 182
184 Welsby and Daniels 1991, 37
185 Gartkiewicz 1990, fig. 71
186 Jakobielski and Medeksza 1990, 167

187 Gartkiewicz 1990, 149ff, figs. 77 and 78
188 Welsby and Daniels 1991, 50, 54-5
189 W. Y. Adams 1996, 87, fig. 21
190 Żurawski 1997c, 182, 188
191 Welsby and Daniels 1991, 89, 45
192 Gartkiewicz 1990, 288ff.
193 Gardberg 1970, 31
194 Gartkiewicz 1982, fig. 66
195 Adams 1994, 20
196 Godlewski 1990c, 129, fig. 1
197 OS, 326
198 Knudstad 1966, 168; Mileham 1910, 43
199 Mileham 1910, 8-9
200 Welsby and Daniels 1991, 42, 91
201 W. Y. Adams 1965b, 91
202 Ibid., 91
203 Sjöström 1998, with additional examples
204 Gartkiewicz 1990, 136
205 Emery and Kirwan 1938, 33, fig. 10
206 Żurawski 1997, 171, fig. 3
207 Godlewski and Medeksza 1987, 198
208 For a detailed discussion of the lock mechanism and of the different types of wooden keys see W. Y. Adams 1996, 154ff.
209 J. Anderson pers. comm. Oct. 2000; W. Y. Adams 2000, 96-8; Allason-Jones 1998, 79. For a fine iron key with a copper-alloy handle see Jakobielski 1998, 162. A massive cast iron key probably of X-Group date came from Qasr Ibrim, see Plumley and Adams 1974, 236, pl. LII.2
210 Plumley and Adams 1974, 236, pl. LIII.1
211 Shinnie and Shinnie 1978, 105
212 Welsby 1992, fig. 1
213 Michałowskii 1965, 70,72, figs. 34-5, 40
214 W. Y. Adams 1996, 74
215 Gartkiewicz 1990, 204
216 Godlewski and Medeksza 1992
217 Godlewski 1998, 175
218 Welsby 1992, 177
219 For the latter see Anderson 1994, 172, pl. 17B.
220 Żurawski 1994, 335
221 Jakobielski 1997, 160; cf. also the pipes in the wall of room 3 in House A, Jakobielski 1979, 234, fig. 6.
222 Żurawski 1997, 178
223 Welsby and Daniels 1991, fig. 90
224 Shinnie and Shinnie 1978, 31
225 Welsby and Daniels 1991, pl. 23
226 Ibid., pl. 17; Shinnie and Shinnie 1978, 17
227 Measured examples were 282.5 x 282.5 x 70 mm and 293.6 x 155 x 52.5 mm.
228 See Morgenstein and

Redmount 1998 for the degree of shrinkage of mud bricks observed in Egypt and for mud bricks in general.
229 Godlewski 1991c, 105
230 Welsby and Daniels 1991, 318-21; Dobrowolski 1987, 2
231 Gartkiewicz 1990, 74, 215. In assessing the module used in a building's construction one must be wary of simply measuring a dimension and then dividing it by what appears to be a logical number of units. The method of laying out a structure is of crucial importance and may well allow a range of dimensions, all derived from the use of the same module, but varying widely. Such an approach applied to a number of bath-houses of the Roman period has illustrated the problems of simply working out a module from the internal or external dimensions of rooms – see Welsby in Gillam et al. 1993, 25-6.
232 Adams 1965, 166
233 Welsby and Daniels 1991, 70, fig. 28 (in room X).

Chapter 8
1 Vercoutter 1966, 162-3 with references; Burckhardt 1819, 10; Myres 1960, 175; Adams 1994b, 113, fig. 2.3
2 Adams and Nordström 1963, 43
3 Tracey and Hewison 1948, 744
4 Pers. comm. C. Delmet
5 Butzer 1976, 30
6 Trigger 1970, 352 with references; for flood damage elsewhere see, for example, W. Y. Adams 1965, 149; 1986, I, 191; Trigger 1967, 79.
7 Allan and Smith 1948, 631
8 Trigger 1965, 123
9 W. Y. Adams 1977, fig. 56
10 Allan and Smith 1948, 628; Tracey and Hewison 1948, 745-6
11 OS, 162-3
12 Only at Old Dongola has the presence of wadi walls designed to impede the movement of flood waters, reducing their erosive potential and allowing the water to percolate into the soil, been identified (Żurawski 1994, 327). However, these are considered to be of relatively modern date (pers. comm. B. Żurawski).
13 OS, 127, 346, 385
14 OS, 605, 649
15 See Bacon 1948, 369-70.
16 Plumley 1975b, 6
17 Rowley-Conwy 1989, 134
18 Plumley 1975b, pl. XIV.4
19 For examples see Shinnie and Shinnie 1978, pl. XLI.
20 For a rotary quern from Qasr Ibrim see W. Y. Adams 1996, pl. 12; from Tamit see Bosticco

et al. 1967, pl. 2.1; identical examples have been found in the medieval town at Sai.
21 Corkill 1948, 254; cf. Edwards 1996b for the importance of beer in the Kushite period and, for its continuing role in the medieval and post-medieval periods, see Edwards 1999b.
22 OS, 511
23 Rowley-Conwy 1989, 135
24 Van der Veen 1991, 271; Cartwright 1998, 260
25 Grzymski 1990, 148
26 Rowley-Conwy 1989, 135
27 Shinnie and Shinnie 1978, 107
28 Ibid., 95
29 Van der Veen 1991, 267; Cartwright 1998, 260
30 Rowley-Conwy 1989, 135
31 OS, 602
32 Reisner 1929, 67; Shinnie 1978, 261
33 Shinnie and Shinnie 1965, 271
34 In el-Maqrizi OS, 613.
35 Godlewski 1998, 178. Grape pips (and olive stones) have been recovered from beneath Building 1 at Hambukol (pers. comm. J. Anderson, Oct. 2000).
36 Pluskota 1997, 235
37 W. Y. Adams 1966
38 In el-Maqrizi, OS 605.
39 Shinnie and Shinnie 1978, 107
40 Van der Veen 1991, 267; Cartwright 1998, 260
41 Rowley-Conwy 1989, 136; for the suggestion of differing farming practices in the north and south of Nubia see Kobischtschanow 1980.
42 Shinnie and Shinnie 1978, 107
43 Grzymski 1990, 155
44 Chaix 1998
45 OS, 274
46 OS, 511
47 Chaix 1998, 241
48 MacDonald and Edwards 1993. For the presence of poultry at Wadi Qitna/Kalabsha South see Strouhal 1984, 263.
49 Ibn Selim in el-Maqrizi OS, 606.
50 OS, 127
51 Heidorn 1997, 111
52 Bruce 1790, 522
53 Cf. Welsby 1996b, 153ff.
54 Burckhardt 1819
55 OS, 603
56 OS, 274
57 Shinnie and Shinnie 1978, 107
58 Chaix 1998, 241
59 W. Y. Adams 1996, 101, pl. 11e
60 Moskalewska in Żurawski 1994, 332-3
61 Plumley 1983, 162
62 W. Y. Adams 1996, 134ff.
63 N. K. Adams 1996, 160ff.
64 Paner 1999, 118
65 OS, 605
66 Bergman 1975, 11-12
67 N. K. Adams 1999, 67
68 W. Y. Adams 1986, I, 39-40

69 For example, the Black Burnished I industry of south-west England which traded throughout Roman Britain from the early second until the mid-fourth century AD, see Gillam 1976.
70 W. Y. Adams 1986, I, 33
71 Analyses of hand-made and wheel-made Kushite ceramics from Meroe has demonstrated that both types were fired in kilns at a temperature of around 1,000°c and that both types may have been produced by the same potters (Robertson and Hill 1999).
72 See Török 1997, 174.
73 Jakobielski et al. 1993, 298
74 Ibid., 298
75 For a Kushite example see Edwards 1999, pls 6.32-34.
76 Pluskota 1990; 1991; Jakobielski et al. 1993, 298-9
77 Pluskota 1994, 362
78 Pluskota 1994, 363-4; 1994b
79 Godlewski 1991b, 94
80 W. Y. Adams 1986, I, 16 -22
81 Jakobielski et al. 1993, 298
82 Żurawski 1994, fig. 15
83 E.g., Debeira West, Shinnie and Shinnie 1978, 78, no. 62.
84 There may have been some continuity in certain areas, for example at el-Khandag, where the post-medieval wares, particularly the utility wares, resemble some of the late Christian pottery although they are heavier walled, have a thicker slip and simpler decorative designs (pers. comm. J. Anderson, Oct. 2000).
85 Welsby and Daniels 1991, 105, 245
86 Trigger 1967, 57
87 W. Y. Adams 1986, I, 42
88 Porter 1991, 336-7
89 E.g. at Soba East, Welsby and Daniels 1991, 246.
90 Welsby and Daniels 1991, 175
91 Grzymski and Anderson 1994, 98-9
92 Godlewski 1991, 107-8. The sample gave a date of AD 510, although the range of dates within which the sample may have actually lain is not stated in the publication.
93 Welsby 1998, 37
94 Shinnie and Chittick 1961, 24
95 Emery and Kirwan 1938, 337-8
96 See Lenoble 1997.
97 Millet 1964, 9, pl. III, fig. 8
98 For the abundant material from Qustul and Ballana see Emery and Kirwan 1938, 283ff.
99 Lenoble 1999, 172ff.; for the opposing view see Shinnie and Robertson 1993; Török 1999, 136.
100 Griffith 1924, 166
101 W. Y. Adams 2000, 25
102 Harden 1978, 89; Morrison 1991, 257

103 Emery and Kirwan 1938, I 186-216, II pl. 37-48
104 W. Y. Adams 1996, 181-3
105 Paner 1998, 118
106 Allason-Jones 1991, 159
107 W. Y. Adams 1996, 183
108 Allason-Jones 1991, 159
109 Żurawski 1994, 341
110 Allason-Jones 1991, 158
111 Ibid., 145-6, pl. 39
112 For a detailed discussion of objects made from these materials from the Late Christian levels on the site see W. Y. Adams 1996, 91ff.
113 Although the rarity of objects made from these material is usually attributed to their poor chances of survival Adams has noted at Meinarti that, notwithstanding the survival issue, there was a marked rarity of wooden objects and gourds (W. Y. Adams 2000, 24).
114 Welsby 1998, 38
115 See W. Y. Adams 1996, 123ff., also Wendrich 1994.
116 W. Y. Adams 1996, 150
117 Simpson 1964, pl. XIV, fig. 17
118 W. Y. Adams 2000, 25
119 W. Y. Adams 1996, 147-9
120 For *angareebs* from the post-Meroitic cemetery at Gabati see Smith 1998b, 112. For examples from the northern part of Lower Nubia see Strouhal 1984, 233-5.
121 Millet 1964, 9, pl. IV, figs 9 and 10
122 Emery and Kirwan 1938, I, 383-4, II pl. 109
123 W. Y. Adams 1996, 177-9
124 Barnard 1994, 52-3
125 Wills 1998, 182-5
126 Ibid., fig. 112, 184. For fine leather shoes from Nag' el-Scheima see Bietak and Schwarz 1987, figs. 48 and 49, taf. 52 and 53.
127 For references see Török 1975, 142, fn. 18.
128 Scanlon 1972, fig. 3; Żurawski 1999b, fig. 42
129 Millet 1963, 153, 159, fig. 7
130 Williams 1991, 77ff., 90ff.
131 Millet 1967, 60. For the possible adoption of Mameluke heraldry in the late medieval period see Millet 1987.
132 Crowfoot 1977
133 Żurawski 1999b, 245-6
134 Vogelsang-Eastwood 1991; 1998
135 References in W. Y. Adams 1996, 171; OS, 385
136 N. K. Adams 1981, 7; 1986, 24-5; W. Y. Adams 1996, 171ff.
137 N. K. Adams 1999, 53
138 El-Masudi OS, 134, Adams 1977, 463
139 W. Y. Adams 1977, 438
140 In el-Maqrizi OS, 604.
141 W. Y. Adams 1996, 196-7
142 See Kirwan 1982; 1987
143 John of Biclar OS, 27-8

144 Török 1978, 300-302
145 For a detailed list see pp. 70-1, Chapter 4.
146 Beshir 1975, 21
147 Emery 1965, 184
148 El-Masudi OS, 133
149 OS, 737-8
150 OS, 135
151 Ibn Selim in el-Maqrizi OS, 603.
152 The reference here must be to kinglets who still required the permission of the Great King of Makuria to travel upstream.
153 OS, 325
154 Ibn Hawqal OS, 168
155 There was presumably also a Christian community at Aidhab although whether these were locals, Copts or Nubians is unclear. A bishop of Aidhab, who was a native of Quft in Egypt, is recorded in the *Synaxaire arabe jacobite* (Cuoq 1986, 51).
156 Plumley 1975, 106; 1983, 162
157 Pers. comm. W.Y. Adams.
158 Reuse was however, common. Sherds were frequently shaped into spindle whorls and counters and used for writing (*ostraca*). Complete pots were occasionally used in an architectural context; large jars set into the spandrels between vaults on Kom H at Old Dongola to help reduce the weight of the filling, *qawadis* used to infill the windows of the cathedral at Faras and amphorae laid across a grave at Faras to form a roofing (Michałowski 1965, fig. 40; Griffith 1927, pl. LIII, 2).
159 Smith 1991
160 W. Y. Adams 1986, I, 55
161 Emery and Kirwan 1938, 401ff.
162 Godlewski 1998, 175, 178
163 From Soba East, see Allason-Jones 1991; from Hambukol see Phillips 1994; at Old Dongola see Pluskota 1997, 235.
164 See Shinnie and Shinnie 1978, fig. 104, nos. 423, 582. For stamps of pottery, wood and stone from Late Christian contexts at Qasr Ibrim see W. Y. Adams 1996, 192-5.
165 Welsby 1998, 92
166 W. Y. Adams 1986, I, 431
167 Cf. W. Y. Adams 1986, I, 43.
168 Beshir 1975, 21
169 Welsby and Daniels 1991, 67
170 El-Idrisi OS, 274
171 El-Qazwini OS, 385
172 El-Maqrizi OS, 649
173 El-Maqrizi OS, 696
174 Translated as teak by Vantini. Teak is a tree of tropical Asian origin although now found in the savannah woodland zone in Sudan (Thirakul 1984, 429).
175 In el-Maqrizi OS, 611.
176 Pers. comm. P. Rowley-Conwy.
177 Welsby and Daniels 1991, 172

178 One room in this building had a tally painted onto one wall and similar tally marks have been found adjacent to a door in a building at Debeira West. What was being recorded is unclear but it may be an inventory of goods stored in these rooms. See Jakobielski 1991, 277, pl. 52; Shinnie and Shinnie 1978, fig. 117.
179 Schneider 1970, 91
180 Welsby 1998, 92
181 W. Y. Adams 1966, 282
182 W. Y. Adams 1986, I, 36l
183 OS, 233
184 Procopius, I.XIX.32
185 See Emery and Kirwan 1938.
186 In el-Maqrizi OS, 615.
187 Ibn Selim in el-Maqrizi OS, 606.
188 W. Y. Adams 1966
189 Cf. Kirwan 1977, 26.
190 OS, 614, 167
191 Kirwan 1972, 170
192 El-Andalusi OS, 415. Sayce noted the discovery by Col. Jackson near Kassinger of a medieval rock inscription which he believed was carved by the workers in the adjacent gold-workings (1910, 267-8).
193 *Sudan Almanac* 1964, 51
194 In el-Maqrizi OS, 613.
195 OS, 613, 615
196 Ibn Selim in el-Maqrizi OS, 603.
197 OS, 274
198 In el-Maqrizi OS, 608.
199 OS, 709
200 OS, 78
201 Shinnie 1955, 60-68; Morrison 1991; Porter 1991; Porter and Hughes 1998; Ward 1998
202 Allason-Jones 1991, 143, 145, pls 38-9
203 Welsby and Daniels 1991, 246
204 Cf. Mallinson 1998, 44; Chittick 1955
205 Weeks 1967, 7
206 W. Y. Adams 1977, 466
207 OS, 333
208 Cf. Connah 1989, 24-66
209 Linant de Bellefonds in Shinnie (ed.) 1958, 173.
210 For a suggestion of very long-range trade contacts between the kingdom of Alwa, the Chad Basin, and as far afield as Igbo-Ukwu, close to the lower Niger in Southern Nigeria, see Sutton 1991, 153; cf. Insoll and Shaw 1997.
211 Török 1988, 33-38
212 Kirwan 1972; Chittick 1982; Fattovich 1982
213 Török 1988, 41
214 See Kirwan 1972, 170.
215 OS, 274-5, 278
216 See Monneret de Villard 1938, 233; Vantini 1975, 274 fn. 14, 411 fn. 16.

Chapter 9
1 Emery and Kirwan 1938, pl. 27B; Michałowski 1965, fig. 9
2 Alexander 1999, 59, pl. 2
3 Ryl-Preibisz 1987, 247
4 Godlewski 1992, 294
5 Gartkiewicz 1990, figs. 100-2
6 Ryl-Preibisz 1986, 379
7 Ryl-Preibisz 1997, 227-8
8 Ryl-Preibisz 1987, figs. 4-6
9 Ryl-Preibisz 1997, 228
10 However, the cross does appear on the early sandstone capitals from Kom E at Old Dongola, see Ryl-Preibisz 1997, 227.
11 For discussions of capitals see Ryl-Preibisz 1986; 1987.
12 Godlewski 1992, 294
13 Ryl-Preibisz 1986, 382
14 These elements are discussed in some detail by Idzikowska 1983.
15 Anderson suggests that this may be partly the result of the limited archaeological work conducted on Makurian and Alwan churches (pers. comm. Oct. 2000).
16 Idzikowska 1983, pl. 5
17 Godlewski 1992, 284
18 Idzikowska 1983, 210
19 Michałowski 1965, 80, fig. 47
20 W. Y. Adams 1996, 74
21 Scanlon 1970, fig. 7
22 Bosticco *et al.* 1967, pl. 10
23 Jakobielski 1972, 30-32, fig. 2; 49, fig. 4
24 However in 1822 Henneker (1823, 160) noted a painting of St John here although if this is correct the painting must have been covered up for several centuries while the cathedral was used as a mosque.
25 Plumley 1970, 130, pls 78-80
26 Jakobielski 1975, 75, pl. 10
27 Shinnie and Chittick 1961, pl. IVa
28 Griffith 1926, 27, pl. XXIV.2, XXVIII.2
29 For the dating of this fortification to the post-Meroitic period see p. 117.
30 Vercoutter 1963, 34, fig. 2
31 Jakobielski *et al.* 1993, fig. 8; Żurawski 1997b, fig. 7; Ryl-Preibisz 1997, 230-1, pl. 31
32 Ryl-Preibisz 1997, 228-9. A very well preserved *higab* of this type survived into the 1960s in the Central Church at Abdullah Nirqi, see Schneider 1970, pl. 38.
33 Welsby 2001, 402. Cat. no. 1385
34 Gartkiewicz 1982, 71, fn. 79
35 Jakobielski *et al.* 1993, 296; Ryl-Preibisz 1997, 229-30, pl. 30
36 Godlewski 1992, 287
37 Gartkiewicz 1990, 203ff., fig. 117
38 Godlewski 1998, fig. 5
39 Ryl-Preibisz 1997, 229, fig. 1.

For the association of some grills with glazing see pp. 179-80, Chapter 7.
40 Godlewski 1992c
41 Plumley 1970, 132
42 Ryl-Preibisz 1987, figs. 9 and 10. Similar representations are also to be seen on pottery (e.g. W. Y. Adams 1986, I, fig. 160.1; Pluskota 1992) and on a *stela* from Qasr Ibrim (Bellucio 1987/88).
43 Martens-Czarnecka 1986, figs. 1-3
44 Plumley 1970, 131, pls 103-8
45 Godlewski 1987/8, fig. 8
46 Żurawski 1997c, 182, 185, 186, 191
47 Anderson 1999, 74. There is also a pebble mosaic panel in the monastery on Kom H (Chmiel 1998b, 11).
48 W. Y. Adams 1965, 166
49 *OS*, 334
50 Norden 1757, 59
51 Clarke 1912, 92
52 For the artists' techniques see Chmiel 1998; also Martens-Czarnecka 1998, 86.
53 Chmiel 1998, 9
54 Godlewski 1992, 287
55 For fragments of paintings of human and divine figures with ornate robes, from the vault in the church at Arminna West, see Trigger 1967, 12.
56 Godlewski 1992, 287-91
57 Ibid., 281
58 Martens-Czarnecka 1986, figs. 1-3
59 Martens-Czarnecka 1987, 264
60 Martens-Czarnecka, 1992, 308
61 Innemée 1995, 280
62 Jakobielski 1982d, 128
63 Jakobielski 1972, 54; 1982d, 128
64 A detailed discussion of these paintings is to be found in Martens-Czarnecka 1982.
65 Martens-Czarnecka 1987, 262
66 Jakobielski 1982d, 129
67 For a discussion of the stylistic characteristics of the various periods of Nubian wall paintings as recognized at Faras see Martens-Czarnecka 1987, 263-66; Godlewski 1992b, 106ff.
68 Martens-Czarnecka 1986
69 For a detailed discussion of late Nubian art, written before the discovery of the paintings on Kom H at Dongola see Martens-Czarnecka 1992.
70 Among the examples of late art singled out by Martens-Czarnecka are two from the Faras cathedral, the head of Christ, no. 7, and the Madonna Eleusa and child no. 88 (Martens-Czarnecka 1992, figs. 9 and 10).
71 Martens-Czarnecka 1997, 222-3; 1998b, 112. The copying of Byzantine models by the Nubians was the natural result

of it being a Christian state ruled by a Christian monarch, unlike Nubia's Coptic neighbours who were under Muslim rule. 'The combination of ecclesiastical and courtly splendour … must have made Constantinople the ideal example for Nubian kings.' (Innemée 1992b, 183-4).
72 Martens-Czarnecka 1987, 266-7
73 Rostkowska 1982c, 210-11
74 Ibid., 211, fig. 3
75 Griffith 1926b, 63-5
76 Jakobielski 1998, 166
77 Martens-Czarnecka 1998, 85-6
78 Jakobielski 1998, 163
79 Martens-Czarnecka 1997, 220-1; 1998b, 98-100
80 Martens-Czarnecka 1997, 223; 1998, 86, fig. 6
81 Martens-Czarnecka 1998b, 100-2
82 Griffith 1927, pl. LXVI.2. For a very similar design in the church at Bawit in Egypt, see Bourguet 1970, fig. 135.
83 W. Y. Adams 1964, 235; 1999c, 11
84 Godlewski 1982, 26
85 Jakobielski et al. 1993, 303
86 Innemée 1992
87 Martens-Czarnecka 1987, 267-8
88 Godlewski 1992, 290
89 Jakobielski 1982, fig. 12
90 Godlewski 1992, 302-3
91 Grzymski and Anderson 1994, 96-7, pl. IIIa; Jonah, Chapters 3-4
92 Shinnie and Shinnie 1978, 9, pl. XIb
93 *OS*, 472
94 Edwards 1991; Welsby 1998, 177
95 Martens-Czarnecka 1987, 266 with references. For possible Ethiopian influences see Martens-Czarnecka 1999.
96 Godlewski 1992b, 111 with references. See also Innemée 1995, 283ff.
97 Rostkowska 1982, 289
98 For a fine wooden example carved from wood with a representation of a man and a child see W. Y. Adams 1996, 189, pl. 55.
99 Griffith 1913, 14-15
100 Ibid., Taf. II
101 *Sonoj* has tentatively been identified as the Nubian term for *eparch* (Plumley 1978, 241).
102 Rostkowska 1982c, 210
103 W. Y. Adams 1986, 41
104 Ibid., I, 242
105 The distinction between Late Kushite and early post-Meroitic in this area is far from clear as the cultural assemblage from el-Hobagi demonstrates.
106 From Berber – Lenoble 1994b, vol. IV, fig. 5; from Gabati - Smith 1998, fig. 6.28

<T5/92c>; from Meroe – Garstang et al. 1911, pl. XLI.9, XLII.3, XLIV.21, XLV.23-26
107 Lenoble 1994b, vol. IV, figs. 7 and 158; Welsby and Daniels 1991, fig. 127, dec. type 124. Also from the post-Meroitic tomb at el-Fereikha (pers. comm. J. Anderson, Oct. 2000).
108 el-Hobagi – Lenoble 1994b, vol. IV, fig. 7; Soba East - Welsby and Daniels 1991, fig. 131, dec. type. 216; Welsby 1998, fig. 48, type 104.2
109 E.g., from el-Hobagi, Lenoble 1994b, vol. IV, fig. 18; Welsby 1998, 119
110 Welsby 1999, colour plate XXI
111 Pluskota 1990; 1991. Note the similarity of the motifs used on this pottery to some of those seen in an X-Group context, for example, W. Y. Adams 1986, I, fig. 180, motifs 16-2 and 26-1. However, it is clear that the Nobadian X-Group ceramic assemblage does not extend south of the Third Cataract.
112 See Welsby 1998, figs. 74-77.
113 See Welsby 1998, 170; Smith 1998, 185-6.
114 Welsby and Daniels 1991, 324ff., figs. 182-188; Welsby 1998, 170ff., figs. 79-105
115 The frog as a decorative motif is a pagan survival seen particularly on moulded lamps (W. Y. Adams 2000, 86).
116 Cf. Martens-Czarnecka 1982, colour table 1; 1982b, fig. 1 and Welsby 1998, decoration types 1221-23, 1265, 1206, 1207.
117 Welsby 1998, fig. 86
118 W. Y. Adams 1986, I, 42, 245
119 W. Y. Adams 1986, I, 247ff. Edwards has suggested that the colour of the pots and the style of decoration may be significant in the social uses to which those pots were put. He draws attention to the change from later Kushite fine white wares to X-Group and Early Christian fine red wares and a return in the Classic Christian period to fine white wares (1999b, 101).
120 For examples see W. Y. Adams 1986, II, figs. 269K, 281K, 284K.
121 See, for example, Welsby and Daniels 1991, fig. 136, decoration type 549 and fig. 138, decoration types 569 and 571.
122 A few rather crude vessels in the same general style of those in production in the north have been recorded at Soba East. It is possible that these are a local attempt to copy the much finer northern products (cf. Welsby and Daniels 1991, 334-5).
123 For the type see Welsby and

Daniels 1991, fig. 128, dec. types 155-157.
124 For these motifs see Welsby and Daniels 1991, figs. 122-133; Welsby 1998, figs. 58-73.
125 For example, Welsby and Daniels 1991, figs. 122-4, dec. types 1-52; see also figs. 82-4.
126 W. Y. Adams 1986, I, 45
127 W. Y. Adams 1996, 219, 222; Plumley 1982b, 18
128 For a discussion of multilingualism in Nubia see Shinnie 1974.
129 The earliest dated inscription in Old Nubian is of 795 (Jakobielski 1972, 36, fn. 11).
130 For the evidence of a decline in literacy at Qasr Ibrim see W. Y. Adams 1996, 223-4.
131 Jakobielski 1974, 299
132 Hägg 1982b, 104-5
133 Ibid., 106
134 Oates 1963, 171. At Qasr Ibrim Greek, Coptic and Old Nubian were used extensively in the period ninth to eleventh century with Old Nubian and Arabic dominating the linguistic scene from the twelfth to fifteenth centuries (Plumley 1975, 102).
135 Griffith 1928, 134ff.
136 Plumley 1975c, 21. On the late use of Greek in Nubia see W. Y. Adams 1996, 221 with references.
137 Godlewski 1998, 179
138 Łajtar 1997, 116
139 Łajtar 1996, 81
140 Jakobielski 1972, 46
141 In el-Maqrizi *OS*, 614.
142 W. Y. Adams 1996, 220-1
143 Michałowski 1965, 80, 176-8, figs. 48, 94 and 95
144 Shinnie and Shinnie 1978, 98, no. 195
145 Török 1999, fn. 167; Griffith 1913, 71
146 Millet 1974, 54
147 Ibid., 57
148 Griffith 1928, 130-1; W. Y. Adams 1991, 1815
149 W. Y. Adams 1996, 223
150 Jakobielski 1972, 190ff.
151 Pluskota 1997, 236ff.
152 Jakobielski 1991, 276
153 Plumley in Michałowski 1975, 103, 104.
154 Among the skins used was that of the crocodile, two documents written on this material were found in the region of Qurta, see Griffith 1928, 131-2. For a description of scrolls from Qasr Ibrim see Plumley 1978, 233.
155 Plumley 1983, 161
156 W. Y. Adams 1996, 219
157 Browne 1984
158 Jakobielski 1991, 277-279

Chapter 10
1 *OS*, 470ff.
2 El-Mufaddal *OS*, 494; el-Maqrizi *OS*, 648ff. For the

possibility of two King Davids, David I being responsible for the attacks on Aidhab and Aswan in 1272 and David II, his son and successor being the protagonist against the Muslims and Shekanda see Munro-Hay 1982/3, 118.
3 OS, 478ff.
4 OS, 679
5 OS, 558
6 OS, 235
7 Hasan 1967, 25, 28-9
8 El-Nuwayri OS, 472ff.; el-Furat OS, 533; el-Maqrizi OS, 648ff., 680ff.
9 OS, 498
10 OS, 425-6
11 Jorays also appears with el-Barsi, the brother of the Makurian king as a member of an embassy to the sultan in 1292, bearing gifts in an attempt to forestall Egyptian attacks owing to non-payment of the Baqt, a mission which was apparently successful. How these events, recorded by az-Zahir (OS, 430-32), are to be reconciled with those described in the main text is unclear.
12 El-Furat OS, 542ff.
13 El-Wardi, OS, 505; el-Maqrizi OS, 690-1; Ibn Iyas OS, 780
14 According to Ibn Selim emery was used to polish gems (in el-Maqrizi, OS, 604).
15 OS, 780
16 Vantini 1981, 186
17 OS, 691
18 El-Maqrizi OS, 692-3
19 OS, 693-4
20 Crawford, 1951, 35, fn. 23
21 OS, 511. The presence of a caravanserai associated with the mosque is also recorded by el-Maqrizi (OS, 616).
22 OS, 562
23 Griffith 1928, 134ff.
24 Munro-Hay 1982/3, 126; el-Maqrizi OS, 695
25 El-Maqrizi OS, 696-7
26 OS, 698ff.
27 OS, 562, 574
28 O'Fahey and Spaulding 1974, 28

29 Plumley 1978
30 Priese 1984, 489
31 W. Y. Adams 1977, 535. Also noted by Griffith who further suggested that the elements of the name Dongola may be Do-ongo-la = Do in the south? (1928, 134).
32 Millet 1967, 61-2. Unfortunately the excavations conducted at Jebel Adda in the 1960s have yet to be published in detail. It is to be hoped that their full publication will provide much new information on the kingdom of Dotawo.
33 Monneret de Villard 1938, 141
34 Griffith 1913, 64-5
35 Ibid., 166
36 Millet 1967, 62
37 Millet in Adams 1977, 752 fn. 85.
38 Jakobielski 1974, 304; Donadoni 1967, 62-4; Sayce 1910, 266
39 Munro-Hay 1982/3, 115
40 Ibid., 129, fn. 145
41 Anderson suggests that it was likely that the vassal king of Dotawo, and perhaps many of the other kinglets, were related to the royal house of Makuria (pers. comm. Oct. 2000).
42 Godlewski 1982, 22 and fn. 4. The abandonment of the Church of the Granite Columns (Church of the Brick Pillars) was dated to the late thirteenth century by Gartkiewicz (1990, 306) who considered that its use was 'broken off abruptly and unexpectedly' in the face of Arab attacks on the city.
43 Gartkiewicz 1990, 307
44 Godlewski 1990b, 44-5
45 Trigger 1967, 15, 24
46 Welsby and Daniels 1991, 87-8
47 Ibid., 62; Welsby 1998, 47-8
48 Godlewski 1991b, 91
49 El-Maqrizi OS, 650, 681
50 Plumley 1975, 102; 1975b, 23; W. Y. Adams 1996, 77
51 Millet 1964, 10
52 Horton 1991b, 12
53 Millet 1967, 61

54 W. Y. Adams 2000, 7
55 W. Y. Adams 1964, 231-3; 1994. For the presence of castle houses as far south as the Third Cataract see Edwards and Salih 2000, 64-5.
56 W. Y. Adams 1965, 175
57 W. Y. Adams 1964, 241
58 W. Y. Adams 1977, 534
59 Jakobielski 1974, 304
60 W. Y. Adams 1996, 254-5
61 OS, 783
62 Alexander 1994; 1997
63 Suleiman reigned from 1520 until 1566.
64 Plumley 1983, 166-7
65 El-Nuwayri OS, 475
66 Az-Zahir OS, 425-6. Although there is the assumption among modern scholars that el-Abwab in the thirteenth century was no longer a province of the kingdom of Alwa this is nowhere stated by the Arab sources. The king of el-Abwab may have remained one of the kinglets under the control of the Great King of Alwa or el-Abwab may have been used as a term to refer to the whole of Alwa.
67 Az-Zahir OS, 425
68 Az-Zahir OS, 431
69 El-Mufaddal OS, 499
70 Az-Zahir OS, 426, 429
71 El-Qalqashandi OS, 577
72 For a detailed discussion of this issue see Crawford 1951, 143ff.
73 OS, 784
74 OS, 787
75 Hasan 1967b, 133 for references.
76 Note however, that David Reubeni in 1523 travelled for ten days through what he calls the kingdom of Soba. There is a strong oral tradition that the Alwan dynasty fled to the upper Blue Nile, the region around Fazugli, and maintained control for some time (see Spaulding 1974). We have no archaeological evidence to substantiate this.
77 Welsby and Daniels 1991, 34

78 Welsby 1998, 278
79 Welsby and Daniels 1991, 26. These graves can be compared with a number in the cemetery at Gabati which, although of medieval date, do not conform to Christian burial practices; see Edwards 1998, 202.
80 OS, 751

Chapter 11
1 W. Y. Adams 1991b, 1803
2 Ibid., 1803
3 Vantini 1970, 141
4 Plumley 1982b, 20
5 For Salih's suggestion that Christianity may not have been deeply rooted in the Nubian psyche see Salih 1982, 88ff.
6 Barnard 1994, 48
7 Gartkiewicz 1990, 308ff.
8 W. Y. Adams 1999b, 35, for the tomb of the saint Sitt Zuleiha. In the church at Sahaba the shaft and chambered tomb in the centre of the nave was crowned by a cenotaph of Sidi Amir el Sahaba (Säve-Söderbergh 1970, 225). For reuse of tombs see for example Debeira East on the 'island' of Fadrus (ibid., 230).
9 Millet 1964, 10-11
10 Alexander 1999, 55ff.
11 Crowfoot 1927, 143, 149; Kronenberg and Kronenberg 1963, 304; 1964, 285; W. Y. Adams 1991b; Vantini 1982; Kołodziejczyk 1982

Appendix
1 Pers. comm. Adam Lajtar
2 Griffith 1928, 118-28
3 For the possibility of another king of this name succeeding David see Munro-Hay 1982/3, 118
4 For the chronology of these rulers see Plumley 1978.
5 Griffith 1913, 54
6 Plumley 1978

Glossary

angareeb	a traditional bed with wooden frame and webbing of leather strips or rope
architriclinus	an official of uncertain function
ardeb	a dry measure of capacity, in modern Sudan equivalent to 198 litres
baqt	a peace treaty, less formal than a *sulh*
bema	the part of the church reserved for the use of the clergy
buqturiyyah	a type of cloth
caravanserai	a building for the accommodation of caravans
comes	a Latin term used to designate a high military rank
chamfron	an element of horse armour used to protect the nasal area
dalmatica	an over-garment of basically triangular form with sleeves, either flaring or narrowing
diaconicon	the room on the southern side of the sanctuary chamber of a church
doka	a large circular ceramic tray on which *kisra* is cooked over a fire
domesticos	an official of uncertain function; in a Byzantine context he was a palace official or an assistant to a minister, governor or general
dromos	the ramp or stairway leading down into a subterranean tomb
emir	any of various high officials in a Muslim state
eparch	a high-ranking deputy of the Makurian king
esonarthex	the innermost of two rooms running across the western end of a church
exarch	a high civil, military or ecclesiastical official of uncertain function
feddan	a unit of measurement equivalent to 0.42 hectares
fellaheen	the Egyptian peasantry
galligaskins	loose breeches, leggings or gaiters of leather
guffa	a two-handled basket
guilloche	an ornamental band of paired lines flowing in interlaced curves
hafir	a water reservoir
haikal	= *presbyterium*
higab	the screen dividing the *haikal* from the *naos* in a church
hmhm	a type of pharaonic and Kushite crown
hypotyrannos	an official within the Blemmyan administration
iconostasis	a screen on which icons are placed separating the sanctuary from the *naos* in Middle Eastern churches
imperium	supreme authority
intonaco	a very fine plaster
intrados	the underside of a vault
jalous	a particular way of using mud as a building material; the wall is formed

from mud shaped by hand, the mud drying *in situ*, in contrast to mud brick where the mud is formed into bricks in a mould and then sun-dried before use

jellabiya	a loose garment, extending from the neck to the lower leg, of a type still worn by Muslim men in Nubia and elsewhere
jihad	a holy war to spread the teachings of Islam
jir	a whitewash made from mudstone and perhaps also from lime
jizya	a tax levied by the Muslims on non-believers
kamelaukion	a crown of Byzantine type
khor pl. *kheeran*	a seasonal or dry water course
kisra	a type of flat, unleavened, bread
mappa	a handkerchief
mek	a local ruler under the Funj Sultanate
meizonauarchos	'admiral supreme' of the fleet
meizoteros	a court official of uncertain function; in Egypt the term is frequently applied to a village bailiff
minbar	a raised platform in a mosque approached by steps, upon which the imam stands to read from the Koran
motiko(l)	an official of uncertain function
mukhmala	velvet or velvet-like fabric
mu'lama	a type of cloth
mutawalli	a person entrusted or commissioned with something
naos	the part of the church designated for the use of the congregation
narthex	a room running across the western end of a church into which the main entrance of the building opens
nauarchos pl. *nauarchoi*	admiral of the fleet
ness	an official of uncertain function
ostracon pl. *ostraca*	a pottery sherd which has been written upon
paenula	a full-circle cloak with a central neck opening
palindrome	a word or verse reading the same backwards as forwards
paludamentum	a semi-circular or trapezoid-shaped cloak
panneau pl. *panneaux*	panel
pastafories	the rooms to each side of the sanctuary chamber of a church
phylarch	an official of second rank below the Blemmyan king
potentiary	an official of uncertain function
presbyterium	the area formed by the extension of the *bema* into the eastern part of the nave of a Nubian church
primicerius	an official of uncertain function
promeizon	an official of uncertain function
prothesis	the room on the northern side of the sanctuary chamber of a church which may have been used for the preparation of the sacred elements for the liturgy

proteicheisma	a lower defensive wall, sometimes on the inner lip of the ditch in front of the main curtain wall
protodomesticos	a palace official of uncertain function
protomeizoteros	a court official of uncertain function
qabati	a type of cloth
qore	'ruler' in Meroitic, the language of the Kushites
qulla	water jar
qadus pl. *qawadis*	pottery vessel used as part of a *saqia* to lift water
qubba	a domed tomb, particularly of the Islamic period
rakuba	a rectangular structure constructed with a wooden framework to which reeds or matting are attached
rinceau	a scroll pattern
saqia	a water-lifting device driven by animal power
schoinos pl. *schoinoi*	Greek unit of measurement equalling 7.862 km
seluka	the land which is inundated by the flood along the Nile banks and on the islands
shaduf	a counterweighted pole used to lift water and also as a crane
silentiary	a palace chamberlain, a court official
sulh	a formal treaty
talus	an elongated dice, a type used in a number of Greek and Roman games
tetrarchos	a ruler of lower status than a king
tibn	chopped straw
tot	an official of uncertain function
tribune	the seating, usually of concentric semi-circular form, in the apse of a church
tricliniaris	an official of uncertain function
tukl	term frequently used to describe a circular hut with a timber frame to which reeds or matting are attached
uraeus pl. *uraei*	an insignia of the Egyptian pharaoh and of the Kushite rulers, in the form of a rearing cobra
wadi	a seasonal or dry water course, larger than a *khor*
wali	a prince or governor
xenon	an institution of Byzantine origin which was a combination of a hospice and a hospital where the efficacy of the treatment was assisted by its proximity to the burials of Holy Men

Bibliography

Abbreviations

AAASH	*Acta Archaeologica Academiae Scientiarum Hungaricae.* Budapest
ANM	*Archéologie du Nil Moyen.* Lille
BzS	*Beiträge zur Sudanforschung.* Wein-Mödling
CRIPEL	*Cahier de Recherches de l'Institut de Papyrologie et d'Égyptologie de Lille.* Lille
GAMAR	*Gdańsk Archaeological Museum African Reports.* Gdańsk
JARCE	*Journal of the American Research Centre in Cairo.* Cairo
JEA	*Journal of Egyptian Archaeology.* London
JNES	*Journal of Near Eastern Archaeology.* Chicago
LAAA	*Liverpool Annals of Archaeology and Anthropology.* Liverpool
MNL	*Meroitic Newsletter.* Paris
PAM	*Polish Archaeology in the Mediterranean.* Warsaw
SARSN	*The Sudan Archaeological Research Society Newsletter.* London
SNR	*Sudan Notes and Records.* Khartoum
WZHU	*Wissenschaftliche Zeitschrift der Humboldt-Universität zu Berlin.* Berlin
ZÄS	*Zeitschrift für Ägyptische Sprache und Altertumskunde.* Berlin

Bibliography

Abdalla, A.M. (ed.) 1974. *Studies in Ancient Languages of the Sudan.* Khartoum.

Adams, N.K. 1981. 'Textile Finds at Qasr Ibrim', *Nyama Akuma* 18, 6-8.

Adams, N.K. 1986. 'Textiles at Qasr Ibrim: an Introductory Quantitative Study', *WZHU* 35.1, 21-6.

Adams, N.K. 1996. 'Textile Materials and Weaves', in Adams 1996, 160-70.

Adams, N.K. 1999. 'The Grave Goods', in Adams *et al.*, 51-71.

Adams, W.Y. 1964. 'Sudanese Antiquities Service Excavations in Nubia: Fourth Season, 1962-63', *Kush* 12, 216-49.

Adams, W.Y. 1965. 'Sudanese Antiquities Service Excavations at Meinarti, 1963-64', *Kush* 13, 148-76.

Adams, W.Y. 1965b. 'Architectural Evolution of the Nubian Church, 500-1400 A.D', *JARCE* 4, 87-139.

Adams, W.Y. 1965c. 'Post-Pharaonic Nubia in the Light of Archaeology. II', *JEA* 51, 160-78.

Adams, W.Y. 1966. 'The Vintage of Nubia', *Kush* 14, 262-83.

Adams, W.Y. 1968. 'Settlement Pattern in Microcosm: The Changing Aspect of a Nubian Village during Twelve Centuries', in Chang (ed.), 174-207.

Adams, W.Y. 1977. *Nubia: Corridor to Africa.* London, Princeton.

Adams, W.Y. 1986. *Ceramic Industries of Medieval Nubia.* Lexington.

Adams, W.Y. 1987. 'Islamic Archaeology in Nubia: An Introductory Survey', in Hägg (ed.), 327-61.

Adams, W.Y. 1991. 'Nubian Languages and Literature', in Atiya (ed.), 1815-16.

Adams, W.Y. 1991b. 'Islamization of Nubia', in Atiya (ed.), 1802-4.

Adams, W.Y. 1992. 'Nubian Church Architecture and Nubian Church Decoration', in Bonnet (ed.), 317-26.

Adams, W.Y. 1994. 'Castle-houses of Late Medieval Nubia', *ANM* 6, 11-46.

Adams, W.Y. 1994b. *Kulubnarti I. The Architectural Remains.* Lexington.

Adams, W.Y. 1996. *Qasr Ibrim. The Late Mediaeval Period.* London.

Adams, W.Y. 1998. 'Towards a Comparative Study of Christian Nubian Burial Practices', *ANM* 8, 13-41.

Adams, W.Y. 1999. 'Introduction', in Adams *et al.*, 1-6.

Adams, W.Y. 1999b. 'The Graves', in Adams *et al.*, 7-50.

Adams, W.Y. 1999c. 'The Murals of Meinarti', *Nubica* IV/V, 3-14.

Adams, W.Y. 2000. *Meinarti I. The Late Meroitic, Ballaña and Transitional Occupation.* London.

Adams, W.Y. 2001. *Meinarti II. The Early and Classic Christian Phases.* London.

Adams, W.Y. and H.-Å. Nordström 1963. 'The Archaeological Survey of the West Bank of the Nile: Third Season, 1961-62', *Kush* 11, 10-46.

Adams, W.Y., N.K. Adams, D.P. Van Gerven and D.L. Greene 1999. *Kulubnarti III. The Cemeteries.* London.

Addison, F. 1951. 'Saqadi' in O.G.S. Crawford and F. Addison. *The Wellcome Excavations in the Sudan, Volume III.* London, New York, Toronto, 111-41, pls LXIII - LXXIV.

Alexander, J.A. 1994. 'Islamic Archaeology: The Ottoman Frontier on the Middle Nile', *SARSN* 7, 20-6.

Alexander, J.A. 1997. 'Qalat Sai, the most Southerly Ottoman Fortress in Africa', *Sudan & Nubia* 1, 16-19.

Alexander, J.A. 1999. 'A New Hilltop Cemetery and Temple of the Meroitic and Post-Meroitic Period at Qasr Ibrim', *Sudan & Nubia* 3, 47-59.

Allan, W.N. and R.J. Smith 1948. 'Irrigation in the Sudan', in Tothill (ed.), 593-631.

Allason-Jones, L. 1991. 'Small objects from the western end of mound B', in Welsby and Daniels 1991, 126-62.

Allason-Jones, L. 1998. 'The small objects', in Welsby 1998, 60-81.

Anderson, J.R. 1994. 'House C-One at Hambukol (Upper Nubia)', in Bonnet (ed.). *Études Nubiennes* II. Geneva, 225-228.

Anderson, J.R. 1997. 'Excavations at the North Kom, Hambukol (Upper Nubia)', *CRIPEL* 17/2, 169-74.

Anderson, J.R. 1998. 'The Graffiti', in Welsby (ed.), 185-209.

Anderson, J.R. 1999. 'Monastic Lifestyles of the Nubian Desert: Seeking the Mysterious Monks of Makuria', *Sudan & Nubia* 3, 71-83.

Anderson, J.R. and S.M. Ahmed (forth.), 'Archaeological Reconnaissance in the Berber-Abidiya Region, 1997. A Post-Meroitic Double-Shaft Tomb in El-Fereikha', *ANM* 9.

Arkell, A.J. 1936. 'Darfur Antiquities', *SNR* 19, 301-11.

Arkell, A.J. 1951. 'An Old Nubian inscription from Kordofan', *AJA* 55, 353-4.

Arkell, A.J. 1953. *Shaheinab. An Account of the Excavation of a Neolithic Occupation Site carried out for the Sudan Antiquities Service in 1949-50.* Oxford.

Arkell, A.J. 1959. 'A Christian Church and Monastery at Ain Farah, Darfur', *Kush* 7, 115-19.

Arkell, A.J. 1961. *A History of the Sudan to 1821.* 2nd edn, London.

Arkell, A.J. 1963. 'The Influence of Christian Nubia in the Chad area between A.D. 800-1200', *Kush* 11, 315-19.

Armelagos, G.J. 1977. 'Disease in Ancient Nubia', in D. Landy (ed.). *Culture, Disease and Healing. Studies in Medical Anthropology.* New York, London, 77-83.

Atiya, A.S. (ed.) 1991. *The Coptic Encyclopedia.* New York, Oxford, Toronto, Singapore, Sidney.

Bacon, G.H. 1948. 'Crops of the Sudan', in Tothill (ed.), 302-400.

Balfour Paul, H.G. 1952. 'Early Cultures on the Northern Blue Nile', *SNR* 33, 202-14.

Barkóczi, L. and Á. Salamon 1974. 'Abdullah Nirqi 1964. Archaeological Investigation of the Settlement Town "A"', *AAASH* 26, 289-336.

Barnard, H. 1994. 'A Description of Three Graves at Qasr Ibrim', *ANM* 6, 47-64.

Bates, O. and D. Dunham 1927. 'Excavations at Gammai', *Harvard African Studies* 8, 1-122.

Bechhaus-Gerst, M. 1991. 'Noba Puzzles: Miscellaneous Notes on the Ezana Inscriptions', in D. von Mendel and U. Claudi (eds), *Ägypten im Afro-Orientalischen Kontext.* Köln, 17-25.

Behrens, P. 1986. 'The "Noba" of Nubia and the "Noba" of the Ezana inscription: a matter of confusion (Part I)', *Afrikanistische Arbeitspapiere* 8, 117-26.

Belluccio, A. 1987/88. 'Le Phénnix dans la Nubie chrétiènne', *Nubica* I/II, 475-97.

Bergman, I. 1975. *Late Nubian Textiles.* Scandinavian Joint Expedition 8, Stockholm.

Bernhard, M.-L. (ed.) 1966. *Melanges offerts à K. Michalowski.* Warszawa.

Beshir, B.I. 1975. 'New Light on Nubian Fatimid Relations', *Arabica* 22, 15-24.

Bietak, M. and M. Schwarz 1987. *Nag' el-Scheima. Eine Befestigte Christliche Siedlung und andere Christliche Denkmäler in Sayala — Nubien.* Wien.

Blackman, W.S. 1927. *The Fellahin of Upper Egypt.* London.

Blanton, R. 1981. 'The Rise of Cities', in J. Sabloff (ed.), *Supplement to the Handbook of Middle American Indians, I: Archaeology.* Austin, 392-400.

Blockley, R.C. 1985. 'Subsidies and Diplomacy', *Phoenix* 39, 62-74.

Bonnet, C. 1982. 'Les Fouilles Archeologiques de Kerma (Soudan). Rapport préliminaire des campagnes de 1980-1981 et de 1981-1982', *Genava* 30, 29-53.

Bonnet, C. 1991. 'Les Fouilles Archéologiques de Kerma (Soudan). Rapport préliminaire sur les campagnes de 1988-1989, de 1989-90 et de 1990-1991', *Genava* n.s. 31, 5-20.

Bonnet, C. (ed.) 1992. *Études Nubiennes.* I. Geneva.

Bonnet, C. (ed.) 1994. *Études Nubiennes.* II. Geneva.

Bosticco, S., E. Bresciani, I. Baldassarre, S. Donadoni and A. Roveri 1967. *Tamit (1964).* Rome.

Bradley, R.J. 1984. 'Meroitic Chronology', *Meroitica* 7, 195-211.

Browne, G.M. 1984. 'Notes on Old Nubian Texts', *Sudan Texts Bulletin* 6, 26-36.

Browne, G.M. 1991. *Old Nubian Texts from Qasr Ibrīm III.* London.

Bruce, J. 1790. *Travels between the Years 1765 and 1773 through Part of Africa, Syria, Egypt, and Arabia, into Abyssinia, to Discover the Source of the Nile.* Edinburgh.

Budge, E.A.W. 1907. *The Egyptian Sudan.* London.

Budge, E.A.W. 1915. *Miscellaneous Coptic Texts in the Dialect of Upper Egypt.* London.

Burckhardt, J.L. 1819. *Travels in Nubia.* London.

Butzer, K.W. 1976. *Early Hydraulic Civilization in Egypt: A Study of the Cultural Ecology.* Chicago.

Caneva, I. (ed.) 1988. *El Geili: the history of a Middle Nile environment, 7000 B.C. - A.D. 1500.* British Archaeological Reports, Int. Ser. S424, Oxford.

Cartwright, C. 1998. 'The wood, charcoal, plant remains and other organic material', in Welsby 1998, 255-68.

Chaix, L. 1998. 'The Fauna', in Welsby 1998, 233-55.

Chang, K.-C. (ed.) 1968. *Settlement Archaeology.* Palo Alto.

Chittick, H.N. 1955. 'An Exploratory Journey in the Bayuda Region', *Kush* 3, 86-92.

Chittick, H.N. 1957. 'Antiquities of the Batn el Hajjar', *Kush* 5, 42-8.

Chittick, H.N. 1982. 'Ethiopia and the Nile Valley', *Meroitica* 6, 50-5.

Chmiel, W. 1998. 'The Medieval Masters of Christian Nubia', *GAMAR* 1, 5-9.

Chmiel, W. 1998b. 'Field Conservation of a Nubian Monastery', *GAMAR* 1, 11-15.

Christides, V. 1992. 'Nubia and Egypt from the Arab Invasion of Egypt until the End of the Umayyads', in Bonnet (ed.), 341-56.

Clarke, S. 1912. *Christian Antiquities in the Nile Valley.* Oxford.

Connah, G. 1989. *African Civilisations: Precolonial Cities and States in Tropical Africa, an Archaeological Perspective.* Cambridge.

Corkill, N. L. 1948. 'Nutrition in the Sudan', in Tothill (ed.), 248-62.

Crawford, O.G.S. 1947. 'Christian Nubia: a Review', *Antiquity* 21, 10-15.

Crawford, O.G.S. 1951. *The Fung Kingdom of Sennar.* Gloucester.

Crawford, O.G.S. 1953. *Castles and Churches in the Middle Nile Region.* Sudan Antiquities Service Occasional Papers no. 2, Khartoum.

Crawford, O.G.S. and F. Addison 1951. *Abu Geili, Saqadi and Dar el Mek.* Oxford.

Crowfoot, E. 1977. 'The Clothing of a Fourteenth-Century Nubian Bishop', in V. Gervers (ed.), *Studies in Textile History.* Toronto, 43-51.

Crowfoot, J.W. 1920. 'Notes. Dongola Province', *SNR* 3, 293.

Crowfoot, J.W. 1927. 'Christian Nubia', *JEA* 13, 141-50.

Crowfoot, J.W. 1941. *Early Churches in Palestine.* London.

Cuoq, J. 1986. *Islamisation de la Nubie Chretienne. VIIe-XVIe siècles.* Paris.

Curto, S., V. Maragioglio, C. Rinaldi and L. Bongrani 1965. *Kalabsha.* Roma.

Davies, W.V. (ed.) 1991. *Egypt and Africa. Nubia from Prehistory to Islam.* London.

Davies, W.V. and I. Welsby Sjöström 1998. 'New Fieldwork at Kurgus', *Sudan & Nubia* 2, 26-9.

Deichmann, F.W. and P. Grossmann 1988. *Nubische Forschungen.* Berlin.

Dinkler, E. (ed.) 1970. *Kunst und Geschichte Nubiens in Christlicher Zeit.* Reckinghausen.

Dinkler, E. 1970b. 'Die Deutschen Ausgrabungen auf den Inseln Sunnarti, Tangur und in Kulb 1968-69', in Dinkler (ed.), 259-79.

Dinkler, E. 1975. 'Beobachtungen zur Ikonographie des Kreuzes in der nubischen Kunst', in Michałowski (ed.), 22-30.

Dobrowolski, J. 1987. 'On a Recently Discovered Church at Old Dongola', *Nubian Letters* 9, 1-6.

Dobrowolski, J. 1991. 'The First Church at Site "D" in Old Dongola (Sudan)', *ANM* 5, 29-40.

Donadoni, S. 1959. 'Un epigrafe Greco-Nubiana da Ikhmindi', *Rivista di Studi Antichi, La parola del passato* 69, 458-65.

Donadoni, S. 1967. 'Le iscrizioni', in Bosticco *et al.,* 61-74.

Donadoni, S. 1969. 'Les débuts du Christianisme en Nubie', *Mémoires de l'Institut d'Égypte* 59, 25-33.

Donadoni, S. 1997. 'A Survey North of the Fourth Cataract', *Mitteilungen der Sudanarchäologischen Gesellschaft zu Berlin E.V.* 7, 10-22.

Driskell, B. N., N. K. Adams and P. G. French 1989. 'A Newly Discovered Temple at Qasr Ibrim. Preliminary Report', *ANM* 3, 11-54.

Dunham, D. 1955. *The Royal Cemeteries of Kush. Volume II. Nuri.* Boston, Mass.

Dunham, D. 1963. *The Royal Cemeteries of Kush. Volume IV. Royal Tombs at Meroë and Barkal.* Boston, Mass.

Dunham, D. 1970. *The Barkal Temples.* Boston, Mass.

Dzierżykray-Rogalski, T. 1985. *Faras VIII. The Bishops of Faras, an Anthropological-Medical Study.* Warszawa.

Dzierżykray-Rogalski, T. and S. Jakobielski 1975. 'La Tombe de l'Éparque Yoannès dans l'église a Colonnes en Granit de Dongola (Soudan)', in Michałowski (ed.), 44-8.

Dzierżykray-Rogalski, T. and E. Promińska 1978. 'Tombeaux de deux dignitaires chrétiens dans l'église cruciforme de Dongola', in *Études Nubiennes,* 91-4.

Edmonds, J.M. 1940. 'A Ruin in the Wadi El Qasr', *SNR*

23.1, 161-7.

Edwards, D.N. 1991. 'Three Cemetery Sites on the Blue Nile', *ANM* 5, 41-64.

Edwards, D.N. 1994. 'Post-Meroitic ('X-Group') and Christian burials at Sesibi, Sudanese Nubia. The excavations of 1937', *JEA* 80, 159-78.

Edwards, D.N. 1996. *The Archaeology of the Meroitic State. New Perspectives on its Social and Political Organisation.* BAR Int. Ser. 640, Oxford.

Edwards, D.N. 1996b. 'Sorghum, Beer and Kushite Society', *Norwegian Archaeological Review* 29.2, 65-77.

Edwards, D.N. 1998. *Gabati. A Meroitic, Post-Meroitic and Medieval Cemetery in Central Sudan. Vol. 1.* London.

Edwards, D.N. 1999. *A Meroitic Pottery Workshop at Musawwarat es Sufra.* Meroitica 17.2. Berlin.

Edwards, D.N. 1999b. 'Christianity and Islam in the Middle Nile: towards a study of religion and social change in the long term', in T. Insoll (ed.), *Case Studies in Archaeology and World Religions.* British Archaeological Reports, Int. Ser. 755, Oxford, 94-104.

Edwards, D.N. 2001. 'The Christianisation of Nubia: some archaeological pointers', *Sudan & Nubia* 5, 89-96.

Edwards, D.N. and Ali Osman M. Salih 1994. *The Mahas Survey 1990. Interim Report and Site Inventory.* Mahas Survey Reports No. 2, Cambridge.

Edwards, D.N. and Ali Osman M. Salih 2000. 'The Archaeology of Arduan Island – the Mahas Survey 2000', *Sudan & Nubia* 4, 58-70.

Eide, T., T. Hägg, R.H. Pierce and L. Török (eds) 1998. *Fontes Historiae Nubiorum. Textual sources for the history of the Middle Nile Region between the eighth century BC and the sixth century AD. Volume III From the first to the sixth century AD.* Bergen.

Eisa, Khider A. and D.A. Welsby 1996. 'A Soba Ware Vessel from the Upper Blue Nile', *BzS* 6, 133-36.

El-Amin, Yousif M. and D.N. Edwards 2000. 'Archaeological Survey in the Fifth Cataract Region', *Sudan & Nubia* 4, 44-50.

Emery, W.B. 1965. *Egypt in Nubia.* London.

Emery, W.B. and L.P. Kirwan 1938. *The Royal Tombs of Ballana and Qustul.* Service des Antiquités de L'Égypte, Cairo.

Et-Tayeb, Mahmoud 1999. 'Rescue Excavations at El Sabeil (Soba West)', *Meroitica* 15, 604-15.

Études Nubiennes 1978. *Études Nubiennes. Colloque de Chantilly, 2-6 Juillet 1975.* Cairo.

Fanfoni, G. 1979. *Sonqi Tino I. L'Architettura della Chiesa.* Roma.

Fattovich, R. 1982. 'The Problem of Sudanese-Ethiopian Contacts in Antiquity: Status Quaestionis and Current Trends in Research', in Plumley (ed.), 76-86.

Fattovich, R. 1984. 'Possible Christian Remains in the Gash Delta, Kassala Province (Sudan)', *Annali dell'Istituto Universitario Orientale* 44, 399-406.

Fattovich, R. 1987. 'Remarks on the peopling of the Northern Ethiopian-Sudanese Borderlands in ancient historical times', in *Studi in onore di Ugo Monneret de Villard (1881-1954). Rivista degli Studi Orientali* 58, 85-106.

FHN - see Eide, T., T. Hägg, R.H. Pierce and L. Török (eds) 1998.

Filer, J. 1998. 'The skeletal remains', in Welsby, 213-32.

Filer, J. 2001. 'The Moving Story of Nubian Burials', *Ancient Egypt,* 2.2, 26-31.

Frend, W.H.C. 1991. 'Nubian Liturgy', in Atiya (ed.), 1816-7.

Fuller, D.Q 1999. 'A Parochial Perspective on the End of

Meroe: Changes in Cemetery and Settlement at Arminna West', in Welsby (ed.), 203-18.

Gardberg, C.J. 1970. *Late Nubian Sites. Churches and Settlements.* Scandinavian Joint Expedition 7, Stockholm.

Garstang, J., A.H. Sayce and F.Ll. Griffith 1911. *Meroe: City of the Ethiopians.* Oxford.

Gartkiewicz, P.M. 1975. 'The central plan in Nubian church architecture', in Michałowski (ed.) 49-64.

Gartkiewicz, P.M. 1980. 'New Outline of the History of Nubian Church Architecture', *Babesch* 55.1, 137-60.

Gartkiewicz, P.M. 1982. 'An Introduction to the History of Nubian Church Architecture', in Jakobielski 1982b, 43-133.

Gartkiewicz, P.M. 1982b. 'New Outline of the History of Nubian Church Architecture', in Van Moorsel (ed.), 9-10.

Gartkiewicz, P.M. 1982c. 'Remarks on the Cathedral at Qasr Ibrim', in Plumley (ed.), 87-94.

Gartkiewicz, P.M. 1986. 'Cathedral in Faras in the light of an architectural re-analysis', in Krause (ed.), 245-79.

Gartkiewicz, P.M. 1987. 'Nubian Church Architecture: Unity or Distinctness?', in Hägg (ed.), 237-45.

Gartkiewicz, P.M. 1990. *The Cathedral in Old Dongola. and its Antecedents. Nubia I. Dongola 2.* Warsaw.

Geus, F. 1991. 'Burial Customs in the Upper Main Nile: An Overview', in Davies (ed.), 57-73.

Geus, F., Y. Lecointe and B. Maureille 1995. 'Tombes napatéennes, méroïtiques et médiévales de la nécropole Nord de l'île de Saï, rapport préliminaire de la campagne 1994-1995 (archéologie et anthropologie)', *ANM* 7, 99-141.

Gillam, J.P. 1976. 'Coarse Fumed Ware in North Britain and Beyond', *Glasgow Archaeological Journal* 4, 57-80.

Gillam, J.P., I.M. Jobey and D.A. Welsby 1993. *The Roman Bath-house at Bewcastle, Cumbria.* Kendal.

Gleichen, A.E.W. 1905. *The Anglo-Egyptian Sudan.* Vol. 1. London.

Glidden, H. 1954. 'The Khor Nubt Tombstones. The earliest dated Arab Remains in the Sudan', *Kush* 2, 63-5.

Glubb, J. B. 1978. *A short history of the Arab peoples.* London, Melbourne, New York.

Godlewski, W. 1979. *Faras VI. Les Baptistères Nubiens.* Warszawa.

Godlewski, W. 1982. 'The Mosque Building in Old Dongola', in Van Moorsel (ed.), 21-8.

Godlewski, W. 1982b. 'Le baptistère de l'église dans le temple de Mandulis à Kalabsha', in Jakobielski (ed.), 134-41.

Godlewski, W. 1987/88. 'The Cruciform Church site in Old Dongola. Sequence of buildings from 6th to 18th century', *Nubica* I/II, 511-34.

Godlewski, W. (ed.) 1990. *Coptic Studies.* Varsovie.

Godlewski, W. 1990b. 'The Northern Church in Old Dongola', *ANM* 4, 37-62.

Godlewski, W. 1990c. 'The Cruciform Church at Old Dongola (Sudan). Some Comments', in Godlewski (ed.), 127-37.

Godlewski, W. (ed.) 1991. *Coptic and Nubian Pottery. Part II.* Warsaw.

Godlewski, W. 1991b. 'Old Dongola 1988-1989 House PCH.1', *ANM* 5, 79-101.

Godlewski, W. 1991c. 'The Fortifications of Old Dongola. Report on the 1990 Season', *ANM* 5, 103-27.

Godlewski, W. 1992. 'The Early Period of Nubian Art', in Bonnet (ed.), 277-305.

Godlewski, W. 1992b. 'Some remarks on the Faras cathedral and its paintings', *Journal of Coptic Studies* 2, 99-116.

Godlewski, W. 1992c. 'La frise de l'abside de la Première Cathédrale de Pachoras (Faras)', in Scholz (ed.), 327-56.

Godlewski, W. 1997. 'Old Dongola. Kom A (1996)', *PAM* 8, 179-87.

Godlewski, W. 1997b. 'Old Dongola. The Early Fortifications', *CRIPEL* 17/2, 175-9.

Godlewski, W. 1998. 'Old Dongola. Excavations 1997 - Kom A', *PAM* 9, 171-9.

Godlewski, W. (forth.). 'The Rise of Makuria (late 5th – 8th century)', Proc. 9th Int. Conference for Nubian Studies, Boston 1998.

Godlewski, W. and S. Medeksza 1987. 'The So-called Mosque Building in Old Dongola (Sudan). A Structural Analysis', *ANM* 2, 185-205.

Gratien, B. 1993. 'Nouvelles empreintes de sceaux à Kerma: Aperçus sur l'administration de Kouch au milieu du 2e millénaire av. J.-C.', *Genava* 41, 27-32.

Griffith, F.Ll. 1913. *The Nubian Texts of the Christian Period.* Berlin.

Griffith, F.Ll. 1924. 'Oxford Excavations in Nubia', *LAAA* 11, nos 3-4, 115-80.

Griffith, F.Ll. 1926. 'Oxford Excavations in Nubia', *LAAA* 13, nos 1-2, 17-37.

Griffith, F.Ll. 1926b. 'Oxford Excavations in Nubia', *LAAA* 13, nos 3-4, 49-93.

Griffith, F.Ll. 1927. 'Oxford Excavations in Nubia', *LAAA* 14, 57-116.

Griffith, F.Ll. 1928. 'Christian Documents from Nubia', *Proc. British Academy* 14, 117-46.

Grossmann, P. 1985. 'Typological Problems of the Nubian Four-Pillar Churches', *Nubian Letters* 4, 23-5.

Grossmann, P. 1987. 'Die Kirche des Bischofs Theodorus im Isistempel von Philae. Versuch einer Rekonstruktion', in *Studi in onore di Ugo Monneret de Villard (1881-1954). Rivista degli Studi Orientali* 58, 107-111.

Grossmann, P. 1990. 'Typologische Probleme der Nubischen Vierstutzenbauten', in Godlewski (ed.), 151-60.

Grzymski, K. 1987. *Archaeological Reconnaissance in Upper Nubia.* Toronto.

Grzymski, K. 1989. 'Trial Excavations at Hambukol and Bukibul', *ANM* 3, 71-91.

Grzymski, K. 1990. 'Excavations at Hambukol (Upper Nubia): 1987 and 1988 Seasons', *JARCE* 27, 139-63.

Grzymski, K. 1993. 'Canadian Excavations at Hambukol, October December 1988', *Kush* 16, 169-76.

Grzymski, K., and J. R. Anderson 1994. 'Three excavation seasons at Hambukol (Dongola Reach): 1989, 1990 and 1991-92', *ANM* 6, 103-18.

Gundlach, R., M. Kropp and A. Leibundgut (Hrsg.) 1996. *Der Sudan in Vergangenheit und Gegenwart.* Frankfurt-am-Main.

Hägg, T. 1982. 'Two Christian Epitaphs in Greek of the "Euchologion Mega" Type', in Säve-Söderbergh (ed.), 55-62.

Hägg, T. 1982b. 'Some remarks on the use of Greek in Nubia', in Plumley (ed.), 103-7.

Hägg, T. (ed.) 1987. *Nubian Culture, Past and Present.* Stockholm.

Hägg, T. 1990. 'Titles and Honorific Epithets in Nubian

Greek Texts', *Symbolae Osloenses* 65, 147-77.

Hägg, T. 1993. 'Magic Bowls Inscribed with an Apostles-and-Disciples Catalogue from the Christian Settlement of Hambukol (Upper Nubia)', *Orientalia* 64, fasc. 4, 376-99.

Hägg, T. 1998. 'Greek in Upper Nubia: An Assessment of the New Material', *CRIPEL* 17.3, 113-19.Hajnóczi, G. 1974. 'Abdullah Nirqi 1964. Architectural Characteristics of the Settlement and Buildings', *AAASH* 26, 339-68.

Hajnóczi, G. 1974. 'Abdullah Nirqi 1964. Architectural Characteristics of the Settlement and Buildings', *AAASH* 26, 339-68.

Hakem, A.M.A. 1979. 'University of Khartoum Excavations at Sururab and Bauda, North of Omdurman', *Meroitica* 5, 151-56.

Harden, D.B. 1978. 'Glass', in Shinnie and Shinnie 1978, 83-94.

Harrell, J. 1999. 'Ancient Stone Quarries at the Third and Fourth Nile Cataracts, Northern Sudan', *Sudan & Nubia* 3, 21-7.

Hasan, Y.F. 1967. 'Main Aspects of Arab Migration to the Sudan', *Arabica* 14, 14-31.

Hasan, Y.F. 1967b. *The Arabs and the Sudan*. Edinburgh.

Heidorn, L. 1997. 'The Horses of Kush', *JNES* 56.2, 106-14.

Henneker, F. 1823. *Notes During a Visit to Egypt, Nubia, the Oases, Mount Sinai and Jerusalem*. London.

Hinkel, F.W. 1979. *Archaeological Map of the Sudan II. The Area of the South Libyan Desert*. Berlin.

Hintze, F. 1959. 'Preliminary Report on the Butana Expedition, 1958, *Kush* 7, 171-196.

Hintze, F. 1962. 'Preliminary Report on the Excavations at Musawwarat', *Kush* 10, 170-202.

Hintze, F. 1963. 'Musawwarat es Sufra: Preliminary Report on the Excavations of the Institute of Egyptology, Humboldt University, Berlin, 1961-62 (Third Season)', *Kush* 11, 217-26.

Hintze, F. 1967-8. 'Musawwarat es Sufra: Report on the Excavations of the Institute of Egyptology, Humboldt University, Berlin, 1963-1966', *Kush* 15, 283-98.

Hirschfeld, Y. 1992. *The Judean Desert Monasteries in the Byzantine Period*. New Haven and London.

Horton, M. 1991. 'Africa in Egypt: New Evidence from Qasr Ibrim', in Davies (ed.), 264-77.

Horton, M. 1991b. 'First Christians at Qasr Ibrim', *Egyptian Archaeology* 1, 9-12.

Hrbek, I. 1977. 'Egypt, Nubia and the Eastern Desert', in *Cambridge History of Africa* Vol. 3, Cambridge.

Hughes, G.R. 1963. 'Serra East. The University of Chicago Excavations, 1961-62. A preliminary report on the first season's work', *Kush* 11, 121-30.

Idzikowska, B. 1983. 'La Decoration En Pierre Des Portes Dans Les Eglises Et Edifices Profanes De Faras', *Études Et Travaux* 12, 195-237.

Innemée, K.C. 1990. 'Relationships between Episcopal and Monastic Vestments in Nubian Wall-painting', in Godlewski (ed.), 161-63.

Innemée, K.C. 1992. 'A Wall-painting in the former Throne-Hall of Dongola', *Études et Travaux* 16, 22-28.

Innemée, K.C. 1992b. *Ecclesiastical Dress in the Medieval Near East*. Leiden.

Innemée, K.C. 1995. 'Observations on the system of Nubian church decoration', *CRIPEL* 17.1, 279-88.

Insoll, T. and T. Shaw. 'Gao and Igbo-Ukwu: Beads, Interregional; Trade, and Beyond', *African Archaeological Review* 14.1, 9-23.

Jackson, H.C. 1926. 'A Trek in Abu Hamed District', *SNR* 9, 1-36.

Jacquet-Gordon, H. and C. Bonnet 1971-72. 'Tombs of the Tanqasi Culture at Tabo', *JARCE* 9, 77-86.

Jakobielski, S. 1972. *Faras III. A History of the Bishopric of Pachoras*. Warszawa.

Jakobielski, S. 1974. 'Inscriptions', in Michałowskii 1974, 279-309.

Jakobielski, S. 1975. 'Polish Excavations at Old Dongola, 1970-1972', in Michałowskii (ed.), 70-5.

Jakobielski, S. 1978. 'Polish Excavations at Old Dongola, 1973-1974', *Études Nubiennes* 129-40.

Jakobielski, S. 1978b. 'Inscriptions from Faras and the Problems of Chronology of the Murals', *Études Nubiennes* 141-51.

Jakobielski, S. 1979. 'Dongola, 1976', *Études et Travaux* 11, 229-44.

Jakobielski, S. 1982. 'The Churches of Old Dongola', in Van Moorsel (ed.), 51-6.

Jakobielski, S. (ed.) 1982b. *Nubia Christiana*. Warszawa.

Jakobielski, S. 1982c. 'Remarques sur la Chronologie des Peintures Murales de Faras aux VIIIe et IXe Siècles', in Jakobielski (ed.), 142-72.

Jakobielski, S. 1982d. 'Portraits of the Bishops of Faras', in Plumley (ed.), 127-41.

Jakobielski, S. 1986. 'Polish Excavations at Old Dongola, 1978/79 – 1982', in Krause (ed.), 299-304.

Jakobielski, S. 1987. 'North and South in Christian Nubian Culture: Archaeology and History', in Hägg (ed.), 231-5.

Jakobielski, S. 1991. 'The inscriptions, ostraca and graffiti', in Welsby and Daniels, 274-96.

Jakobielski, S. 1997. 'Old Dongola. Kom H, Site NW', *PAM* 8, 161-8.

Jakobielski, S. 1998. 'Old Dongola. Kom H', *PAM* 9, 160-9.

Jakobielski, S. 1998b. 'The Monastery in Old Dongola: Excavations of the Western Annex 1995-1997', *GAMAR* 1, 55-61.

Jakobielski, S. 1999. 'Old Dongola: Excavations, 1998', *PAM* 10, 137-47.

Jakobielski, S. and S. Medeksza 1990. 'The North-West Church at Old Dongola', in Godlewski (ed.), 165-74.

Jakobielski, S. and A. Ostrasz 1967-68. 'Polish Excavations at Old Dongola. Second Season-December 1965-February 1966', *Kush* 15, 125-42.

Jakobielski, S., K. Pluskota and B. Żurawski 1993. 'Polish Excavations at Old Dongola, Twenty Fifth Season, 1991/92', *Kush* 16, 288-333.

Jeuté, P. 1994. 'Monasteries in Nubia – An Open Issue', *Nubica* III/I, 59-97.

Johnson, S. 1983. *Late Roman Fortifications*. London.

Junker, H. 1925. 'Die christlichen Grabsteine Nubiens', *ZÄS* 60, 111-48.

Junker, H. 1925b. *Ermenne. Bericht über die Grabungen der Akademie der Wissenschaften in Wein auf den Friedhöfen von Ermenne (Nubien) im Winter 1911/12*. Vienna and Leipzig.

Kákosy, L. 1975. 'Abdullah Nirqi 1964. Burials', *AAASH* 27, 103-17.

Karkowski, J. 1981. *Faras V. The Pharaonic Inscriptions from Faras*. Warschau.

Karkowski, J. 1986. 'A Few Remarks on Stone used in Christian Constructions at Faras', in Krause (ed.), 311-15.

Kirwan, L.P. 1937. 'A Contemporary Account of the Conversion of the Sudan to Christianity', *SNR* 20, 289-95.

Kirwan, L.P. 1937b. 'Studies in the Later History of Nubia', *LAAA* 24, 69-105.

Kirwan, L.P. 1939. *The Oxford University Excavations at Firka*. London.

Kirwan, L.P. 1963. 'The X-Group Enigma: a little known people of the Nubian Nile', in E. Bacon (ed.), *Vanished Civilisations*. London, 69-78.

Kirwan, L.P. 1966. 'Prelude to Nubian Christianity', in Bernhard (ed.), 121-28.

Kirwan, L.P. 1972. 'The Christian Topography and the Kingdom of Axum', *Geographical Journal* 138.2, 166-77.

Kirwan, L.P. 1974. 'Nubia and Nubian origins', *Geographical Journal* 140.1, 43-51.

Kirwan, L.P. 1977. 'Rome Beyond the Southern Egyptian Frontier', *Proceedings of the British Academy* 63, 13-31.

Kirwan, L.P. 1980. 'The Emergence of the United Kingdom of Nubia', *SNR* 61, 134-9.

Kirwan, L.P. 1982. 'Some Thoughts on the Conversion of Nubia to Christianity', in Plumley (ed.), 142-5

Kirwan, L.P. 1987. 'The Birth of Christian Nubia: some archaeological problems', *Rivista del Studi Orientali*, 58, 119-34.

Kirwan, L.P. 1988. 'Meroe, Soba and the Kingdom of Alwa', *Meroitica* 10, 299-304.

Knudstad, J. 1966. 'Serra East and Dorginarti. A Preliminary Report on the 1963-64 Excavations of the University of Chicago Oriental Institute Sudan Expedition', *Kush* 14, 165-86.

Kobischtschanow, Y.M. 1980. 'Agriculture and Economic-cultural Types in Medieval Nubia. On the Cultural Heritage of Meroe in the Middle Ages', *Meroitica* 7, 472-82.

Kolodziejczyk, K. 1982. 'Some Remarks on the Christian ceramics from Faras', in Jakobielski (ed.) 1982b, 173-89.

Krause, M. (ed.) 1986. *Nubische Studien*. Mainz am Rhein.

Krautheimer, R. 1969. *Studies in Early Christian, Medieval and Renaissance Art*. New York and London.

Krautheimer, R. 1975. *Early Christian and Byzantine Architecture*. 2nd edn, Harmondsworth.

Kromer, K, 1967. *Römische Weinstuben in Sayala (Unternubien)*. Wien.

Kronenberg, A. and W. Kronenberg 1963. 'Preliminary Report on Anthropological Field-Work 1961-62 in Sudanese Nubia', *Kush* 11, 302-11.

Kronenberg, A. and W. Kronenberg 1964. 'Preliminary Report on Anthropological Field-Work in Sudanese Nubia, 1962-63', *Kush* 12, 282-90.

Krump, T. 1710. *Hoher und Fruchtbarer Palm-Baum*. Augsburg.

Kubińska, J. 1974. *Faras IV. Inscriptions Grecques Chrétiennes*. Warszawa.

Kuper, R. 1988. 'Neuere Forschungen zur Besiedlungsgeschichte der Ost-Sahara', *Archäologisches Korrespondenzblatt* 18, 127-42.

Lajtar, A. 1991. 'Two Greek Funerary Stelae from Polish Excavations in Old Dongola', *ANM* 5, 157-66.

Lajtar, A. 1995. 'Greek Inscriptions from the Monastery on Kom H in Old Dongola', in M. Starowieyski (ed.), *The Spirituality of Ancient Monasticism*. Tyniec-Cracow, 47-61.

Lajtar, A. 1996. 'Three Christian Epitaphs from the area of Gebel Barkal', *Journal of Juristic Papyrology* 26, 73-89.

Lajtar, A. 1997. 'Greek Funerary Inscriptions from Old Dongola: General Note', *Oriens Christianus* 81, 107-26.

Lajtar, A. 1998. 'The epitaph of Iesonsinkouda, eparch of Nobadia(?), domestikos of Faras and nauarchos of the Nobadae, died A.D. 1102', *GAMAR* 1, 73-80.

Lajtar, A. and J. van der Vliet 1998. 'Rich Ladies of Meinarti and their Churches', *Journal of Juristic Papyrology* 28, 35-53.

Lajtarukaszewicz, A. 1990. 'Some Remarks on the Iconography of Anchorites from the Faras Cathedral', *Nubica* I/II, 549-56.

Leclant, J. and G. Soukiassian 1982. 'L'Eglise de Nilwa a Sedeinga', in Plumley (ed.), 155-61.

Lenoble, P. 1987. 'Quatre tombes sur mille de Djebel Makbor. AMS NE-36-O/3-X-1', *ANM* 2, 207-47.

Lenoble, P. 1989. '"A New Type of Mound-Grave" (continued): Le Tumulus à enceinte d'Umm Makharoqa, pres d'el Hobagi (A.M.S. NE-36-O/7-O-3)', *ANM* 3, 93-120.

Lenoble, P. 1991. 'Chiens de païens, une tombe postpyramidale à double descenderie hors de Méroé', *ANM* 5, 167-88.

Lenoble, P. 1992. 'The "End" of the Meroitic Empire: The Evidence from Central Sudan', *SARSN* 3, 9-12.

Lenoble, P. 1994. 'Une Monture pour Mon Royaume, Sacrifices Triomphaux de Chevaux et de Méhara d'el Kurru à Ballana', *ANM* 6, 107-30.

Lenoble, P. 1994b. 'Du Méroïtique au Postméroïtique dans la région méridionale du Royaume de Méroé. Recherches sur la période de transition.' Unpublished doctoral thesis, University of Paris, Sorbonne.

Lenoble, P. 1995. 'La Petite Bouteille Noire, un Récipient Méroéen de la Libation Funéraire', *ANM* 7, 143-62.

Lenoble, P. 1996. 'Les "Sacrifices Humains" de Meroe, Qustul et Ballana. I. Le Massacre de Nombreux Prisonniers', *BzS* 6, 59-87.

Lenoble, P. 1997. 'Enterrer les flèches, enterrer l'empire I: Carquois et flèches des tombes impériales à el-Hobagi', *CRIPEL* 17/2, 137-52.

Lenoble, P. 1999. 'The Division of the Meroitic Empire and the End of Pyramid Building in the 4th Century AD: an Introduction to further Excavations of Imperial Mounds in Sudan', in Welsby (ed.), 157-98.

Lenoble, P., R.-P Disseaus, A. Ali Mohammed, B. Ronce and J. Bialais 1994. 'La fouille du tumulus à enceinte el Hobagi III. AMS NE-36-O/7-N-3', *MNL* 25, 53-88.

Lepsius, C.R. 1853. *Discoveries in Egypt, Ethiopia and the Peninsula of Sinai in the years 1842-1845*. 2nd. edn, London.

Lepsius, C.R. 1913. *Denkmäler aus Aegypten und Aethiopien, Text V*. Leipzig.

MacDonald, K. C. and D. N. Edwards 1993. 'Chickens in Africa: the importance of Qasr Ibrim', *Antiquity* 67, 584-90.

Maddox, J. 1991. 'Analysis of mortar fragments', in Welsby and Daniels, 349.

Malek, J. 1984. 'The date of the water-cisterns discovered along the desert crossing from Korosko to Abu Hamed in 1963', *Göttinger Miszellen* 83, 47-50.

Mallinson, M. 1998. 'The SARS Survey from Omdurman to Gabolab 1997. The Survey', *Sudan & Nubia* 2, 42-5.

Martens-Czarnecka, M. 1982. *Faras VII. Les elements decoratifs sur les peintures de Faras.* Warszawa.

Martens-Czarnecka, M. 1982b. 'General results of using decorative ornaments and motifs on Faras murals as a criterion for their dating', in Jakobielski (ed.), 214-22.

Martens-Czarnecka, M. 1986. 'Observations on repainted murals from Faras', in Krause (ed.), 329-35.

Martens-Czarnecka, M. 1987. 'Nubian Wall Paintings', in Hägg (ed.) 261-74.

Martens-Czarnecka, M. 1992. 'Late Christian Painting in Nubia', in Bonnet (ed.), 307-16.

Martens-Czarnecka, M. 1997. 'New Mural Paintings from Old Dongola', *CRIPEL* 17/2, 211-25.

Martens-Czarnecka, M. 1998. 'An Attempt to Define the Function of Selected Rooms at the Monastery in Old Dongola', *GAMAR* 1, 81-94.

Martens-Czarnecka, M. 1998b. 'Mural Paintings from Old Dongola', *GAMAR* 1, 95-113.

Martens-Czarnecka, M. 1999. 'Certain common aspects of Ethiopian and Nubian painting', *Nubica* IV/V, 551-64.

Mathews, T. F. 1971. *The Early Churches of Constantinople: Architecture and Liturgy.* London.

Maystre, C. 1970. 'Fouilles Americano-Suisses aux Églises de Kageras, Ukma Est et Songi Sud', in Dinkler (ed.), 181-208.

Michałowski, K. 1964. 'Polish Excavations at Faras, 1962-63', *Kush* 12, 195-207.

Michałowski, K. 1965. *Faras. Fouilles Polanaises 1961-1962.* Warszawa.

Michałowski, K. and G. Gerster 1967. *Faras: Die Kathedrale aus dem Wüstensand.* Einsiedeln, Zurich and Cologne.

Michałowski, K. 1970. 'Open Problems of Nubian Art and Culture in the Light of the Discoveries at Faras', in Dinkler (ed.), 11-28.

Michałowski, K. 1974. *Faras. Wall Paintings in the Collection of the National Museum in Warsaw.* Warsaw.

Michałowski, K. (ed.) 1975. *Nubia. Récentes Recherches.* Varsovie.

Mileham, G.S. 1910. *Churches in Lower Nubia.* Philadelphia.

Millet, N.B. 1963. 'Gebel Adda Preliminary Report for 1963', *JARCE* 3, 147-65.

Millet, N.B. 1964. 'Gebel Adda Expedition Preliminary Report, 1963-64', *JARCE* 4, 7-14.

Millet, N.B. 1967. 'Gebel Adda Preliminary Report for 1965-66', *JARCE* 6, 53-63.

Millet, N.B. 1973. 'The Kharamadoye Inscription', *Buletin d'Information Meroitique* 13, 31-49.

Millet, N.B. 1974. 'Writing and Literacy in the Ancient Sudan', in Abdalla (ed.), 49-58.

Millet, N.B. 1984. 'Meroitic Religion', *Meroitica* 7, 111-21.

Millet, N.B. 1987. 'Nubian Heraldry', *Society for the Study of Egyptian Antiquities* 17, 1/2, 33-5.

Mills, A.J. 1982. *The Cemeteries of Qasr Ibrim, a Report of the Excavations Conducted by W.B. Emery in 1961.* Egypt Exploration Society Excavation Memoir 51, London.

Mohamed, Abdul Rahman Ali 2000. 'Rescue Excavations at Soba East', *Sudan & Nubia* 4, 27-31.

Monneret de Villard, U. 1932. 'Note Nubiane', *Aegyptus* 12, fasc. 4. 305-16.

Monneret de Villard, U. 1935-57. *La Nubia Medioevale.* 4 vols. Cairo.

Monneret de Villard, U. 1938. *Storia della Nubia Cristiana.* Rome.

Morgan, G. 1998. 'Analysis of the mortar and plaster', in Welsby 1998, 280-1.

Morganstein, M.E. and C.A. Redmount 1998. 'Mudbrick Typology, Sources, and Sedimentological Composition: A Case Study from Tell el-Muqdam, Egyptian Delta', *JARCE* 35, 129-146.

Morrison, H. 1991. 'Vessels of glass', in Welsby and Daniels 1991, 246-59.

Müller, C.D.G. 1970. 'Deutsche Textfunde in Nubien', in Dinkler (ed.), 245-58.

Munro-Hay, S. 1982-83. 'Kings and Kingdoms of Ancient Nubia', *Rassegna di Studi Etiopici* 29, 87-137.

Myres, O.H. 1960. 'Abka Again', *Kush* 8, 174-81.

Nautin, P. 1967. 'La Conversion du Temple de Philae en Église Chrétienne', *Cahiers Archéologiques* 17, 1-43.

Norden, F.L. 1757. *Voyage d'Égypte et de Nubie III.* Paris.

Oates, J.F. 1963. 'A Christian Inscription in Greek from Armenna in Nubia', *JEA* 49, 161-71.

O'Fahey, R.S. and J.L. Spaulding 1974. *Kingdoms of the Sudan.* London.

OS — see Vantini 1975.

Paner, H. 1998. 'The Hamdab Dam Project. Preliminary Report from Work in the 4th Cataract Region, 1996-1997', *GAMAR* 1, 115-32.

Papadopoullos, T. 1966. *Africanobyzantina — Byzantine Influences on Negro-Sudanese Cultures.* Athens.

Penn, A.E.D. 1931. 'The Ruins of Zankor', *SNR* 14, 179-84.

Petrie, W.M. 1927. *Objects in Daily Use.* London.

Petrie, W.M. 1937. *Funeral Furniture and Stone Vases.* London.

Phillips, J. 1994. 'Jar-sealings from Hambukol', in Bonnet (ed.), 229-36.

Pliny. *Naturalis Historia.* Trans H. Rackham, Loeb Classical Library, London and Cambridge 1942.

Plumley, J.M. 1970. 'Some Examples of Christian Nubian Art from the Excavations at Qasr Ibrim', in Dinkler (ed.), 129-40.

Plumley, J.M. 1975. 'The Christian Period at Qasr Ibrim. Some Notes on the MSS Finds', in Michałowski 1975, 101-07.

Plumley, J.M. 1975b. 'Qasr Ibrim, 1974', *JEA* 61, 5-27.

Plumley, J.M. 1975c. *The Scrolls of Bishop Timotheos.* London.

Plumley, J.M. 1978. 'New Light on the Kingdom of Dotawo', in *Études Nubiennes*, Cairo, 231-42.

Plumley, J.M. (ed.) 1982. *Nubian Studies.* Warminster.

Plumley, J.M. 1982b. 'New Evidence on Christian Nubia in the Light of Recent Excavations', in Jakobielski (ed.), 15-21.

Plumley, J.M. 1982c. 'Nubian Christian Numerical Cryptograms: Some Elucidations', in Van Moorsel (ed.), 91-9.

Plumley, J.M. 1983. 'Qasr Ibrim and Islam', *Études et Travaux* 12, 157-70.

Plumley, J.M. and W. Y. Adams 1974. 'Qasr Ibrim, 1972', *EA* 60, 212-38.

Pluskota, K. 1990. 'Early Christian Pottery from Old Dongola', in Godlewski (ed.), 315-33.

Pluskota, K. 1991. 'A pottery production centre from the Early Christian Period', in Godlewski (ed.), 34-56.

Pluskota, K. 1992. 'A Liturgical Vessel from Old Dongola', in Scholz (ed.), 411-14.

Pluskota, K. 1994. 'Old Dongola - Kiln R 2 (Post-Classic Christian Pottery Deposit)', *Nubica* III/1, 361-77.

Pluskota, K. 1994b. 'Some Remarks on the Post-Classic Christian Pottery from Old Dongola', in Bonnet (ed.), 219-20.

Pluskota, K. 1997. 'Old Dongola. Recent Pottery Finds', *CRIPEL* 17/2, 235-42.

Polanyi, K. 1968. *Primitive, Archaic and Modern Economies*. New York.

Porter, V. 1991. 'The Islamic pottery from the trial trenches and from the western end of mound B', in Welsby and Daniels, 336-7.

Porter, V. and M. Hughes 1998. 'The Glazed Pottery', in Welsby 1998, 174, 176-7.

Presedo, V.F. 1964. *La Fortaleza Nubia de Cheikh-Daud, Tumas (Egipto)*. Madrid.

Priese, K.-H. 1973. 'Articula', *Études et Travaux* 7, 155-62.

Priese, K.-H. 1984. 'Orte des mittleren Niltals in der Über lieferung bis zum Ende des christlichen Mittelalters', *Meroitica* 7, 484-97.

Procopius. *History of the Wars*. Trans. H. B. Dewing, Loeb Classical Library, London and New York, 1914.

Promińska, E. 1978. 'Les Ossements des Tombes des Églises de Dongola', in *Études Nubiennes*, 243-6.

Ratynski, Z, 1982. 'Hand and Pectoral Crosses from Faras', in Jakobielski (ed.), 223-82.

Reisner, G. 1929. 'Ancient Egyptian Forts at Semna and Uronarti', *Bulletin of the Museum of Fine Art, Boston* 27, 64-75.

Ricke, H. 1967. *Ausgrabungen Von Khor-Dehmit Bis Bet El-Wali*. The University of Chicago Oriental Institute Vol. 2, Chicago.

Robertson, J.H. and E.M. Hill 1999. 'Two Traditions or One? New Interpretations of the Hand-made/Wheel-made Ceramics from Meroe', in Welsby (ed.), 321-329.

Rostkowska, B. 1982. 'Nobadian Painting. Present State of Investigations', in Jakobielski (ed.), 283-304.

Rostkowska, B. 1982b. 'The Visit of a Nubian King to Constantinople in AD 1203', in Van Moorsel (ed.), 113-16.

Rostkowska, B. 1982c. 'The Patronage of the Arts in Nobadia', in Plumley (ed.), 208-214.

Rowley-Conwy, P. 1989. 'Nubia AD 0-550 and the "Islamic" agricultural revolution: preliminary botanical evidence from Qasr Ibrim, Egyptian Nubia', *ANM* 3, 131-8.

Ryl-Preibisz, I. 1986. 'On the Types of Capitals in Christian Nubia', in Krause (ed.), 379-84.

Ryl-Preibisz, I. 1987. 'Nubian Stone Architectural Decoration', in Hägg (ed.), 247-60.

Ryl-Preibisz, I. 1997. 'Architectural Decorative Elements Recently Discovered at Old Dongola', *CRIPEL* 17/2, 227-33.

Salih, Ali Osman M. 1982. 'Medieval Nubia: Retrospects and Introspects', in Van Moorsel (ed.), 69-92.

Salih, Ali Osman M. and D.N. Edwards 1992. *The Mahas Survey 1991*. Cambridge.

Säve-Söderbergh, T. 1964. 'Preliminary Report of the Scandinavian Joint Expedition: Archaeological Investigations between Faras and Gemai, November 1962-March 1963', *Kush* 12, 19-39.

Säve-Söderbergh, T. 1970. 'Christian Nubia – The Excavations carried out by the Scandinavian Joint Expedition to Sudanese Nubia', in Dinkler (ed.), 219-44.

Säve-Söderbergh, T. (ed.) 1982. *Late Nubian Cemeteries*. Scandinavian Joint Expedition 6, Solna.

Sayce, A.H. 1910. 'Karian, Egyptian and Nubian-Greek Inscriptions from the Sudan', *Proc. Society for Biblical Archaeology* 32, 261-8.

Scanlon, G.T. 1970. 'Excavations at Kasr el-Wizz: A preliminary report. I', *JEA* 56, 42-57.

Scanlon, G.T. 1972. 'Excavations at Kasr el-Wizz: A preliminary report. II', *JEA* 58, 7-42.

Schneider, H.D. 1970. 'Abdallah Nirqi: Description and Chronology of the Central Church', in Dinkler (ed.), 87-102.

Scholz, P.O. (ed.). 1992. *Orbis Aethiopicus*. Albstadt.

Shaw, W.B.K. 1936. 'The Ruins at Abu Sufyan', *SNR* 19, 324-6.

Shinnie, M. (ed.) 1958. *Linant de Bellefonts, Journal d'un Voyage à Méroé dans les années 1821 et 1822*. Khartoum.

Shinnie, P.L. 1954. 'Excavations at Tanqasi, 1953', *Kush* 2, 66-85.

Shinnie, P.L. 1955. *Excavations at Soba*. Sudan Antiquities Service Occasional Papers 3, Khartoum.

Shinnie, P.L. 1974. 'Multilingualism in Medieval Nubia', in Abdalla (ed.), 41-7.

Shinnie, P.L. 1978. 'Trade in Medieval Nubia', in *Études Nubiennes*, 251-63.

Shinnie, P.L. 1987-8. 'Christian Nubia and the Crusades', *Nubica* I/II, 603-9.

Shinnie, P.L. and H.N. Chittick 1961. *Ghazali - a Monastery in the Northern Sudan*. Sudan Antiquities Service Occasional Papers 5, Khartoum.

Shinnie, P.L. and J. H. Robertson 1993. 'The End of Meroe. A comment on the paper by Patrice Lenoble and Nigm ed Din Mohamed Sharif', *Antiquity* 67, 895-8.

Shinnie, P.L. and M. Shinnie 1965. 'New Light on Medieval Nubia', *Journal of African History* 6, 263-73.

Shinnie, P.L. and M. Shinnie 1978. *Debeira West. A Mediaeval Nubian Town*. Warminster.

Simpson, W.K. 1964. 'The Pennsylvania-Yale Expedition to Egypt: Preliminary Report for 1963: Toshka and Arminna Nubia)', *JARCE* 4, 15-23.

Sinclair, P.J., T. Shaw and B. Andah 1993. 'Introduction', in T. Shaw, P.J. Sinclair, B. Andah and A. Okpoko (eds) 1993, *The Archaeology of Africa. Food, metals and towns*. London and New York, 1-31.

Sjöström, I.Y.W. 1998. 'The inscribed bricks', in Welsby 1998, 209-13.

Sjöström, I.Y.W. 1998b. 'New Fieldwork at Kurgus. The Cemetery and the Fort', *Sudan & Nubia* 2, 30-4.

Sjöström, I.Y.W. and D.A. Welsby 1991. 'Excavations within the Capital City of Alwa: Soba, 1989-90', *ANM* 5, 189-204.

Smith, L.M.V. 1991. 'Petrographic and electron probe analysis of ceramics from Soba', in Welsby and Daniels, 337-49.

Smith, L.M.V. 1998. 'The Post-Meroitic and Medieval Pottery', in Edwards 1998, 178-93.

Smith, L.M.V. 1998b. 'Post-Meroitic and Later Finds. Part I: Finds from the Test Excavations', in Edwards 1998, 112-23.

Sodini, J.-P and K. Kolokotsos 1984. *Aliki, II: La Basilique Double. Études Thasiennes* X. Athens and Paris.

Spaulding, J. 1971. *Kings of Sun and Shadow: a History of the 'Abdallab Provinces of the Northern Sinnar Sultanate, 1500-1800 AD*.

Spaulding, J. 1974. 'The Fate of Alodia', *Meroitic Newsletter* 15, 12-30.

Steinborn, M. 1982. 'Harness in Nubian Wall Paintings', in Jakobielski (ed.) 1982b, 305-50.

Steindorff, G. 1935. *Aniba 1. Service des Antiquitiés de l'Egypte. Mission Archéologique de Nubie*. Gluckstadt and Hamburg.

Stenico, A. 1960. 'Ikhmindi, una citta fortificata medievale della Bassa Nubia', *Acme* 13, 31-76.

Strabo. *Geography*. Trans. H. L. Jones, Loeb Classical Library, London and Cambridge, 1917, 1930, 1932.

Strouhal, E. 1978. 'Hand-made Pottery of the IVth to VIth Centuries A.D. in the Dodecaschoinos', in Plumley (ed.), 215-22.

Strouhal, E. 1984. *Wadi Qitna and Kalabsha South*. Prague.

Strouhal, E. 1986. 'Archaeological character of some X-Group sites of the Dodecaschoinos', in Krause (ed.), 187-90.

Strouhal, E. 1990. 'Family Structure of the Wadi Qitna Population (Egyptian Nubia, 3rd-5th cent. A. D.)', *Nubica* I/II, 611-29.

Strouhal, E. and J. Jungwirth 1971. 'Anthropological Problems of the Middle Empire and Late Roman Sayala', *Mitteilungen d. Anthropol. Gesellsch. (Wien)* 101, 10-23.

Sutton, J.E.G. 1991. 'The International Factor at Igbo-Ukwu', *African Archaeological Review* 9, 145-60.

Switsur, R. 1991. 'The radiocarbon ages from Soba East', in Welsby and Daniels, 350-1.

Thirakul, S. 1984. *Manual of Dendrology. Bahr el Ghazal and Central Regions*. Quebec.

Titherington, G.W. 1939. 'The Kubinat. Old Forts of the Fourth Cataract', *SNR* 22, 269-71.

Török, L, 1974. 'Ein Christianisiertes Tempelgebäude in Musawwarat es Sufra (Sudan)', *AAASH* 26, 71-103.

Török, L. 1975. 'Abdullah Nirqi 1964. The Finds from the Excavation of the Hungarian Mission 2', *AAASH* 27, 135-43.

Török, L. 1978. 'Money, Economy and Administration in Christian Nubia', *Etudes Nubiennes*, 287-312.

Török, L, 1980. 'To a History of the Dodekaschoinos between ca. 250 B.C. and 298 A.D.', *ZÄS* 107, 76-86

Török, L. 1986. 'The Chronology of the Qustul and Ballana Cemeteries', in Krause (ed.), 191-7.

Török, L. 1987. 'A Contribution to Post-Meroitic Chronology: The Blemmyes in Lower Nubia', *in Studi in onore di Ugo Monneret de Villard (1881-1954). Rivista degli Studi Orientali* 58, 201-43.

Török, L. 1988. *Late Antique Nubia*. Budapest.

Török, L. 1989. 'Kush and the external world', *Meroitica* 10, 49-215.

Török, L. 1997. *Meroe City. An Ancient African Capital*. London.

Török, L. 1999. 'The End of Meroe', in Welsby (ed.), 133-56.

Tothill, J.D. (ed.) 1948. *Agriculture in the Sudan*. London.

Tracey, C.B. and J.W. Hewison 1948. 'Northern Province', in Tothill (ed.), 736-61.

Trigger, B.G. 1965. *History and Settlement in Lower Nubia*. New Haven.

Trigger, B.G. 1967. *The Late Nubian Settlement at Arminna West*. New Haven and Philadelphia.

Trigger, B.G. 1970. 'The Cultural Ecology of Christian Nubia', in Dinkler (ed.), 347-79.

Trigger, B.G. 1972. 'Determinants of Urban Growth in Pre-Industrial Societies', in P.J. Ucko, R. Tringham and G.W. Dimbleby (eds), *Man, Settlement and Urbanism*. London, 575-99.

Van Gerven, D.P. and D.L. Greene 1999. 'The Human Remains', in Adams *et al.,* 73-88.

Van Moorsel, P. 1970. 'Die Stillende Gottesmutter und die Monophysiten', in Dinkler (ed.), 280-90.

Van Moorsel, P. 1972. 'Die Nubier und das glorreiche Kreuz', *BABesch* 47, 125-34.

Van Moorsel, P. (ed.) 1982. *New Discoveries in Nubia*. Leiden.

Van der Veen, M. 1991. 'The plant remains', in Welsby and Daniels, 264-73.

Vansĺeb, J.M. 1677. *Histoire de l'église d'Alexandrie … écrite au Caire même, en 1672 et 1673*. Paris.

Vantini, G. 1970. *The Excavations at Faras, a Contribution to the History of Christian Nubia*. Bologna.

Vantini, G. 1970b. 'Le Roi Kirki de Nubie a Baghdad: un ou deux Voyages?', in Dinkler (ed.), 41-48.

Vantini, G. 1975. *Oriental Sources concerning Nubia*. Heidelberg and Warsaw.

Vantini, G, 1975b. 'A propos de deux Rois de 'Alwa mentionnés par Ibn Hawqal', in Michałowski (ed.), 130-2.

Vantini, G, 1981. *Christianity in the Sudan*. Bologna.

Vantini, G, 1982. 'Christian relics in Sudanese tradition', in Jakobielski (ed.) 1982b, 25-42.

Vantini, G. 1999. 'The Remotest Places Reached by Nubian Christianity in the Sudan', *Nubica* IV/V, 347-50.

Vercoutter, J. 1962. 'Un Palais des "Candaces", contemporain d'Auguste', *Syria* 39, 263-99.

Vercoutter, J. 1963. 'Excavations at Aksha. September 1961-January 1962', *Kush* 11, 131-9.

Vercoutter, J. 1966. 'Semna South Fort and the Records of Nile Levels at Kumma', *Kush* 14, 125-64.

Vercoutter, J. 1970. 'Les Fouilles Chrétiennes Françaises à Aksha, Mirgissa et Sai', in Dinkler (ed.), 155-62.

Vila, A. 1976. *La Prospection Archéologique de la Vallée du Nil, au Sud de la Cataracte de Dal (Nubie Soudanaise). Fascicule 3. District de Firka, Est et Ouest*. Paris.

Vila, A. 1977. *La Prospection Archéologique de la Vallée du Nil, au Sud de la Cataracte de Dal (Nubie Soudanaise). Fascicule 5. Le district de Ginis, Est et Ouest*. Paris.

Vogelsang-Eastwood, G. 1991. 'The Textiles', in Welsby and Daniels, 300-8.

Vogelsang-Eastwood, G. 1998. 'The textiles', in Welsby 1998, 177-82.

Ward, R. 'The Glass Vessels', in Welsby 1998, 83-7.

Weeks, K.R. 1967. *The Classic Christian Townsite at Arminna West*. New Haven.

Welsby, D.A. 1992. 'Windows in Medieval Nubia: The Evidence from Soba East', *Antiquaries Journal* 72, 174-8.

Welsby, D.A. 1996. 'The Medieval Kingdom of Alwa', in Gundlach *et al.* (Hrgs.), 179-94.

Welsby, D.A. 1996b. *The Kingdom of Kush. The Napatan and Meroitic Empires*. London.

Welsby, D.A. 1998. *Soba II. Renewed excavations within the metropolis of the Kingdom of Alwa in Central Sudan*. British Institute in Eastern Africa Memoir 15. London.

Welsby, D.A. 1999. 'Saqadi - form, function and chronology', in W. V. Davies (ed.), *Studies in Egyptian Antiquities. A Tribute to T. G. H. James*. London, 103-9.

Welsby, D.A. 1999b. 'Roman Military Installations along the Nile South of the First Cataract', *ANM* 8, 157-82.

Welsby, D.A. (ed.) 1999c. *Recent Research in Kushite History and Archaeology: Proceedings of The Eighth International Conference of Meroitic Studies*. London

Welsby, D.A. 2000. 'The Amri to Kirbekan Survey', *Sudan & Nubia* 4, 51-7.

Welsby, D.A. 2001. *Life on the Desert Edge. 7000 years of Human Settlement in the Northern Dongola Reach, Sudan*. London.

Welsby, D.A. (forth.). *Survey above the Fourth Nile Cataract*. London.

Welsby, D.A. and C. M. Daniels 1991. *Soba. Archaeological research at a medieval capital on the Blue Nile*. British Institute in Eastern Africa Memoir 12, London.

Wendrich, W.Z. 1994. 'Recording the 1990 Qasr Ibrim Basketry: A Matter of Edging', in Bonnet (ed.), 205-7.

Williams, B. 1991. *Noubadian X-Group Remains. From Royal Complexes in Cemeteries Q and 219 and from Private Cemeteries Q, R, V, W, B, J, and M at Qustul and Ballana*. Oriental Institute Nubian Expedition IX, Chicago.

Wills, B. 1998. 'The Leather Sandals and Shoes', in Welsby 1998, 182-5

Woolley, C.L. 1911. *Karanog. The Town*. Oxford.

Woolley, C.L. and D. Randall-MacIver 1910. *Karanòg: The Romano-Nubian Cemetery*. Philadelphia.

Zurawski, B. 1986. 'Bishops' tombs in Faras', in Krause (ed.), 413-18.

Zurawski, B. 1987. 'The Nubian Mortuary Complex', in Hägg 1987, 275-8.

Zurawski, B. 1992. '*Magica et ceramica*: Magic and Ceramics in Christian Nubia', *Archaeologica Polona* 30, 87-107.

Zurawski, B. 1993. 'Nubia and Ethiopia in the Christian Period – Some Affinities', in P.B. Henze (ed.), *Aspects of Ethiopian Art from Ancient Axum to the 20th century*. London, 33-42.

Zurawski, B. 1994. 'The Service Area in North-Eastern Corner of the Monastery on Kom H in Old Dongola. A preliminary report', *Nubica* III/1, 319-360.

Zurawski, B. 1994b. 'Some Christian Foundation Deposits from the Region of Old Dongola', in Bonnet (ed.), 211-7.

Zurawski, B. 1997. 'Old Dongola. Kom H, Southwestern Unit', *PAM* 8, 169-78.

Zurawski, B. 1997b. 'The Cemeteries of Dongola. A Preliminary Report', *CRIPEL* 17/2, 195-210.

Zurawski, B. 1997c. 'The Early Church on Kom E near Old Dongola. Excavations of 1993 and 1994 Season', *CRIPEL* 17/2, 181-93.

Zurawski, B. 1998. 'Pliny's 'Tergedum' discovered', *Sudan & Nubia* 2, 74-81.

Zurawski, B. 1998b. 'Nubian and Ethiopian horned headgears of the Medieval Period', in Muzeum Archeologicznre w Gdansku and Orbis Aethiopicus (eds), *Ethiopia and its neighbours. Orbis Aethiopicus (the 3rd Academic Conference of Orbis Aethiopicus)* Frankfurt, 121-35.

Zurawski, B. 1999. 'Medieval Nubian Regalia: Innovation versus Tradition', in Welsby (ed.), 223-34.

Zurawski, B. 1999b. 'The Monastery on Kom H in Old Dongola. The monk's graves', *Nubica* IV/V, 201-53.

Zurawski, B. 1999c. 'Dongola Reach: the southern Dongola Reach Survey, 1998', *PAM* 10, 149-60.

Zurawski, B. 1999d 'Faith-healing, Philanthropy and Commemoration in Late Christian Dongola', in S. Emmel, M. Krause, S.G. Richter and S. Schaten (Hrsg.), *Ägypten und Nubien in spätaniker und christlicher Zeit* (Akten d. 6 Internationalen Koptogenkongreß Münster 1996), Wiesbaden, 423-48.

Zurawski, B. and Mahmoud et-Tayeb 1994. 'The Christian Cemetery of Jebel Ghaddar North', *Nubica* III/1, 297-317.

Index